THE HISTORY OF HUMAN SOCIETY

General Editor: J. H. PLUMB, LITT.D.

Vice-Master of Christ's College, Cambrid-

THE S

SEABORNE EMPIRE

THE HISTORY OF HUMAN SOCIETY

General Editor: J. H. Plumb

THE SPANISH
SEABORNE EMPIRE

J. H. PARRY

Hutchinson of London

Hutchinson & Co (Publishers) Ltd
3 Fitzroy Square, London W1

London Melbourne Sydney Auckland
Wellington Johannesburg and agencies
throughout the world

First published 1966
Second impression September 1967
Third impression November 1971
Reprinted 1977
© J. H. Parry 1966
Introduction © J. H. Plumb 1966

Printed in Great Britain by litho at The Anchor Press Ltd,
and bound by Wm Brendon & Son Ltd
both of Tiptree, Essex

Contents

PART V   THE DISINTEGRATION OF EMPIRE

List of plates

List of maps

Preface

THE book which follows is an attempt to summarise the growth of the Spanish Kingdoms in the Americas, and the interactions between those kingdoms and metropolitan Spain, from the late fifteenth century to the early nineteenth. The volume of writing on the subject is immense; but even so our understanding of it remains uneven and our knowledge of some aspects, at least, is slight. An author who tries to tell, even in outline, the story as a whole, must rely heavily on the help of friends and specialised colleagues. In a short Preface I can acknowledge only my most pressing debts. I wish particularly to thank Dr Woodrow Borah for much illuminating talk about the Indians of New Spain; Dr Neil MacKay for information, so far unpublished, about eighteenth-century Buenos Aires; and Dr David Brading for valuable details, also as yet unpublished, on colonial local government and finance, particularly in the mining areas of New Spain. They and many others supplied me with information: if I have misinterpreted it the fault is mine. Dr Holden Hall of the Newberry Library and Dr Helen Wallis of the British Museum gave me patient and expert help in the search for illustrations. Finally I should like to thank those who helped with manuscript, proofs and index: my wife, my daughter Katherine, and Miss Harriet Rees.

J. H. P.

Swansea

Introduction

BY J. H. PLUMB

I

OVER the last fifty to a hundred years, man's belief that the historical process proved that he was acquiring a greater mastery over nature has received a brutal buffeting. In his early youth H. G. Wells, a man of vast creative energy, of rich delight in the human spirit, and of all-pervading optimism, viewed the future with confidence; science, born of reason, was to be humanity's panacea. When, in the years of his maturity, he came to write his *Outline of History*, his vision was darker, although still sustained with hope. World War I, with its senseless and stupid slaughter of millions of men, brought the sickening realisation that man was capable of provoking human catastrophes on a global scale. The loss of human liberty, the degradations and brutalities imposed by fascism and communism during the twenties and thirties, followed in 1939 by the renewed world struggle, these events finally shattered Wells's eupeptic vision, and in sad and disillusioned old-age he wrote *Mind at the End of its Tether*. His hope of mankind had almost vanished. Almost, but not quite: for Wells's lifetime witnessed what, as a young writer, he had prophesied—technical invention not only on a prodigious scale but in those realms of human activity that affected the very core of society. And this extraordinary capacity of man to probe the complexities of nature and to invent machinery capable of exploiting his knowledge remained for Wells the only basis for hope, no matter how slender that might be.

If the belief of a man of Wells's passionate and intelligent humanism could be so battered and undermined, it is not surprising that lesser men were unable to withstand the climate of despair that engulfed the Western World between the two world wars. The disillusion of these years is apparent in painting, in music, in literature—everywhere in the Western World we are brought up sharply by an expression of anguish, by the flight from social and historical reality into a frightened, self-absorbed world of personal feeling and expression. Intellectual life, outside science, has pursued much the same course as artistic life, although it has shown greater ingenuity and a tougher-minded quality. Theology, philosophy and sociology have tended to reduce themselves to technical problems of exceptional professional complexity, but of small social importance. Their practitioners have largely ceased to instruct and enliven, let alone sustain the confidence of ordinary men and women.

In this atmosphere of cultural decay and of professional retreat, history and its philosophy have suffered. As in so many intellectual disciplines its professional workers have resolutely narrowed the focus of their interests to even more specialised fields of inquiry. The majority of historians have withdrawn from general culture in order to maintain, at a high intellectual level, an academic discipline. They have left the meaning and purpose of history to trained philosophers and spent their leisure hours tearing to shreds the scholarship of anyone foolish enough to attempt to give the story of mankind a meaning and a purpose: writers as diverse as H. G. Wells and Arnold Toynbee have been butchered with consummate skill. The blunders of scholarship and the errors of interpretation have counted everything; intention nothing. Few academic historians, secure in the cultivation of their minute gardens, have felt any humility towards those who would tame the wilderness. In consequence, an atmosphere of anarchic confusion pervades the attitude of Western man to his past.

A hundred years ago, in the first flood of archaeological discovery, scholars possessed greater confidence: the history of mankind seemed to most to point to an obvious law of human progress. The past was but a stepping-stone to the future. First adumbrated by the philosophers of the late Renaissance—Bodin in France and Bacon in England— the idea of progress became an article of common faith during the Enlightenment. And progress came to mean not only the technical progress that had preoccupied Bacon but also moral progress. By the nineteenth century the history of man demonstrated for many an improvement in the very nature of man himself as well as in his tools and weapons. Such optimism, such faith in man's capacity for rational behaviour, was shaken both by discoveries in science and in history as well as by events. By the middle of the twentieth century man's irrational drives appeared to be stronger than his intellectual capacities. Freud and Marx laid bare the hollow hypocrisy of so-called rational behaviour either in individuals or in society. Also, the rise and fall of civilisations, laid bare by the spade, seemed to point to a cyclical pattern in human destiny which made nonsense of any idea of continuous progress; and this naturally attracted the prophets of Western doom. Yet more persuasive still, and, perhaps, more destructive of confidence in human destiny, was the utter loss of all sense of human control brought about by global wars and violent revolutions. Only those men of societies who felt life was going their way, the revolutionaries and, above all, the Marxists, believed any longer in the laws of historical progress. For the rest, retrogression seemed as tenable a thesis as progress.

This disillusion in the West suited academic historians. It relieved them of their most difficult problems. If they happened to be religious they were content to leave the ultimate meaning of history to God; if they were rationalists they took refuge either in the need for more historical knowledge or in the philosophic difficulties of a subject that by its very nature was devoid of the same objective treatment that gave such authority to scientific inquiry. In the main they concentrated upon their professional work. And this was an exceptionally important and necessary task. What the common reader rarely recognises is the inadequacy of the factual material that was at the command of an historian one hundred years ago or even fifty years ago. Scarcely any archives were open to him; most repositories of records were unsorted and uncatalogued; almost every generalisation about a man or an event or an historical process was three-quarters guesswork, if not more. Laboriously, millions of facts have been brought to light, ordered and rendered coherent within their own context. Specialisation has proliferated like a cancer, making detail livid, but blurring the outlines of the story of mankind, and rendering it almost impossible for a professional historian to venture with confidence beyond his immediate province. And that can be very tiny—the Arkansas and Missouri Railway Strike of 1921; the place-names of Rutland: twelfth-century Rouen; the oral history of the Barotse; the philosophy of Hincmar of Rheims. And so it becomes ever more difficult for the professional historian to reach across to ordinary intelligent men and women or make his subject a part of human culture. The historical landscape is blurred by the ceaseless activity of its millions of professional ants. Of course, attempts at synthesis have to be made. The need to train young professional historians, or the need to impart some knowledge of history to students of other disciplines, has brought about competent digests of lengthy periods that summarise both facts and analysis. Occasionally such books have been written with such skill and wisdom that they have become a part of the West's cultural heritage. A few historians, driven by money or fame or creative need, have tried to share their knowledge and understanding of the past with the public at large.

But the gap between professional knowledge and history for the masses gets steadily wider: professional history becomes more accurate, more profound, whilst public history remains tentative and shallow.

This series is an attempt to reverse this process. Each volume will be written by a professional historian of the highest technical competence; but these books will not exist *in vacuo*, for the series is designed to have a unity and a purpose. But perhaps first it is best to say what it is not.

It is not a work of reference: there are no potted biographies of the Pharaohs, the Emperors of China or the Popes; no date lists of battles; no brief histories of painting, literature, music. Nor is this series a Universal History. All events that were critical in the history of mankind may not necessarily find a place. Some will; some will not. Works of reference, more or less factually accurate, exist in plenty and need not be repeated. It is not my intention to add yet another large compilation to what exists. Nor is this a 'philosophic' history. It does not pretend to reveal a recurring pattern in history that will unveil its purpose. Fundamentally philosophy, except in the use of language, is as irrelevant to history as it is to science. And lastly this series will not cover all human societies. There will be two volumes devoted to Russia, none to Germany. There will be histories of China and Japan but not of Indonesia. The Jews have a volume to themselves, the Parsees do not. And so on. Yet the series is called *The History of Human Society* for very good reasons. This history has a theme and a position in time.

The theme is the most obvious and the most neglected; obvious because everyone is aware of it from the solitary villages of Easter Island to the teeming cities of the Western World; neglected because it has been fashionable for professional and Western historians to concern themselves either with detailed professional history that cannot have a broad theme or with the spiritual and metaphysical aspects of man's destiny that are not his proper province. What, therefore, is the theme of *The History of Human Society*? It is this: that the condition of man now is superior to what it was. That two great revolutions—the neolithic and the industrial—have enabled men to establish vast societies of exceptional complexity in which the material well-being of generations of mankind has made remarkable advances; that the second, and most important, revolution has been achieved by the Western World; that we are witnessing its most intensive phase now, one in which ancient patterns of living are crumbling before the demands of industrial society; that life in the suburbs of London, Lagos, Djakarta, Rio de Janeiro and Vladivostok will soon have more in common than they have in difference: that this, therefore, is a moment to take stock, to unfold how this came about, to evoke the societies of the past whilst we are still close enough to many of them to feel intuitively the compulsion and needs of their patterns of living. I, however, hope, in these introductions, which it is my intention to write for each book, to provide a sense of unity. The authors themselves will not be so concerned with the overriding theme. Their aim will be to reconstruct the societies on which they are experts. They will lay bare the structure of their societies—their economic basis, their social organisations, their aspirations, their cultures, their religions and their conflicts. At the same time they will give a sense of what it was like to have lived in them. Each book will be an authoritative statement in its own right, and independent of the rest of the series. Yet each, set alongside the rest, will give a sense of how human society has changed and grown from the time man hunted and gathered his food to this nuclear and electronic age. This could only have been achieved by the most careful selection of authors. They needed, of course, to be established scholars of distinction, possessing the ability to write attractively for the general reader. They needed also to be wise, to possess steady, unflickering compassion for the strange necessities of men; to be quick in understanding, slow in judgement and to have in them some of that relish for life, as fierce and as instinctive as an animal's, that has upheld ordinary men and women in the worst of times. The authors of these books are heart-wise historians with sensible, level heads.

The range and variety of human societies is almost as great as the range and variety of human temperaments, and the selection for this series is in some ways as personal as an anthology. A Chinaman, a Russian, an Indian or an African would select a different series; but we are Western men writing for Western men. The Westernisation of the world by industrial technology is one of the main themes of the series. Each society selected has been in the main stream of this development or belongs to that vast primitive ocean from whence all history is derived. Some societies are neglected because they would only illustrate in a duller way societies which appear in the series; some because their history is not well enough known to a sufficient depth of scholarship to be synthesised in this way; some because they are too insignificant.

There are, of course, very important social forces—feudalism, technological change or religion, for example—which have moulded a variety of human societies at the same time. Much can be learnt from the comparative study of their influence. I have, however, rejected this approach, once recorded history is reached. My reason for rejecting this method is because human beings experience these forces in communities, and it is the experience of men in society with which this series is primarily concerned.

Lastly, it need hardly be said that society is not always synonymous with the state. At times, as with the Jews, it lacks even territorial stability; yet the Jews provide a fascinating study of symbiotic social groupings, and to have left them out would be unthinkable, for they represent, in its best known form, a wide human experience—a social group embedded in an alien society.

As well as a theme, which is the growth of man's control over his environment, this series may also fulfil a need. That is to restore a little confidence in man's capacity not only to endure the frequent catastrophies of human existence but also in his intellectual abilities. That many of his habits, both of mind and heart, are bestial, needs scarcely to be said. His continuing capacity for evil need not be stressed. His greed remains almost as strong as it was when he first shuffled on the ground. And yet the miracles created by his cunning are so much a part of our daily lives that we take their wonder for granted. Man's ingenuity—based securely on his capacity to reason—has won astonishing victories over the physical world—and in an amazingly brief span of time. Such triumphs, so frequently overlooked and even more frequently belittled, should breed a cautious optimism. Sooner or later, painfully perhaps and slowly, the same intellectual skill may be directed to the more difficult and intransigent problems of human living—man's social and personal relations—not only directed, but perhaps accepted, as the proper way of ordering human life. The story of man's progress over the centuries, studded with pitfalls and streaked with disaster as it is, ought to strengthen both hope and will.

Yet a note of warning must be sounded. The history of human

society, when viewed in detail, is far more often darkened with tragedy than it is lightened with hope. As these books will show, life for the nameless millions of mankind who have already lived and died has been wretched, short, hungry and brutal. Few societies have secured peace; none stability for more than a few centuries; prosperity, until very recent times, was the lucky chance of a small minority. Consolations of gratified desire, the soothing narcotic of ritual and the hope of future blessedness have often eased but rarely obliterated the misery which has been the lot of all but a handful of men since the beginning of history. At long last that handful is growing to a significant proportion in a few favoured societies. But throughout human history most men have derived pitifully little from their existence. A belief in human progress is not incompatible with a sharp realisation of the tragedy not only the lives of individual men but also of epochs, cultures and societies. Loss and defeat, too, are themes of this series, as well as progress and hope.

2

In 1492 the American Dream was born. Columbus, proud of his success and eager to triumph, wrote his account of the New World. Although the importance of his discoveries and the vast nature of the continents that he had brought within the reach of European enterprise were not fully appreciated for many decades, his account quickly spread in humanist and intellectual circles and fired the imagination of many complex and sensitive men who were disturbed by the violence and corruption of their world. Naked savages, sharing what they possessed: needs simple, lives harmonious: natural goodness, a golden world which had escaped the Fall, that had never known original sin: these hallucinatory phantoms bewildered minds weary with tribulations of their time. Soon the Americas were peopled with Utopias. Transmogrified by time, and modified by knowledge, this theme, given its first great prominence by Sir Thomas More, became a part of the European consciousness. The belief that life was simpler, more devout, less corrupt, more human in the great open plains and savannahs of the Americas; that there is a purity about the pioneer life grappling with the vast forces of nature; that freedom and liberty and true democracy were to be found there, such concepts have haunted the European imagination since the first great discoveries were made, and become a part of the political rhetoric of America which strives to impress an idealistic identity upon its peoples.

This was not the only dream that Columbus's discoveries unleashed. After all, he too had been captive of his fantasy—gold, silver, gems, riches that would slake the greed of the world. These tumbled and gleamed across the great waste of waters: drawing hard-faced, desperate men, willing to kill and be killed; willing to torture and enslave; willing to grind men into utter poverty so that they might fulfil their lust for power and riches: and this, too, began with the first Spanish colony in Hispaniola, the endless killings, lootings, brutalisations of primitive, peasant people: that exploitation that has gone on for centuries and still has not ceased. And in the wake of both dreams came two ugly realities—slavery and war.

The rapid obliteration of the Caribs by the Spaniards made a new labour force essential. Slave trading was, of course, more than half a century old by the time Columbus discovered the West Indies, for the Portuguese had begun the trade between Africa and Europe in 1441 and slaving had an older history than that, reaching far back: but the Atlantic trade which was well under way by 1510 was larger, crueller, more systematic than anything Europe had known before. In many ways it is the most inhuman aspect of European history—for the middle passage remained for centuries one of the most brutal experiences inflicted by man upon men. And the results of this trade still lie heavily on the conscience of America, and more particularly on the United States, for it has given rise to a massive problem—the attempt to create a multi-racial society in which all men have equal rights: a form of human society that, as yet, has never been achieved in the history of mankind. The moral problems involved both in forced labour of primitive Indians and in Negro slavery were clear to many Spaniards as soon as the practices started, and they gave rise to one of the greatest debates on the nature of Christian obligation to primitive, non-Christian peoples, between Las Casas and Sepúlveda at Valladolid in 1550 before the Emperor Charles V. By that time not only had the Caribs been largely wiped out but the populous barbaric empires of Mexico and Peru had been captured, subjugated and exploited ruthlessly, so ruthlessly that, it has been calculated, the population of Mexico fell from eleven to six and a half millions between 1519 and 1540, the years of the conquest and settlement. Las Casas had witnessed the wholesale killings, the burning, the torture, the rapine, the senseless destruction of human life, and Christian human life at that, for the Mexicans had proved easy converts. Sensitive, single-minded, obsessed by the need for justice yet verbose in writing and garrulous in speech, Las Casas had fought his crusade for a humane and Christian treatment of the Indians until he had reached the Emperor himself. His opponent, Sepúlveda, possessed a better mind and a cooler temperament. His arguments have a familiar ring: natural authority of Europeans, natural servitude of Indians, the necessity to place pagans and barbarians under the tutelage of civilised Christians, if need be by force, for their own good: the habitual crimes of barbarians against the natural law: furthermore subjection to Spain had led to commercial prosperity, or would do so: *ergo* the natives could only gain from a long period of subjection. At the heart of this great debate was, of course, the problem that was to rack the European conscience for centuries, that was, indeed, to haunt the empires of France, Britain and the Netherlands as well as Spain, and one that still bites deep into the heart of the world's problems. Sepúlveda was the highly intelligent advocate of pragmatism and expediency in conflict with Las Casas's warm-hearted humanism which as the centuries revolve is seen to be not only more just but so much more sensible, so much more likely to give rise to social stability as well as fulfilling the needs of a human justice than the seemingly sensible views of Sepúlvada.

Within a few decades of Columbus's discoveries Spain had been forced to face all the major problems of empire, some of which did not confront other European colonial powers—such as the Dutch—for centuries. With considerable foresight the Spanish monarchy kept a very firm hold over the government of New Spain and rapidly developed what was for the sixteenth century a complex bureaucratic system: but, of course, its effectiveness was partially vitiated by distance. To be effective, administrative decision needs to be prompt. Decisions, even on minor matters, often took six to twelve months, so that opportunities for prevarication and delay were almost endless; yet once a decision was taken, it was usually obeyed. And one of the most amazing facets of the Spanish Empire in America is the continuing, absolute authority of the Crown. The same was true, even, of royal policy towards the Indians. The Crown leaned somewhat towards the views of Las Casas, largely because the powerful ecclesiastical lobby at the Escorial was more concerned with conversion than with exploitation. Naturally the Spaniards in America were very lukewarm towards the royal policy: it was often evaded: its decrees misinterpreted and frequently neglected. In the last resort the King was obeyed, and the Spanish Crown was far more effective than any other European power except, perhaps, France in the late seventeenth century, but Louis XIV's problem was, in comparison, small—the control of a few garrisons, settlers and Indians—whereas the Spanish court ruled the greatest empire since antiquity.

How a relatively backward, poor and isolated country of Europe achieved such a mastery and such security is a problem as yet unsolved by historians. And it must be remembered that Spain in the sixteenth century did more than this. There were Spanish dominions in Italy and the Netherlands: war with the Turks, war with the Dutch and war with the English. The dynamic and explosive force of Western European societies was demonstrated for the first time, and in the most dramatic fashion, by Spain between 1500–50. And Professor Parry has explored the dynamics of that explosion with a matchless scholarship and sharp historical insight that takes us nearer to a solution than anyone has yet achieved. And perhaps equally important he evokes the quality of Spanish as well as Amerindian life, and so helps us to understand one of the most remarkable transformations of society in the history of man, for within less than a century not only had the great Aztec, Maya and Inca civilisations vanished but they had been replaced by a culture that was irremediably Catholic and Spanish no matter how strong its pagan undertones and so gave the possibility of unity to more than half a continent—at least at a cultural and social level, for the last hundred years of revolution and war have destroyed, for the foreseeable future, all hope of political unity for South and Central America.

The strength of the Spanish Empire lay in its institutions and its comparatively sophisticated bureaucracy in marked contrast to the subsequent empires of Britain and the Netherlands in the seventeenth century whose sinews were almost entirely commercial. At first there was little commercial conflict between Spain and the other maritime powers in Europe, and German banking firms were active in the exploitation of Spanish American silver-mines: in the middle decades of the sixteenth century Dutch and English slaving ships were welcome in the ports of the Caribbean. This did not last.

Hostility towards the British and war with the Dutch led to an attempted closure of the Spanish ports in America to other European trading nations; a situation which was influenced by the activities of Francis Drake, who managed to cloak his piracy not only with patriotic fervour but also religious zeal. The enormous hauls of bullion that Drake seized from the Spaniards cast a golden haze of optimism in the British mind about the wealth of the Indies. And Protestant pirates were soon lurking like sharks about the Spanish Main. English appetites were not the only ones to be whetted by the prospects of a vigorous, if illicit, trade with the Spanish Empire. As Spanish power decayed in Europe, its possessions overseas became an object of European cupidity and were one of the reasons for the involvement of Britain and the Netherlands in the War of the Spanish Succession. By then the Spanish Empire was clamped in an iron mould of bureaucratic tradition, and as irrevocably lost amidst medieval dreams and illusions as Spain itself. In 1700 the great powers of Europe stood poised like great vultures, ready to swoop, once the childless Charles II, a pathetic Hapsburg, inbred idiot, was dead. In October he was dying: dying in spite of the presence of San Isidro's mummified body or of San Diego of Alcala's corpse sitting in its urn: in spite of bits of saints, vestiges of Christ's Agony and shrouds or garments of the holy: in spite of the freshly killed pigeons on his head and the catharides on his feet: in spite, even, of the steaming entrails of freshly killed animals on his stomach. Nothing availed. And yet this was the world of Newton, of Leibniz, of Boyle, of Leeuwenhoek; of the early, sophisticated days of the European enlightenment: barbarous though the habits of Western courts might seem, they were centuries removed from the obscurantism and medievalism of Spain, where the solemn ritual burning of Jews and heretics still provoked a cathartic sense of holiness to Court, Church and people alike. And here lies the heart of the matter. The dynamic explosion of Spain's energies in the sixteenth century had taken place within the firm structure of medieval thought and belief and had not altered them one iota. True, for a time it seemed as if the transformation of Spain might take place: Erasmus was more widely read there than anywhere in Europe: for a time, Spanish doors were open to the entrepreneurs of the rest of Europe. But by the reign of Philip II that moment had gone and the world of Don Quixote had taken its place, a tragi-comic world of down-at-heel knights, improbable chivalry and nostalgia for that heroic Christian past which had driven the Moors from Spain and acquired the New World in the name of Christ. As Professor Parry so clearly shows, even the great debate between Las Casas and Sepúlveda was essentially a medieval dispute, one which in thought and language would have seemed natural enough to the great medieval doctors of the Church. And perhaps the enduring success of Spain in America lay in the static, medieval, Catholic ethos which it imposed on the peoples of Mexico and Peru. After all, their lives, too, had been bound to a cyclical universe of birth and renewal, a world in which change and growth and empirical novelty played no part; hence it was so easy to replace their savage gods by gods more benign perhaps, but still gods of a cyclical ritual of birth, death and renewal.

As the maritime nations of the North-West, aggressive, piratical and Protestant, threatened Spain in Europe as well as in America, it was natural that Catholicism in Spain and in America should become more intransigent, more suspicious of empiricism and rationalism and the new sciences of Europe. Spain, to preserve its identity, anchored itself both to the Church and to the past. There were, of course, other causes, economic and social, at work in Spain that ossified its energies, inhibited industrial growth, weakened commercial development and rendered rigid a social structure that belonged essentially to the late Middle Ages—a society of knights, priests and peasants, factors which are too complex for discussion here. Although almost incapable of change, the strength of seventeenth-century Spain must not be underestimated, for it possessed a vast inertia that brought with it, at least for a century or more, a capacity to survive the disasters of war and the buffets of fortune. And nothing illustrates this better than Spain's fate after the death of Charles II. Once he was dead, Louis XIV claimed Spain in Italy, Spain in the Netherlands, Spain in the New World, Spain in Asia and Spain itself: Austria, Britain, the Dutch, a miscellany of German princelings, set to, and the greatest and bloodiest war Europe had ever known was unleashed. Spain won. True, territories were lost in Italy and the Netherlands, and Louis XIV's grandson occupied the Escorial, but Spain triumphed. Philip V was quietly absorbed into the Spanish system, hierarchical, bigoted, resistant to change: and his court was the court of Philip II not Louis XIV. And the few trading rights that the powers wrested from the reluctant Spanish proved almost meaningless. The great Spanish Empire remained closed, and so became one of the prizes for which France and Britain fought for the next hundred years, with little success.

In the end the liberal ideas of France and the military success of

Britain in the Napoleonic Wars led to the break-up, to the fragmentation and Balkanisation of Spanish America, and yet the essential nature of its society did not change and it required the great social revolutions of the twentieth century to begin the painful transformation to the modern world.

The story of Spain and its empire is one of the most fascinating in the history of human society. The Spaniards alone discovered fabulous new worlds: as Bernal Díaz, the *conquistador*, wrote when he saw Mexico City: 'It all appeared to us like the enchanted things we read in the book of Amadis'. And yet within a few decades the strangeness was obliterated and all rendered commonplace and static. It was left to the enemies of Spain to feed their imagination and their greed on the wonders of the New World. Discovery is not necessarily a social catalyst, nor the possession of empire the harbinger of change. What worked like yeast in the societies of Britain and the Netherlands crystallised in the joints of Spain and rendered it arthritic. And yet their achievements will always amaze: the last, the most heroic, exploits of the medieval world, that reached back through the chronicles of the Crusades to the sagas of Viking and Norman, such were the conquests of Cortés and Pizarro, who toppled empires in the name of Christ and in the quest of gold.

The tradition of conquest

THE Spanish dominion in America has been a fruitful source of dramatic material for chroniclers and of puzzling paradoxes for historians. It was the first in time of the great seaborne empires of Western Europe, for long the richest and most formidable, the focus of envy, fear and hatred. It was created with astonishing speed, in little more than two generations, by a series of hazardous improvisations, the work of obscure private adventurers who explored vast areas, crossed great mountain ranges and conquered populous and highly organised native kingdoms. Despite the haphazard character of its origin, it proved remarkably enduring. Government and informed opinion in Spain reacted with a speed and vigour which matched the speed of conquest. The existence of conquest evoked, within two generations, a self-conscious, responsible imperialism, which profoundly influenced the development both of political theory and administrative practice. The administration of empire, after the initial free-for-all of conquest, was centralised, meticulously conscientious and by the standards of the time effective. It strove to protect the interests of a conquered people of alien race and religion, who were nevertheless regarded as direct subjects of the Crown, and to curb the exuberance of the *conquistadores* while profiting from their achievements. It sought to preserve for the Crown a source of wealth, and of the military strength which wealth could buy, which was for a time the wonder and terror of Europe. The objects of empire proved incompatible; no one was fully attainable. The strain of maintaining the system contributed powerfully to the impoverishment and defeat of Spain. The very effectiveness of the administration was, in part, the cause of its eventual undoing. All settler aristocracies, especially if they depend upon the labour of subject peoples, tend to resent centralised control, and the Spanish-American

Creoles were no exception. The administration was run, necessarily, by peninsular Spaniards. When the empire outgrew its strength, as all empires eventually do, and broke under the blows of war and invasion at the centre, its administration, lacking local roots, disintegrated, leaving the whole vast area a prey to economic instability and political disorder. It was not the conquered Indians, nor other envious Europeans, but the descendants of the *conquistadores*, who seized their opportunity and carved out, from the débris of empire, a whole series of new successor states, furnished with revolutionary theories and liberal constitutions, but aristocratic in social structure, conservative in temper, Catholic in religion, Spanish in language, culture and tradition. Conquest both preceded and outlived empire; and the interplay between conquest and empire is the theme of this story.

The story of conquest and empire in the Indies is comprehensible only against the background of the older story of conquest and monarchy in Spain. The successive Arab and Berber armies which from the eighth century entered Visigothic Spain from Africa were small in numbers, but their conquest was thorough and their influence lasting. They never subdued the whole peninsula; their hold on the arid highlands of Castile was never strong, for the *meseta* offered little to attract them; and north of the Cantabrian mountains they hardly penetrated at all. Toledo was the most northerly of the major Muslim cities. The southern half of the peninsula, however, from the eighth to the thirteenth century was predominantly Muslim. Under Muslim princes, Christian, Muslim and Jewish communities lived side by side, and while often feeling for one another little respect and no affection, grew accustomed to one another's ways. Many native Spaniards embraced Islam, and such conversions led to mixed marriages and mixed blood. A rich, varied and complex civilisation soon developed, compounded of Roman, Arab and native Spanish elements, the Arab predominating. Arab-Berber influence made itself evident especially in the immense and varied vocabulary of the Spanish language, in social habits such as the seclusion of women, in architecture and the lay-out of towns, in commercial practices, and in a great range of practical devices: irrigation and water-lifting appliances; the design and rig of boats and ships; saddlery and harness. Many Spanish Muslim cities were famous for centuries throughout Europe and the Near East for their specialised manufactures: Toledo for arms and armour, Córdoba for leather-ware, Granada and Almería for silk, Málaga and Valencia for pottery. In less material ways also southern Spain, Al-Andalus, had much to teach to a rough and primitive Europe dependent for its culture upon a half-forgotten Roman inheritance. Greek science and learning found their way to medieval Europe—in so far as they were known at all—largely through Arabic translations. Even the elaborate conventions of medieval chivalry were to some extent imitated from Arab customs and Arab romances. When the petty monarchs of northern Spain, proclaiming themselves the heirs of the Visigothic Kings, pushed beyond the Cantabrians to the south, they were attacking a civilisation which they resented for its infidel religion and its alien presence on Spanish soil, but which they admired and envied for its learning, its sophistication and its wealth.

For considerable periods in the Middle Ages, Al-Andalus possessed a unified political organisation and wielded a military power commensurate with its economic and cultural leadership. The Caliphate of Córdoba, established early in the tenth century by 'Abdu'r-Rahman III, challenged comparison with the great empires of the Near East. It was not only the ruling authority, both politically and spiritually, over all Muslim (and much of Christian) Spain; it was the protecting power of most of the Maghreb. The Caliph, by virtue of his title, was a semi-sacred figure, surrounded by an elaborate ritual and inaccessible save to a small circle of officials and intimates. Unlike European rulers, he defended his territories not by feudal levies or temporarily hired mercenaries but by a professional standing army recruited among the Berber warriors of North Africa. He demanded from his subjects a veneration and a docility quite alien to European notions of the relation between lord and vassal. This docility helps to explain the remarkable wealth and success of the Andalusian economy. It was an economy based on irrigation, producing not only an abundance of the traditional food plants, wheat, olives, vines, but also sub-tropical luxury crops, citrus, sugar, saffron, cotton, silk. In a society lacking powerful mechanical appliances, large-scale irrigation—indeed any large-scale system of public works—depends upon the ability of rulers to direct and organise large concentrations of labour more or less at will; it requires, therefore, a numerous and extremely docile peasant population. This Al-Andalus possessed; and this was its weakness and its strength. A docile peasantry is a source of strength and wealth to a strong ruler who can organise its capacity for labour and for paying taxes, who can keep vassals in order and invaders at bay; but under a weak or disintegrating government such a peasantry will, without much spontaneous resistance, render passive obedience to an invader from outside or to a rebellious local magnate. In such a society the road travelled by a ruling dynasty from obscurity to omnipotence, from omnipotence to defeat and ruin, is often short. Only the machinery of production and of government is permanent, ready to the hand of any ruler who can seize the controls.

The caliphate of the Umaiyad dynasty lasted little more than 100 years. Its last great ruler, Al-Mansur, 'the Victorious', was not himself one of the Umaiyads, but—nominally at least—their official. After his death, disintegration began; local governors set themselves up as independent rulers; and Al-Andalus broke up into twenty or thirty successor states or *taifas*. The *taifa* princes were of varied origin—Arab, Berber or Islamised Spaniard—and constantly at war with one another. As time went on, the stronger *taifas*, such as the Arab principality of Seville and the Berber state of Granada, tended to swallow up their weaker neighbours. The Muslim culture of Andalusia continued to flourish in these independent city states, despite political uncertainty; and the stronger *taifas* preserved the characteristics of the caliphate: sophisticated urban life, highly developed craft industries, a productive agriculture based on irrigation and forced labour, and a highly organised autocracy. None of the *taifa* rulers, however, wielded the military power of an 'Abdu'r-Rahman or an Al-Mansur. The *taifas* were an irresistible temptation to invaders, whether from the Christian North or from Morocco. Their rulers, like the Christian kings of the North, sought alliances where they could, alliances which often cut across religious boundaries. Some, to secure support or immunity from raiding, paid to Christian allies sums of money which, according to the prevailing balance of power, could be regarded either as tribute or as subsidies to mercenary allies; but when the demands of these fierce and rapacious allies became too heavy to be borne the *taifa* princes sometimes invited instead the intervention of warrior leaders from North Africa. So Al-Mu'tamid of Seville rejected the demands of Alfonso VI, declaring that he would 'rather tend the camels of the Almoravids than graze swine in Castile'. The Berber war-lords were as alien to the Spanish *taifa* rulers, in every respect save religion, as were the Christian kings; but they were formidable fighters. The caliphate of Al-Andalus was twice restored by such invaders from Africa proclaiming a Holy War: by the Almoravids at the end of the eleventh century and by the Almohads in the twelfth. Each group successfully evicted intruding Christian princes from Al-Andalus and carried the war against them back to the North. Both the Berber caliphates were relatively short-lived, however. Each was succeeded by a new age of *taifas* and of shifting alliances. It was in these circumstances, between the early thirteenth century and the late fifteenth, that the northern kingdoms completed the conquest of Spain by Christian arms.

Among the Christian kingdoms of northern Spain, the most tenacious resistance to the Almoravids, and later the most aggressive expansion, came not from the ancient kingdom of León but from upstart Castile, whose rulers in the tenth century first succeeded in establishing their territory as a separate and hereditary county, and which under Ferdinand III in the thirteenth century re-incorporated León as a secondary realm in a united kingdom. Castile displayed, in every aspect of its life, a dramatic contrast with the cultivated states of the Muslim south. It was, from its first emergence, a frontier kingdom, whose people, prompted by pugnacity, land hunger and religious zeal, looked to expansive war and conquest for the satisfaction of their ambitions. Its thin soil and arid climate, its immense and monotonous horizons with their repeated outcrops of tawny rock, all prompted its people to mobility, to dissatisfaction with a sedentary life of labour in the fields. Except for Old Castile, the region about Burgos—a region of early peasant resettlement—the economy of the *meseta* was predominantly pastoral, the only predominantly pastoral economy in Western Europe. It was based on the grazing of immense flocks of sheep, herds of pigs and half-wild cattle. Such an economy accorded well with the political scene of shifting frontiers and incessant fighting. Grazing on a large scale in semi-arid conditions was necessarily transhumant, covering great areas of open range. The flocks grazed on the southern *meseta* and in Extremadura in the winter and were driven away to summer pastures in the northern mountains. Their migratory cycle coincided with the alternation of winter peace and summer campaigning. The master of flocks and herds fitted well into such a restless scene. The peasant, conversely, tied to his land, was economically vulnerable and socially despised.

Like its economy, the social structure of Castile differed from that of the rest of Western Europe. The castles perched on every suitable crag throughout Castile—whether the strongholds of great men or the fortified priory-towns of the fighting Orders—were primarily fortresses. They were not, for the most part, the administrative centres of territorial fiefs, for the wealth which supported them was constantly on the move. Feudal ties were loose, based upon personal loyalty rather than on territorial dependance or jurisdiction. A gentleman was not primarily a man who held land by a particular kind of tenure. He was a man who owned a horse and was prepared to ride it into battle in his lord's support. His horse, no less than his sword, marked him off from the earth-bound peasant; it was the emblem of the mobility, the pride and the independence of the fighting man. Hence the love of horses, the feeling of comradeship with them, which pervaded the fighting class, the lesser nobility, of Castile. The Cid, the great traditional hero of medieval Castilian epic, was a man of this class, of the *infanzonía*. His patrimony was small, his personal prestige immense; and Babieca, his charger, was almost as famous as the man himself. Such a man acknowledged the duty of loyalty and obedience to his king or his overlord, but he expected the king to respect his personal dignity and to consult him about major decisions. The disciplined restraint, tempering the warrior's courage, which lends nobility to the character of the Cid, arose from within himself, owing nothing to fear or the hope of favour.

The kingdom of Castile was tough, resilient and predatory. Its knights regarded the rich principalities of the South as their natural prey. The surrender of Toledo to Alfonso VI in 1085 was the great turning point in the story of Castilian expansion; in the next century the Castilians were already confidently discussing, in treaty negotiations with other Christian states, the delimitation of their future conquests, not only in the peninsula but even in North Africa. The tide of war was to ebb and flow several times after the fall of Toledo, but Castile, with its towers and its cavalry, successfully resisted the attacks of Almoravids and Almohads, and in the thirteenth century embarked upon an offensive which extended its territory to the southern coast of Spain. Murcia was taken in 1243, and the King of Aragon, himself already in possession of Valencia, recognised the right of Castile to this new acquisition. Ibn al-Ahmar, the ruler of Granada, purchased a limited independence by an offer of tribute and of assistance against Seville. By this means Granada survived for 200 years more as the only Muslim *taifa*, connected with North Africa by a tenuous bridgehead at Gibraltar and Algeciras. Seville itself surrendered to Fernando III in 1248. It is hard to exaggerate the importance of this event. The richest, most productive and most civilised territory in all Spain, the greatest and most industrious city, a thriving port which was to become the gateway to Atlantic trade and discovery, became incorporated in Castile, the most warlike, the most powerful, economically and socially the most backward kingdom in Spain. A whole armoury of new weapons had been placed in the hands of the successors of the Cid.

After the conquest of Andalusia the destinies of the Iberian kingdoms diverged. Navarre, long excluded from the great advance, had already turned towards France. In Aragon, Cataluña had began to establish its merchant colonies in the wake of those of Genoa throughout the Mediterranean, and the Aragonese crown was turning to the annexation of Mediterranean islands and the conquest of southern Italy. León, having vested its imperial pretensions in Castile, was losing its political individuality. Portugal remained in association with Castile, but only until Gibraltar and Tarifa were secure in Christian hands; once there was safe transit between ocean and inland sea, the confluence of Mediterranean and Atlantic shipping at Lisbon was to open for the Portuguese a new career of oceanic trade and discovery. Granada, between the upper and nether millstones of Castile and Morocco, preserved a precarious independence by intrigue and alliances. Castile itself, with its primitive social and economic structure and its crusading tradition, held to a career of colonisation and conquest.

Andalusia, once conquered by Castile, was rapidly and extensively colonised. For over a hundred years Seville was the favourite residence of the Castilian kings, and naturally they sought to people Andalusia with loyal subjects. Castilian noblemen secured great fiefs in the south, including huge cattle ranges in the drier upland areas, and in the valleys productive irrigated estates tilled by a docile *mudéjar* peasantry. In the wake of the conquering armies, also, came colonists from all over the north of Spain, from Castile, from León, from Aragon and the Basque country, attracted by good land, by an easy climate, by the luxurious and sophisticated life of the southern cities, and by the prospect of lording it over a Muslim population reduced by conquest to an inferior status. Seamen from Biscay, from Galicia and from Portugal settled not only in Seville but in the many small ports of the *condado* of Niebla, which were to become the outports of Seville, sharing modestly in its commercial prosperity. All these settlers brought their own local customs and speech; but in the Andalusian melting-pot they gradually lost their regional differences and became Spaniards, adopting the speech of Castile, which became the dominant language of Spain. For more than two hundred years this steady drift to the south continued, and with it a steady shift of the centre of economic gravity. In Andalusia the Castilians developed their own domestic imperialism and formed the habits of conquest and settlement which they would inevitably, sooner or later, seek to exercise beyond the boundaries of Spain.

Granada remained a more or less tolerated Muslim enclave. Fernando III had originally welcomed the emergence of this independent mountain kingdom as a rival to Seville and to Murcia. After the conquest of the rest of Andalusia, Granada was protected by its vassalage; and though its Nasrid rulers sometimes withheld tribute and defied Castile, the warfare for many years had something of the character of the tournament. Its independent existence helped to exercise the martial skill of the Castilians and to keep the crusading spirit alive, without presenting any very dangerous threat to Castile. North Africa was a more obvious object of Castilian acquisitiveness; but in the second half of the thirteenth century a new and vigorous dynasty, the Marinids, united Morocco, held the southern tip of Spain and presented too formidable a front to be lightly assaulted. On occasion, indeed, they made raids into Andalusia which gave the Castilians cause to be grateful for the neutrality of their Granadine vassal. In the fourteenth and fifteenth centuries, moreover, Castile was repeatedly torn by internal fighting, by minorities and disputed regencies, by succession wars. The offensive against Islam was not effectively resumed for more than two hundred years after the capture of Seville; not until Isabella, married to Ferdinand of Aragon, was firmly seated on the Castilian throne after a last bitter succession war with the King of Portugal. Isabella was the true successor of Fernando III, the reviver of the military and religious policy for which he had stood; but with important differences.

By the fifteenth century, European civilisation had developed to a point where it no longer depended upon the Arab world for inspiration and instruction, and in Spain Africanising fashions tended to become a sterile affectation. At the hedonistic and disorderly court of Henry IV of Castile this affectation was pushed to extremes in which the Christian religion was derided, Moorish customs openly adopted and the war against Islam forgotten or deliberately postponed. The Succession War and the accession of Isabella brought a sharp reversal. The Queen was inspired not only by her own intense religious conviction but also by

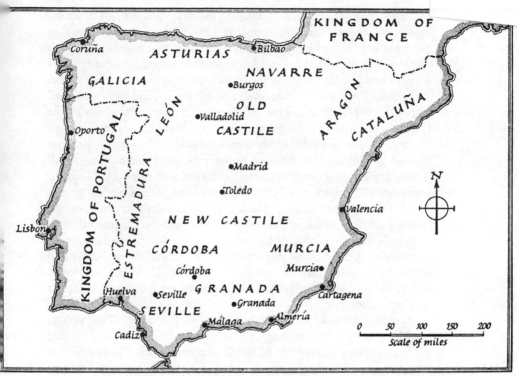

1. The kingdoms of Spain in the late fifteenth century

the need to forestall the danger of a new Holy War. The Ottoman Turks had extinguished the Byzantine Empire, and were engaged in conquering and unifying the Muslim states of the Levant. Already they were threatening the Christian kingdoms of the Balkans; in 1480 Muhammad II actually invaded Italy, and the invasion was stopped only by the Sultan's death. Castile could ill afford what in later Spanish history was to be called a fifth column. Isabella determined to press ahead with preparations against Granada (whose rulers, emboldened by the Succession War, had again withheld tribute) and if possible eventually to carry the war into North Africa, as the Portuguese had already done at Ceuta in 1415. Systematic operations for the conquest of the Moorish kingdom, village by village, began in 1482. Spaniards embarked on this last European crusade with a complex mixture of attitudes towards the Muslim enemy. The mixture included intense religious exaltation; abhorrence of unbelief, modified (on the part of feudal superiors) by concessions to economic expediency; acquisitiveness, in the sense not only of hope of plunder but of determination to exploit the Moors as vassals; social dislike, modified by long familiarity; economic envy (for the Moors were usually better farmers and craftsmen, and often sharper traders, than their Spanish rivals); and finally political fear—fear not of Granada but of the powerful support which might reach Granada if that kingdom were not brought under Christian control. As for Granada, isolated and divided within itself, the issue was never in serious doubt. The capital city surrendered in 1492. All Spain, for the first time in many centuries, was ruled by Christian sovereigns. The territory of Granada was placed under Castilian governors by the terms of a treaty which in other respects was generous and which initially guaranteed the free practice of Muslim law and religion.

Isabella, however, advised by the uncompromising ecclesiastics who surrounded her, was little disposed to allow the Moors of Granada to settle down peacefully as Muslim vassals of Christian overlords. Religious zeal, for her, must find expression not only in conquest and suzerainty but in conversion. After the capture of Granada she inaugurated a new policy of vigorous proselytising. This policy, initially confined to preaching and persuasion, met with very limited success, despite the devotion of the Observant Franciscans to whom it was entrusted. The impatience of the Queen and her minister Cisneros soon insisted upon sterner measures: systematic persecution and a drastic stiffening of ecclesiastical discipline. The expulsion of the Jews, the violent baptism of the Moors of Granada, the extraordinary powers entrusted to the new Inquisition, were all departures from medieval tradition in Spain. In former centuries, in most parts of Spain, the three 'peoples of the Book' had lived side by side in separate but neighbouring communities. Spanish rulers, while willing enough to subdue the infidel, had appreciated his civilised standing, his abilities and his knowledge. Archbishop Raymond of Toledo in the twelfth century had founded schools where Muslim, Jewish and Christian scholars collaborated in work which, when communicated to the learned centres of Europe, opened a new era in medieval science. Alfonso X had gathered into his court the learned of three religions, for he was as eager to sift the wisdom of the East as of the West. Fernando III, king and saint, is proclaimed by his epitaph to have been a king who tolerated infidel cults in mosque and synagogue. But times had changed; Isabella's

severities were, on the whole, publicly approved, as they would not have
been a hundred years before; and in Castile (though not in Aragon)
they were vigorously enforced, as a hundred years before they could
not have been. They represented both a reaction against the intensified
Muslim pressure on Christendom since the fall of Constantinople, and
an intensification of religious fervour, and so of religious intolerance,
in Spain. They represented also a deliberate rejection on the Queen's
part of the African element in Spanish culture; an equally deliberate
affirmation of Spain's community with the rest of Christian Europe;
and, by implication, a new assertion of social and racial superiority. These
were the feelings of a self-confident people, apt for empire. Granada
was to the Spaniards what Constantinople, in its last enfeebled years,
had been to the Turks: the culmination of one series of conquests
and the beginning of another.

The conquest did not relieve Spain of the fear of Islam; nor did
the Spanish invasion of North Africa, which began with the capture
of Melilla in 1492, prevent the advance of the Turks. Early in the sixteenth century they conquered Syria and Egypt and extended their
suzerainty along the whole North African coast. The immense power
of the Ottoman Empire could then be summoned to defend the Muslim
rulers of the coast, and possibly even to support rebellion among disaffected Moors in Spain. It was a power too strong to be challenged, as
yet, by the forces of the Spanish kingdoms. Meanwhile, the enthusiasms
and ambitions quickened by the war against Granada persisted, only
partially satisfied by victory. An outlet for this pent-up martial energy
was suggested, only a year after the fall of Granada, by Columbus's
report of islands in the western Atlantic, and by his insistence that
those islands might be used as stepping-stones to China. Within a
generation, the feelings which had rallied Spaniards against Granada
developed into a bold and methodical imperialism which, casting about
for new provinces to conquer, found its opportunity overseas. While
Portuguese imperialism in West Africa sought, among other objects,
a back door through which to attack the Arab and the Turk, Spanish
imperialism, by opportune discovery, was led to operate in a new
world.

CHAPTER I

Islands and mainland
in the Ocean Sea

THE conquest of most of Andalusia in the thirteenth century opened for Castile new windows on the world. To Bilbao and the smaller harbours of Galicia and Biscay, through which Castilian wool, carried down by mule train from Burgos, was shipped to Flanders, the conquest added the ports of Murcia and Valencia, with their access to Italian supplies of grain, and, most important of all, the great harbour of Seville, with its busy dockyards and its thriving trade to North Africa. Fernando III had employed Galician ships to blockade Seville in his final attack, and when the city was in his hands he did all in his power to restore and encourage its shipyards. Castile became an important naval power. Naval, not initially maritime. Castilian horsemen did not immediately take to the sea. The harbour of Seville was regarded as a military instrument, to serve as a base in the coming struggle for control of the Straits and for safe communication between the Atlantic and Mediterranean seaboards of Castile. Officers and men employed in these naval operations were mostly, in the early days, Italian mercenaries, and for many years the traditional seaborne trades of Seville also remained in the hands either of Muslims or of Pisans or Genoese. The steady immigration of Basque and Galician seamen into Seville and its outports in the fourteenth and fifteenth centuries, however, bred new trades. A Spanish maritime community developed in western Andalusia. The immigrant seamen of Seville, Cadiz and the Río Tinto ports sought outlets for their enterprise in northern Europe, in Portugal, in Africa and in the Atlantic islands.

In many of these maritime enterprises the Portuguese had already shown the way. Portugal possessed a long ocean seaboard, a considerable fishing and seafaring population, and a powerful commercial class largely emancipated from feudal interference. Portuguese fishermen were the first Europeans to exploit the Mauretanian fisheries; and Portuguese shippers were eager and able to graduate from an Atlantic trade in wine, fish and salt to more widespread and lucrative ventures in slaves, gold and spices. They found in West Africa the first two of these commodities, and even a substitute—*malagueta* and Benin peppers —for the third. At the time of the outbreak of the Castilian Succession War they already had the beginnings of a thriving trade with the Gulf of Guinea. The Río Tinto ports are very close to Portugal, and in those days the precise nationality of seamen was often difficult to establish. Andalusian sailors shipped in Portuguese expeditions, and Andalusian skippers followed the Portuguese down the coast. Naturally the presence of these foreign poachers was resented by the Portuguese monopolists; and resentment was quickened by the possibility that islands lying within easy reach of the coast might be used as interlopers' bases. Of the four principal groups of islands lying in the middle latitudes of the eastern Atlantic, three—Madeira, the Azores and the Cape Verde Islands —were claimed and partly settled by Portuguese in the course of the fifteenth century. All three groups proved valuable not only as ports of call but as sources of marketable subtropical products. The fourth group, the Canaries, which was also the largest and the nearest to the African coast, was claimed by Castile by virtue of a papal grant of 1344. Unlike the other island groups, the Canaries—or some of them—were inhabited by a primitive but numerous and warlike people, the Guanches. The European settlement of these islands proved a long and arduous business, not indeed completed until well after the discovery of America and the opening of West Indian trade. Early in the fifteenth century various adventurers, mostly Normans, had planted settlements in Lanzarote, Ferro and Fuerteventura, and did homage for them to the King of Castile. These plantations became modestly prosperous, producing sugar, wine and wheat; and Andalusian traders found another means of profit, by collecting sea-shells in the islands and shipping them to the Guinea coast for use as coin. The Portuguese not only tried to drive away or capture these

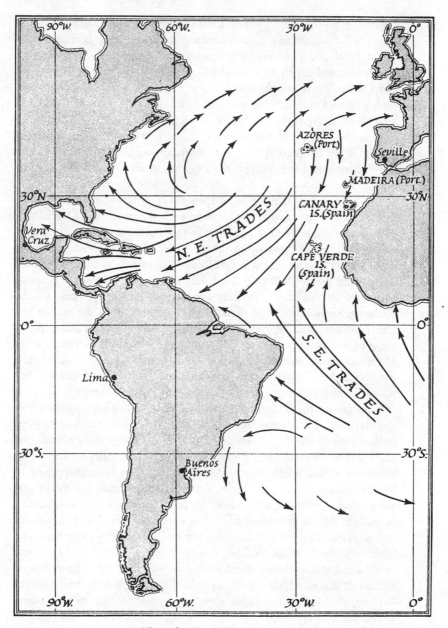

2. The Atlantic wind system (summer)

interlopers on the coast but also tried to neutralise Castilian bases in the Canaries by establishing rival settlements in unoccupied islands within the archipelago. The savage, unorganised sea-fighting which ensued was swallowed up in 1475 in the Succession War between Portugal and Castile. Portugal, though heavily defeated by Isabella's forces on land, achieved considerable successes at sea. In the Treaty of Alcaçovas which ended the war—the first European treaty to deal with oversea possessions—the Spaniards undertook to respect the Portuguese mono-poly of trade in West Africa and of settlement in Madeira, the Cape Verde Islands and the Azores; the Portuguese abandoned all claims in the Canaries.

The Spaniards had established themselves in Grand Canary during the war, and after the peace pushed on with the conquest of the island. They began the settlement of Palma in 1490, of Tenerife in 1493. Mod-est harbour towns grew up in the principal islands, each with its little fleet of fishing and trading caravels. The Guanches, as they were sub-dued, were divided with the land they occupied, as Moorish peasants had been in Andalusia, in fiefs among the leading settlers. In the Canaries, Spaniards served their first apprenticeship in the arts of co-lonial empire, and had their first experience of converting and exploit-ing a primitive subject race. The Canaries lie near the northern edge of the north-east trade-wind zone; a comfortable wind for sailing into the Ocean Sea. In later years the last vanishing sight of Europe, for many Spanish adventurers, was the towering cone of Tenerife.

Throughout the fifteenth century sailors were discovering islands in the Atlantic. There was no apparent reason why the discovery of fresh islands should not go on indefinitely. Of all legendary islands, the most famous and most persistent was Atlantis or Antilla, the isle of the seven cities, where seven Portuguese bishops were supposed to have migrated with their flocks, during the barbarian invasions, and where their descendants had lived in prosperity and piety ever since. It was one of the dreams of fifteenth-century sailors to rediscover this mythical country, its Christian people and its gold. A cloudbank can look very like an island at dusk, and probably in the Atlantic harbours of Portugal and Andalusia there were men who claimed to have sighted Antilla. It was into such a world of sailors' yarns, where anything might happen, that Columbus came peddling the 'enterprise of the Indies' round the courts of Europe.

That a great Iberian explorer should be the son of an obscure weaver in Genoa was not in itself surprising. The Genoese went everywhere in Europe, and had close commercial contacts with Seville and Lisbon. All the major European centres of geographical knowledge at that time were in Italy. Every citizen of Genoa, however humble, depended directly or indirectly upon the city's maritime connections. Nearly all the professional explorers—nearly all professional seamen, indeed— were men of comparatively humble origin. Columbus himself was not a professional sailor. He was a self-taught and extremely persuasive geographical theorist, with some knowledge of cartography and a grounding in navigation. The precise nature of his theories, their origin, and the practical proposals which he based on them, have been the subject of much learned controversy. By the agreement under which he sailed in 1492 he was to 'discover and acquire islands and mainland in the Ocean Sea'. This was a standard formula. In this instance it probably included Antilla, if any such place existed; but almost certainly the phrase 'islands and mainland' was also understood to mean Cipangu and Cathay, the resounding names by which Marco Polo had described Japan and China. There was nothing fantastic, at least in theory, in a proposal to reach Asia by sailing west. Since the earth was known to be round and there was no suspicion of an intervening continent, the practical possibility depended on winds, on currents, above all on distance; and on this there were many theories and no certainty.

According to Barros and others, Columbus made his first proposal in 1484, to the Portuguese Crown. This, too, was natural. Enthusiasm for exploration was then at its height in Lisbon, and government and investors alike were anxious to profit by Italian commercial experience and cartographical skill. While in Portugal, Columbus made at least one voyage to Guinea in a Portuguese ship. While in Portugal, also, he acquired, by marriage with the daughter of a leading Madeira settler, contacts with circles interested in island discoveries. Nevertheless, his proposal for an expedition at royal expense was declined, after a careful hearing. Columbus's geographical reasoning presumably failed to convince. Diogo Cão's first voyage, moreover, had raised hopes of a surer way to the East; hopes which Bartolomeu Dias, in 1489, was triumphantly to confirm. Columbus, having tried France and England without success, turned finally to Castile.

In Spain, Columbus's difficulties arose not chiefly from vested interests and geographical scepticism but from the pressure of other concerns which made the government reluctant to consider maritime exploration of any kind. After many importunities, however, he succeeded in enlisting the support of a great officer of state, Luis de Santángel, keeper of the privy purse to the King of Aragon and treasurer of the Santa Hermandad. Santángel himself raised a considerable part of the money needed to finance the enterprise. Through his good offices the consent and participation of the Spanish monarchs was secured, and once committed they agreed to all Columbus's terms, including the rewards, listed in the agreement, which he was to receive in the event of success. The fleet was fitted out in the Río Tinto, at Palos, home port of lateen caravels similar to those which the Portuguese used for West African exploration and coastal trade, and of seamen familiar with Portuguese expeditions. The sovereigns provided Columbus with well-found ships: the Palos caravels *Niña* and *Pinta*, and as flagship the Galicean square-rigged *nao Santa Maria*. With royal money he could man the ships with reliable crews and capable and experienced officers. Columbus himself was a careful and accurate, though not very up-to-date navigator; to picture him as an unpractical mystic is mere caricature. Sailing from Palos in August 1492, he made for the Canaries, where he stayed for several weeks, taking in wood and water and refitting. This was to become standard Spanish practice. From the Canaries he set his course due west. In that latitude, on its northern fringe, the trade-wind is unreliable, and Columbus, discovering this, made his later passages considerably further south; this too became standard practice. In 1492, however, he was lucky in having a fair wind all the way out. After thirty-three days of uneventful sailing, with nothing but floating gulf weed and the bosun birds to keep hope alive, his people sighted their first island in the Bahamas. Threading their way to the south-west between the cays, they found the north-east coast of Cuba and the north coast of Hispaniola, modern Haiti, clothed to the water-line in high forest. Here prospects brightened. Hispaniola yielded a little alluvial gold, and a few gold nose-plugs and bracelets were obtained by barter from the natives. On the north coast of Hispaniola, however, Columbus lost his flagship, wrecked by grounding, and decided to return home, leaving some of his men behind with instructions to build houses and search for gold-mines.

On his return passage Columbus made one more important discovery: the necessity, on leaving the West Indies, of standing well to the north and out of the trade-wind before attempting the Atlantic crossing. He found a westerly wind, as thousands of his successors were to do, in about the latitude of Bermuda, and ran down before it to the Azores. On approaching Europe, however, he ran into foul weather, and was compelled to put in for shelter, first in the Azores and then in the Tagus. Here the Portuguese authorities demanded an explanation of his activities. With previous experience of Italian exaggeration, they were sceptical of his story, contemptuous of his geographical reasoning and unimpressed by his description of the Tainos of Hispaniola. They had been alarmed by a recent revival of Andalusian poaching on the coast of Upper Guinea and, with an expedition to India under discussion, were extremely suspicious of all Spanish maritime activity in the Atlantic. John II decided to lay claim to Columbus's discoveries on the grounds that they came within the provisions of the Treaty of Alcaçovas, that they lay close to the Azores and might even be regarded as forming part of that group.

Columbus himself claimed, and believed until his death, that he had found islands lying off the coast of eastern Asia, and possibly part of the mainland too. His belief was based chiefly on a somewhat uncritical reading of Marco Polo and of Ptolemy. We cannot be sure whether his claims agreed with his original intentions and promises, nor whether Ferdinand and Isabella entirely accepted them. Some intelligent contemporaries certainly did not; and doubt in the minds of Columbus's own men is suggested by the alternative name of Antilles, from Antilla or Atlantis. But beyond doubt Columbus had found an extensive archipelago of hitherto unknown islands, which were inhabited by a peaceful and tractable, though primitive, people, and which produced gold. If they should prove stepping-stones to India, so much the better; but in any event they were worth careful investigation, and the decision to settle them with Spaniards was made almost at once. Ferdinand and Isabella therefore opened negotiations both with Portugal and with the Papacy, to get the islands formally recognised as a Spanish possession, and to open the way for the acquisition of further territory beyond them to the west.

The Papacy first: the Papacy was necessarily concerned in the discovery and settlement of territories outside Europe, for the Pope and the Pope alone could authorise missions to the heathen; further, the Pope alone could allot to a particular Christian community—kingdom or religious Order—the exclusive right of proselytising in a particular heathen area. The West African activities of the Order of Christ and of the Portuguese Crown had been covered by bulls of this type. It was even sometimes argued—but not generally accepted—that the Pope, in order to benefit the Faith, might lawfully allot to Christian princes the lands and temporal possessions of heathen rulers. Certainly a Christian prince could gain important diplomatic advantages by securing formal papal approval of his actions or intentions, and such approval the Catholic monarchs proceeded to seek. The pope of the time, Alexander VI, was himself a Spaniard, already under heavy obligations to the Catholic sovereigns and looking to them for support in his endeavour to create a principality in Italy for his son. He issued a series of bulls, each successively strengthening and extending the provisions of the preceding, in accordance with successive demands made by Ferdinand and Isabella upon Columbus's advice. Their effect was to grant to the sovereigns of Castile all lands discovered, or to be discovered, in the regions explored by Columbus. The most important of the bulls, the famous *Inter caetera*, drew an imaginary boundary line from north to south a hundred leagues west of the Azores and Cape Verde Islands, and provided that the land and sea beyond the line should be a Spanish sphere of exploration. *Dudum siquidem* extended the previous grants to include 'all islands and mainlands whatever, found or to be found . . . in sailing or travelling towards the west and south, whether they be in regions occidental or meridional and oriental and of India'.

The bulls of 1493 constituted for Spaniards the basic legal claim of the Spanish Crown to the lands of the New World. Immediately, however, they were preliminaries to the negotiations with Portugal. The Portuguese had no intention of going to war over a few distant islands inhabited by naked savages or of defying the authority of the Pope; but they were very much concerned, in view of *Dudum siquidem* with its specific reference to India, to restrict Spanish maritime activity, to push it to the west where (as they thought) it could do little harm, and to reserve for themselves as wide an area as possible in the south Atlantic. John II therefore dropped his claim to the islands and agreed to accept the bull of demarcation, *Inter caetera*, as a basis for discussion. He only asked that the boundary line be moved 270 leagues further west, ostensibly to protect his African interests. The Spanish monarchs, secure in the delusions which Columbus had fostered about the western route to Asia, agreed. Both sides must have known that so vague a boundary could not be accurately fixed, and each thought that the other was deceived. The treaty of Tordesillas was duly signed in 1494, a diplomatic triumph for Portugal, confirming to the Portuguese not only the true route to India but most of the south Atlantic with the imaginary land of Antilla and—as shortly afterwards appeared—the real land of Brazil.

The treaty did not affect the newly discovered Indies, and the sovereigns had not waited for its conclusion before sending Columbus out again. He left Cadiz in September 1493, in command of a large fleet, ships, caravels and pinnaces, seventeen sail in all. The fleet carried few arms, and no trade goods other than small trinkets for barter. Its chief cargo was men—twelve hundred people, priests, gentlemen-soldiers, artisans, farmers—and agricultural stock—tools, seeds and animals: a whole society in miniature. Its immediate purpose was not to open a new trade, or to conquer oriental kingdoms, but to settle the island of Hispaniola, to found a prospecting and farming colony which should produce its own food, pay for the cost of the voyage by remitting gold to Spain, and serve as a base for further exploration in the direction of India or Cathay. For such adventurous and rewarding service there were many volunteers. The settlement of Atlantic islands was already a familiar idea in the Iberian kingdoms, and no doubt Columbus's knowledge of the development of Madeira affected his plans. The fleet was fitted out under the direction of Juan Rodríguez de Fonseca, Archdeacon of Seville and a member of the Council of Castile, who was to have a long and influential connection with the Indies. Columbus complained bitterly of Fonseca, whom he thought obstructive and dilatory. Sea-going commanders are often impatient of dockyard administration, and the two men seem to have disliked one another personally. In fact, the fitting-out was done with considerable efficiency: five months was a short time for the preparation of so large a fleet in fifteenth-century Spain. Fonseca's only serious mistake was failure to provide the colony with enough food for the first year; over-optimism about the extent to which Europeans could live off the country in the Tropics was a common feature of these early explorations and was one of the chief causes of the difficulties which Columbus encountered.

The fleet made a prosperous passage and a good landfall at Dominica, the wild Carib island whose sharp volcanic spires were to be for thousands of Spaniards their first sight of the New World. They passed along the beautiful arc of the Lesser Antilles, through the Virgin Islands, past Puerto Rico, and came to the north coast of Hispaniola.

Here they found that the settlement of Navidad, planted on the first voyage, had been destroyed. In selecting as the site for his second settlement the unprotected, unhealthy shore which he named Isabela, Columbus made his first serious blunder. Isabela never prospered. Even with a better site, it would have been no light task to maintain discipline among those early Spanish settlers—touchy, adventurous and greedy as they were—to make them clear forest, build houses and plant crops, instead of roaming about the island in search of gold or slaves. Certainly the task was beyond Columbus. He was a foreigner and the son of an artisan tricked out with an empty title and a new coat of arms. By choice and temperament he was an explorer, not a colonial governor. His energies, during this second visit to the Indies, were concentrated on the exploration of the south coast of Cuba and the discovery of Jamaica. Early in 1496 he returned to Spain, to report progress and to deal with complaints carried there by malcontents from Isabela. In his absence, but with his approval, his brother Bartholomew, whom he left in charge, organised the removal of the settlement from Isabela to a better site on the south coast. There, in 1496 or 1497, the colonists began to build the town of Santo Domingo, which was to be for half a century the capital of the Spanish Indies, and which survives as a thriving city today.

The Catholic monarchs still had no return on their investment except for a few 'Indian' slaves whom the Queen ordered to be released and sent back home. They still trusted Columbus's judgement, however, and respected their agreement with him. He was allowed a third expedition at royal expense in 1498. On this occasion he sailed to the south of his former courses, to discover the island of Trinidad and the mouths of the Orinoco, by far the largest river then known to Europeans, whose great volume of fresh water proved the new-found coast to be part of a mighty continent. From the Venezuelan coast he sailed directly, by a remarkable feat of navigation, to Hispaniola, to the new settlement which his brother had founded. He found the colony in an uproar. The Tainos, unwarlike gatherers of roots and shellfish, lacking all but the most rudimentary agriculture, had been exasperated to the point of war by incessant demands for food and women. Half the settlers, disillusioned and hungry, were in open revolt against Bartholemew's authority. Columbus had no choice but to buy off the rebels with pardon and restoration to office, with land grants, and —more significant still—with a general division of the Indians of the island among the Spanish settlers as estate labourers. This *repartimiento* system, imported from the Canaries, later became general in a modified form throughout the Spanish Indies. Rebellious discontent was thereby, for a time, appeased; but the damage had been done. In the spring of 1499 the sovereigns appointed Francisco de Bobadilla to supersede Columbus and to investigate the complaints against him. Bobadilla sent the Admiral home in irons. Though his sovereigns restored his title and revenues and treated him with courtesy to his death, Columbus was never again allowed to exercise his offices of admiral and viceroy or to interfere in the government of the Indies.

The real beginnings of settled government in the Indies date from the arrival of Bobadilla's successor, Frey Nicolás de Ovando, Knight Commander of Alcántara. It was characteristic of the time that this task should be entrusted to a high officer of an order founded to garrison the Christian outposts in Spain against Islam. Ovando arrived in 1502 with a great fleet of thirty ships and brought 2,500 people to reinforce the 300 or so surviving settlers. He governed Hispaniola ably for six years, with a severity far harsher than Columbus had ever dared to exercise. Discipline, indeed, was what the settlers chiefly needed. From the subjugated Indians the invaders exacted a tribute of produce and forced labour, by means of the *repartimiento* system introduced under Columbus, extended and legalised under Ovando. Against the wild Indians they waged relentless war. Probably the Tainos were doomed already. The shock, the despair and the social dislocation caused by forced labour; the ravages of measles and smallpox; the destruction of crops by imported animals; all contributed to a rapid decline in their numbers. Ovando's severities only hastened their extinction. Spanish landholders, on the other hand, achieved in his time a modest prosperity, producing increasing quantities of gold-dust from the streams, and pasturing great herds of pigs and horned cattle upon open range. Little attempt was made to survey boundaries. Cattle were sorted and calves branded at periodic round-ups, but many escaped the branding and took to a completely wild existence in the forests. Within a few years *montería*—the hunting of feral cattle and pigs—became a recognised right held in common by the settlers in each locality. Unable to subsist adequately on tribute in kind, the settlers also grew some crops of their own: native cassava, imported yams and even a little sugar-cane which they ground in ox- or water-mills. In the 1520s, as the gold became exhausted, sugar took its place, along with pastoral products, as an exportable commodity. Oviedo gave the number of mills in his time as twenty-four, which represented a considerable capital investment. Lack of labour was the chief hindrance to development. The settlers resorted to slave-raiding in the Bahamas in order to replace the dying Tainos, and a little later occasional Negro slaves began to be brought in, but there was never enough labour. To men of the temperament of the early Spanish settlers land was useless without hands to work it. No Spaniard cared to engage in agricultural labour in the Tropics. Even gold prospecting, the primitive washing of gold-dust from the gravel of the streams, was tedious work calling for docile unskilled labour. Lack of labour, as much as greed, missionary zeal or simple restlessness, drove many newcomers on from Hispaniola to settle in other islands and mainlands where the native population might prove more numerous and more hardy. Hispaniola became, as its founders had intended, the base for further exploration and the source of bacon, dried beef and cassava bread to victual the exploring expeditions which sailed out in ever-increasing numbers during the government of Ovando's successor, the old admiral's son, Diego Colón.

In 1509 Juan de Esquivel began the settlement of Jamaica. In 1511 the much larger enterprise of settling Cuba was undertaken by Diego Velázquez, who had been Ovando's lieutenant in Hispaniola. Velázquez was an *entrepreneur* rather than a discoverer. Having put down initial native resistance, he settled in rude state at Santiago, where he could command communications with the other islands, and left the work of exploration to agents and subordinates. The conquest was swift, brutal and successful. Velázquez retained the royal confidence; Spanish settlements were duly incorporated, and enjoyed—until the gold ran out—a rough prosperity. Cuba produced considerable quantities of gold, and being less mountainous than Hispaniola it offered better opportunities for ranching, farming and sugar-planting. As in Hispaniola, the labour for mines and farms was procured in the early years through *repartimientos* of the native population.

While the Greater Antilles were thus being subdued and settled, other longer, more dangerous and more speculative expeditions were sailing from Hispaniola to explore the mainland coasts of the Caribbean. Columbus's own monopoly of exploration on the mainland coast, based on his 1492 agreement, was less clear than his monopoly in the islands, and had, indeed, been infringed in his lifetime. Authorisation for these infringements was granted to some of Columbus's former companions through the agency of his old enemy Fonseca. In 1499 Vicente Yáñez Pinzón, former captain of the caravel *Niña*, had coasted part of northern Brazil and Guiana. Alonso de Ojeda, earlier in the same year, had followed up the Admiral's third voyage and explored the coast of Venezuela from Margarita to Maracaibo. With him had sailed Amérigo Vespucci, whose ready pen and sound geographical judgement were to bring him a fame which for a time eclipsed that of Columbus himself. Ojeda's first voyage had little immediate result—his cargo of brazil-wood, sold in Cadiz, failed to cover his costs; but subsequent exploration by Nicolás Guerra on the same coast revealed that the oysters fished by the local Indians were rich in pearls. The little island of Cubagua became the site of the Spanish settlement of New Cadiz, founded to exploit the pearl fishery. For about twenty-five years, until over-fishing destroyed its source of wealth, New Cadiz was one of the most prosperous places in the Caribbean, and the centre of a thriving and brutal trade in slaves to serve as divers.

More permanent and more significant for the future were the settlements in Central America, on the isthmus coast which Columbus had found on his fourth voyage and where the Columbus family later held their only mainland possession, the little duchy of Veragua. The shores of the Gulf of Darien had been visited in 1500 by Rodrigo de Bastidas, accompanied by Columbus's old pilot and cartographer Juan de la Cosa; and in 1504 da la Cosa carried out a more thorough exploration. By that time it was generally accepted in Europe that a hitherto unknown continent had been found, a barrier—to all except the Portuguese an unwelcome barrier—between Europe and Asia. The continent, nevertheless, had its own attractions, and de la Cosa's reports decided the Crown in favour of mainland settlement. Despite the protests of Diego Colón, two licenses were issued, one to Diego de Nicuesa for the settlement of Veragua, the other to Alonso de Ojeda for what is now the north coast of Colombia. The two expeditions, which sailed at the end of 1509, numbered together over a thousand men, but hunger, sickness and poisoned arrows soon killed all but a few score. This was the most serious loss which the Spaniards had suffered in America up to that time, and one of the earliest casualties was Juan de la Cosa, whom Spain could ill spare. Reinforcements eventually arrived under the command of an official from Hispaniola, Martín Fernández de Enciso, later noted as the author of a valuable geography of the Indies. Enciso was out of his element among starving cut-throats, and the real leadership devolved, by common consent, upon a stronger personality, Vasco Núñez de Balboa. Balboa had the advantage of local knowledge, having sailed with Bastidas in 1500; he was decisive, unscrupulous and no respecter of persons. He shipped Enciso back to Hispaniola (Ojeda had gone already), turned Nicuesa adrift to drown and assumed command of the whole enterprise. Balboa was the first of the great *conquistadores* of the American mainland. He founded the city of Darien; he achieved ascendancy over the Indians of the isthmus by a combination of force, terror, conciliation and diplomacy; he collected from them great quantities of food and gold, but at the same time compelled his own people to make provision for the future by building houses and planting crops. The settlements begun under his leadership proved productive and lasting. The isthmus within a few years became so important in the colonial trade of Spain that it earned the name of Castilla del Oro, Golden Castile. Most important of all, in 1513, following up an Indian report, Balboa led an expedition through the forests of the isthmus to the shores of the Pacific.

Balboa's discovery not only revealed to Europeans the existence of the 'South Sea': it revealed also how narrow a strip of land separated the two oceans, and so gave new encouragement to those who hoped to find a strait through Central America and a westward all-sea route to the East. It was partly that hope which prompted the exploration of the Caribbean coasts of the isthmus and, as soon as boats could be built, the Pacific coast also. The conquest of Central America was thus in a sense an incident in the race between Spaniards and Portuguese to reach the East. In the same year (1513) that Balboa crossed the isthmus, the first Portuguese ships reached the Moluccas. In the same year (1519) that Cortés landed in Mexico, Magellan sailed on the voyage which was to reveal both the true western route to the East and the daunting size of the Pacific. Magellan's voyage also revealed that the Spaniards had lost the race; but in Central America they had a reward of a different kind: though they failed to find a strait, they founded a great empire.

CHAPTER 2

Seville and the Caribbean

EMPIRES, however acquired, must be governed. More immediately, the despatch of trans-Atlantic expeditions, some of them very large; the equipping and victualling of distant pioneer settlements; the receipt and disposal of return cargoes including appreciable quantities of gold —all these tasks called for an organised home base and a centralised administration. Down to the end of the fifteenth century, or thereabouts, the choice of a port of departure and return of an Indies expedition lay largely in the hands of the commander; to the government it mattered little. It was natural that Columbus should originally have chosen the corner of Spain with which he was most familiar and where, thanks to his Franciscan friends at La Rábida, he had wide and useful contacts. Of the ports in that area, he might have been expected, perhaps, to prefer Cadiz; but Cadiz harbour in 1492 was choked with shipping, under Crown charter to carry deported Jews away from Spain. Among the small harbours of the Odiel and Río Tinto estuaries —Palos, Moguer, Huelva—there was little to choose. All had efficient small fleets of fishing and coasting caravels. All were the homes of seamen with Atlantic experience. Palos, however, had recently committed a municipal misdemeanour for which it was fined the use of two caravels for twelve months; and Palos was the chosen port.

Palos was, and is, a modest little place, too small to grasp the opportunities which Columbus put in its way. His second expedition sailed from Cadiz; but the administrative headquarters of the enterprise was Seville and probably much of the work of fitting-out was done there. Columbus's third voyage started from San Lúcar de Barrameda at the mouth of the Guadalquivir; his fourth from Seville itself, but with short stays at San Lúcar and Cadiz to pick up additional stores. The first Indies expedition made outside Columbus's command, that of

Ojeda in 1499, sailed from Puerto de Santa María, across the bay from Cadiz. Palos and Moguer continued to send out expeditions at least to the end of the century. Vicente Yáñez Pinzón sailed from Palos in 1499—he was a native there; the first Guerra expedition fitted out at Moguer. These were small fleets, however, comprising two or three caravels and no large ships. By 1500 the Río Tinto ports had almost entirely dropped out. Ovando's great fleet sailed from Cadiz; again the administrative work in connection with it, and much of the fitting-out and storing, was done at Seville. In all these developments can be seen the growing centripetal attraction of the great port on the Guadalquivir; and the influence, no doubt, of that assiduous but unlovable functionary, the Aragonese Fonseca.

Cadiz resisted strongly the influence of Seville, and for the first ten years after Columbus's discovery the primacy among Andalusian ports in the Indies trade remained in doubt. With Ovando's appointment, however, and the acceleration of West Indian settlement which followed, a decision had to be made. In 1503 the first organ of colonial administration, the *Casa de la contratación de las Indias*, formed to promote and regulate trade and navigation to the New World, was established by royal decree at Seville. For many years thereafter sailings to the Indies, with rare permitted exceptions, were to clear from Seville; and all Indies fleets, without exception, were required to return there. Cadiz, for the Indies trade, was to be a mere port of call, though an important one. Seville had its disadvantages. It lay sixty miles up a winding, muddy river. In later years the delays of river navigation, and the dangers of the sand-bar of San Lúcar at the mouth, to say nothing of the red tape of the *Casa* itself, were seriously to impair the efficiency of the Indies trade. The Seville monopoly has often been cited as an example of Spanish indifference to commercial interest, of a preference for bureaucratic regulation over economic enterprise. In fact, the Crown was merely giving official approval to a choice already made by most commanders experienced in the Indies navigation. The ships then employed in the trade were neither large enough to run much risk of grounding on the San Lúcar bar, nor numerous enough to strain unduly the harbour facilities of Seville. None of the possible alternatives was satisfactory. The Río Tinto ports were too small, too remote from the main centres, too near the frontier. The Crown had no wish to see the hard-won gold of the Indies smuggled into Portugal, where bullion was in high and urgent demand to finance the newly opened trade with India. Cadiz had a far better harbour than Seville, but it was more exposed, both to rough weather and—as events later in the century were to prove—to enemy attack. More serious, it was isolated. Perched on its rocky peninsula, it had no adequate hinterland. Stores intended for fleets at Cadiz had mostly to be taken there by water, with consequent risk of loss and delay. San Lúcar was a small place on an open road, without facilities, a mere downriver outport of Seville. As for other Castilian ports further afield, the question of their participation in the Indies trade in these early years had hardly arisen. Apart from the royal interest in creating a manageable monopoly, no other part of Castile enjoyed the natural advantages of the Atlantic coast of Andalusia. Málaga and Cartagena, the principal Mediterranean harbours of Castile, had nearly all their commercial contacts with Italy and with North Africa. Even if their merchant communities had wished to trade across the Atlantic, their ships would have had to make the difficult passage of the Straits, with fluky winds and a contrary current, and run the gauntlet of the Barbary corsairs on every voyage. There were many busy ports on the north coast, in Galicia and Biscay; and having ready access to suitable timber they built their own ships, often bigger and better than those launched in the Seville yards. Columbus's flagship, it will be remembered, was built in Galicia, and in later years the northern shipyards were to contribute many good ships to the *Carrera de Indias*. But a ship from Coruña or Bilbao, in order to reach the trade-winds which alone assured a quick passage to the Indies, had to navigate along the whole length of the Portuguese coast, always dangerous and sometimes hostile, and accept the consequent increase in the length and the cost of the voyage. In fact, in the early years of the Indies settlements no other part of Spain showed any serious desire to dispute the monopoly enjoyed by Western Andalusia; and no other harbour in Western Andalusia could effectively dispute the primacy of Seville.

Seville was the commercial centre of the richest area in Spain, and already possessed the population, the harbour accommodation and the financial organisation needed to develop a new trade. Its communications with its hinterland were good. The river was an important artery of internal trade, and in the gently rolling arable country of the Andalusian plain waggon transport was easy. The settlers of Hispaniola could, at a pinch, subsist on cassava bread and maize, but they naturally preferred the diet to which they were accustomed. They demanded live cattle, wheat flour, oil and wine in considerable quantities, and after the initial years of hardship they had the means to pay for their imports. They not only washed for gold: they grew a little sugar, and as their herds increased they produced hides, in constant demand for saddlery, protective clothing and hangings, and tallow, used not only for candles but for coating the hulls of ships as a protection against ship-worm. Indies cargoes entering Spain were valuable and needed efficient marketing. The wine, oil and flour required for the outward cargoes could easily be procured in Seville; and in the *Casa* at Seville the gold of the Indies was in relatively safe custody. For the administrative capital of the Indies in the early years Seville was a logical and natural choice.

It is possible that in establishing the *Casa* at Seville the advisers of the Crown had in mind a system of direct royal trading similar to that operated by the *Casa da India* at Lisbon. The Crown of Castile, however, had at its disposal neither the capital nor the experience for such an undertaking. The trade of the West Indies was left to private enterprise, and the *Casa* from its foundation was a regulating, not a trading organisation. The officials appointed in 1503 were a treasurer, an accountant and a factor or business manager; and initially its functions were those of any customs house. It checked cargoes in and out and collected the appropriate duties; in particular, the royal share of all precious metals and stones. Royal gold from the Indies was sent directly from the *Casa* to the Seville mint; and from 1503 the mint was required to coin it without fee other than the technicians' wages, so that it passed promptly into circulation. The business of the *Casa*, however, soon expanded beyond these purely fiscal duties. It acted as trustee of the estates of those—and they were many—who died in the Indies leaving heirs in Spain. It licensed and recorded all passengers to the Indies; the Castilian Crown, busy converting its Muslim subjects and deporting its Jews, was anxious to prevent members of either group from migrating to the Indies to extend there the damage they were thought to have done to religious purity and political loyalty in Spain. Besides its regulating duties, the *Casa* exercised a considerable degree of technical control. It was responsible for fitting out fleets sailing on the account of the Crown, such as the great armament which accompanied Pedrarias de Avila to his appointment as governor of Castilla del Oro in 1513. It was not concerned, of course, with fitting out the privately owned vessels which carried most of the trade, but it inspected them before sailing, to ensure their seaworthiness, and in the interests of safety enforced upper and lower limits on their size. It licensed navigators; as early as 1508 a *piloto mayor*—chief pilot—was appointed for this duty. Amérigo Vespucci was the first holder of the office. He was succeeded first by Juan de Solís and then by Sebastian Cabot, both eminent explorers. Under their direction a school of navigation developed—the first of its kind in Europe—which not only examined pilots for their licences but also gave instruction in the techniques of trans-Atlantic navigation. The technicians of the *Casa* kept a careful and systematic record of all discoveries in the Indies, maintained an up-to-date standard chart, the *padrón real*, and inspected charts issued to ships in the trade to ensure that they conformed to the *padrón*. Historians of the Indies trade have emphasised, perhaps unduly, the vexatious and restrictive aspects of the *Casa's* activities; in the early years of development it rendered essential services. Without the continuous oversight exercised by the officials of the *Casa*, without the technical experience which they acquired, royal control of the Indies administration would hardly have been possible. Vexatious the *Casa* undoubtedly was, especially to the local authorities of the proud city in which it worked. From its beginnings it exercised judicial powers, both in civil suits arising from the trade and in criminal cases concerning breaches of its own rules or offences committed on board ship. This wide jurisdiction was confirmed and defined by royal decree in 1511; inevitably it often conflicted with the jurisdiction of the municipal magistrates, and, more seriously, with that of the Seville high court, the *Audiencia de las Gradas*. Vexatious though the *Casa* might be, however, the trade monopoly which it governed was an important source of local profit; the threat of removing it to Cadiz usually sufficed to silence complaints in Seville.

The officials of the *Casa* were concerned with the execution of policy, not directly with its formulation. During the troubled years after Isabella's death, when the Castilian succession was in doubt, the *Casa* and the governor of Hispaniola were left very much to their own devices; but when Ferdinand reasserted his authority in Castile both Hispaniola and the *Casa* came once more under effective control. The Indies were the Indies of the Crown of Castile, and all major decisions affecting them were made, in theory, by the monarch, advised by the Council of Castile. That august body, the highest in the kingdom, combined, in a manner characteristic of the time, the functions of a supreme court of appeal with those of a cabinet council, advising on major administrative matters and proposing legislation. Most of its members were either prelates or eminent lawyers. The affairs of the Indies naturally claimed a very small share of the council's attention. It dealt with Ovando's *residencia*—the judicial inquiry into his conduct of the government of Hispaniola held after his return to Spain; it drafted the decree of 1511 which defined the jurisdiction of the *Casa*, and another decree of the same year creating a high court, an *audiencia*, in Santo Domingo; and it adjudicated in the various conflicts of jurisdiction which arose between this new court and the viceroy Diego Colón. In these and similar matters the council acted as supreme court, deciding lawsuits and creating or defining subordinate jurisdictions. Administrative matters, questions of policy affecting the Indies, on the other hand, rarely if ever came before the whole body of the council. The King referred them instead to individual councillors, almost always to Fonseca, assisted by another Aragonese, the royal secretary Lope de Conchillos. Conchillos resided at the court, as his duties required him to do; and Fonseca, though bishop successively of Badajoz, Córdoba, Palencia and Burgos, spent much of his time there. Fonseca held no specific office connected with the Indies; he was simply that councillor who specialised in Indies affairs; but he was, in effect, in complete control. To the end of Ferdinand's reign he and Conchillos drafted, issued and despatched through the *Casa de la Contratación* almost all decrees concerning the Indies. They selected, with the King's full approval, almost all senior officials. They created their own informal secretariat to deal with the increasing volume of paperwork. They even organised a special postal service to carry correspondence between the court and the *Casa*, and between the *Casa* and the Indies. This service, by the standards of the time, was remarkably efficient. It could convey urgent despatches between Seville and Madrid, over rough country where no paved roads had been made since Roman times, in four days. By this means the *Casa*, the administrative centre of the Indies, was tied firmly to the source of policy decisions at court, wherever the court happened to be. The government of the Indies, in theory directed, with the government of Castile, through a deliberative council, was in practice a narrow and tightly centralised bureaucracy controlled by Fonseca in the name of the King. The outward sign of this control was the inauguration in 1514 of a separate royal seal, entrusted to Fonseca, for the formal authentication of all decrees and decisions pertaining to the Indies.

The administration in the Indies, with which Fonseca, through the *Casa*, corresponded, was a sketchy affair. Columbus had been granted, as viceroy, administrative and judicial authority over the territories which he discovered, and as admiral, jurisdiction over the seas of the New World. Further, he was to receive one-tenth of all revenue which the Crown derived from the discoveries. In 1499 he lost his government; but he retained his emoluments and his admiralty jurisdiction until his death in 1506. Ovando, who went out in 1502 as governor of Hispaniola, governed as an autocrat. The treasury officials, responsible for the collection, disbursement and shipment of royal revenue, worked under his disciplinary authority; a situation of which, according to complaints in his *residencia*, he took full advantage. The only other subordinate agents of law and order in his day were the towns—mostly little groups of thatched huts, towns only in name—seven of which were formally incorporated in 1507. Incorporation entitled them to local government by their own councils, and to a local jurisdiction exercised by magistrates whom the councils elected. Appeals from their decisions went before the governor. When Diego Colón succeeded as governor and, later, viceroy, he sought to interpret his inherited rights in the widest possible fashion; but his claims were resisted and his independent authority increasingly limited by decisions made in Spain. His general claim to patronage throughout the Indies was ignored; patronage, the right to appoint to lucrative offices, was in Spain reserved to the Crown, save by express delegation, and when the offices of the Indies began to have some value the Crown assumed its prerogative of appointment there. Jurisdiction, also, was a royal duty, not lightly delegated; and, when delegated, always apt to be withdrawn. Diego's admiralty jurisdiction could not easily be challenged, though his attempts to extend it by construction were resisted. His judicial powers within the islands, however, soon came under hostile scrutiny. In 1511, in response to petitions from the settlers for an appellate jurisdiction independent of the governor, the *audiencia* of Santo Domingo was created, a bench of school-trained civilian lawyers, in imitation of the courts at Valladolid, Granada and Seville, which had performed notable service in the unification of Castile. The new *audiencia*, an effective check upon the authority of the governor, was to be the forerunner of many such courts in America. At the same time, the rudimentary treasury organisation of Hispaniola—treasurer, comptroller and factor, with their triple-padlocked strongbox—was made independent of the authority of the governor and directly responsible to Fonseca's bureau in Spain; a reasonable provision, in view of Diego's extensive claims on the royal revenue. By 1512, therefore, there were in Hispaniola three more or less independent organs of royal authority: the governor, the *audiencia* and the treasury.

The beginnings of settlement on the mainland introduced fresh complications. Down to 1513 the little colony on the isthmus had acknowledged, however perfunctorily, the authority of Santo Domingo; but when its potential value became known, Diego's claims were once more set aside. His claims to govern and to draw a share of revenue were recognised only in the islands. A separate mainland government was established, and a governor sent out from Spain, accompanied not only by a formidable fighting force but by a secretarial staff and a second team of treasury officials. Balboa, by the standards of his time, had deserved well of his comrades and his king; but his forceful independence offended the bureaucratic and autocratic temper of Fonseca. His treatment of Nicuesa and of Enciso had affronted the royal authority. His report of the South Sea, his contributions of gold and pearls, arrived in Spain too late to reinstate him in favour. He too was passed over. The first governor of Castilla del Oro was Pedrarias de Avila, the ferocious old man whom his associates nicknamed *furor Domini*. Pedrarias drove on with great energy the work of exploration and settlement, but abandoned entirely Balboa's policy of conciliating the Indians and undid much of Balboa's constructive work. Quarrelling inevitably with Balboa, who had many friends, he had him arrested in 1519, on a charge of conspiracy and treason, and beheaded. Appropriately, the man entrusted with the task of arresting him was an obscure cut-throat named Pizarro who later, in South America, was to outdo Balboa in achievement and Pedrarias in ferocity. For sixteen years Pedrarias and his captains ruled, exploited and devastated the isthmus, enriching themselves—such of them as survived—and sending a gratifying store of treasure home to Spain.

Ferdinand, unlike the Queen whom he survived, concerned himself little with the well-being of the settlers in the Indies—who, after all, had gone there of their own volition—and hardly at all with that of the native Indians. His primary, almost his only, interest lay in the revenue to be drawn from the New World. Fonseca interpreted his duties in the same spirit. He was, naturally, an interested party. It was customary for members of the royal councils to receive, besides their salaries, extra emoluments for special work. These emoluments often took the form of a share of the royal patronage, a grant of fee-earning office, with the right to appoint deputies. Fonseca in the course of his career received, in addition to his steady ecclesiastical preferment, many honoraria charged on the Indies revenue. So did Conchillos, a notoriously grasping official. He was appointed in 1508 Chief Notary of the Mines of the Indies. Other councillors, who took an occasional hand in the work, received a share of the spoils. When the Indies postal service was created, the office of *correo mayor*, postmaster-general, for example, was given to a councillor of Castile, Dr Galíndez de Carvajal; he deputed the actual work to the officials of the *Casa* (who performed it very efficiently) and paid them a share of the fees which he received. Tello, the *fiscal* of the Council, besides the considerable fees which he drew for dealing with lawsuits appealed from the Indies, held the office of *alguacil mayor*, chief constable of the Indies, and sold deputations of the office to emigrants. Not only the Crown, therefore, but many individual councillors and officials had a vested interest in the Indies revenue.

The revenue, in the early years, included a half-share (at least in theory) of precious metals and stones captured as legitimate booty in war; a royalty, fixed in 1504 at one-fifth, of metals and stones got by mining or washing; duties on goods entering the Indies, or entering Spain from the Indies; and tribute levied from the Indians. In the islands this last item was negligible; having parted with their few gold trinkets, the Tainos had nothing left worth taxing, save their cassava and maize crops, and the tribute share of those went mainly to the *encomenderos*. In practice the increase of royal revenue depended chiefly on increasing the production of precious metals, and that depended on forced labour. Fonseca and his colleagues, therefore, were extremely reluctant to place obstacles in the way of the free use of Indian labour by the settlers. Fonseca's reception of the Dominican missionaries who, from 1511 onwards, attempted to plead the cause of the Indians and to secure some protection for them, was frigid. Neither he nor Conchillos played any part in the drafting of the Laws of Burgos, the first Spanish code of rules concerning the treatment of natives; their obstructive attitude in the matter, indeed, prevented any serious attempt to enforce the vaguely pious provisions of the code. Nor did Fonseca interfere in any way with the slave-raids in the Bahamas, by means of which the Hispaniola settlers sought to recruit additional labour. Later, after about

1520, the *Casa* under his direction facilitated, by the ready issue of licences, the purchase of considerable numbers of Negro slaves from Portuguese sources to replace the dwindling Tainos; and eventually these slaves came to constitute the principal labour force of the West Indies.

During Ferdinand's reign the fiscal and economic policy of Fonseca, in its limited and immediate intentions, achieved considerable success, and justified the confidence which that avaricious monarch placed in his councillor for the Indies. The Spanish settlements grew steadily in number and in size. There were seven incorporated towns in Hispaniola in 1507, fourteen in 1514. Santo Domingo, in particular, became a town and harbour of some importance. Ovando had begun the work of building a permanent stone and brick city, laid out on the spacious rectilinear plan which was to become characteristic of most Spanish towns in the New World. Even after the conquest of other islands and the beginnings of settlement on the mainland, Santo Domingo remained the centre for the distribution of Spanish goods throughout the Caribbean, and ships usually congregated there before sailing on the return passage. So long as settlements remained confined to the Caribbean shores and islands, and so long as their chief requirements were for the products of Andalusia, Seville handled the other end of the Atlantic trade route easily, without competition or serious complaint. The volume of shipping between Seville and Santo Domingo—leaving out of account exceptional fleets such as those of Ovando, Diego Colón and Pedrarias Dávila—fluctuated considerably from year to year, but the peak years showed a steady increase. In 1508, according to a recent and carefully documented study, sixty-six ships crossed the Atlantic, outward or homeward; in 1514 seventy-seven; in 1520 108. They were all small ships, probably few or none exceeding 100 *toneladas*, roughly equivalent at that time to about eighty modern capacity tons. Many went out and never returned. Either they were lost, or broken up in the islands for the sake of their fittings; or else—since the bulk of outward cargoes greatly exceeded that of return cargoes—they could find no return freight, and remained in the Indies to serve local needs. Those which did return brought to the royal treasury a revenue still small compared with that derived from European sources, but steadily increasing, and doubly acceptable because most of it was in gold. By 1516 it already reached 35,000 ducats. The success of the settlements, however, was achieved at heavy cost—a rapid and careless depletion of natural resources, appalling human suffering, the progressive destruction of an inoffensive primitive people, the extinction of an entire way of life.

Responsible opinion in Spain could not ignore indefinitely the demographic tragedies which settlement had brought to the islands. The death of Ferdinand, and the accession of the slow, awkward, deeply conscientious youth who was to become the Emperor Charles V, made possible both a change of attitude and a change of organisation. The aged Cardinal Jiménez, who governed as regent while awaiting Charles's arrival, had been deeply shocked by Dominican reports from Hispaniola. Nothing is known of the personal relations between the Cardinal and Fonseca, but the inflexible and sternly religious Jiménez probably had no great opinion of the worldly episcopal absentee, and must have held him responsible, at least in part, for the atrocities which were being fiercely and publicly denounced by Fray Bartolomé de las Casas. Fonseca and Conchillos were both removed, informally and apparently without written decree, from control of the affairs of the Indies during the two years of the regency. The business was entrusted to two other councillors, assisted by another of the royal secretaries. Charles arrived in Spain, and Jiménez died, in 1517; Fonseca's signature reappears on Indies papers early in 1518. Conchillos, on the other hand, was dismissed; and though he received a pension for his services as secretary, his Indies offices and emoluments were taken from him. At the same time, all officials resident in Spain (including Conchillos) who held *repartimientos* of Indians were deprived of them—the first practical step towards a reform of native policy.

When Fonseca returned to the Indies administration he did not return alone. He still did most of the work, but associated with him by royal decree were two of the most powerful men in Spain: the Grand Chancellor Sauvage, and the Cardinal Adrian; three other councillors; and Francisco de los Cobos as secretary. This was a major and permanent reform, a change from a centralised personal bureaucracy in which Fonseca had been an all-powerful minister, back to the collegiate, deliberative system traditionally used in Spain in the formulation of royal policy. The new group of councillors was a standing committee of the Council of Castile. It soon acquired an identity and a name of its own. In March 1519 the King first addressed it as '*Los de mi Consejo que entienden en las cosas de las Indias*'; by September 1519 the cumbersome title had been shortened, apparently informally, by usage, to '*Consejo de las Indias'*—Council of the Indies. The time was opportune for a reform and a strengthening of the central administration of the Indies. Rumours of great mainland territories to the north of the isthmus were already reaching Spain. In 1519 Cortés sailed from Cuba on his momentous voyage into the Gulf of Mexico. Charles was about to become the sovereign of distant kingdoms far more extensive and populous, incomparably richer and more powerful, than the pitiful empire of the islands.

CHAPTER 3

The kingdoms of the sun

COLUMBUS did not discover a new world; he established contact between two worlds, both already old. He revealed to Europeans the existence of continents and islands which were already inhabited and had been so for many centuries. So far as we know, there was no truly aboriginal American man; but there were, and are, American cultures. Man in the 'New World' was probably cut off at a primitive stage in his cultural development from Asia, whence he came; cut off, certainly, from regular contact. The Amerindians developed their characteristic cultures in America in the course of wandering and settlement extending over thousands of years. Considering the immense range of conditions between Alaska and Cape Horn, it is not surprising that these cultures differed widely one from another. They all differed much more radically, however, from any Old World culture. Even where similar habits or artefacts occur in both Old and New Worlds, the presumption of independent origins is strong. We have no ground for supposing a connection between the ancient Mexicans and the ancient Egyptians, for example, merely because both built pyramids.

Some Amerindian peoples, living in areas rich in fish and game, found their hunting and gathering economy so satisfactory that they never abandoned it. In California one of the densest populations in the Americas maintained itself into modern historic times without any form of agriculture. Planting or sowing societies grew up in areas where a relative scarcity of game and wild fruit made agriculture necessary to a growing population; and where the combination of soil, climate and suitable plants made agriculture possible by man's unaided effort. Without ploughs and plough beasts, the farmer can make little impression on prairie grassland, savannah or heavy clay. He is confined to soft soils—to alluvial silts, to semi-arid upland soils, or to leaf-mould on the forest floor; and he must find plants which can be made to yield adequately by means of hoe and digging-stick cultivation.

Among the many food plants of the Americas the most widespread and important were maize and various kinds of beans. Maize is a native American plant, and Europeans first encountered it, as a totally unfamiliar crop, in the New World. Its original centre of dispersal seems to have been Middle America between the fourteenth and twentieth parallels, in which area were concentrated many early centres of intense cultivation and rapid cultural growth. Maize and beans, supplemented by chiles and by various species of squash and other gourds, formed a crop complex well adapted to preserve soil fertility in conditions of hoe cultivation. Maize was the staple; the squashes gave shade and conserved moisture round the roots of the growing maize; the beans performed a double function, supplying protein in a diet impoverished by the killing out of game, and fixing nitrogen in the soil. From Middle America maize and beans were diffused in all directions, and by the time of the European conquest were grown in most parts of America where agriculture was practised. In North America east of the mountains they superseded less satisfactory plants such as the sunflower and the giant ragweed, formerly grown for their seed. In South America their spread was less uniform. The Andean highland region—another great area of cultural origination and growth—developed an agriculture based not on grain but on potatoes, and the potato was supplemented, not ousted, by the spread of maize and beans. In Brazil and the West Indies primitive forest groups lived by growing cassava and accepted the spread of maize and beans slowly and late.

The development of agriculture, in America as elsewhere, liberated man from the tyranny of the constant search for food; and naturally the areas which first produced a stable complex of cultivated crops were also the areas which first developed highly organised societies and recognisable cultures. The higher civilisations of these areas were formed not by innovating conquerors or immigrants but by gradual evolution, a progressive sophistication of archaic skills and habits. The process of development took place in a number of different centres, independent one of another, but undoubtedly influencing one another. In Guatemala the Mayas evolved a ceremonial civilisation centred in great temple cities. In the Mexican state of Oaxaca the Zapotecs were the creators of a rich civilisation, of which the ruins of Monte Albán form the chief remaining monument. In the forests of Tabasco and coastal Vera Cruz there are evidences of other high civilisations, Totonac and Olmec. Just north of Mexico City, on the fringe of the area of high civilisation, another little-known people built the huge pyramids of Teotihuacán and the complex of sacerdotal buildings which surrounds them. These city-building cultures differed considerably one from another, but all had one important feature in common. The cities were not primarily dwelling-places, or fortresses, or even in any modern sense administrative capitals; they were ceremonial cities. The demands of a forest agriculture did not permit the occupation of large permanent towns. To clear forest land for planting maize, trees had to be girdled and, when they were dead, burned. Land cleared in this way yielded good crops, from its thin surface of leaf-mould, for two or three years, and then became exhausted. Whole villages had then to be moved; or else each family had to be allowed enough land to move its fields every two or three years, allowing the exhausted patches to fallow and revert to bush. Throughout ancient Middle America, therefore, most people lived in scattered villages, in flimsy and impermanent dwellings; but they expressed their social unity by building temples, which rose above the forest villages much as the abbeys of medieval Europe towered above the fields and hovels of a devout and patient peasantry. The cities of Middle America were devoted chiefly to religious observance, and secondarily to the social gatherings and market meetings of an intensely religious people.

Of all the city-building cultures that of the Mayas, though not necessarily the earliest, was the most widespread, the most influential and the most impressive in its religious, scientific and artistic achievements. The Maya area includes three distinct regions: a southern region in highland Guatemala; a central region in Petén and British Honduras; and a northern region, the Yucatán peninsula. The highland region is physically the most rewarding. Its temperate climate and friable volcanic soil make primitive agriculture easy, and in ancient times it yielded many of the most valuable commodities of Maya society: obsidian for knives and spearheads, iron pyrites for mirrors, specular haematite for ceremonial red paint, feathers of trogons and other brightly coloured birds used for tapestry and for the mantles of chiefs, and jade. All these articles were traded throughout Middle America and beyond; and the beans of the cacao tree, which grew on the Pacific slope, were used as currency by all the settled peoples. Despite these natural advantages, however, the highland region lagged behind the other two in science and the arts. The heartland of Maya culture in its best, its 'classical', period was Petén, an undulating, low-lying limestone area, with scanty soil, heavy rainfall and high dense forest. In classical Maya times the area probably held much more surface water than it does today—a network of shallow lakes affording easy communication between the settlements. Today Petén is almost uninhabited, but the ruins of ancient cities, half hidden by the forest, are scattered throughout the region. Yucatán also is limestone country, but arid and covered with scrub forest, with little surface water except where the limestone crust has broken through to form *cenotes* or natural wells. Here, too, ruined cities, usually in association with accessible *cenotes*, are numerous and widely scattered.

The principal buildings in all these Maya centres are temple-pyramids and massive, many-chambered community houses which probably housed priests and novices during religious fasts and feasts. These characteristics are general throughout Middle America, but the Maya buildings have peculiar features of their own. In decoration the richness and inventiveness of Maya sculpture—executed entirely with stone tools—is unsurpassed in the Americas and holds a high place throughout the world. In construction the Mayas, alone among Amerindian peoples, supported roofs by means of corbelled vaulting, in which the two legs of the vault draw together until the space between can be bridged with capstones. No American people discovered the true arch. Most interesting and characteristic of all was the custom of erecting series of commemorative stelae or calendar stones in connection with public buildings. These great monolithic shafts, covered with glyphs and sculptured figures in relief, occur only in the Maya lowlands, but there they are widespread. A preoccupation with time was characteristic of Maya religion. Astronomy, or astrology, was studied as an aid in measuring time, in predicting the future and in fixing the propitious dates for sacrifices and major undertakings. The astronomical knowledge collected, through long observation, by a numerous and highly trained priesthood, was very extensive, and the calendar based on it was complex and remarkably accurate. All the developed civilisations of Middle America practised this science in some degree, and all possessed sacred calendars; but none equalled the Mayas either in the fullness of their knowledge or in the effectiveness of their means of recording it. Since the Mayas also—alone among Amerindian peoples—possessed an embryonic form of writing, using glyphs or symbols and not mere pictographs, they were able to record on their stelae astronomical and calendric information and, it may be presumed, historical data also, a form of annals carved in stone. This last point is presumption only, because only the calendric glyphs can as yet be deciphered with any confidence; but at least the stelae enable archaeologists to date ancient Maya sites with some approach to certainty. According to the most generally accepted interpretation, the earliest surviving stele, at Uaxactún, was erected in A.D. 328. The latest, near La Muñeca in Campeche, may possibly be as late as A.D. 928, but it is a much battered and obviously degenerate example. Most of the Maya cities ceased to erect stelae in the course of the ninth century. Five or five and a half centuries was the span of the classical period of Maya civilisation; approximately the span, in Europe, from Constantine to Charlemagne.

In the central Maya region the ninth century saw not only the end of the stele cult but the total cessation of building activity in the ceremonial centres. One by one the temple cities were abandoned to decay, and in some at least the abandonment was sudden, for buildings were left half finished. Many causes have been suggested. Soil exhaustion would not have caused a sudden desertion. Epidemic disease might have done; but the main killing diseases of the area—yellow fever, smallpox, hookworm, malaria—are Old World importations, and there is no evidence that the countryside was depopulated. Petén was certainly populous when the Spaniards arrived. Nor does the evidence suggest foreign invasion and destruction due to war. The most plausible explanation, perhaps, is revolution, a peasant revolution spreading from city to city. Possibly the burden of building temples and supporting a priestly hierarchy grew intolerable. Possibly the priesthood, by devotion to astronomy and to sky-gods, and by neglect of the homely gods of earth and rain and fertility, lost the confidence of a farming peasantry. Whatever the cause, the Maya cities of lowland Guatemala were swallowed up by the forest and never recovered.

The cities of Yucatán survived to encounter a different fate: foreign infiltration and eventually conquest. The Mayas never founded any large-scale political unit. Their cities differed considerably in language or dialect and in architectural style, and politically were independent one of another. The peaceable reputation ascribed to the Maya by some

scholars was undeserved; they often made war. The Itzá clan, who towards the end of the tenth century possessed themselves of the Yucatec
city of Chichén, may have entered the Maya area as mercenaries. Certainly they were better armed and better organised for war than any
Maya group. They were of Mexican origin; both their own traditions
and similarities in art and customs link them with the Toltec centre of
Tula on the Mexican plateau. They introduced new gods—a sun-god,
a war-god and (most famous of all, becaue of his impact on the imagination of the Spaniards) Quetzalcoatl or Kukulcan, 'feathered serpent',
god of learning and of priesthood and introducer of maize. The
Mexicans believed that these gods required to be nourished constantly
with blood, preferably human blood. The sun-god, for example,
passed through the underworld each night and arose weary and thirsty
for blood each morning. The Toltecs, indeed most Mexican peoples,
practised human sacrifice on a scale far greater than was usual with the
Mayas, and this practice in turn intensified the Mexican preoccupation
with war as a means of acquiring captives for sacrifice. The Toltecs
were great builders; and the Itzás at Chichén and elsewhere introduced
new building styles, supplementing the Maya corbelled vault with
more spacious but less durable constructions, with roofs supported on
columns and wooden beams. In sculpture they lacked the inventiveness and the serenity of the Mayas. A monotonous repetition of restless
feathered serpents is the principal characteristic of their decorative
styles.

The Itzás were few in number. Outside the neighbourhood of
Chichén Itzá their influence was at first indirect, and even there they
adopted many Maya habits and devices. But in the thirteenth century
they were reinforced by other more numerous Mexican groups, who
succeeded, after much fighting among themselves, in establishing a
league of cities, of which Chichén Itzá and Mayapán were the chief.
This alliance controlled the whole of northern Yucatán and could, by
a slight stretch, be described as an 'empire'. The decline of art and
architecture, especially religious architecture, is obvious at Mayapán.
Mayapán was not a ceremonial centre but a fortified city, built to be
inhabited by a race of warriors who lived by the labour of a conquered
and tributary people. The military dominion of Mayapán lasted until
the fifteenth century. Its Mexican rulers, however, gradually became
absorbed by the Maya majority and lost not only their identity but
their ability to rule. In the fifteenth century their empire broke into

warring fragments. The last hundred years before the arrival of the Spaniards in Yucatán were a period of disorder and progressive barbarisation.

A somewhat similar sequence of events occurred in Mexico. The great centres of early civilisation—Monte Albán of the Zapotecs, for example, and Teotihuacán—were ceremonial centres similar in purpose to the 'classical' Maya cities, with which they were roughly contemporary. Teotihuacán, the largest and most impressive of all ruined sites in Mexico, must have been famous over a wide area in its day. It retained its sanctity long after it ceased to be inhabited, and was still venerated by the Aztecs when the Spaniards came. Like the central Maya cities, after at least one rebuilding to meet new religious requirements, it was abandoned in the tenth century, apparently in the full tide of achievement. Ixtlilxochitl, the Christianised Aztec annalist, attributed its downfall to crop failure, religious conflict and revolt. All are possible explanations. To reshape the immense buildings of Teotihuacán in the interests of religious change vast quantities of lime were used. To reduce limestone on primitive open kilns whole forests must have been destroyed. The consequent desiccation and erosion may well have caused crop failure, and the combination of labour exactions and food shortages may have led to revolt. Attacks from outside may also have hastened the desertion of the site; there is some evidence of deliberate destruction.

Teotihuacán stood on the northern frontier of civilised Middle America, exposed to recurrent pressure from groups of nomadic barbarians from the arid north who moved into the fertile land, settled, and in time built up settled cultures of their own. Such a group, the Toltecs, were engaged in the tenth century in building up a formidable power at Tula, in the modern state of Hidalgo. The Toltecs greatly surpassed the people of Teotihuacán, as they surpassed the Mayas, in military skill and organisation. They used the spear thrower (*atl-atl*) and a sheaf of javelins instead of a single long spear; they possessed highly organised and respected military Orders, the eagles and the jaguars; they introduced to Mexico, as they did later to Yucatán, a society in which the warrior shared the privileged position of the priest. The Toltecs in Mexican traditional history were described as the master-builders. Tula lacks the massive ordered bulk of Teotihuacán, but is architecturally splendid, with beautifully proportioned buildings. Unlike Teotihuacán, the site includes extensive refuse heaps; like Chichén in its later period, it marks a transition from purely ceremonial centres to cities lived in and defended by dominant warrior tribes.

The break-down of highly developed societies and their capture by immigrant barbarians, who in turn took over and adapted their ways of life, was a recurrent feature of Mexican history. When in time Toltec society disintegrated and Tula was abandoned, fresh centres of power grew up in the Puebla-Mixteca area and in Anáhuac, the central valley of Mexico. The last group of settlers in the valley were the celebrated Aztecs, who were in possession when the Spaniards arrived. Far more is known about the Aztecs than about any other native American people. More than any other, they caught the imagination of Europe. Nevertheless, the Aztecs added little to the achievements of Middle American culture. Their distinction was military and political. They made notable improvements in the art of war and in organisation for war, accompanied by a great extension of the sacrificial cults, not only of Quetzalcoatl, but of war-god, sun-god, rain-god and many others, so that their festivals sometimes took on the wholesale aspect of ceremonial massacre accompanied by ritual cannibalism. They achieved by war a degree of political unity in central Mexico which led European chroniclers to describe their dominion as an empire and Montezuma, the war-chief of Tenochtitlán, as an emperor.

The extraordinary ferocity of the public life of the Aztecs, the constant recurrence of war and ritual massacre, the indifference to human life and preoccupation with death, are hard to explain in a people who as individuals (if Spanish missionaries are to be believed) were gentle and affectionate, lovers of music, of poetry and of flowers. Much of the mental and spiritual nature of this strange people must remain an impenetrable mystery to Europeans; but a possible partial explanation lies in the fact that for a century or more before the Spanish invasion they were engaged, with others, in a grim struggle for survival, due to the increasing pressure of population upon cultivable land. The Mexican economy was based primarily upon maize, an extremely productive crop, dependable and relatively easy to grow. Like other productive crops—rice, potatoes, cassava—maize can support, at a low subsistence level, a very dense peasant population. Such a population, unless regularly thinned by migration or disease, tends to expand to the limits of subsistence, and ultimately to destroy, by land exhaustion and erosion, the means of its subsistence. Central Mexico, when the Spaniards arrived, was still prosperous and productive, but it already had its areas of old erosion, particularly in the Mixteca Alta, and its rural population was very numerous, probably more numerous than it is today. In the fertile valley of Anáhuac, where the Aztec power grew up, pressure of population upon land became acute in the fifteenth century. The Aztecs, thereafter, had to conquer or to starve.

The Aztecs had emerged as a separate people, or group of peoples, with a recognisable culture of their own, in the thirteenth century. They occupied a number of villages dotted round the shores of the lake which then filled much of the valley floor of Anáhuac. The villages were independent one of another; throughout the whole of Mexican history before the Spanish conquest, the village tribe, living on the produce of its own fields, was the unit of political organisation. This remained true even when a tribe grew to many thousands of members and the village became a city state. When a city became too large to be supported by its own productive labour it had either to split up, some of its members departing to found new colonies elsewhere, or else to prey upon other cities or villages in the neighbourhood. In central Mexico no suitable land remained for new colonies; aggressive parasitism was the only solution open to the Aztecs. The Tenochcas, a small but warlike group living on islands in the lake of Texcoco, became the most successful of a number of competing predatory tribes. Tenochtitlán, their island stronghold, was settled about 1325. As the islands became built over, the Tenochcas added to their arable land by making *chinampas*, islands compounded of matted growing weed and mud dredged from the lake bottom. Outgrowing this resource, they secured their first foothold on solid ground, by means of alliances among the growing towns which ringed the lake shore, in the early fifteenth century. For the next hundred years their power grew, at the expense both of their allies and of other settlements.

Raiding expeditions went out regularly and the city drew tribute in kind, services and captives for sacrifice from conquered and terrorised peoples throughout the valley of Mexico, throughout the Puebla-Mixteca area, as far south as Guatemala and as far east as Vera Cruz. Tenochtitlán became a great city, whose temples, community houses and markets provoked the startled admiration of Spanish soldiers. It was linked to the shore by causeways, and drew drinking water by aqueduct from the hills of Chapúltepec. It was at the height of its power and splendour when, in 1519, Cortés landed at Vera Cruz and began his march inland.

The Tenochcas became an aristocracy of predators rather than of rulers. They performed no duties in return for the tributes they exacted, other than the elementary duty of protecting their vassals against other predators. Their administration, their elaborate pictographic records, their system of communication, all were designed to maintain military initiative and to exact tribute. The vassal towns felt, apparently, no loyalty to a central authority. They were separate communities, bound to Tenochtitlán only by fear of punitive expeditions if tribute were withheld. Neither the Aztecs, nor any other North or Central American people, had yet developed a clear conception of a political unit wider than a single city state; though Tenochtitlán, when the Spaniards arrived, was well on the way towards it.

Such a conception had already developed in South America. Like central and southern Mexico and Guatemala, the northern and central Andean region, both coast and mountain, produced a series of highly developed societies extending over a long period of time. As in Middle America, areas of growing civilisation began to emerge from the general level of archaic culture in the first centuries of the Christian era. The most striking of these nascent high cultures were the Tiahuanaco culture of the highlands, and in the coastal plain the Nazca culture of southern, the Moche culture of northern, Peru. Both these coastal peoples developed valley economies, irrigating their arid fields from the rivers, using adobe bricks to build their towns and erecting great pyramidal adobe mounds as temples and as fortresses. Both peoples are justly celebrated for their pottery. Moche pots are modelled with vigorous and realistic, often humorous, relief. Nazca polychrome ware is famous for its simple and beautiful designs and for the variety and brilliance of its colour. Both peoples were great weavers, the Nazca especially remarkable for the variety and unsurpassed beauty of their cotton fabrics. The highland culture was a grimmer, more austere, affair. It grew up in the bleak wind-swept basin of Lake Titicaca and derives its name from its principal site, the great ruins of Tiahuanaco, just south of the lake, in modern Bolivia. Its most striking achievements were its buildings, of massive cut-stone masonry, and its stiff, conventional, equally massive relief sculpture. Its artefacts were in general markedly inferior to those of the coastal cultures. On the other hand the Tiahuanaco people displayed considerable expansive vigour. For a period after the sixth century they strongly influenced, perhaps overran, the Moche of the northern coast; but by the eleventh century both of these very different cultures had lost their vitality and disappeared.

In the centuries immediately preceding the Spanish invasion new cultures grew up among the dense populations of the coastal plain of Peru, Chimu in the north, Ica in the south, inferior in many of the arts to their Moche or Nazca predecessors, but superior in their capacity for political organisation. This was a period of city-building and consolidation of kingdoms. Chanchan, the Chimu capital, in particular, is an impressive and extensive site, the ruin of a great city. The central fact of this period, however, was the rise of a new power in the highlands: that of the Incas, one among many groups of llama-tending, potato-growing mountaineers, of Quechua stock and language. Their home was a long, shallow, grassy depression, the Cuzco valley, lying at ten to twelve thousand feet between the central and eastern ranges of the high Cordillera. In the middle fourteenth century the Incas took to a predatory career and began to expand. Within a few decades their pugnacity and the astuteness of their chiefs enabled them to subjugate their immediate neighbours in the valley. Their war-chiefs succeeded in establishing themselves as a dynasty, and the tribe as a whole became an aristocracy among other tribes. The Incas, alone among Amerindian peoples, thus early possessed two essential instruments of empire—a hereditary monarchy and a hereditary ruling class. The ability of their rulers, generation after generation, and the characteristic docility of the Peruvian character, enabled them to govern and not merely to prey upon the peoples whom they conquered. Early in the fifteenth century the Inca army crossed the Desaguadero into the country of the Colla peoples, the country of ancient Tiahuanaco. There they learned the art of ashlar masonry, an immense improvement on the *pirca* walling—rough stones set in mud—which they had used until that time. Cuzco became a city of massive cut-stone walls, many of which stand to this day. It was an open city, without defences; instead, the mmense fortress enclosure of Sacsayhuamán was built on a height above the town as a refuge, if the tide of conquest should turn. Sacsayhuamán was never needed, however, before the Spaniards came. The tide of conquest by the end of the fifteenth century had carried Inca arms north to southern Ecuador and south to the Maule river in central Chile, where their advance was stopped—as the Spaniards were later to be halted in their turn—by the primitive valour of the Araucanians.

The snow-covered ranges of the Cordillera run roughly north and

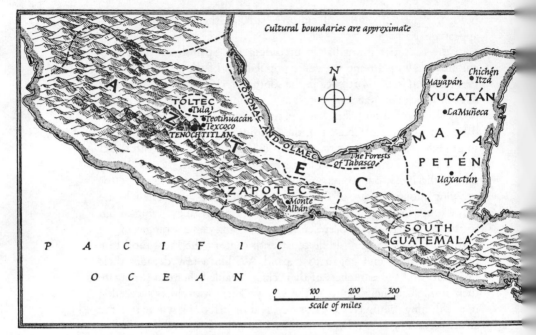

3. The kingdoms of the sun, Central America

south, and the high plains and basins—of which the Cuzco valley is
one—lying between them are separated by relatively modest saddles.
Passage north and south is not unduly difficult. From the east or the
west, however, the high valleys are extremely difficult of access. Most
of the major rivers rising in the Peruvian Andes flow towards the
Atlantic. They cut through the eastern Cordillera in deep but passable
gorges, such as that of the Urubamba, in which there are two major
Inca sites: Macchu Picchu and the fortress of Ollantaytambo. Once
clear of the foothills, however, the rivers plunge into the Amazonian
forest, more impassable than the sea. The Inca armies rarely ventured
there, and never remained for long. In Inca times the chief objects of
conquest lay to the west, in the coastal plain. The way there lay over
precipitous ranges, barren foothills and arid desert. The rivers were
short and small, and there were few usable passes. Communication, as
the Spaniards were to discover, was appallingly difficult. Nevertheless,
the piecemeal conquest of the coast, and the assimilation by the Incas
of coastal art and skill, took less than a hundred years. Inca armies

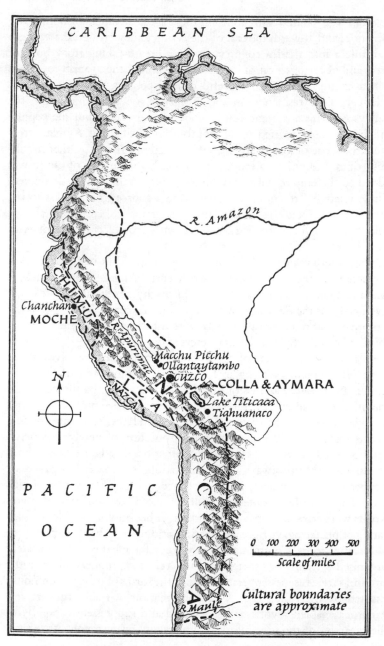

4. The kingdoms of the sun, South America

overran the Chimu kingdom in the 1460s, advancing south from
Ecuador; and towards the end of the century they crossed the western
Cordillera into the Ica country. It was a breath-taking story both of
arms and of organisation, at least as remarkable as the Spanish conquests
half a century later. The peaceful coastal peoples, it is true, offered
relatively little resistance. In the highlands, on the other hand, the
valleys running north and south offered easier access, but the peoples
inhabiting them resisted more stoutly. The Colla and Aymara areas
were the scene of long wars and subsequently of revolts. Other mountain tribes held out even longer: the great highland area of Quito was
added to the empire only a few decades before the Spaniards arrived.
These relatively recent acquisitions were a source of weakness to the
Inca state. In Quito, especially, the inhabitants, still resentful of Inca
rule, received the European invaders with acquiescence, if not with
enthusiasm.

The society over which the Incas ruled differed in many important
respects from the high civilisations of Central America and Mexico. It
was a real empire, administered by a hierarchy of officials whose effective head was the *Sapa Inca*, with his capital at Cuzco. Throughout the
empire all but minor local officials were Incas, and the highest officers,
those whom the Spaniards later described as 'governors' or 'viceroys',
were normally members of the imperial family, close relatives of the
Sapa Inca himself. Nothing in Inca history is more remarkable than
the sustained ability and vigour of this great dynasty. Its authority was
maintained by all possible physical and psychological means. Garrisons
of loyal subjects were stationed in strategic places; sometimes whole
towns were moved to hasten the incorporation of newly conquered
provinces. Alone among the ancient Amerindians, the Peruvians built
roads, or rather footways, of beaten adobe on the coast, paved or
stepped in the mountains, to facilitate the passage of armies or of officials. The main Inca routes can still be traced for hundreds of miles.
Rivers were crossed by means of bridges: either 'monkey-bridges', with
cables of plaited agave fibre, or floating bridges supported on pontoons
of buoyant reeds. Communications were maintained by an elaborately
organised system of post-stations, and relays of runners all over the
empire; service as messengers was one of the forms of tribute commonly
exacted by the ruling clan. The combination of roads, runners and
garrisons enabled revolts to be detected and suppressed as rapidly as
the weapons of the time allowed; but in any event revolts were rare.

The sanctity of the *Sapa Inca* was maintained by a court ritual of great complexity. The Hispanicised Inca historian Garcilaso—son of a *conquistador* and an Inca princess—describes in detail the ceremonial abasement—the symbolic burden, the bare feet and the downcast eyes—of all who approached the ruler, and the splendour of his ceremonial appearances, whether on civil occasions or in rites designed to ensure the fertility of crops or the abundance of animals. The Inca Empire, moreover, had a state religion which supplemented, though it never entirely supplanted, the older animistic beliefs and fertility cults. Its principal object of worship was the sun, of which the *Sapa Inca* was held to be a descendant, and in whose ceremonial worship he played a central and indispensable part.

The sun-worship of the Incas served, or at least upheld, the interests of empire. To generalise broadly, the Andean peoples directed their energies towards the material technique of supporting life and organising large-scale societies, rather than to the cultivation of supernatural knowledge and power. The Incas held their captives ruthlessly to forced labour; they never sacrificed them wholesale, as did the Aztecs, to appease implacable gods. Their great ruins—buildings, roads, irrigation systems—are secular in character. They had no great ceremonial centres, inhabited by a dedicated priesthood; their cities from their beginnings were built to be lived in and defended. They erected no stelae. Their temples never equalled the magnificent and lavish sculptured pyramids and corbelled shrines of Middle America. Inca masonry, in general, though it is massive, durable and beautifully dressed, demanded for its construction neatness and laboriousness rather than architectural genius or spiritual drive. The specialised priestly arts did not flourish greatly in the Inca state. There was no elaborately developed astronomical and calendric science, and no writing. The nearest Andean approach to writing was the *quipu*, a series of knotted strings used in conjunction with a rudimentary abacus for calculating and recording tribute. On the other hand, some of the secular arts flourished exceedingly. Ancient Peruvian pottery had no peer in the Americas. Its manufacture was slow and laborious, since the potter's wheel was unknown and vessels were built up from coils of wet clay; but this very fact encouraged rich, elaborate and highly individual design. The arts of painting and firing pottery were well understood. Surviving examples of jewellery and ornaments wrought in soft metals—gold, silver and copper—are also among the treasures of their kind. Above

all, weaving was developed to a point perhaps unequalled by man in
the whole course of human history. For this last purpose the Peruvians
possessed a wide range of raw materials. They had, it is true, no silk;
but in addition to many of the coarser vegetable fibres the coastal
peoples grew several species of cotton. The highlanders, for their part,
had three species of wool-bearing animals—llama, alpaca and vicuña—
whose fleeces offered a great variety of textures and natural colours.
The exchange of lowland cotton for highland wool was probably the
most important trade of the empire, and characteristically was organised by the state.

The word 'monolithic' has often been used to describe the Inca state.
The *Sapa Inca* certainly inspired a veneration more complete, and
wielded a power more absolute, than any European monarch. Inca rule
succeeded in imposing a remarkable uniformity on its subjects, regulating in great detail the labour tribute demanded from each class and
age group, regimenting their religious, political and economic activities
in the interests of the empire as a whole, but in return protecting them
from war or violence, and to a considerable extent also from want.
The Inca state, nevertheless, might more aptly be described as multi-
cellular than as monolithic. The *ayllu*, the village clan, remained and
remains to this day the fundamental unit of social organisation. The
Incas themselves, before their rise to power, were only a highland
ayllu led by a temporary war-chief. They built upon a foundation which
they understood, retaining the ancient *ayllus* and their chiefs under the
supervision of the hierarchy of imperial officials. The *ayllus* themselves
were in most respects self-sufficient and self-contained. In spite of their
common subjection to Inca discipline, and the uniformity which
discipline imposed, they had little contact one with another. Indeed,
one of the most characteristic features of Peruvian life was its immobility. Except when the government, for its own purposes, caused whole
tribes to move their homes, ordinary people travelled very little. Incaic
highways were for the use of officials and imperial runners. Even trade
was local and limited for the most part, confined either to rarities for
the use of the nobility or to objects of state monopoly such as vicuña
wool. There was relatively little long-range commerce, such as the
Middle Americans enjoyed; a curious circumstance, considering that
the Peruvians, alone among the Amerindian peoples, possessed a beast
of burden, though a feeble and unadaptable one usable only in its native
highlands. The self-sufficiency of the *ayllus* and the immobility of their

members were important factors in the Inca rise to power. The villages could be conqured one by one and ruled uniformly but separately. The effective geographical extension of the system, on the other hand, was limited, for the strain of maintaining garrisons and communications increased disproportionately with every increase in area. By the sixteenth century the effective limits had been reached and probably overreached. Finally, the system was likely to break down when, as eventually happened, a serious split occurred in the ruling dynasty.

The native cultures of the Americas displayed an immense variety of attainment, and ranged from the naked savages of some of the West Indian islands to the sophisticated nobilities of Middle America or the Andes. The most developed societies differed greatly one from another, but they all had one characteristic in common. In all of them remarkable levels of attainment—religious, social, political, artistic—were reached with very limited technical equipment. They had no hard-metal tools, except for a relatively rare use of bronze among the Incas; no wheeled vehicles; no boats except flimsy canoes or primitive balsas; few and inferior domestic animals. They lacked even that most fundamental of agricultural implements the plough. In compensation they commanded, characteristically, a very high degree of social conformity, of docility—the willing submergence of the individual in the personality of the tribe. Their technical deficiencies were such, indeed, that without the closest social co-operation, enforced by detailed and continuous ritual compulsion, they could barely have supported life, much less built up impressive civilisations. Compulsion was particularly necessary to the Incas, because of the dependence on irrigation in coastal Peru, and to the Aztecs because of the need for flood control in the valley of Mexico. In America, as in the East, wherever agriculture has depended on large-scale hydraulic works an authoritarian central control has emerged to mobilise and direct the population for the labour required. The same is true in lesser degree in places where religious feeling or the needs of defence have demanded unusually massive and elaborate public building. Mayas, Aztecs, Incas, accordingly, found means of extending Amerindian conformity, docility, from the scale of a village to the scale of a city state, a network of conquered cities, a large empire. Their systems of rule naturally tended to encourage passive acquiescence rather than active loyalty, except among the ruling castes or clans. The systems, moreover, were peculiarly vulnerable to an enemy who combined a technical superiority in weapons with a relatively high mobility.

Such an enemy, even if loosely commanded and few in number, could paralyse the organisation by striking swiftly at the centres, and so demonstrating the powerlessness of the gods in whose name ritual compulsion was enforced.

The achievements of the higher civilisations of America were such as to astonish the first Europeans who saw them. Their combination of wealth and technical weakness was their undoing. No *conquistador* could resist the temptations offered by civilised but infidel peoples, possessing land and gold; subject peoples accustomed to obey and to render tribute; ruling peoples ready indeed to fight, but armed only with weapons of wood and stone.

CHAPTER 4

The conquerors

THE isthmus, Castilla del Oro, had been settled from Hispaniola. The men who explored and invaded Mexico came from Cuba, and the leading spirit in the work of preparation was that sharp speculator, governor Diego Velázquez. Velázquez' people had for some time been slave-raiding in the Bay Islands off the Honduras coast, and there probably found evidence of trade with the more developed societies of the mainland. Small expeditions were sent from Cuba in 1517 and 1518 to reconnoitre the coasts of Yucatán and the Gulf of Mexico. In 1519, as a result of their reports, Velázquez fitted out a much larger fleet, and appointed as its commander Hernán Cortés, who had been his secretary and was financially a partner in the enterprise. Cortés was personally popular, and the project attracted a force of about 600 volunteers, a large number for that sparsely settled country. Velázquez and Cortés distrusted one another; and probably, although Velázquez had in mind only exploration, slaving and trade, Cortés from the start contemplated the conquest of an independent kingdom. He left Cuba in clandestine haste, and on landing lost no time in repudiating Velázquez' authority. From that moment the enterprise was Cortés' own.

The conquest of Mexico is the best-known and best-documented of all the Spanish campaigns in the New World. Of the surviving contemporary accounts, two at least are of unusual literary and historical merit. Cortés' own letters are graphic and detailed, though inevitably affected by political considerations and by a natural tendency to represent all decisions as Cortés' own. The corrective is to be found in the *True History* of Bernal Díaz del Castillo, which tells the story from the point of view of a loyal and intelligent foot-soldier who happened to possess a remarkable memory. Besides being well known

and well told, the story of the conquest represents perfectly and characteristically the three main strands in the psychological make-up of the
conquistadores—their restless greed for gold, for land and for slaves; their
traditional ambition to strike down the heathen and to win souls for
Christ; and, more subtle but no less compelling, their love of great
deeds for their own sake. It was this pride in doing great deeds, this
thirst for reputation, which made the rank and file so susceptible to
the oratory of a leader such as Cortés; which made them applaud
decisions which they knew to be imprudent, held them together in
the face of disaster and led them to attempt the seemingly impossible.
They had little formal discipline, little loyalty save to leaders whom
they respected personally. They were individualists, who thought of
themselves not as imitators, but as equals and rivals of the heroes of
ancient times. Certainly there are no stories in classical legend or
medieval romance more dramatic than this conquest of a splendid,
if ill-equipped, empire by a handful of down-at-heel swordsmen.

Cortés' first mainland landing was on the coast of Tabasco, where he
fought his first serious battle and gained his first reliable intelligence
of Aztec power and wealth. Passing along the coast, he next landed
near what is now Vera Cruz, where he spent four months establishing
a base and cultivating relations with the coastal people in preparation
for his march inland. The beginning of the major operation, the march
on Mexico, was marked by two symbolic acts. The first was the destruction of the ships in which he had come. By so doing Cortés prevented malcontents returning to Cuba, freed the sailors to march with
the army and satisfied the *conquistador's* love of a dramatic gesture with
a classical analogy. The second—for which there was ample precedent
in Reconquest Spain—was the ceremonious founding of a municipality. To the magistrates of the 'town' of Vera Cruz, Cortés resigned
the commission he had received in Cuba; from them, as representatives of the Crown in Mexico, he received a new commission, and
wrote at once to the King for confirmation of it. Having thus legalised
as best he could his assumption of an independent command, he led his
army up the long and rugged climb from the steamy forests of Vera
Cruz to the high plateau of Central Mexico.

To the modern traveller Cortés' route seems almost perversely difficult. It included two high passes: that between Orizaba and the Cofre
de Perote in Vera Cruz State, and the Paso de Cortés between the twin
snow peaks Popocatépetl and Ixtaccíhuatl. Neither pass carries a usable

road today. The route was dictated largely by political considerations, by the need to travel as far as possible through friendly territory. In the neighbourhood of Vera Cruz were many recently conquered *pueblos* which paid tribute unwillingly to their Aztec overlords. By a mixture of force and diplomacy, Cortés had been able to quicken the resentment of Cempoala, the Totonac capital, into open defiance of Tenochtitlán. Cempoala helped the Spaniards with food, with porters and with information. There Cortés first heard of Quetzalcoatl, the god-hero of Toltec mythology, whose return to earth was expected by Mexican augurers. The Cempoalans advised him on his route to Tenochtitlán and suggested the possibility of alliance with Tlaxcala, the one city of the plateau region which still maintained its independence. Here was a situation which the Spaniards thought they understood; a situation which recalled that of Muslim Granada a generation or two earlier. But whereas Granada had only been tolerated in loose vassalage until the Castilian rulers felt strong enough to seize it, Tlaxcala was tolerated in permanent independence by the Aztecs as a source of captives for sacrifice. At regular intervals, and with due notice, Tenochtitlán made war on Tlaxcala with the intention not of reducing it to vassalage but of capturing prisoners. These repeated and inconclusive wars caused a constant drain upon the resources of Tlaxcala; and though they fiercely and instinctively resisted the Spaniards at first, the Tlaxcalans after defeat agreed to the alliance which Cortés proposed.

From the seasoned warriors of Tlaxcala, Cortés learned something of the military strength and weakness of the Aztecs. Embassies from Tenochtitlán also arrived in the camp, seeking to dissuade him from advancing by threats and by pleas of poverty; but the pleas were belied by the presents which they brought, whose value and workmanship revealed the wealth of Mexico to the greedy eyes of the waiting Spaniards. Cortés wisely sent the best of this glittering treasure home to the King (though some of it was intercepted by French pirates and never reached Spain). From the threats he divined the mixture of defiance and superstitious dread in the mind of the Aztec war-chief and saw the use which could be made of Montezuma's fears. Cortés' greatness largely consisted in his power of appreciating the psychological factors in the situation, and in the skill with which he built up his own prestige alike among allies and enemies. Politely but firmly he insisted on making a friendly visit, to which Montezuma eventually agreed. The advance of the army was orderly and swift, and soon the

Spaniards, escorted by their Aztec hosts, marched along the causeway
into Tenochtitlán in a peaceful display of martial pageantry. The Spaniards were lodged in a great community-house or palace in the city,
while the allies camped outside, on the shore of the lake. It was remarkable evidence of Aztec powers of organisation that, in a country
where all transport was by canoe or on men's backs, so many extra
mouths could be fed at such short notice.

Peace was short-lived. The first interruption was the arrival at Vera
Cruz of a powerful force under Pánfilo de Narváez, one of the original
conquerors of Cuba, who had been sent by the governor to apprehend
Cortés. Cortés rushed down to the coast, out-manœuvred Narváez,
and by a mixture of threats, bribes and promises enlisted the men from
Cuba under his own command. In his absence, however, the zeal of
his lieutenants in destroying temples, and their incessant demands for
food, had exasperated the Aztecs to the point of war. The Spaniards
under Pedro de Alvarado had anticipated war by an unprovoked attack
during a religious festival; and both sides, in sullen hostility, awaited
Cortés' return. Cortés, trusting in Montezuma's authority and his own
prestige, was allowed to re-enter the city and rejoin Alvarado, so that
the whole army was entrapped. The Aztecs had elected a new war-
chief. Montezuma, by now a discredited puppet in Spanish hands,
attempted at Cortés' urging to pacify his people and was stoned to
death. Cortés had to fight his way out along the broken causeways by
night, losing in that one night a third of his men and most of his
baggage. The allies, however, remained loyal to their agreement. The
army was able to retire on Tlaxcala and re-form for a more thorough
and less spectacular advance. The city was besieged and its food and
water supply cut off. Its buildings were systematically destroyed and
the rubble shovelled into the lake in order to avoid the hazards of
street-fighting, as the Spaniards and their allies advanced. Under the
direction of a master shipwright in his company, Cortés had sailing
boats built of local timber, and mounted in them the guns he had
brought from Vera Cruz. These *bergantines* rendered essential service
in battering the adobe buildings of the city, in protecting Spanish
troops passing along the causeways and in intercepting canoe-borne
supplies. The attackers, moreover, were preceded by a sinister ally,
smallpox, which they had brought with them from Cuba, and which
raged throughout the city. In 1521 the surviving Aztecs surrendered.
In the beautiful Spanish town which Cortés began to build upon the

site hardly a trace of Indian building remains. The place was built over as completely as the Roman cities of Europe, and the lake is now a dusty plain.

The loot of the conquest proved disappointing; it could hardly have been otherwise, so high were the soldiers' expectations. Cortés was blamed for it, and even accused of hiding treasure for his own profit. His remedies were the standard ones: the distribution of Indian villages among his followers as tributary fiefs—*repartimientos* or *encomiendas*—and the despatch of the most ambitious captains upon further expeditions. Cortés never forgot that the discovery and conquest of New Spain had originated in attempts to find a route to the Pacific and so to the Far East. Mexico occupied and its valley secure, Cortés resumed the search, whether for a strait between the oceans or for harbours which could become bases for Pacific exploration. Between 1522 and 1524 Michoacán and most of the Pacific coast area as far north as the Santiago river were conquered and distributed in *encomienda*. In 1524 Pedro de Alvarado led a well-equipped force through Tehuántepec into the region of the Maya cities of Guatemala, and Cristóbal de Olid was sent by sea to the Bay of Honduras. Both these expeditions encountered not only physical obstacles and stout Indian resistance but also opposition from an unexpected quarter—from Pedrarias Dávila's men exploring north from Darien. The two great streams of mainland conquest met along the southern borders of what are now the republics of Guatemala and Honduras, and a dangerous armed clash seemed imminent. To complicate the situation further, Olid repudiated Cortés' authority and set up an independent command. Cortés thought it necessary to deal with mutiny and possible civil war in person. It was the one serious blunder of his career. His army marched to Honduras across the base of the Yucatán peninsular, through appallingly difficult country in which abrupt mountain ranges alternated with dense rainforest. One river and its riparian swamps had to be crossed by means of a floating bridge whose construction required the felling of over a thousand trees. Few horses survived the march, and the men who survived emerged from the forest broken in health and even, for a time, in spirit. Nevertheless, Cortés' presence sufficed to restore order among the Spaniards in Honduras—Olid had been murdered before his arrival —and to make an arrangement with the men from Darien which attached Honduras, for a time, to Mexico. Meanwhile Alvarado had carried out a successful, rapacious and brutal campaign in Guatemala.

The Mayas, vigorous, intelligent, with a developed though decaying culture, lacked political unity, and Alvarado profited by the enmity between two principal peoples, Cakchiquel and Quiché, to support one against the other and ultimately to subdue both. The Spanish city of Guatemala, on the first of its three successive sites, was founded in 1524, and *encomiendas* were distributed among its founding citizens in the usual way. Alvarado succeeded in holding his men together and in standing off incursions from Darien. He visited Spain in 1527 and returned to America a Knight of Santiago, with his government of Guatemala confirmed.

Cortés returned by sea from Honduras to Mexico in 1526, and resumed with his old vigour the business of organising New Spain, exploring its coastal provinces and pursuing the search for a sea route to the East. In 1527 he despatched a fleet of three ships, all built in Mexico, across the Pacific to the support of the little garrison which Magellan's men had stationed in the Moluccas. Meanwhile, however, hostile tale-bearers had been busy in Spain, and Cortés thought it necessary to go there himself to defend and explain his proceedings in Mexico and to urge his claims upon the royal gratitude. He presented himself at court, with appropriate gifts and a troupe of Indian acrobats, in 1529. Charles V greeted him warmly, created him marquis of the valley of Oaxaca, and confirmed his huge *encomienda* there, officially of 23,000 tributaries, in fact many more. Cortés was too famous and too powerful, however, to be entirely trusted. The Emperor named him captain-general—a general without an army—but would not entrust to him the civil government of New Spain. Already in 1527 an *audiencia*, a court of appeal, had been established in Mexico to safeguard Crown interests and keep an eye on Cortés. It is true that the senior members of this body proved both brutal and dishonest, and that the president, Nuño de Guzmán, soon deserted his post and went off on an unauthorised and destructive conquest of his own in New Galicia, to the north-west; but Nuño was replaced by an eminent ecclesiastic, and the *audiencia* system was retained. In 1535 the Emperor sent out a viceroy with both civil and military powers: Antonio de Mendoza, soldier, diplomat, cadet of a great noble house. Again Cortés was passed over. He offered to lead troops against Nuño de Guzmán in New Galicia, but the offer was refused. His plans for expeditions in search of the rumoured 'cities of Cíbola' in the north were thwarted by Mendoza, who had similar ambitions. His energies were more and more confined to business activities, to the management of his sugar and cattle properties in Oaxaca and his house property in Mexico City. Finally in 1539 Cortés wearied of the New World and returned to Spain, where he lived on the revenues of his *marquesado*, in bored and litigious retirement. His reputation as a commander of expeditions against semi-barbarous tribes was little valued in Europe. Neither his services nor his advice was sought by the Crown, even in fields such as North Africa, where they might have been of value. He died at his house of Castilleja de la Cuesta, near Seville, in 1547.

While officials and lawyers were busy organising New Spain for the King, and whittling down Cortés' power and authority, another equally formidable empire in South America was being subdued by Spanish arms. Ever since the occupation of Darien rumours had been current among the Spaniards there of civilised and prosperous kingdoms to the south; but because of the barriers of sea, desert and mountain protecting it, the reality long eluded discovery. Serious exploration was begun in Darien by a syndicate comprising two obscure soldiers of fortune from Extremadura, Francisco Pizarro and Diego de Almagro, and a priest named Luque. All three had settled in Darien as *encomenderos*, dabbling also in farming and gold-prospecting. Luque, though he took no active part in the conquest of Peru, seems to have provided most of the initial capital. The partners spent four years in voyages of coastal exploration, in which they collected enough evidence to encourage them to approach the Emperor for a formal capitulation. Pizarro's journey to Spain coincided with the triumphal appearance of Cortés at the court, a favourable omen; and Pizarro secured an appointment as *adelantado* and governor of the kingdom which he undertook to conquer. He returned to Panama with his four half-brothers and a few other volunteers. Leaving Almagro in Panama to recruit more men, Pizarro finally set out in 1530 with about 180 men and twenty-seven horses for the conquest of Peru.

The arrival of Pizarro at Túmbez on the northern coast of Peru coincided with the final stage of a succession war. The reigning Inca, Huáscar, had been defeated by his half-brother Atahualpa. The victor was still encamped with his army near the little town of Cajamarca in northern Peru. Reports of this situation encouraged Pizarro, after establishing himself in the Túmbez region and founding the 'city' of San Miguel, to march inland in 1532 to Cajamarca. Here, by means of a surprise attack under cover of a formal conference, the Spaniards succeeded in killing most of Atahualpa's immediate retinue and capturing the ruler himself. Aided by surprise, by a favourable political situation and by a breath-taking boldness which frightened the conquerors themselves, Pizarro and his men decided the fate of the Inca Empire in a single afternoon. Almagro arrived shortly afterwards with reinforcements from Panama. The Inca forces, deprived of the authority of their ruler, were unable effectively to resist the conquerors' march, with about 600 men, on Cuzco. The inhabitants did not even attempt to retire to the defences of Sacsayhuamán. They remained passively in the city, which was taken and sacked in November 1533. The gold and silver looted from Cuzco, together with the roomful of gold vessels which Atahualpa collected at Cajamarca in the vain hope of buying his freedom, was melted down, the royal fifth subtracted and the rest distributed; enough to make every man in the army rich for life, though few lived long to enjoy it.

Hitherto the campaign had followed approximately the same lines as that of Cortés in Mexico, but after the capture of Cuzco the pattern of events diverged. Pizarro, unlike Cortés, did not establish the centre of his power in the ancient capital of the kingdom, but founded in 1535 an entirely new Spanish capital—Lima, the City of the Kings, close to the sea in the Rimac valley. The choice was natural on military grounds, for Cuzco was remote from the harbours on which Spanish Peru depended for reinforcements and supplies from the outside world, and its mountainous surroundings made the use of cavalry, the chief Spanish arm, difficult if not impossible; but by this decision Pizarro emphasised the division between Spanish coast and Indian mountain, and lost one means of attaching the Peruvians to a new allegiance. Pizarro, moreover, was a man of very different stamp from Cortés. In Spain he was an illegitimate son, brought up by obscure peasants; in the Indies a warrior, owing his leadership to ambition, boldness and skill in fighting. He was illiterate, and so dependent on secretaries, who sometimes abused their power and made enemies for their master. Shrewd though he was, he lacked Cortés' charm and subtlety, his sensitive understanding of human situations, his genius for attaching even defeated enemies to himself. The judicial murder of Atahualpa was a blunder, condemned by many Spaniards. Pizarro, moreover, had jealous rivals in his own camp, and serious disputes soon arose among the conquerors. The first news of trouble came from San Miguel, whose governor, Belalcázar, had left his post and marched north into the Quito area at the invitation of some of its inhabitants to rid them of their Inca governors and to establish a conquest of his own. The situation was complicated by the unexpected arrival from Guatemala of the restless and warlike Alvarado, who also had designs on Quito. First Almagro and then Pizarro hastened north to avert civil war. Almagro and Belalcázar (who were *compadres*) made common cause against Alvarado, who after an interview with Pizarro agreed to return to his own government. Before leaving, however, Alvarado sold much of his equipment and ammunition to Almagro for a huge sum in bar silver. Many of the men from Guatemala joined Almagro, who thus became strong enough to be a serious rival to Pizarro.

Meanwhile Hernando Pizarro—who alone among the half-brothers was legitimate and had some claim to education—had been sent to Spain with reports and with the royal share of the loot of Cajarmarca. He returned in 1535 with despatches granting to Francisco Pizarro the title of marquis, and to Almagro that of *adelantado* in a necessarily undefined area to the south of that governed by Pizarro. Almagro promptly claimed Cuzco as part of his grant; Pizarro refused to give up the city, and civil war again seemed imminent. The two chieftains were persuaded, however, to a face-saving reconciliation, and Almagro departed on an expedition to explore and conquer his southern kingdom. He was away for two years, during which his army traversed the bleak *Altiplano* of what is now Bolivia and penetrated far into Chile, returning by way of the coastal desert of Atacama. Almagro's people suffered great hardships from cold and hunger, from heat and thirst; they lost most of their horses and many of their own number; found no more cities and no plunder worth the name; and returned to Cuzco in April 1537 still more bitterly jealous of Pizarro's good fortune.

During Almagro's absence Pizarro had to face a dangerous and widespread Indian rising led by Manco Inca, a successor of Huáscar whom Pizarro tried unsuccessfully to use as a puppet ruler. Manco failed to make any impression on Lima, but invested Cuzco closely. His people occupied the deserted fortress of Sacsayhuamán, and from its height hurled incendiary missiles into the city, setting the thatch roofs blazing and driving the Spaniards to camp in the central plaza. For a time they cut the city off from reinforcements sent from the coast. Indian armies were too large, however, to keep the field for long periods, with the primitive means of transport available, and after a few months Manco's

army began to dwindle; but before Pizarro could take advantage of
this weakening, Almagro arrived with the survivors of his army from
Chile, took Manco in the rear and defeated him, marched into Cuzco
and seized the government of city and province. This was the origin
of the first of the civil wars of Spanish Peru, the war of Las Salinas.
Like many subsequent disturbances in Peru, the war was a quarrel not
only between two factions of Spaniards but between the coast and the
mountains, between the cities of Lima and Cuzco. Lima won; Almagro, after many vicissitudes, was defeated in 1538 and strangled by
order of Hernando Pizarro, who took him prisoner. He had been an
open-handed and popular leader, and his death made many enemies
for the Pizarros. Francisco Pizarro's turn came three years later. In
1541 he was murdered in Lima by a group of the 'men of Chile'.
Manco Inca survived them both. He lived on as a fugitive ruler in the
fastnesses of Vilcabamba, periodically raiding the smaller Spanish
settlements. He was murdered ten years later by two runaway Spaniards
whom he befriended.

The war of Chupas, which broke out in 1541 between the partisans
of the two dead chieftains, differed from the earlier quarrels in that a
royal governor despatched from Spain was actively engaged. The
licentiate Vaca de Castro, president of the new *audiencia* of Panama
but sent on to Peru to investigate the disorders there, held a commission to succeed Pizarro in the event of the marquis's death; and accordingly on arrival assumed command of the Pizarro faction, turning
it thereby into a royal army operating against an armed rebellion.
The Almagro party was defeated and many of its leaders executed.
More difficult, Castro, with a lawyer's skill and patience, dissuaded
Gonzalo Pizarro from claiming, sword in hand, the succession to his
brother's authority. Peace was short-lived, however. In 1543–5 the
government in Spain began a sweeping attack on the *encomienda*
system, and sent to Peru as viceroy an unintelligent martinet, Blasco
Núñez de la Vela, with orders to confiscate *encomiendas*. Núñez's insistence, against every counsel of prudence, on the immediate enforcement of his instructions provoked an armed rising led by Gonzalo
Pizarro and a fresh civil war, in which Núñez was killed, early in 1546.
Gonzalo Pizarro became for a time the effective ruler of Peru. Had he
repudiated his allegiance altogether, as his grim camp-master Carbajal
advised, he might have established an independent kingdom. Habits of
loyalty to the Crown, however, though loose, were strong. Gonzalo

attempted to negotiate for royal recognition of his authority, and the consequent delay enabled Núñez's successor in the government, the priest Pedro de la Gasca—having already, from Panama, secured command of the sea—to land in Peru, to detach many jealous individuals from Gonzalo and eventually to raise an army which defeated him. Gonzalo and his principal lieutenants were beheaded in 1548. Of the five violent and ungovernable brothers who had conquered Peru, only Hernando survived, to languish for twenty years in a Spanish prison.

The area under Spanish government had expanded greatly during the civil wars. Belalcázar, after the defeat of the Almagro faction in 1539, had lost the government of Quito, which Francisco Pizarro had conferred on his brother Gonzalo. With his followers he pushed on further north, through forest country inhabited by primitive tribes, to Popayán. From there he embarked on a bold expedition through the mountains of the eastern Cordillera, adding a new technique to the methods of conquest by driving a great herd of pigs along with his army as a source of food on the march. Eventually he broke through the encircling rampart of mountains into the populous savannahs of Bogotá, inhabited by an isolated but settled town-dwelling people, the Chibchas; but his discovery had been forestalled. Gonzalo Jiménez de Quesada, marching from Santa Marta on the Caribbean coast, had forced his way up the precipitous valley of the Magdalena and so reached Bogotá from the north. On this occasion the two leaders, approximately equal in strength, sensibly agreed to refer the division of territories to the government in Spain. Belalcázar was confirmed as governor of Popayán; Santa Fe de Bogotá became eventually the capital of a separate Spanish kingdom, New Granada.

Gonzalo Pizarro in 1541–2 led an extremely arduous expedition from Quito through the vast forests on the eastern slope of the Andes, attracted—so he said—by reports that cinnamon trees grew there; and by equally unfounded but more persistent rumours of 'El Dorado', the gilded king. The people of this expedition, lost and hungry— having devoured their pigs and many of their horses—came upon the Napo river and built a boat of timber felled on the bank in order to explore the river in search of villages and food. It was in this boat that Francisco de Orellana and a handful of companions, unable to return against the stream, followed the entire length of the Amazon to its mouth in 1542. Gonzalo, with his surviving company, struggled back

on foot to Quito, where he dictated his report to the Emperor, a master-
piece of understatement and brevity. Meanwhile, far to the south,
Almagro's reconnaissance of Chile had been followed up by Pedro de
Valdivia, who founded the city of Santiago in 1541. Valdivia's conquest
was unusual in two respects. As a result of Francisco Pizarro's death
he found himself without a master and became one of the few elected
governors in the Indies by the choice of the householders of Santiago,
much as Cortés had been 'elected' at Vera Cruz. Finding no gold and
no elaborate Indian culture, he succeeded in establishing a modest but
soundly based Spanish farming community in one of the loveliest and
most fertile valleys in the world.

Manco Inca, in his mountain exile, might well have reflected on the
ironical fate which befell the conquerors of his people—little bands of
armed marauders seeking one another out and fighting to the death
among great mountains, with an empire at their feet awaiting an organising hand. The disorders which confused and delayed the Spanish
settlement of Peru were due almost entirely to Spanish quarrels. As far
as the Inca government was concerned, the conquest was achieved by
1535. The span of a single generation sufficed for the defeat of all the
principal settled societies of the Americas. The dramatic and extraordinarily rapid success of these Spanish campaigns calls for explanation. Some Amerindian societies, at least, were familiar with organised,
large-scale war. Some of them—the Aztecs in particular—made a cult
of it. They had specialised war-chiefs, clans or Orders of professed
warriors, and a well-organised system of territorial levy whereby
large numbers of armed men could be assembled under their local
chiefs at comparatively short notice. They had systems of runners by
means of which messages could be conveyed over long distances at
least as rapidly as in contemporary Europe. Their weapons were primitive by European standards, but formidable nevertheless. The Mexican
maquauhuitl, a battle-axe made of a stout staff with obsidian blades,
could cut off a horse's head. For throwing missiles they had slings,
spear-throwers and in some places long-bows. Their body armour,
made of quilted cotton, was light, and effective against arrows; some
Spaniards, in the tropical heat, abandoned their own armour of
leather and steel and took to wearing native armour instead. Their
tactical conventions were comparatively simple, and their habit of
fighting in dense masses in the open made them vulnerable to fire-
arms; but they learned quickly, and sometimes showed considerable

adaptability in making use of cover, in preparing ambushes and stratagems and in selecting positions on rough ground where cavalry could not manœuvre.

The Spanish preparations for the American campaigns, in a period when warfare both at sea and on land was developing and changing rapidly, had a haphazard and curiously old-fashioned quality, recalling the earlier crusades or the romances of late medieval chivalry. The ships employed were not fighting vessels but small coasters bought or hired for use as transports. This did not matter, since there was no resistance by sea and little on the coasts. The fighting forces were not organised armies in the European sense, but motley groups of adventurers, each arming himself as best he could, or attaching himself to a leader who would provide him with arms. There were men among them, professional or semi-professional soldiers, who had served with the Great Captain; there were also blacksmiths, bakers, silversmiths, carpenters; men who lived by their wits; men of no occupation at all, whose only experience of fighting had been gained in pot-house brawls. Men who had been implicated in civil commotions, such as the revolt of the *comuneros*, sometimes took themselves off in haste to the Indies. So did those who had cause to fear the Inquisition; Jews, *moriscos, conversos*, were early among the ranks of the settlers in America. They all came, however, from a harsh country and were accustomed to a hard and frugal life; they made extremely formidable fighting material. The leaders were mostly poor gentlemen, bred to arms as was the custom of the time, but not professional soldiers; a few were cut-throats of undiscoverable origin. Both discipline and tactics were informal, largely improvised; this was just as well, since the *conquistadores* found themselves in novel situations which no drill-book could have foreseen. The arms and equipment were as heterogeneous as the men; they included few weapons which in Europe would have been considered modern, and certainly did not, in themselves, confer an overwhelming superiority upon the Spanish forces. The possession of fire-arms was naturally an important, but probably not a decisive factor. A ship carries its armament wherever it goes, but on land cannon had to be dragged over mountains and through swamps by human strength. The army with which Cortés invaded Mexico had a few cannon, taken out of the ships at Vera Cruz and carried along with the army. They were hauled first by sailors, then by Indian auxiliaries, and finally mounted in boats for the siege of Tenochtitlán. They must have been small and not very effective pieces, though no doubt their noise and smoke made a great impression. Apart from the cannon, Cortés had thirteen muskets. Horses were more important than fire-arms. The *conquistadores* owed much to the experience gained through centuries of crusading of transporting horses by sea. Bernal Díaz on several occasions attributed victory 'under God, to the horses'; but Cortés had only sixteen horses when he landed, and some of these were soon killed in battle. Most of his men fought on foot with sword, pike and crossbow. They had the advantage of steel over stone, but they were not a well-equipped European army fighting a horde of helpless savages.

The opposition, of course, was not united; the invaders were usually able to form alliances and encourage one Indian tribe to take arms against another. The small numbers of the Spanish forces proved in some situations to be an advantage. In a region where there were no carts or beasts of burden and all supplies had to be carried on the backs of porters the large Indian armies could only keep the field for short periods. When they had eaten the food they carried with them they had to return home. The Spaniards could move much more swiftly and live off the country as they went. This was the main reason for the defeat of Manco Inca. It was also the reason why Cortés' army, in the first disastrous flight from Tenochtitlán, was not long pursued, and after a few days' hurried march was able to re-form in friendly territory. The docility of the mass of the Indian population, and the thoroughness with which it was organised for communal labour, was of great service to the Spaniards. Without Indian labour Cortés could not have built his *bergantines*, nor have pulled down the buildings of Tenochtitlán. Without the roads, which the Incas had built with tributary labour, the Spaniards could not have moved, horse and foot, about the high Andes, and might never have reached Cuzco.

Moral factors counted for much. The Spaniards were able to exploit some of the legends and beliefs of their adversaries in such a way as to paralyse opposition, at least temporarily. They themselves never doubted that they were fighting mortal men; but to the Indians, horses and guns could be represented, while they were still new and unfamiliar, as trappings of divinity. In Mexico the conventional formalism of the Aztecs in war, and their preoccupation with capturing prisoners for sacrifice, put them at a disadvantage in fighting tough and desperate men who took no prisoners. Finally, the Spaniards had the advantage

I a *Inca masonry: Macchu Picchu*
  b *Inca masonry with Spanish colonial houses superimposed*
    (*from H. Ubbelohde-Doering*, Auf den Königsstrassen der Inka)

II *A Maya stela at Copán, Honduras*
a *front view*   b *side view*
   (*from drawings by A. de Waldeck*)

of their truculent missionary faith. The feeling of 'bringing light to those who were in darkness' was general even among the humbler soldiers, and helps to explain their conviction that, however unsanctified their own lives might be, the Saints fought on their side. This is not to suggest an unsophisticated credulity. The stories of the actual appearance of St James in battle were invented by chroniclers, not by *conquistadores*; Bernal Díaz treats these 'miracles' with ironic contempt. Nevertheless, the *conquistadores* prayed to St Peter and St James before their battles, and the feeling of divine support was strong among them. In the Old World this, though a stimulus to aggression, had not been a military advantage, because the enemy, usually Muslim, also possessed an optimistic faith, whose attitudes towards war, victory and death were similarly encouraging. Amerindian religion, by contrast, was profoundly pessimistic, the sad, acquiescent faith of the last great Stone Age culture. The Indian believed that his religion required him to fight and, if need be, to die bravely. The Spaniard believed that his religion enabled him to win.

Some of them did win. The exploits of Pizarro, Cortés and their like attracted the attention of their contemporaries and of historians because of their conspicuous success. In the settled and populous areas where these commanders operated no other outcome was possible. Significantly, the only lasting military defeats suffered by Spaniards were inflicted by wild people living a scattered life in wild country. The Araucanians of southern Chile, the Chichimecas of northern Mexico, the Caribs of the lesser Antilles, having no great temples or capital cities, were less vulnerable, more mobile, more dangerous. Spanish armies, moreover, could be defeated not only by wild men but by the wilderness itself. It should be remembered that by far the greatest part of the Americas at that time was neither populous nor productive. Immense areas were traversed by Spanish explorers who, as *conquistadores*, were failures, in that they found nothing which they considered to be of value. Sixteenth-century knowledge of the vast area which later became the southern and south-western United States was derived mainly from two expeditions, that of Hernando de Soto and that of Francisco Vázquez Coronado. De Soto in 1539 explored from Tampa Bay in Florida north to the Appalachians and west to the Mississippi. Coronado in 1541 set out from New Galicia across the Río Grande and the Pecos into the great prairies west of the Mississippi, and reported immense herds of 'cows' and primitive people parasitic upon them, 'living like Arabs'. These exploits added much to geographical knowledge, but they had no immediate results and added nothing to the wealth or the contemporary reputation of those who took part in them. The same is true of the men who first explored California, or 'Cíbola' (the *pueblos* of New Mexico), or ascended the rivers of Guiana in search of El Dorado, or discovered the route, later much used by smugglers, up the Río de la Plata and the Paraguay river, into Upper Peru. Wounds, sickness, disappointment and early death were the lot of most of these eternal optimists.

The rule of the *conquistadores* was quarrelsome and brief. They had gone to America at their own expense, endured great hardships, risked their lives and (such as they were) their fortunes, without much practical help from the government at home; and the government never fully trusted them. Most of the leaders died violent deaths. Among those who survived the hardships, the campaigns and the knives of jealous rivals, very few were permanently entrusted with administrative power. Obviously they were not men of a kind likely to settle down as obedient bureaucrats; and it was natural that the Crown should supplant them—once their conquests were secure—with men of its own choice: officials, lawyers, ecclesiastics. Their followers and successors, however—the second and third ranks of the conquest, a wave of emigration representative of almost every class and group in Spain, except the highest nobility—settled in considerable numbers in the lands they had conquered, and created their own characteristic society, highly resistant to bureaucratic regulation. This society—turbulent, aristocratic, loosely organised and jealous—was to set an enduring stamp upon the whole story of Spanish America.

CHAPTER 5

The society of conquest

THE small and informal armies which invaded the Americas were bound together by personal loyalty, by joint hope of gain and by debt. Loyalty and hope of gain bound associated groups of leaders, the officers of the army, to their commander; but each officer, including the commander, had his personal followers, often armed and equipped with money which he had advanced. When a particular conquest had been achieved the commander—usually himself in some kind of contractual relation with the Crown and with investors—had three urgent preoccupations: to ensure his supplies for the future; to reward his companions; and to create a territorial administration.

The three aims naturally interlocked. To achieve the first, the commander had to pacify an Indian community temporarily stunned by the shock of conquest—its chieftains killed, captured, or in subordinate alliance, its temples defaced, its gods discredited, its peasantry frightened, bewildered, apt to revert to a narrow subsistence economy within their villages if central authority were not quickly replaced. Peace had therefore to be restored and random marauding stopped, to encourage the villagers to resume their old productive ways; and means had to be found for the systematic collection and distribution of tribute.

The problem of rewards was equally urgent. The army was a loosely organised band of fortune-hunting individualists. With victory, discipline relaxed and the men fell to whoring, gambling and quarrelling over the spoils. Some of the more ambitious among the officers hoped to command new *entradas* of their own and carve out territorial fiefs for themselves. Many a feckless foot-soldier had no other ambition than to stagger back to Spain with a sackful of silver on his back, or else to move on to fresh adventures and further rapine. If the conquest were to be permanent and profitable, however, the army had to be held together, as a safeguard both against Indian risings and against attack by other European marauders. Its members had to be induced to settle, and provided with the means to do so. The artisans among them—smiths, farriers, tailors, saddlers, shoemakers—could easily find profitable occupation; so could those with access to capital or credit, who set up as local shopkeepers. The leaders, however, considered themselves primarily as fighting men, and expected as a right of conquest to be supported by the labour of others.

In every successful *entrada* the initial rewards (apart from a share of the booty, if there was any) normally took the form of grants of *encomienda*. The *encomienda* system was not new; something like it had long existed in Spain in territory taken from the Moors, and in the Canaries; in the West Indian islands a labour force had been recruited in rough-and-ready fashion by the allocation to leading settlers of groups of natives as labourers or personal servants. In the islands these allocations were originally known as *repartimientos*, divisions; but when the practice of division spread to the populous and settled areas of the mainland the older term, *encomienda*, with its implication of duties as well as privileges, came to be preferred. An *encomienda* was basically the right to demand tribute, and initially also labour, from the Indians of a specified district. The district might be very large; Cortés arrogated to himself a vast *encomienda* in the valleys of Mexico and Oaxaca, comprising officially 23,000 tributary heads of households, in fact many more. This was exceptional; but *encomiendas* of 2,000 or more tributaries were not uncommon. From the income of his grant the *encomendero* could build a house, maintain a household and continue to feed and arm his personal followers. In return he was required to protect his Indians against other would-be exploiters, appoint and pay parish priests in his villages, and bear his share of the military defence of the province. He had no other administrative or judicial duties; *encomiendas* were not feudal manors. Nor were they slave-worked estates; the first conquerors were not particularly interested in land or agriculture. For them, as for most Spaniards, town life meant sophistication and companionship, country life isolation and boredom. It would, moreover, have been dangerous for them to live scattered among a sullen and hostile peasantry; both from choice and from prudence they lived together in urban settlements and left their Indians to till their own land in their own way. In most of the densely settled areas Indian land custom had long made provision for the payment of tribute to overlord peoples and for the support of priests and chieftains, temples and community houses. In a rough-and-ready fashion the Spanish *encomenderos* stepped into the places of the Aztec or Inca rulers and drew the tributes and services formerly rendered to them. In practice this usually meant that an *encomendero* would demand, from the head-men of the principal town of his grant, the largest amount which the grant seemed able to provide, and would leave the headmen to collect and deliver it. The headmen would endeavour to collect enough to satisfy the *encomendero*, to defray communal expenses and provide a livelihood for themselves. The *encomendero* would not concern himself with the details of the levy, so long as he received regular service and a regular income. Other rewards followed later: grants of land; grazing rights for the pasturage of sheep, cattle and horses; and, later still, mining rights; but the *encomienda* was the first step. By its means, with royal approval, the army was settled upon the country as a quasi-feudal militia.

The third preoccupation of the commander of an *entrada* was to provide a legal method whereby the temporary and informal organ-isation of his army could be transformed into an official and permanent organisation for local government. The normal method was that of municipal incorporation. The *conquistadores* brought their civic ideas with them from Spain. In medieval Castile fortified corporate towns had occupied a position of great privilege and power, as was natural in a country whose history had been filled with intermittent war, with constantly shifting frontiers. Noblemen, though they drew their in-come from land or from the ownership of transhumant flocks and herds, built their palaces in the towns, and made their influence felt in municipal administration and politics. In the reconquest of Christian Spain from the Moors the occupation or the establishment of fortified towns had been an essential precaution. Similarly, it was natural for the Castilian conquerors of the New World, while looking to the country-side for their support, to establish themselves in corporate towns. The traditional municipality, already in decay in sixteenth-century Spain, entered upon a new lease of life in the Indies.

Every leader of a conquering army made it his care either to occupy existing towns or to found new ones; to get them legally incorporated by the Crown; and to install his own immediate followers as the officers of municipal government. Of course, the majority of such towns were not Mexicos or Limas or Cuzcos. Many of them were at first mere temporary camps of thatched huts; but they all had the essential characteristics of legal incorporation, with jurisdiction over the surrounding country, control of Indian labour and dependence upon Indian supplies for their subsistence. Most of them quickly developed Spanish centres and Indian suburbs. The soldiers of the army became the *vecinos*, the legally enrolled householders, of one or other of the incorporated towns in each conquest, and usually most of them, including the officers, settled in the capital city. In the early years the administration of the capital was the key to the administration of the province. From among his officers the commander nominated the first city government, the *cabildo* of twelve *regidores* or councillors (in small towns the number of councillors was smaller). The *regidores* were to elect, not from their own number but from among the general body of *vecinos*, the two *alcaldes* or municipal magistrates; with them were to hold office for a year; and then to elect their own successors, subject to the commander's approval. Election in this sense meant presenting a list of names to the commander, who made the final choice. Office was thus to circulate among a restricted group of leading *vecinos*, who were usually also *encomenderos*. Practice differed to some extent. Sometimes the leader of a conquest might be authorised by the Crown to appoint *regidores* for life. Pizarro, for example, was permitted to appoint three such life councillors in the *cabildo* of Lima, and Valdivia enjoyed a similar concession in Santiago. This was a rare and valuable privilege. At the other extreme, in some small towns, some or all of the *regidores* might be elected by the whole body of householders. In Havana, for example, popular election was the rule until about 1570, and similarly a little later in Buenos Aires. To sixteenth-century Spaniards, however, popular election was a dangerously anarchical proceeding. Respectable citizens understood and expected that offices should circulate among the heads of the leading families of the neighbourhood; initially, the military leaders. To crown the structure, the commander himself usually sought royal approval to transform his own authority from that of the leader of an irregular army to that of a formally appointed governor, entitled in that capacity to preside over the deliberations of the *cabildo*.

Encomienda and *cabildo* were the basic institutions of the society of conquest in its first generation. The *encomienda*, however, provided a very narrow economic base for a growing European population. It was politically inexpedient to commend all the villages of an area;

usually more than half remained directly tributary to the Crown. In the wilder areas the inhabitants would not submit to commendation at all, and even when conquered their tributes and services were of little value. The number of *encomiendas* of adequate size to support individual Spanish leaders was thus limited. The humbler soldier who received no *encomienda*—unless he possessed trading capital and accounting skill, or was trained in a craft and was willing to practise it—had initially only two choices. He could move on to fresh conquests and hope eventually to secure Indians of his own; or he could remain the follower, the *paniaguado*, of a great *encomendero* and live on his bounty. Society in these circumstances was necessarily restless, factious and disorderly. *Encomiendas*, moreover, tended to decline in value, partly because of government interference, partly through decline in the Indian population. At best, Indian agriculture, on which the *encomienda* rested, could not provide the European products—European food especially—which the Spanish towns demanded and which were too bulky or too perishable to import in sufficient amount; nor could Indian labour regularly produce, by way of tribute, adequate quantities of valuable commodities—gold, silver, cochineal—for export to Spain. Within a generation these considerations led many settlers, whether or not they possessed *encomiendas*, to seek other ways of making a living without outraging their prejudices on the subject of work suitable for gentlemen. The most favoured occupations were estate agriculture, stock-ranching and mining.

The Spanish towns insistently demanded wheat flour, wine and oil. All could be imported, but at very high prices. Vineyards and olive groves proved difficult to establish in the Indies—vines and olive trees also being naturally slow to come into bearing—and the only places where wine and olives were produced in quantity in the sixteenth century were the irrigated valleys of coastal Peru. The first grape crop of significant size in Peru was picked in 1551. Olive groves did not become established until the 1560s, and for many years the olives were pickled whole and sold in that form. Oil production on a commercial scale began at the very end of the century. In 1602 the Seville shippers secured legislation prohibiting the further extension of both vineyards and olive groves, an indication of the growing importance of these industries. Wheat, on the other hand, was early produced in favoured localities throughout the Indies, especially in the Puebla valley southeast of Mexico City, where Spaniards acquired large tracts of arable land by purchase (or seizure) from Indian communities in the 1540s, employed Indian labour and found a ready market both in Mexico itself and in Vera Cruz for victualling the convoys. Later in the century, Antioquia in New Granada—a rare example of Spanish agricultural settlement—performed a similar service for Cartagena and the galleons. Within the *marquesado*, the huge Cortés *encomienda* in Oaxaca, also, large arable tracts were brought under European management. Here sugar was the principal crop; it was shipped not only to Spain but down the Pacific coast to Peru. Most valuable of all, in these warm areas of southern Mexico—Oaxaca and Mixteca—the collection of cochineal, the little blood-red beetle parasitic upon the *nopal* cactus, came more and more to be organised by Europeans. Among the exports of New Spain in the sixteenth century cochineal was second only in value to silver, though admittedly a long way behind.

In the arid uplands of Castile from which most of the *conquistadores* came, pastoral pursuits, the grazing of semi-nomadic flocks and herds, had long been preferred to arable farming. The preference was social and military as well as economic; and in the New World, as in the Old, the man on horseback, the master of flocks and herds, was the man best adapted to frontier conditions. The military conquest of the Indies depended heavily upon Spanish horses; the economic conquest depended even more upon that humble and indomitable beast of burden, the mule. Mules revolutionised the transport of the Americas. They supplied the essential links between Vera Cruz and Mexico, between Nombre de Dios and Panama, between Lima and Cuzco. Mules, with wheat and sugar, were prominent among the valuable products raised by the stewards of the *marquesado* and exported to Peru. As mules revolutionised transport, cattle and sheep revolutionised land use. Brought in from Spain and from the islands, they multiplied prodigiously on land which had never before been grazed. By the time of the first viceroy, Mendoza, cattle- and sheep-raising in many parts of the Indies had become the principal livelihood of the richer Spaniards. Every sixteenth-century chronicler of New Spain mentioned, usually with astonishment and delight, the vast numbers of beasts which the country supported. Mendoza himself introduced the merino sheep, the basis of a woollen textile industry which earned a sinister reputation for coercion and ill-treatment of Indian labourers in its workshops. Of the spread of cattle, in the 1530s, the price of beef in the Mexico market is eloquent evidence: in 1538, seventeen *maravedís* the *arrelde* (about 9 lb);

in 1540, 10 mrs; in 1542, 4 mrs. The price was fixed at the last figure by municipal ordinance, and penalties exacted for selling cheaper; for the city *regidores* were almost all ranch-owners. With beef so cheap, no Spaniard need starve, or work for wages, and great men who owned cattle ranges could always keep open house and feed their bands of retainers. Production, in such conditions, was necessarily on a very large scale. Ranges were loosely defined, initially in terms of radius from a fixed spot, and little attempt was made to survey boundaries. The beasts ran wild. They were rounded up and slaughtered at annual intervals, and often the carcasses were left to rot where they lay. Except in the neighbourhood of towns the beef was comparatively unprofitable. The chief value of the beasts lay in their hides and tallow. After silver, sugar and cochineal, hides and tallow became the most valuable products of sixteenth-century New Spain.

Encomiendas, arable estates and stock-ranches between them produced the accumulations of capital which made large-scale mining possible. The exploitation of sources of precious metals in most parts of the Indies developed in three well-marked stages. The first stage was simple collection, the acquisition by plunder or by barter of gold and silver objects in the possession of native people at the time of the conquest. In some places, notably in Cajamarca and Cuzco, the quantity obtained in this way was very large, but within a short time the accumulations of years had been collected and for the most part melted down. The Spanish invaders then turned to prospecting on their own account, employing native labour to wash out surface gold from the beds of streams. This primitive exploitation was practised in most parts of the Indies and also yielded considerable quantities, but the process was slow, uncertain and extremely wasteful of labour. Silver, moreover, could not be produced in this way. In the 1530s enterprising Spaniards began to take seriously to mining, to digging out ore, especially silver ore, from rich veins below the surface. By 1540 the silver sent from the Indies to Spain already formed above 85 per cent of the total official shipment of precious metal, measured by weight. It was still only 40 per cent of the total shipment measured by value; but the quantity of silver produced increased steadily as new mines were discovered and new techniques came into use, while gold production stood still. By the 1560s, silver shipments had come to exceed gold shipments in value also.

Silver-mining, unlike surface prospecting for gold, was narrowly localised. With primitive techniques, lacking effective pumps, the miners could operate deep shafts only in places where the danger of flooding was small. On the other hand, since mining required a large and concentrated labour force, it could not be carried on in absolute desert; for though food, at a price, could be transported over big distances, water could not. In New Spain the exploitable mines were confined to a relatively narrow belt of territory in the north, in New Galicia. The area was remote from settled land, inhabited only by primitive and warlike nomads to whom the Spaniards gave the general name of Chichimecas, the wild people. The hostility of these Chichimecas made life in the camps precarious, and travel impossible except for large and well-armed parties; some mines, indeed—San Luis Potosí for example—were left unworked for many years because of the danger of native attack. The most productive veins, however, those of Zacatecas and Guanajuato, discovered in 1548, were promptly exploited. A silver-rush began, and disorderly shanty towns sprang up at the principal sites. In Peru the corresponding critical balance between habitability and adequate drainage in silver-producing areas was found not in semi-arid hills but in high mountains. Silver-mines in the mountains near Cuzco had been exploited in Inca times, and Spaniards took them over; but in 1545 they were eclipsed by the discovery of the immensely rich veins of Potosí, the prodigious mountain of silver in what is now Bolivia. Potosí lies at the extreme limit of habitability, at a height—over 12,000 feet—where heavy manual labour, whether above ground or below it, is difficult and dangerous. Nevertheless Potosí became, almost overnight, a vast and teeming shanty town, drawing in people of all races from all over the Indies. It is not a great exaggeration to say that the discovery of Potosí was one of the turning points in the history of the Western World. Certainly silver became, in the middle decades of the sixteenth century, the chief motive force in the European economy in the New World.

Although some Spaniards and more Indians worked small claims by hand, the typical silver-miner was a capitalist on a fairly large scale. Extensive plant—extensive for those days—was needed for the reduction of the ore, initially by simple smelting, but increasingly, after about 1560, by a mercury amalgamation process. Peru had its own sources of mercury, the famous Inca mine of Huancavélica; a circumstance which greatly enhanced the productivity of Potosí. New Spain sometimes imported Huancavélica mercury by sea, but more commonly drew its supplies from Spain. The supply of mercury, carried awkwardly in leather bags, was in itself a vital and lucrative trade, and naturally the subject of constant official regulation and concern. Besides mercury, the miners needed steady supplies of beef, on the hoof the most portable form of food, leather and tallow candles. They needed also great numbers of mules to carry supplies to the mines and to take the silver back to civilisation. Mining and ranching were therefore complementary, and often the same people were concerned in both. Above all, mining created a great demand for labour, both pick-and-shovel labour and the labour of skilled craftsmen in the *ingenios*. High wages were enough to attract craftsmen in a society where a money economy was spreading very quickly. Indians soon acquired the necessary skills, and most of the skilled work was done by them. The demand for pick-and-shovel labour was met partly by the import of Negro slaves; but most of this work also was done by Indians who, though paid, had to be recruited largely by coercion. Mine-owners who were also *encomenderos* naturally tried to draft their own Indians into the mines; but this method of recruitment was uneconomic, because of the distances often involved, and was repeatedly prohibited by royal legislation. All Indian communities, however, whether commended to individuals or directly tributary to the Crown, were liable to a loosely organised system of public forced labour, known confusingly in New Spain as *repartimiento*, in Peru (where the Incas had operated a similar system) as *mita*. Under this system Indian communities in any particular area could be called upon in turn to contribute a fixed number of labourers, for a fixed period of weeks and at a fixed wage for public purposes. Silver production—understandably, in view of its importance to the royal revenue—was usually regarded as a public purpose, and much of the unskilled labour in the mines was recruited in this way.

Much of the silver which came from the mines was sent to Spain, but much also remained in the Indies and was coined and spent there. New Spain, having in the sixteenth century a bigger European population and a more intense, more varied, economic life, retained a higher proportion of its silver production than did Peru; but both in New Spain and in Peru a steady stream of new wealth flowed to the capital cities, where it served both to pay for European imports and to stimulate local industry. The mining camps, though busy and populous— Potosí was the biggest single concentration of population in the Spanish Empire—never lost their makeshift character, never became major administrative or social centres. They were too remote from the sea and from contact with Spain, too disorderly, too uncomfortable. The production of Potosí was controlled from Lima, to a lesser extent from Arequipa; that of Zacatecas from Mexico, to a lesser extent from Guadalajara. The main sources of wealth in the Indies—*encomiendas*, estates, cattle- and sheep-ranches, mines—were often owned by the same people, and nearly always by the same kind of people. These rich men, many of them sons and grandsons of old conquerors and settlers, ran their enterprises through overseers and stewards. They themselves lived for most of the year in the capital cities, which their fathers had founded, and which, through the institution of the *cabildos*, they effectively governed.

The *cabildos* provided one of the means whereby groups of associates rewarded themselves for the risks and hardships which they—or their fathers—had undergone. In most provinces the *regimientos* of the chief towns were removed from the gift of the military commander within a few years of the conquest. Many old conquerors and settlers secured for themselves, by special grants from the Crown, *regimientos* for life, sometimes with the right to nominate their own successors. *Cabildos*, at least in the main cities, tended to become closed oligarchies of rich men. *Regidores* usually received no salary; the 9,000 *maravedís* a year which they were paid in Mexico was exceptional. They had, however, many perquisites. For example, the leading settlers, as individuals, required land; as *regidores* they were responsible for distributing land. As ranchers, they produced the beef and some at least of the other provisions with which the towns were fed; as *regidores* they fixed the prices at which those provisions were to be sold. As land-owners and mine-owners they needed labour; as *regidores* they influenced, directly or indirectly, the administration of native labour under the *repartimiento* system. As private individuals they could be sued by those whom they wronged; but as *regidores* they elected, from among men of their own type and interest, the municipal magistrates before whom, in the first instance, the suits would be heard. The *cabildos* were the chief institutions for safeguarding the interests and expressing the opinions of the *conquistador* class.

Because the early *cabildos* were self-perpetuating and often venal, however, we must not assume that they were necessarily incompetent or devoid of public spirit. On the contrary, the minute books of Mexico, Lima and many minor capital cities indicate that the *regidores* took their work seriously. The *cabildo* of Mexico met twice a week, and sometimes oftener, throughout the sixteenth century. Absentees were expected to ask leave beforehand, and to give their reasons. Meetings were orderly and discussion serious, though often repetitive. A strict discipline was observed; members spoke in order of seniority; brawling, or even abusive words, were relatively rare—rarer than in some modern assemblies; though quarrels about precedence occurred, and it was characteristic of that gathering of old conquerors that members were required to leave their swords outside. Matters discussed were very various. The old conquerors were not above such topics as the disposal of garbage and the procedure for impounding pigs found straying in the streets. Public works, water supply, the allocation of building sites and garden lots, the organisation of Indian labour, the management of municipal property, police regulations—these were the regular concerns of the *regidores*. In 1533, for example, the *cabildo* of Mexico took alarm at the extravagant cutting of forests to provide building timber, which was already causing erosion and silting in the lake. It set aside forest reserves in the neighbourhood, and forbade the cutting of trees within the city. A little later, in 1538, it introduced a licence requirement for the felling of timber anywhere in its area of jurisdiction. In addition to these administrative duties, much time was spent in discussing the details of public ceremonies and of decorations, processions, bull-fights and the like in connection with them. If such concern appears trivial it must be remembered that these were virtually the only urban entertainments available, apart from gaming and carousing—both frowned upon—in a limited and monotonous social round. Besides these routine matters, the *cabildos* debated at great length the instructions and terms of reference of their *procuradores*, the envoys whom they sent either to other towns to discuss boundaries and similar matters of common interest, or to Spain to solicit municipal privileges. Frequently, also, they discussed topics of wider import. The letters and reports despatched by *cabildos* to the King often contained unsolicited advice on matters of general concern to the empire.

In carrying out their administrative duties the big *cabildos* employed a double tier of municipal officers. The major offices, in the early days, were shared among the *regidores* themselves. One served as *alférez* or standard-bearer, in charge of public ceremonial; another as *alguacil mayor*, or chief constable; another as *fiel ejecutor*, inspector of weights and measures; and yet another as *obrero mayor* or commissioner of public

works. These prominent citizens drew their remuneration from fees
and fines levied from the public whom they served or the offenders
whom they prosecuted, but they relied upon salaried underlings to do
the actual work. The chief salaried officer of every city was the *escribano
de cabildo* or town clerk, not a member of the *cabildo*, but its servant.
He kept the records and dealt with the correspondence. In a big city he
was a responsible and highly paid official. The inspector and the chief
constable, who were *regidores*, usually recruited their own assistants
and paid them wages out of the perquisites of office. The *obrero mayor*
obviously needed a trained staff, and his men were usually paid by the
city. From a very early date in the big cities we read of a *medidor* or
surveyor and an *alarife* or municipal architect. We have a fairly complete list of the *alarifes* of Mexico in the sixteenth century. One of the
earliest, Alonso García Bravo, was a soldier in Cortés' army, but a
mason by trade. He was almost certainly responsible for the celebrated
traza, the master plan upon which the Spanish city was laid out. Another prominent *alarife* was appropriately named Juan de Entrambas
Aguas; he designed and partly executed the permanent water supply
of the Spanish city, brought by aqueducts from the heights of Chapúltepec. He also designed, at municipal expense, a public inn on the road
half-way between Mexico and Vera Cruz, in the shadow of the Cofre
de Perote.

The income from which the cities defrayed the cost of their ceremonies and their public works and paid the wages of their servants
came from a variety of sources. No American city had any right of
direct taxation; there were no municipal rates. A few cities, including
Mexico, secured from the Crown the right to charge customs duties
on goods brought into the city; but usually these grants were for specific purposes and for a limited period of time. Most of the income came
from municipal property. In allocating land to its *vecinos*, a city usually
retained areas of common land immediately outside the building area.
Muleteers bringing goods to the city, and drovers bringing in cattle
for slaughter, pastured their beasts upon the commons and paid a rent
to the city. The *portales* or colonnades which lined the principal streets
in most cities were considered to be public property, and the municipality charged a rent to the shopkeepers who set up their stalls there.
Finally, some cities were *encomenderos* in their corporate capacity. Mexico
City held the *encomienda* of Ixtapalapa, which was a source both of
labour and of tribute income for the city. Municipal income, however,

was never adequate for extensive public works, and the *cabildos* made free use of their powers of coercion to make householders, at their own expense, pave, drain and illuminate the streets, and conform to municipal ground plans and building standards. If we criticise the *cabildos* as rapacious associations of rich men we must remember also that only such groups of leading citizens could have exercised enough power to insist on the order and uniformity in private building which contemporaries so much admired.

Some of the earliest accounts of Mexico City were written between 1550 and 1575 by Englishmen, mostly seamen captured from privateering ships. They had no cause to love Spaniards or to admire Spanish achievements; but they all expressed amazement at the size of the city, at the breadth and regularity of its streets, at the monumental character of the central plaza and the flanking buildings. They had cause for amazement. The population of the city in the middle of the sixteenth century, Spanish and Indian, cannot have been much less than 100,000, and may have been much more; larger by far than Seville or Toledo, or any of the Spanish cities with which the *conquistadores* had been familiar. The city, moreover, differed fundamentally in lay-out from Spanish cities, as anyone familiar with the older parts of Toledo or Seville can see at a glance. It is impossible to say exactly how the familiar grid-iron plan of the American cities originated. It is, of course, a fairly obvious design, which could come independently to the minds of town-planners in different parts of the world. In some places, notably Mexico, the streets followed to some extent the causeways and ceremonial avenues of the antecedent Indian city, but this was a rare instance. In the southern viceroyalty Indian Cuzco was too massive to be destroyed as Indian Mexico had been, and too remote to be conveneint as a Spanish administrative centre. Lima, having no antecedent native city, was initially much smaller and meaner than Mexico; its early history rather resembled that—for example—of Santo Domingo; but Lima also, enriched by Potosí, soon acquired the same monumental character, the same regularity of design, and so on a smaller scale did most of the cities of the *conquistadores*. Probably the inspiration came, in part at least, from the neo-classical books on town-planning which were then current in Europe. Certainly the cities of America, in their physical aspect, approximated much more closely to Italian Renaissance ideas of what cities ought to be like, than to actual Spanish cities of the time.

Spanish American cities were, for the most part, unfortified. Only coastal cities, such as Cartagena and Havana, which might be attacked from the sea, ever possessed extensive formal fortifications. Most of the major cities were inland, safe from foreign invaders. It is true that in some capitals—Mexico, Lima, Cuzco—the early *conquistadores* often built themselves fortified houses, with thick walls pierced only by loopholes and embrasures. They did this chiefly as a security against local riots, or against the armed envy of their own neighbours and rivals. For dealing with Indian insurrections they relied not upon defensive works but upon the offensive operations of mobile, usually mounted, bands. By the late sixteenth century the private fortresses had disappeared, replaced by more elegant and more convenient dwellings. The cities of Spanish America, unlike those of Europe, were untrammelled in their growth by the encumbrance of massive encircling walls. They developed as modern cities, seats of government and industry, undefended and open to commerce and travel. They possessed proud and powerful oligarchic government, considerable wealth, abundant Indian labour and bold ideas on town planning. The *conquistadores* and their successors were by preference, as well as by force of circumstance, town-dwellers and town-builders. Their *encomiendas*, their estates, their ranches and their mines provided them with revenue and with occasional rural diversion; but the cities which they built were the principal reflection of their energy, their power and their pride.

This feverish building activity, this heavy social superstructure, necessitated drastic changes in the native Indian society. In the major centres the Indian rulers, priests or chieftains, in effect disappeared. Either they were killed or driven into remote exile; or else they came to terms, accepted baptism, adopted European ways and lived on as land-owners, as appointed local governors, even as *encomenderos*, in the manner of leading Spaniards. Many humbler Indians also early accepted the implications of a money economy and the economic and social privileges which they could secure by close association with the conquerors. In this connection Cortés' decision to rebuild Tenochtitlán-Mexico and make it his capital was highly significant. He was wise enough to appreciate the prestige of the place, its 'renown and importance', as he expressed it, despite its economic and strategic disadvantages, its limited area, its easily invested causeways. By reoccupying Tenochtitlán, by building churches and dwellings upon its temple sites, rather than leaving its ruins as a monument to Aztec grandeur, the Spaniards not only destroyed the pre-conquest appearance of the city: they also identified themselves with its traditions as a religious and political centre. Mexico grew as a mixed city in which Spaniards and Indians lived side by side in their respective *barrios*. The rebuilding took a fearful toll of Indian lives and labour, but it also began a fruitful intermingling of Spanish and Indian ways which has remained characteristic of Spanish North America ever since. To their own highly developed native skills Indian craftsmen quickly added new skills learned from Spaniards. They could gain admittance—though not without opposition from time to time—to many of the Spanish craft gilds which made their appearance in the big cities in the later sixteenth century. Without their co-operation the vast work of church- and city-building throughout the Indies would have been impossible. In Peru the intermingling was less free and less fruitful. The European population was relatively smaller and more segregated; Lima, as we have seen, was originally a purely Spanish settlement. Indian resistance to Europeanising influences, though mainly passive, was long-lived and determined. In Peru, as in New Spain, however, the Spanish communities soon gathered an Indian population, including skilled craftsmen, shopkeepers and pedlars, attracted both by wages and by the possibility of escaping the burden of tribute and forced labour exacted from their villages. In the mines, quite apart from the thousands of unskilled labourers drafted in by compulsion, there were many skilled and highly paid Indian technicians, who carried on the complex processes of silver extraction and—according to many contemporaries— understood them better than did the Spanish overseers. Indians usually handled, and often owned, the strings of mules which plodded ceaselessly from Lima to Cuzco, from Arequipa to Potosí, from Vera Cruz to Mexico, to Guadalajara, to the mines of New Galicia. These Indian muleteers often employed Negro slaves, especially on the Mexico road. The *arriero* was a familiar social figure, picaresque and violent, in New as in Old Spain; he was also a capitalist on a considerable scale. Many of the muleteers at Zacatecas owned strings of fifteen or twenty beasts; a valuable property, in a vast and wild region where transport was the key to economic development, and where an unbroken mule was worth, at the close of the century, twenty silver *pesos*.

The intermingling of cultures was accompanied inevitably by the intermingling of races. Many *conquistadores* took Indian women, and on occasion during the conquest owed their lives to information given them by loyal mistresses. Some of the leaders formally married the daughters of chiefs; and some of the *mestizo* sons of such unions became prominent figures. Garcilaso Inca de la Vega, the historian, was a *mestizo*. So was the ill-fated Martín Cortés, the son of Cortés and Marina and half-brother of the second marquis. In the years immediately after the conquest there were very few Spanish women in the Indies, and social prejudice did not inhibit mixed marriage. Even the offspring of casual and temporary unions were often recognised and provided for by their Spanish fathers. Legally, *mestizos* were treated as Spaniards, and were exempt from tribute and *repartimiento* labour. Except for the legitimate sons of prominent fathers, however, they were considered by Spaniards as social inferiors. As the number of Spanish women increased, mixed blood tended more and more to be associated with illegitimacy, and a complex hierarchy of nicknames, mostly derogatory, was employed to describe the various degrees of racial mixture. *Mestiza* women, in particular, occupied an equivocal social position and rarely succeeded in marrying Spaniards of standing. The *mestizo* population steadily increased, especially in New Spain, largely by marriage within its own ranks. *Mestizos* formed a middle class of farmers, traders and clerks; and many of the poorer and more rootless among them came to swell the crowds of vagabonds and hangers-on which thronged the streets of Mexico.

The great mass of settled Indians remained in their own towns and villages, tilling their own fields in the old way and rendering their tribute to their new masters. They accepted, by a selective process of acculturation, certain European commodities and devices. They acquired, to a slight extent through the agency of the *encomienda*, to a larger extent through the activities of missionary friars, a smattering of Christian religion and European customs. They also acquired European diseases. The impact upon their agrarian economy of grazing animals was almost wholly destructive. The heavy demands for labour, caused by the growth of silver-mining and by the Spanish mania for building, broke into the rhythm of village life. The operation of these factors among the Indian communities is a complex story and requires a separate chapter to itself; but in general terms, for the great mass of settled peoples in many, perhaps in most parts of the Spanish Indies, the incursion of Europeans produced an economic, and above all a demographic, catastrophe.

It remains to consider the effect of these developments upon Spain. Spain was already the home of societies of conquest. The north had conquered the south, and the idea of living by the labour and skill of a conquered people was already familiar. The conquest of the Indies represented an immense extension of the area available for settlement, investment and exploitation. It gave new wealth, power and self-confidence to Castile, and confirmed the political and military predominance of that kingdom over the rest of Spain. Within Castile, as might be expected, the steady drift of population from north to south, which had been going on since the capture of Seville by Fernando III, was greatly accelerated. Men went to Seville from all over Castile—indeed from all over Spain—to try their luck in the Indies; but many of the northern immigrants got no further than Andalusia. The population of Seville itself more than doubled in the sixteenth century. The influx of people was accompanied by an influx of investment capital, much of which came, in the first half of the century, from the old manufacturing and trading centres of the north. Old Castile participated indirectly in the development of the Indies; its capitalists invested in trans-Atlantic trade money which they had made in the old wool trade with Flanders.

The Indies trade at first consisted chiefly, as we have seen, in the export of wine, oil and flour, together with small quantities of manufactured goods; and the import of precious metals, tropical products such as sugar, cochineal and tobacco, and hides. Hides were the raw material of a wide range of leather-working industries in Spain. Tropical goods were in demand all over Europe; Spanish merchant houses re-exported sugar and, as the taste for it grew, tobacco, both in small quantities, but at considerable profit. The import of precious metals, as is well known, encouraged a general rise in prices; but in the first half of the sixteenth century the influx was comparatively small and consisted mostly of gold. Its effect, on an economy long starved of specie, was highly stimulating. Again the stimulus worked most vigorously and rapidly in the south-west, not only because specie took time to travel outwards from Seville but also because the products which the colonists demanded most insistently were southern in origin. Among urban manufacturing centres the stimulus was strongly felt in Toledo, source of iron tools and steel weapons, of woollen cloth, felt hats and tiles. It was felt more directly still in the towns of Andalusia which produced leather goods, pottery and textiles. The woollen manufacturers of Old Castile and the iron industry of Cantabria were little affected. Similarly, the production of oil and wine, both Andalusian in origin, was greatly stimulated. The prices of these two commodities, significantly, rose much more rapidly than did that of wheat, which was grown extensively in Old Castile, as well as in Andalusia. In Old Castile the only group much enriched by the Indies trade were the financiers of Burgos and Medina del Campo. Most of the money made in the trade—apart, of course, from the Crown's share—stayed in Andalusia. The men who became rich by it were the ship-owners and exporting merchants of Seville and the big Andalusian land-owners.

After the middle of the century the pattern of the trade changed profoundly. Demand in the Indies shifted from Andalusian foodstuffs to manufactured goods, which Spanish industry could not supply in adequate quantity. Return cargoes included more and more bullion, especially silver; a stream of treasure for which Spain paid a heavy price. The cost of empire to Spain, in political, social and economic terms, like the demographic catastrophe of the Indies, requires chapters to itself; but to generalise roughly, in the second half of the century the silver of the Indies seriously upset the bimetallic ratio, turned a stimulating price rise into a severe and damaging inflation, and put Spain at a serious disadvantage in international trade. At the same time it encouraged the Crown in an over-ambitious military policy abroad and excited the envy and the fear of other European kingdoms. The possession of the Indies, moreover, by assuring the Crown of an independent and expanding revenue, encouraged Philip II and his successors more and more to ignore unwelcome advice from the *Cortés*, from the nobility and from public opinion generally, in Castile. Public opinion grudgingly acquiesced in the growth of absolutist practices born of successful imperialism; bureaucratic absolutism spread, as it were by contagion, from the Indies to Castile.

No nation can live, or fancy itself to be living, by the efforts of subjects overseas without some demoralisation of its social and public life. Not only the Crown, but a wide section of the official classes in Spain, came to regard the Indies as a source of sinecure office and easy wealth. For the minor gentry, the *conquistador* provided an exciting but demoralising example of the way in which arms could relieve a man of the need to work. In all these ways the society of conquest in America encouraged the growth of a society of parasitic dependence in Spain.

CHAPTER 6

The maritime life-line

Two major systems of European oceanic trade grew up in the first half of the sixteenth century: the one between Portugal and India, specifically between Lisbon and Goa; the other between Spain and America, specifically between Seville and various harbours in the Caribbean and the Gulf of Mexico. One was a public monopoly operated by the Crown; the other a system of private enterprise operated by a limited group of firms and individuals. Both were controlled by close governmental regulation; and from contemporary descriptions and surviving records it is possible to compare both the scale and the manner of their operations in some detail. Of the two systems, that of Spain was the larger both in bulk and in value. Trans-Atlantic trade between Spain and Spanish America in the sixteenth century employed far more shipping and moved far more goods than the trade from Portugal to India—paradoxically, since the one served the needs of, at most, a few hundred thousand Spanish settlers, *mestizos* and Hispanicised Indians, while the other connected Western Europe directly with the great populations of the East. But precisely because it was a colonial society Spanish America, much more than the highly developed societies of the East, was the economic complement of Europe. The early settlers depended on Spain for almost all the commodities which they required, above the needs of bare subsistence; and for a steady stream of human reinforcement to enable them to explore and conquer the vast spaces of America. While Portuguese Indiamen went out in ballast, carrying only passengers to staff factories and man garrisons, Spanish ships sailed for the West Indies carrying passengers, to be sure, in large numbers, but loaded also with casks of wine, barrels of flour, jars of oil, tools, agricultural implements, seed and domestic animals. Even ballast was a marketable commodity, for ships were often ballasted with bricks and dressed stone, to be unloaded and used for building; and the ships themselves often remained in the Indies for local employment. To pay for all this, the settlers developed their ranching, planting and mining economy, producing goods for sale in Europe. The increasing volume of trans-Atlantic traffic, at least until the middle of the century, was the measure both of the increasing Spanish population of the Indies and of its continued dependence on Spain.

Thanks to the meticulous record-keeping of the *Casa de la Contratación* the volume of traffic between Spain and the Indies can be estimated with some confidence from year to year. It varied greatly, influenced by the vicissitudes of conquest and settlement, by the fluctuations of demand, of prices and of freight rates in Spain and in the Indies, by the availability of shipping and of cargoes, by war and peace and the incidence of privateering and piracy. Peaks of activity occurred at roughly decennial intervals, with many fluctuations between them, each peak higher than the preceding one, until the middle of the century. In this long growth three roughly defined stages can be distinguished: an island stage, a Mexican stage, and an Isthmian or—better— Peruvian stage. The three stages naturally overlapped. The island stage, the period of the undisputed leadership of Santo Domingo, amounting almost to a monopoly, lasted from the first discovery until the early 1520s. It is true that during those years many small settlements were established on the mainland coasts of South and Central America; but these settlements were so cut off from their hinterlands and from one another, so dependent for survival upon their seaborne communications with Spain or with Santo Domingo, that they may for practical purposes be considered as though they were islands. Traffic between Spain and the islands during this period reached a peak in 1520, with seventy-one ships sailing from Spain to the islands. In the same year thirty-seven ships sailed from the islands to Spain. Disparity between outward and homeward sailings was significantly widening. Cortés was engaged in the conquest of Mexico. To the ordinary causes of disparity—losses at sea, lack of return cargoes (since gold, high in value, was small in bulk) and purchases of ships for local use—was added the attraction of mainland adventure and of an incipient passenger traffic, from the islands to Mexico, of men hastening to join in the plunder. Of the seventy-one ships which arrived in the islands in 1520, only thirty-two returned to Spain the following year.

In the next few years the traffic between Spain and the islands declined sharply. To some extent this was due to a decline in the attractiveness of the islands themselves as a market. The alluvial gold on which their early, easy prosperity had been based was becoming exhausted; it had indeed reached and passed its peak of production about 1515. More serious for the future, the native labour which had been employed in gold production was dwindling fast. The settlers were less able to pay for imported food and wine, and their harbours could offer little except hides by way of return freight. At the same time—and probably a more important consideration—circumstances in Europe combined to reduce sailings to the Indies. The war with France which broke out in 1521 loosed fleets of French privateers against Spanish Atlantic shipping; and bad harvests caused, in 1522, an acute shortage of grain, leaving little for export. In the years 1521-3, therefore, the volume of outward traffic dropped to the level of 1513-15. Of the reduced number of men and ships reaching the islands, a considerable proportion continued to be drawn away to the mainland, and did not return to Spain.

Recovery began in 1524; by 1525 the volume of traffic was back to its 1520 level and continued to rise. Political circumstances again played a part; for though the war went on, it was on the whole a successful war. Pavia was won in 1525. Unexpected and alarming French and English incursions into the Caribbean in 1527 caused a sharp drop in sailings in 1528, but the interruption in the upward trend was brief, and was not repeated for some years. The war ended in 1529, and 1530 was a peak year, seventy-eight ships sailing to the Indies and thirty-three from the Indies to Spain. In the islands, it is true, the euphoria induced by gold had passed, but a new source of wealth—sugar—was being developed and a new supply of labour—African slaves—was being imported to grow it. Being both valuable and bulky, sugar gave return employment to an increasing number of ships. Santo Domingo, the old capital, still retained its commercial pre-eminence; but no longer undisputed. New mainland settlements were developing commercially: Cartagena, Nombre de Dios, Cubagua. The German settlements in Venezuela, under Welser management—ultimately a failure, but momentarily promising—were attracting attention. Most important of all, conquered New Spain, through its harbour of Vera Cruz-San Juan de Ulúa, was clamouring for imports. Some ships were already sailing from Seville directly to Vera Cruz with oil, wine, grain and passengers. A larger number made Santo Domingo their first stop, but sailed on to Vera Cruz, often with cattle. New Spain could, as yet, offer few return cargoes, since silver and cochineal, like gold, occupied little space; so most ships clearing from Vera Cruz called again at Santo Domingo to pick up hides and sugar for the return passage to Spain. These longer and more hazardous voyages demanded more stores and larger ships. A decree of 1522 had prohibited ships of less than eighty *toneladas* from making voyages to the Indies. The decree was probably dictated chiefly by considerations of defence, and arose from official concern, in time of war, over the small size and feeble fire-power of most of the ships then engaged in the trade. In itself it probably had little effect—small ships, indeed, were never eliminated from the *Carrera de Indias*—but it was reinforced by economic considerations, and from 1522 the average size of ships crossing the Atlantic, as well as the number year by year, began slowly but steadily to increase.

The 1530s were a time of rapid advance in the numbers and prosperity of the European and Europeanised population of New Spain. Emigrants sailed from Seville to Vera Cruz during those years at the rate of 1,000 to 1,500 a year. Cattle and sheep were overrunning the hills of central New Spain. Silver-mining was beginning to yield its first rich results; in this decade, indeed, the ratio between gold exports, the product of the islands, and silver exports, the product of New Spain and the loot of Peru, as measured by weight, was completely reversed. Between 1521 and 1530 it had been 97 to 3 per cent; between 1531 and 1540 it was 12·5 to 87·5 per cent. The share of the islands in the total trade of the Indies, as measured by the movement of ships, dropped from about three-quarters to about one-third during the 1530s, despite the continued practice of calling in at the islands for bulky cargoes on the return passage. In absolute terms the volume of shipping plying to the islands in 1540 was little more than half of what it had been in 1530. At the same time the total trade of the Indies increased year by year. In 1540 seventy-nine ships went to the Indies and forty-seven returned. The number was not much greater than in 1530, but the ships were larger, and the total tonnage was greater by more than 50 per cent. The lawful minimum size of ships in the trade was raised to 100 *toneladas* in 1544. The decree enacting this rule, like its predecessor of 1522, originated in the perils of war and the necessity for self-defence. The small vessels, the caravels, which had been used extensively in earlier decades both in discovery and in trade, were now almost confined to the island trade and to the carriage of foodstuffs from the Canaries. In the trade from Seville to the mainland ports their place was taken by *naos*, square-rigged merchant ships of greater capacity and capable of carrying more formidable armament. By this means New Spain gained all that the islands lost, and more.

In the middle and late 1530s the increasing demand for tonnage led, apparently for the first time, to a serious shortage of shipping in the Indies trade. From 1534 to 1540 freight rates at Seville were very high, ships were regularly and dangerously overloaded, and many worn-out ships were pressed into service. Difficulty was experienced—as constant complaints from the *Casa de la Contratación* revealed—in finding seamen to man and qualified officers to navigate them. The need for economy in trained men was an important additional reason for employing larger ships. One ship of 500 tons needed fewer seamen than five ships of 100 tons, and only one navigating officer. The shortage of seamen persisted, and, despite larger ships and organised convoys, grew worse. It was attended, as might be expected, by a steady rise in the rate of losses at sea. The Indies were a graveyard of shipping for other reasons also; in particular because of the high prices paid for old ships by ship-breakers. Ships' timbers were always in demand; houses and stores in shore-side towns such as Nombre de Dios were largely built of them. Even more valuable were iron and brass fittings, especially when shipyards were set up at Pacific ports to build ships for exploration and coastal trade to Peru. When an old and worn-out ship arrived in the Indies and discharged its out-bound cargo the master often had difficulty in getting a homeward freight and found it more profitable to sell the ship to the breakers. The imbalance between outward and homeward sailings was thus perpetuated, and the heavy demand for shipping space at Seville maintained.

Shipping increased, nevertheless; and the most striking advance of the century was still to come, in the decade 1540-50. During those years the richest silver discoveries were made, and a new continent entered the trade. The principal conquests in Peru had been won, and the richest plunder secured, before 1535; but civil war, combined with shortage of Pacific shipping, had delayed the full impact of these dramatic events upon trans-Atlantic trade until the 1540s. Whether Peru at that time produced more silver than New Spain is hard to say, but it certainly exported more. Its conquest had been more destructive than that of New Spain; its conquest economy was less diversified, less lively, less productive in general. It produced, indeed, little of interest to Europeans except silver. Consequently, it used less silver for its own internal purposes than New Spain, had more available for export to Spain and in proportion to its European population imported more European goods. In the 1540s shipping to the isthmus, carrying goods destined for Peru, and returning to Spain with Peruvian silver, already considerably exceeded the volume of shipping to Vera Cruz. The distribution of trade between the islands, New Spain and the isthmus at the end of the decade, measured in recorded volume of shipping, was roughly in the proportion 29, 32 and 39 per cent; and probably many ships recorded as plying to or from the islands in fact merely called there *en route* to or from the mainland. The total annual volume of shipping increased between 1540 and 1550 in a steady progression broken only by a sharp temporary decline in 1544, again caused by war. Recovery after this lean year was rapid. 1545 and 1546 were good years; 1547, 1548, 1549 and 1550 each in succession a record year. In 1550, 133 ships crossed the Atlantic west-bound, eighty-two east-bound. The total tonnage in 1550 was more than double that of 1540.

The year 1550 was a major turning point in the development of the Indies trade. In the next four years the volume of shipping declined steeply year by year. The figures for 1554 were the lowest for thirty-two years: only twenty-three ships west-bound—of which twenty sailed from the Canaries and only three from the Guadalquivir—and thirty-six east-bound. Circumstances in Europe combined to cause a decline in trade in these years; they were years, for the Emperor and for Spain, of fierce and disastrous war, in which French privateers were more active and bolder than ever before. In the second half of 1553 and throughout 1554 the coast of Andalusia was in a state of virtual blockade. Twenty-five trans-Atlantic ships were lost by enemy action in these two years. The brief interlude of peace in 1556–7 did not greatly reduce the activities of privateers and pirates, and the reduction of the rate of loss from 1555 onwards was due chiefly to the vigorous naval measures inaugurated by Alvaro de Bazán. Apart from the danger of loss by sea, the 1550s were years of commercial depression in Spain; the prices of most commodities, measured in silver, not only ceased temporarily to rise but actually dropped. The depression came to an end, and so eventually did the war, with the peace of Câteau-Cambrésis in 1559; the Indies trade might then have been expected to reach, and soon to surpass, the volume of 1550, but it did not. The year 1559, it is true, was the beginning of a long period of expansion, which culminated in the huge fleets of the first decade of the seventeenth century, but the expansion was steady and slow. The 1550 record, measured in number of ships, was not equalled until 1589. For thirty years after 1559 sailings remained fairly steady, sixty or sixty-five ships on average each year west-bound, rather less east-bound. The average size of ships continued to increase; ships of from 300 to 600 tons began to appear in the trade in considerable numbers in the 1560s. The increase, however, was dictated more by the necessity of carrying heavier armament than by an increased demand for cargo space, and even the total tonnage did not again reach the 1550 figure until 1572. While the volume of the trade increased only by slow, steady degrees from the low levels of the middle 1550s, its value—even after making allowance for a steady rise in prices—increased by leaps and bounds. The average annual value of Spanish goods imported into the Indies in the early 1560s, measured by the amount of duty levied, was more than four times the value in the early 1540s, or, allowing for the rise in prices, about two and one-half times; yet the volume of shipping required was only about 30 per cent greater. The explanation lies in a change in the nature of the goods carried. In the first half of the sixteenth century the chief demand in the Indies had been for imported European food, but by the middle of the century a generation of New World Spaniards had grown up who either were accustomed to Ameri-can food—since many of them had Indian wives or mothers—or, if they wanted European food, could buy it locally grown. Wheat was be-coming plentiful, vineyards, olive groves and orange orchards were coming into bearing. The carriage of bulky foodstuffs to the Indies became less and less profitable. During the years of war, depression and contraction of trade in the 1550s their export from Spain ceased almost entirely; only relatively expensive manufactured goods, of relatively small bulk, were worth shipping from Seville; only the Canary islanders, employing their own small ships, continued to send oil, wine and flour to the less favoured Caribbean harbours. When the war ended, and the Seville trade began to grow once more, recovery in the oil and wine export trades was accompanied by a much more rapid growth in exports of textiles, weapons and cutlery, glass, paper and similar commodities of urban civilisation. Books, too, were an important item, for though universities had been established in Mexico and Lima in 1551, printing presses in the Indies were few. A small press was established in Mexico in 1539; between that date and 1600, 174 titles were certainly printed there, all in small editions. In Peru no press existed until 1584. Universities, schools, catechising missionaries and private citizens alike imported most of their books from Spain.

As might be expected, corresponding changes occurred in the homeward trade. The Spanish population in the big mainland centres of the Indies was increasingly able to pay for expensive imports. The discovery of new mines in the later 1540s, and even more the spread of the *patio* process of extraction in the early 1560s, made possible a rapid expansion of silver production. Returns in the mainland trade were made more and more in silver, with cochineal, tobacco and indigo a long way behind. An increasingly sharp division appeared between the trade from the West Indian islands—small ships, sailing singly or in small groups, carrying hides and sugar—and that from Vera Cruz and Nombre de Dios—big, well-armed ships, sailing in convoy, carrying silver and tropical luxuries. Manufactured goods out, silver home; this had become by 1560 the dominant pattern of the *Carrera de Indias*, and was to remain so for many years. In the Indies the change in the character of the trade marked the end of the age of conquest; in Spain it led to an increasing dependence on American silver for financing both public and private activity. In the first half of the sixteenth century the Indies had been heavily dependent upon Spain; in the second half Spain came more and more to depend upon the Indies.

The expanding trade of the Indies, increasingly diverse, increasingly valuable, carried in ever-larger ships, was still confined to a few harbours, all of which had their inconveniences and their dangers. After the middle of the century, indeed, harbours rather than ships were the principal physical factors limiting the expansion of the trade. At the European end of the *Carrera* Seville maintained both a legal and an effective monopoly from which only the small ships of the Canaries escaped. In its early days the monopoly had been a result of sensible choice, not merely or mainly one of government regulation. In size and wealth, in commercial experience, in security, in easy communication with a rich hinterland, Seville had no effective competitor for the Indies trade. So long as the trade remained an affair of small ships, exporting the agricultural products of Andalusia, the Seville monopoly caused no serious inconvenience. When in 1529 Charles V permitted a number of other Spanish harbours, including Coruña, to freight ships for the Indies—in compensation, perhaps, for the loss of oriental possibilities, caused by the Treaty of Zaragoza in the same year—no serious attempt was made to exploit the opportunity; nor —except for occasional smuggling visits to Lisbon under cover of repairs, stress of weather or navigational error—did ship-masters seriously try to evade the rules requiring them to return from the Indies directly to the Guadalquivir. Seville served all the needs of the trade; the machinery of dockyard services, of financial and commercial organisation and of governmental control were all established there, and the monopoly acquired the force of long-accepted custom. In 1543, after repeated petitions, the merchant houses of Seville trading with the Indies were legally incorporated in a *Consulado* or merchant gild in which the monopoly of the trade was formally vested. The *Consulado* took over a considerable part of the civil jurisdiction over its members, formerly exercised by the *Casa de la Contratación*. It was a rich and powerful body, well able to defend its privileges by litigation, and to pay for them through the loans which it made to an impecunious government. As the nature of the trade changed, and Seville exported more and more manufactured goods which were not products of Andalusia, or even necessarily of Spain, but which came to Seville by sea, the members of the *Consulado* developed a vast agency and commission business, consigning goods to the Indies on behalf of merchant houses all over Europe. Custom and vested interest thus continued to protect the Seville monopoly long after the volume and value of the trade and the size of the ships engaged had outgrown the port's facilities.

Seville was a small-ship harbour. Its shipyards excelled in building the numerous and very varied small craft which plied up and down the winding Guadalquivir and carried the local trade of the adjacent coast. Few big ships were launched in the river, and those few were of inferior construction. Suitable timber of appropriate size was not to be had; large oaks were rare, the local pine was too soft and fragile. This was not an unsurmountable handicap; throughout the second half of the sixteenth century the great majority of ships used in the Indies trade were built in the north of Spain; some ships were bought in from abroad; very few were Andalusian built. More serious, the facilities for maintaining and refitting big ships in the river were poor. In the mid-sixteenth century dry-docking was still an uncommon and very expensive operation. Caulking and paying of seams and all underwater maintenance was commonly done with the ship hove down in shallow water; but in most parts of the Seville river the current was too strong for this to be done easily and safely. The only safe careenage was in a quiet bend of the river at San Juan de Aznalfarache, a few miles down stream from Seville, and in the first half of the sixteenth century most of the maintenance work was done there. Later, docks and slips for repairing large vessels were constructed at Los Horcades, much further downstream, below the *marismas*; and later still at Borrego, only a few miles above San Lúcar. Berthing facilities were equally scanty and equally scattered. A small number of ships of moderate size could berth alongside at Seville itself, and some also at Triana on the opposite bank; its only connection with Seville being a flimsy pontoon bridge further upstream. Most ships anchored in the stream wherever they could find room, and took in cargo from lighters. The port of the Indies was not merely Seville, but the whole stretch of swift, winding, muddy river from Seville to San Lúcar, crowded with ocean-going ships and hurrying small craft.

The port was difficult and dangerous of access, and its difficulties and dangers grew in direct proportion to the increase in the size of ships. Officials of the *Casa* and the officers of the *Consulado* frequently complained that ships in the trade were too big, and sought legislation to control their size. Just as a minimum limit was set in order to exclude ships too small to defend themselves at sea, so a maximum limit was set to exclude vessels too big to use the river safely. The maximum was no more effectively enforced than the minimum, for the economy in freight charges made possible by bigger ships constantly tempted merchants and ship-owners to take risks. Ships above a certain draught, when fully loaded, could not cross the sand-bar at San Lúcar without risk of grounding; the biggest ships entered or left the river lightly loaded, sometimes even without their ballast, and took in or discharged cargo lying in the open road, a highly dangerous proceeding. Outward bound, they often put into Cadiz to complete their loading, a practice which was much disliked by the *Casa* officials because of the opportunities it gave to smugglers, and by the *Consulado* because it kept alive the claims of Cadiz as a possible rival to Seville. Most of the wine consumed in America was loaded at Cadiz. Within the river, cargo had to be lightered between Seville and the point of loading or unloading, which was expensive; and the ships themselves ran dangers of grounding and collision. Big ships lying high in the water were hard to control under sail, and galleys had to be stationed at strategic points along the river to

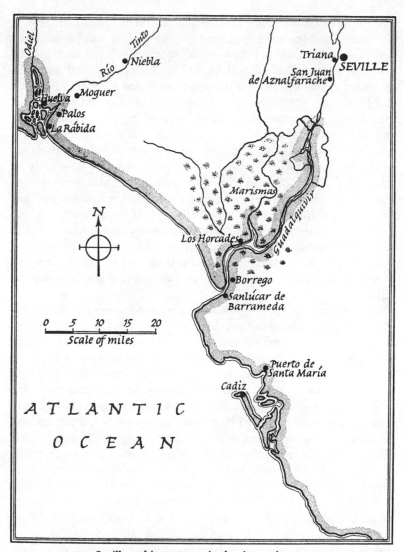

N

0   5   10   15   20
Scale of miles

5. Seville and its outports in the sixteenth century

tow them round the more difficult bends—again, expensive. The
galleons, the escorting warships which carried the royal silver, were
always big ships, and usually berthed in the lower reaches of the river,
sending their silver up to Seville in armed galleys provided by the *Casa*.

The ships of a trans-Atlantic fleet, therefore, whether discharging cargo after arrival, or repairing, or fitting out, or loading and preparing to depart, might be scattered anywhere along the river or in the outports, some in berths many miles from Seville. Naturally communication presented constant problems: the transport of goods between the ships and the Seville warehouses; the transport of the *Casa* officials, whose duty it was to examine ships, crews, cargoes, papers and passengers; and the transport of the passengers themselves. The passenger business was a lucrative branch of the Indies trade, but the carriage of passengers in the river was forbidden to sea-going ships; it was a monopoly in other hands. Trans-Atlantic passengers embarked and disembarked at San Lúcar, and a frequent service of passenger tenders operated between San Lúcar and Seville throughout most of the sixteenth century. The complex operation of the whole harbour estuary depended on the services of hundreds of auxiliary river and coastal craft—barges, lighters, galleys, despatch boats, bum-boats, passenger tenders—all of which added their quota to the cost of carrying goods across the Atlantic.

The immense volume—immense by sixteenth-century standards—of shipping, of men and of goods which squeezed through the bottleneck of the Guadalquivir after many weeks at sea entered corresponding bottlenecks in the Indies; though there the periods of choking, instead of being more or less continuous, were seasonal and relatively brief. There were dozens of small harbours dotted round the coasts of the Caribbean and in the islands, but most of them served only restricted, sparsely inhabited hinterlands (economically, if not geographically, islands), depended upon local or Canarian shipping for their needs and rarely saw a ship from Spain. For the *Carrera*, the main-route traffic in the middle decades of the sixteenth century, only three harbours were important: Santo Domingo for the islands, Vera Cruz–San Juan de Ulúa for New Spain, Nombre de Dios for Peru. Between them they handled more than 90 per cent of the trade. Santo Domingo was physically the best harbour of the three, nearer to Spain in terms of distance, far nearer in terms of time, danger and cost; but, as we have seen, Santo Domingo was declining in importance while the trade of the other two places steadily expanded. The Gulf coast of New Spain was deficient in good harbours and notoriously dangerous, exposed to hurricanes in the summer and to violent 'northers' at most times of the year. Vera Cruz, on its second site among the marshes and dunes

III a *The temple known as El Castillo, at Tulum in Yucatán. This fortified coastal city greatly impressed the Spanish invaders*

  b *Aztec weapons: two mace heads and a battle-axe with obsidian blades*
     (*from drawings by A. de Waldeck*)

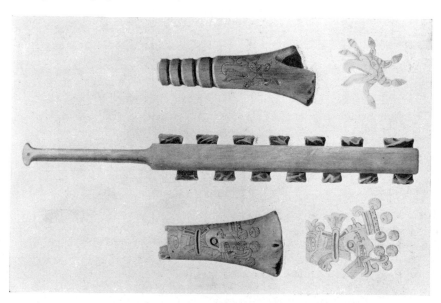

IV a *Indians washing for gold in a stream in sixteenth-century Hispaniola*
   b *Gold-mining in sixteenth-century Hispaniola*
   (*from engravings by T. de Bry in* Peregrina in America)

at the mouth of the Antigua river, had one advantage: it stood at the point where the mountains jutted nearest to the sea, so that the journey from the fever-ridden coast to the healthier, more populous, plateau was relatively short. It was in itself an inhospitable place—an open road, a river closed by a shallow and dangerous bar. It was used chiefly by small ships engaged in coasting trade with the ports of Tehuántepec and Yucatán, and with the islands. The masters of the bigger trans-Atlantic ships preferred when they could—for space was limited—to anchor or secure in the lee of the little island of San Juan de Ulúa, fifteen miles down the coast. Throughout most of the century, therefore, Vera Cruz was not one harbour but two; it suffered, like Seville, from the inconvenience and expense of constant trans-shipment, for which the local supply of small craft was never adequate. Not until 1600 was the decision made, and the money provided, to move the town to a new site directly opposite the island. This conservative inertia is the more surprising in that Vera Cruz was never a city of importance. It was a shanty town, housing only customs and treasury officials, local traders and tavern-keepers, and the labour, largely Negro, employed in loading or discharging cargo. Its coasting trade was insufficient to employ any considerable population, and the place came to life only when a fleet was expected from Spain. When the fleet was in, the captain-general, with several thousand sailors under his command, virtually took over the government of the town. The representatives of the importing merchants, the guards of the silver shipments, the muleteers with their rowdy and violent crews, all came down from Mexico. When the ships sailed and the mule trains set out on their long haul back to the capital, Vera Cruz returned to its malarial torpor. Mexico, not Vera Cruz, was the real terminus of the *Carrera* in New Spain. There the goods were sold from one fleet while the silver was stored against the arrival of the next. From Mexico the tributaries of trade stretched out, to New Galicia, to the northern mines and to the Pacific coast; later in the century, after the conquest of the Philippines, through Acapulco across the Pacific to Manila.

The harbours of the viceroyalty of Peru were all on the Pacific coast and virtually inaccessible to Atlantic commercial shipping. The passage of Magellan's Strait was prohibitively slow and dangerous for the ships of that time, and Tierra del Fuego was generally believed—at least until Drake's circumnavigation—to be part of a continent bounding the Pacific to the south. The discoverers of Peru had coasted south from Panama, and trade followed the same route. The Caribbean terminus of the *Carrera* to Peru was Nombre de Dios, at the narrowest point of the isthmus; but just as Vera Cruz was only a place of trans-shipment for Mexico, Nombre de Dios similarly served the needs of Lima, until 1598, when Puerto Belo superseded it. Nombre de Dios was a shanty town on an open beach, lacking even a strong and defensible treasury, since the main silver store on the isthmus was at Panama. Like Vera Cruz, it came to life only when a fleet was expected, and the representatives of the Lima merchant houses came across from Panama to buy European goods with Peruvian silver. Ships anchored off-shore—the road was less dangerous than Vera Cruz, being too far south for hurricanes—and discharged into lighters or surf-boats. Goods were lightered up the Chagres river to its headwaters, and thence packed by mule train to Panama; loaded again into ships on the Pacific coast, and after a long and arduous passage landed at Callao for Lima. Goods for Cuzco had to be packed from Lima over high mountain passes; for Potosí, carried on by sea to Arica and packed from there *via* Arequipa. There was another route from Europe, up the Río de la Plata and the Paraná into the heart of South America, and by mule train across Tucumán to Potosí. This back-door route involved fewer trans-shipments and, being illicit, paid no duties; it was exploited later in the century by *peruleiros*, Brazilian smugglers and slave-dealers who imported goods from Europe and Africa in Dutch or Portuguese ships, and was also used to some extent by Spaniards. In the seventeenth century it was accorded a limited and grudging official recognition, and a custom-house was set up in 1623, at Córdoba, where a 50 per cent transit duty was supposed to be collected. It never became the main channel of trade, however, for good reasons. Official restriction was a minor reason; more important was the poverty of the immediate hinterland of the hamlet, which in 1583 became Buenos Aires; most important of all, for ships sailing from Spain, the difference in distance. In those days of small ships and slow passages sheer distance mattered much more, portages and trans-shipments mattered much less, than they do today, in all except very bulky trades. In the Mediterranean trade in oriental goods *via* Cairo or Aleppo survived by a hundred years and more the opening of the all-sea route to India. Similarly, trade *via* Panama, manufactured goods one way, silver the other, held its own despite the competition of the *peruleiros*.

The coasting trade of the Spanish Pacific in the mid-sixteenth century already employed a considerable volume of shipping, not only between Panama and the ports of Peru but also between the two vice-royalties. The Spaniards in Peru were a small community with a good deal of specie at their disposal and an avid desire for consumers' goods. New Spain was industrious and productive, and was relatively short of specie, because of the efficiency of silver-tax collection and the large private remittances made to Spain. From the 1530s it became profitable to import goods of Spanish origin into Peru from New Spain, to supplement the costly trickle of supplies across the isthmus. With these trans-shipments went a much larger volume of Mexican products: mules, sugar, preserved fruit; European-type wares made in New Spain by Spanish or Indian craftsmen; and an assortment of Indian wares—polished obsidian mirrors, lacquered gourds, feather-work tapestry and the like. The return cargoes were almost entirely silver, except for a period in the 1560s and 1570s when large shipments of quicksilver from the Huancavélica mine were sent to New Spain. The ships in the trade, or at least their hulls and spars, were built at Huatulco and other small ports on the coast of Tehuántepec, a region which pro-duced not only timber but *pita* and *caguya* fibres from which rope could be made. Discarded sails and rigging from *flotas*, and all necessary iron and brass fittings, were brought across from Vera Cruz. In the second half of the sixteenth century a ship-building industry also developed at Guayaquil. Some of the ships were as large as 200 or 250 tons, and a dozen or more might make the New Spain–Peru voyage in a year. Though built in Central America, they were mostly owned in Peru, whence came the capital to build them. From Callao they were sent to Panama when a trans-Atlantic fleet was expected, at other times to the Pacific ports of New Spain.

The greatest profits of the coasters, however, were in connection with the trans-Pacific trade. The expedition of Miguel López de Legazpi in 1564, which led to the conquest of the Philippines, was planned at a time when the Portuguese spice trade was in great difficulties, and when a new route to the Far East offered even more attractions than usual. The project of opening a spice trade by way of the Philippines and Mexico was quickly dropped in face of the immediate and jealous reaction of the Portuguese in the East; but Legazpi himself suggested the alternative of a trade in silk, which could be bought readily from Chinese junks which frequented the islands. Over the next thirty years

the jealousy of the Portuguese changed to a willing naval and commercial co-operation. The Spanish settlement at Manila became a
principal market for the merchants of Macao, who, in defiance of
prohibitions, sold Canton silk for American silver, and soon controlled
a large part of the business of the Philippines. When, in the seventeenth
century, the Portuguese lost their access to Japan, and when the Dutch
closed the Malacca Strait against them, the Manila trade helped to
save Macao from commercial extinction.

The trans-Pacific trade established direct contact between a society
in which silver bullion was in high demand and one in which it was
plentiful and cheap. The Spaniards were able, therefore, to buy silk
in Manila at prices which justified an appallingly long and hazardous
voyage between two very hot and unhealthy places. Acapulco, the
Mexican terminus, was the best harbour on the Pacific coast; but, like
Vera Cruz and Puerto Belo, it was only occupied when the galleons
were in. For the rest of the year its population moved to higher and
healthier ground. From Acapulco to Manila was a trade-wind run of
eight or ten weeks. As in the Atlantic, the return passage was the
dangerous one. After leaving Manila the ships spent some two months
struggling north-eastward, in a region of normally light and variable
winds but subject to frequent typhoons. This was the worst region of
shipwreck. In the thirties or forties of north latitude, the latitudes of
Japan, a westerly wind could usually be found which would take the
ships to the coast of California and thence south-east to Acapulco. The
whole return voyage took from four to seven months, and on the
longer passages hunger, thirst and scurvy could reduce a ship to a
floating cemetery. The ships used in the trade were mostly built in the
Philippines, of local teak, by European designers and Eastern craftsmen. They had the reputation of the strongest and most durable ships
in the world. Their size was limited by legislation in 1593 to 300 tons,
and their number to two sailing in any one year, in a characteristic
attempt to keep the export of bullion within bounds. The number was
rarely exceeded, and often not attained; but the ships were often much
larger than 300 tons. Their size was governed by the requirements of
the trade at the time of building.

The best years of the trade were the last decades of the sixteenth
century and the first decades of the seventeenth. In the peak year—1597—
the amount of bullion sent from Acapulco to Manila reached the
enormous total of 12,000,000 *pesos*, a figure exceeding the total value

of the official trans-Atlantic trade. This was exceptional; in the last decade of the sixteenth century the annual export of bullion was usually between 3,000,000 and 5,000,000 *pesos*, of which perhaps two-thirds came from Peru. The trade was disliked in official circles in Spain, because it diverted Peruvian silver to New Spain and thence into the specie-hungry Orient, and because it flooded Peru with Chinese goods and spoiled the market for textiles from Spain. Not all the silk landed at Acapulco was trans-shipped to Peru, however; New Spain itself absorbed some; and the European demand for silk was so insistent, and the supply from all sources so inadequate, that until about 1640 it was worth while to carry considerable quantities from Acapulco by pack train through Mexico to Vera Cruz, where it was shipped to Spain.

Fed from these diverse sources, Spanish Atlantic trade grew and, to all appearance, prospered. It was, however, always hazardous. Many ships were lost, both through navigational errors and through foundering at sea; many also—despite steady improvement due to accumulated experience—by grounding in the open harbours which the fleets had to use. Old wrecks were a serious danger to navigation in the Guadalquivir itself. Apart from shipwreck, fleets carrying valuable cargoes by well-defined and predictable routes through the Caribbean and across the Atlantic were in constant danger of attack, by enemy warships or privateers in time of war, by pirates at any time. French privateers were active off the Azores and in the Caribbean from the 1530s; in 1556 a party of them landed in Cuba and sacked Havana; and down at least to the Treaty of Câteau-Cambrésis they constituted the principal danger to Spanish shipping. To this danger, armed convoy was the natural and obvious answer.

Ships for the Indies from the beginning normally sailed in company, not only for the sake of mutual help in fighting or foul weather but also in order to pool navigational knowledge. Experienced ocean navigators were few, and in the work even of the best there was a good deal of estimation and guess-work; so the navigating officers of a fleet consulted one another at frequent intervals, and everyone felt safer. If minimum standards of size, speed and armament could be enforced, so much the better. The first tentative attempts to enforce convoyed sailings were made in the 1520s. Regular convoys were organised during the war with France which broke out in 1542, and from 1543 it was forbidden to leave for the Indies in fleets of less than ten sail. In the

1550s—a decade of fierce and almost continuous fighting against the French—strenuous efforts were made, under the influence of the great admiral Alvaro de Bazán, to develop the galleon: a specialised fighting ship, often of 500 tons or more, with finer lines than a merchant ship and with a heavy broadside armament. These formidable vessels were employed by Bazán to keep open the shipping lanes between Seville, the Canaries and the Azores, and could when required escort fleets right across the Atlantic. A regular routine for trans-Atlantic convoys was worked out in the 1560s by another distinguished admiral, Pedro Menéndez de Avilés—not a great tactician, as Bazán was, for he never commanded a fleet in a major action, but a naval strategist of great ability and wide vision. From 1564 almost all shipping for the Indies, in peace or war, sailed in armed convoy. A fleet for New Spain was expected to leave San Lúcar every May, and usually entered Caribbean waters by the Mona passage. Once inside the Caribbean, ships for Honduras and the Greater Antilles parted company; the main body passed south of Hispaniola and Cuba, through the Yucatán channel, across the Gulf to Vera Cruz. The isthmus fleet left San Lúcar in August, and set a slightly more southerly course, passing through the Windward Islands. Some ships put into small harbours on the Main, but the main body anchored off Nombre de Dios, where it unloaded goods for Peru and loaded silver. It then retired to the sheltered harbour of Cartagena, where it took in stores. Cartagena was not a commercial harbour of much importance, but it was an essential naval and military base, and in the second half of the century it was heavily fortified. Both fleets normally wintered in the Indies. The isthmus fleet began its return voyage in January, steering north-west—usually a comfortable reach with the wind on the starboard beam—until it could round Cape San Antonio and put into another sheltered harbour at Havana. Meanwhile the Mexican *flota* in February made its tedious three- or four-week beat against the trade-wind from Vera Cruz, for a rendezvous at Havana in March. Because of the prevailing wind, Havana guarded the only convenient exit from the Gulf of Mexico for sailing ships. Like Cartagena, it was a place of military rather than commercial importance, and like Cartagena it had eventually to be heavily fortified. The concentration of the fleets there contributed directly to the commercial and political decline of Santo Domingo. The fleets refitted and victualled at Havana, and endeavoured to sail for Spain in the early summer in order to get clear of tropical waters before the hurricane season. They beat out through the Florida channel—a tedious and dangerous stretch, with headwinds and with pirates lurking among the Bahama cays— and then stood to the north until they could pick up a westerly wind for the Atlantic crossing. Each convoy was escorted by armed galleons, from two to eight according to the international situation and the shipping available; and these warships, besides protecting the merchant- men in convoy, carried the royal silver.

The main objection to the system was its expense. The unavoidable delays of convoys made rapid turn-rounds and the economical use of shipping impossible. The cost of the escorts, moreover, had to be met by a heavy additional duty—the *avería*—levied on the goods carried. Naturally merchants and ship-masters conspired with venal officials to evade this duty. The examination of goods—other than silver— was usually perfunctory, and assessments of value arbitrary, so that the rate on lawfully declared cargoes was unnecessarily high. The warships carried illicit cargoes, usually on the private account of the captains- general and their staffs. Menéndez de Avilés, a notably able sea commander and a stern disciplinarian, made a fortune by smuggling. Another admiral was reported as sailing in a flagship so heavily loaded that her lower gun-ports were under water. The venality of naval officers and fiscal functionaries intensified what a recent French writer aptly calls a 'psychosis of fraud', and added still further to the costs. High transport costs, heavy duties, restrictive regulations, shortage both of shipping and of port facilities, and chronic fraud were the salient econo- mic characteristics of the *Carrera de Indias*. Nevertheless, the system served its purpose. The power of combination and weight prevailed, on the whole, against manœuvrability and speed. Philip II's confidence in Menéndez' advice was, on the whole, justified. Reasonably regular sailings were maintained for a century and a half. Though stragglers were often captured, shipping in convoy was protected against mere pirates or individual privateers. Open attack on convoys or major harbours was made prohibitively dangerous for anything short of a powerful naval force. The maritime life-line of the Indies was kept intact, save for a few brief intervals, by a constant, brave, well-organised and enormously costly *tour de force*.

CHAPTER 7

Rights and duties

THE Spanish Crown in the sixteenth century governed its wide and diverse kingdoms through a hierarchy of councils. Most of these bodies were composed predominantly of lawyers, of men trained in the academic study of Roman Law. The law schools of the universities were the training ground of the Crown's advisers. They taught not only knowledge of law but an absorbing interest in jurisprudence; a field in which sixteenth-century Spain led the rest of Europe. Spanish jurists worked out theories of sovereignty which were distinct equally from the narrow kingship of the Middle Ages and from the unbridled absolutism later described by Hobbes; theories of a constitutional state, possessed of the right of legislation and unrestricted in its sphere of action, but restricted in its exercise of power by man-made law and custom as well as by natural law. Writers such as Azpilcueta and Covarrubias were behind their times, no doubt, in describing as constitutional a monarchy which in practice was becoming more and more absolute. Mariana, later and more observant, noted and deplored the decline of the *Cortés*; but whether or not they noticed the signs of change, a horror of absolutism was common to them all. Throughout the century, books insisting on the legal rights of free peoples, and even in extreme cases advocating tyrannicide, continued to circulate freely, were read without scandal, and exercised a profound influence not only upon thought but upon administration.

In such an atmosphere the discovery and conquest of a new world naturally gave rise to juridical problems. Lawyers, theologians and policy-makers alike sought clearer definition of the rights and wrongs, the purposes and the limits of imperial responsibility. Officially, the Spanish Crown based its right to rule the Indies upon prior discovery and just conquest, reinforced by the bulls of 1493, in particular by *Inter caetera*, which granted to Spain 'islands and mainlands . . . towards the West and South . . . with all their rights, jurisdictions and appurtenances', excepting only lands already held by Christian princes. None of the lands subsequently colonised by Spaniards had Christian rulers, but all were inhabited. Of the inhabitants, though some were very primitive, all lived under some kind of political discipline, all appeared to obey recognised chiefs. Presumably those rulers all had some sort of title to the territory which they governed and to the obedience of the people who occupied it. The Crown lawyers argued that the titles of the native rulers were probably usurped; that their rule was tyrannical and therefore indefensible; and that in any event the papal grant had over-riding force. This was a highly contentious argument. The doctrine of universal papal dominion, in temporal as in spiritual matters, usually associated with the name of Henry of Susa (Ostiensis), was, it is true, well known to canonists in the fifteenth and early sixteenth centuries, but was certainly not universally accepted.

Ostiensis had argued that infidels might retain their lands and possessions only by the favour of the Church. If they refused to recognise papal authority the Pope might direct the steps necessary for bringing them into obedience, even to the extent of appointing Christian rulers over them. In accordance with this doctrine, the distinguished jurist Palacios Rubios of the Council of Castile was commanded in 1510 to draw up a *requerimiento* calling on the Indians to submit peacefully and receive the Faith. This long and complicated legal document was to be read aloud to the Indians on all occasions before military operations were undertaken against them. The obligation was taken literally, if not always seriously; as late as 1542 the viceroy Mendoza ordered the *requerimiento* to be read to the Chichimeca warriors encamped in the *peñoles* of Mixton and Nochistlán. The reading was made in the Nahuatl language and was entrusted to a friar who, according to the chroniclers of the Mixton War, was compelled to stand out of range of arrows, and presumably, therefore, out of earshot; but the requirements of law and justice were held to have been fulfilled.

For scrupulous minds this solemn pantomime was not enough. Many jurists, in Spain as elsewhere, rejected the Ostiensian doctrine not only because it was theologically unsound but because it was unrealistic. Ostiensis, writing in an age of Mediterranean crusades, had had in mind the Muslims of the Levant, militant enemies of Christendom despite ample opportunity of studying Christian doctrine. It might plausibly be argued that their infidelity was deliberate, malicious and punishable. The great discoveries, however, demonstrated more power-fully than any theory the error of regarding 'the world' and 'Christen-dom' as more or less coterminous. It was clearly absurd to call on the Americans to acknowledge the authority of a pontiff of whom they had never heard. Moral, intellectual and legal scruples about the justice of the enterprise of the Indies could be quieted only by arguments independent of the temporal sovereignty of the Pope.

Whatever else they might purport to be, the bulls of 1493 were a clear instruction to the Crown of Castile to undertake the conversion of the American Indians to Christianity. No Catholic—and discussion of these matters was long confined to Catholics—could deny the right of the Pope to give such an instruction, or the duty of the Spanish monarchs to carry it out. To what extent, however, were they authorised to use secular means to this spiritual end? Could the duty of conversion be held to justify armed conquest, the deposition of native rulers—if indeed the Indians had legitimate rulers—the assertion of Spanish sovereignty over the Indians in general? This was the central question. If it could be answered affirmatively it gave rise in turn to subsidiary questions. If the Indians should be reduced, by a just con-quest, to the position of subjects of the Spanish Crown, what legal and political rights remained to them? Should they be converted by com-pulsion? Were they to be subject to Spanish courts and Spanish law, civil or ecclesiastical? Might they be commended to individual Spanish feudatories, deprived of their land, put to forced labour, enslaved?

The question of the validity of Spain's title to the Indies exercised some of the best minds of the sixteenth century. The most distinguished and in many ways most original discussion of the problem was con-tained in a series of lectures delivered at Salamanca in 1539 by the great Dominican jurist Francisco de Vitoria. Vitoria was not directly con-cerned with America, and never went there; his interest was academic, part of a wider interest in the rights and wrongs of war and conquest. He was the first serious writer to reject firmly and unequivocally all claim of Pope or Emperor to exercise temporal jurisdiction over other princes, Christian or infidel. He considered that the Pope possessed a 'regulating' authority, recognised among Christian peoples, by virtue of which a single prince might be charged, to the exclusion of others, with the task of supporting missions among a heathen people. This regulating power might authorise certain secular acts, such as the provision of armed force for the protection of missionaries, but it could not authorise war or conquest.

War, like all relations between independent states, was for Vitoria governed by rules of law. He maintained that there was a Natural Law connection between all nations, and that this connection, though not expressed in any authority exercised by an earthly overlord, nevertheless involved a system of mutual rights and duties. He conceived this Law of Nations as a law binding *inter se* upon states which were still in a state of nature in virtue of their sovereignty, and binding upon them in exactly the same way as the pre-political Natural Law had been binding upon individuals when they were living in a state of nature. To this newly conceived Law of Nations, Vitoria gave the old Roman name, *Jus gentium*; but he redefined the term in his own highly original fashion. *Jus gentium* had originally meant that part of the private law of Rome which was supposed to be common to Rome and other peoples; but Vitoria treated it as a branch of public law governing the relations between one people and another. He was quite clear that the Amerindians were 'gentes' in this sense; they formed organised and independent states; their princes ruled by accepted title and were subject, equally with the princes of Europe, to *Jus gentium*. Just cause for waging war against them could be found, not in any papal edict, probably not in their idolatry or alleged barbarity or wickedness, but certainly if they denied to other peoples those rights to which, by the Law of Nations, all peoples were entitled.

The principal rights possessed by every nation were those of peaceful commerce and intercourse with every other nation, and the peaceful preaching of the Gospel. The Spaniards originally shared with other nations the right to visit the Indies on such errands. The Pope, however, by virtue of his regulating authority, had confided the duty of evangelising in the New World to the Spaniards alone, partly as the nation best fitted for the task, and partly to avoid strife, since the Spaniards possessed the subsidiary claim of prior discovery. The papal decree was binding upon all Christian princes, though not upon the Indians; but the Indians, equally with the Christians, were bound by the wider rules of the Law of Nations to receive the Spaniards peacefully and to hear the Gospel. The Spaniards, for their part, must behave as Christians, offer peaceful trade, refrain from provoking resistance and present the Gospel fairly. The Indians would not incur the penalty of conquest merely by rejecting the Gospel after hearing it; but refusal to hear, refusal to admit strangers, unprovoked attacks on traders or missionaries—any of these offences would at once give the Spaniards just ground for war and conquest.

The Law of Nations in Vitoria's thought did not require universal acceptance in order to claim universal validity. *Jus gentium* derived originally from Natural Law. The nearest approximation on earth to a formulation of Natural Law was 'a concensus of the greater part of the whole world, especially in behalf of the common good of all'. The supposed majority of peoples constituted by Christian Europe was considered, therefore, to be the guardian of Natural Law and to have a secondary right and duty (since the Indians were members of the 'natural society and fellowship') to exercise a paternal and benevolent guardianship over peoples living in ignorance or open defiance of Natural Law. Typical offences against Natural Law—quite distinct from offences against the Law of Nations—were tyranny, human sacrifice and bestiality, all of which crimes were attributed to the Indians by Spanish colonists, most circumstantially and authoritatively by Oviedo. Vitoria, however, was charitably sceptical of these reports, and would not base a right of conquest on Natural Law offences alone.

The possibility that a majority of Indians might elect to live under Spanish rule; the duty of protecting converts from the dangers of persecution or relapse; the right of assisting a friendly nation in a just war against a neighbour (such as the war of the Tlaxcalans against the Aztec confederacy, of which Cortés made such adroit use), all were recognised as additional minor justifications for Spanish armed intervention in the New World.

Whatever the justifications, Vitoria clearly would have preferred an empire based on peaceful trade to one formed by conquest. He believed commerce to be at least as effective as conquest in spreading the Gospel, in satisfying a legitimate desire for individual profit and in increasing the royal revenue. He cited in support of this belief the successes of the Portuguese in the East—a subject on which he cannot have been well informed. He admitted, however, that once the Spaniards were established in the Indies they could not well withdraw and leave colonists and converts to perish. He thought that Spanish government, even in a purely secular sense, could be an advantage to the Indians: 'Those people are not unintelligent, but primitive; they seem incapable of maintaining a civilised State according to the requirements of humanity and law . . . their government, therefore, should be entrusted to people of intelligence and experience, as though they were children . . . . But this interference must be for their welfare and in their interests, not merely for the profit of the Spaniards; for otherwise the Spaniards would be placing their own souls in peril.' Finally: 'The prime consideration is that no obstacle should be placed in the way of the Gospel. . . . I personally have no doubt that the Spaniards were compelled to use force and arms in order to continue their work there; though I fear that measures were adopted in excess of what is allowed by human and divine law.'

Vitoria's justification of the Spanish title to the Indies was unenthusiastic and tentative. It showed a penetration and a liberality of mind remarkable in its time, but also an anxious searching of conscience, which was shared by many sensitive Spaniards throughout the life of the Empire. It embarrassed the government; it called forth a reprimand from the Emperor and a strong hint to the Dominicans not to discuss such matters in public. Nevertheless, Vitoria's great academic prestige and his considered humanity could not fail to influence public opinion, even in some degree public policy. In a still wider field his attempt to formulate rules governing the conduct of civilised states, both towards one another and towards weaker peoples, was a permanent and valuable addition to European political theory. He was the principal founder of the study of International Law.

Most other writers on the Indies were less academic in their approach, less interested in justifying the conquest (which was a fact, and had to be accepted), more concerned with the nature of the lordship which the Castilian rulers actually exercised. During the middle decades of the sixteenth century the Crown was bombarded with memorials on colonial policy, and the government of the Indies—more specifically, the treatment of the Indians—became the subject of a bitter pamphleteering war. The propagandists, very roughly, fell into two groups: those who wished to safeguard the freedom of the Indians and, by implication, the exclusive influence of the missionary friars; and those who wished to extend the liberty of action and the quasi-feudal authority of the Spanish settlers. Of the first group, the most famous and most influential was another Dominican, Bartolomé de las Casas.

Las Casas spent most of his long working life in the Indies, as missionary, as bishop and as writer. He had gone to Hispaniola as a settler in 1502, had held a *repartimiento* of Indians and had participated in the conquest of Cuba. In Cuba, in 1514, he experienced the spiritual upheaval which led him eventually to enter the Dominican Order and which made him the most powerful and most vociferous of humanitarian agitators. His writings and his whole life were governed by his affection for the Indians, his zeal for their spiritual well-being, his determination to defend their rights, his passionate indignation at the treatment which they received. His major works, the *Historia* and the *Apologetica historia*, are full of valuable information, but because of their verbosity and their lack of orderly arrangement, have been little read. His numerous polemical writings are vituperative, one-sided and at times extravagant. The best known of them, the *Brevísima relación de la destrucción de las Indias*, is a hair-raising catalogue of atrocities. It was widely published in Protestant countries, later in the century, as anti-Spanish propaganda: in Latin in the Netherlands and in Germany, with De Bry's ghoulish engravings, and in English in a translation with the succinct title *Casas' horrid massacres*. Nevertheless, taken as a whole, Las Casas' writings reveal a theory of man and of government which, through all the passion and the verbiage, is clear and consistent.

The key to Las Casas' thought was his insistence upon liberty. He laid down as the essentials of civilised existence that men should live in politically organised communities, but that, subject to the minimum of restraint necessary to make such organisation possible, they should be entirely free. Reason, which all men possessed, naturally inclined them to live in peace together, to seek good and to avoid evil. The free exercise of reason was a right by Natural Law, and should be unrestricted. The right belonged as well to infidels as to Christians, and not even the Vicar of Christ, in his zeal for the extension of the Faith, might lawfully invade it. Las Casas insisted more strongly than any other writer of his century on free and willing conversion; to use any form of coercion in missionary work was worthy only of Mahomet. He consistently denounced the Ostiensian doctrine as heretical, and maintained that the Pope in ordinary circumstances held no authority whatever over infidels, to punish their sins or to depose their princes.

Like Vitoria, Las Casas attributed to the Papacy a limited and indirect temporal authority in matters relating to the spiritual welfare of Christendom. The Pope might lay upon a prince the task of defending

Christians against infidels who openly attacked the Faith, and might delegate to him the duty of carrying the Gospel to infidels who were ignorant of it. In this limited sense Las Casas attributed Spanish authority in the Indies to the papal commission; but that authority, he insisted, was delegated exclusively to the Spanish monarchs, not to Spaniards in general. Spanish conquerors and settlers in America had no authority, no special rights, save as agents and subjects of the Crown. Las Casas' views on colonial government were based, therefore, not on a theory of superior civilisation but on a theory of kingship—an older and in some ways more primitive theory than that commonly held by the contemporary writers of the Spanish juridical school; for while those writers in general attributed kingship to some form of secular election, Las Casas clung to the medieval idea of divine ordination. The kingly rank was ordained by God for the sake of justice, and in his own sphere of activity, in the administration of justice and the protection of rights, the King had no peer. His sphere of activity was limited, however; the law of God, the rights of subjects according to their station, the laws and customs of the realm, were above the power of the King. He could not create, nor even define, such rights and laws. They existed; the King's part was to uphold and enforce them. He must provide justice and keep the peace; he must uphold and defend the Church and further the spreading of the Faith; he must maintain the rights of his subjects according to custom; he must preserve the realm and the royal authority, which were not his own, intact for his successors. So long as he performed these duties faithfully and confined himself to them, a legitimate king was entitled to the implicit obedience of all his subjects. If he seriously neglected or overstepped them he became a tyrant, and might lawfully be disobeyed, deposed or even killed.

This reasoning, though distinctly old-fashioned in the Spain of Las Casas' day, was not unorthodox, at least in so far as it related to the 'natural realms' of the Spanish Crown. But were the Indies—territories which the King's vassals had conquered by their own efforts and at their own expense—to be regarded as 'natural realms'? Las Casas insisted that they were. The Indians, equally with the people of Spain, were the natural subjects of the King and enjoyed, from the moment of their entering into Spanish obedience, all the guarantees of liberty and justice provided by the laws of Castile. The King owed to them, in the Indies, the same duties, the same respect for rights, as in Spain he owed to Spaniards. Conversely, he was entitled to their direct allegiance. The leaders of the conquest, by deposing Indian rulers, making grants of land, distributing Indians in *encomienda*, had usurped royal authority and invaded rights which the King was sworn to protect. The Crown's advisers, by issuing confirmations of these acts, had granted away part of a patrimony which should be kept inalienable and intact. They had given away the King's subjects.

As subjects, the Indians had duties as well as rights. Las Casas consistently maintained that they were rational men, intellectually able to grasp the implications of their allegiance, to perform the duties of loyal subjects and to receive the Faith. He knew the Indians better than most Spaniards, and few in Spain could contradict him. He could not, of course, deny that most Indians were uninstructed heathen and in need of tutelage, but he did emphatically deny that *encomenderos* and Spanish settlers generally were acceptable tutors. He considered that the Indians should live in their own villages under the day-to-day government of their own chiefs; and that the chiefs should be supervised by royal officials who should administer justice, instruct them in European customs and discourage barbarous practices. The Church, for its part, should be allowed a free hand in the work of peaceful evangelisation and spiritual care. Europeans, as private persons, if they were to be allowed in the Indies at all, should live apart from the Indians and live by their own labour. Las Casas would allow the colonist no privilege and no special reward, except that of spiritual achievement.

Las Casas' arguments were powerful enough to persuade the Crown to authorise administrative experiments: a brief attempt in Hispaniola at Indian self-government under missionary supervision; a settlement of self-supporting Spanish farmers in Cumaná—designed to give effect to his theories. These experiments, as might be expected, failed. The ideal empire was far from American reality. The interests of *encomenderos*, proprietary officials and town councils were well entrenched. His propaganda could not simply be shrugged off, however, as fanatic extravagance. He had powerful friends. His vehement persistence could overcome both opposition and indifference. Some of his ideas were congenial to Charles V and his ecclesiastical advisers, and made a wide appeal to humanitarian feeling. Indications of approval in high places in Spain help to explain the hatred with which Las Casas was pursued by Spaniards in the New World. The old conquerors and settlers considered his ideas a challenge not only to their livelihood but to their respectability. These men were by no means all mere cut-throat adventurers. Many of them took serious pride in their achievements, and thought of themselves as champions of civilisation and religion against a cruel and superstitious barbarism. These ideas also had their theoretical defenders, among whom the most distinguished was Juan Ginés de Sepúlveda.

Sepúlveda wrote his *Democrates Alter* in 1542. He was then at the height of his reputation as a humanist, an Aristotelian scholar and a master of Latin style. Like many learned Spaniards, he had counted Erasmus among his friends. As with Vitoria, his concern with the Indies was academic, unaffected by personal interest. He never went to America. Like Vitoria, he founded his thought on the subject on his own individual view of Natural Law. Natural Law governed men's behaviour one towards another. It had two aspects: an instinctive aspect, which caused men to reproduce their kind and to repel force by force; and a rational aspect, which impelled them to respect their parents, to seek good and avoid evil, to keep promises and to believe the teachings of true religion. The second aspect of law was as natural as the first, and in case of conflict overrode it; for since man was rational by nature, no prompting of instinct which failed to conform to reason could be deemed truly natural. Natural Law in its rational aspect was made explicit in *Jus gentium*, the body of rules supposedly common to all organised peoples. Unlike Vitoria, Sepúlveda regarded *Jus gentium* as regulating the relations between individuals; he had no conception of an international law between states. Reason impelled men to formulate a common opinion on all matters of universal importance, and in particular enabled them to deduce from Natural Law —itself rational—the explicit rules of *Jus gentium*. Some men, however, were more rational than others; and the common opinion which deduced and defined the Law of Nations was not the opinion of all men, nor even of the 'greater part'. The Law of Nations was to be found only among the *gentes humanitiores*, not among those on the fringe of civilisation; and even among civilised peoples the duty of declaring what was or was not Natural Law was confined to the wisest and most prudent men of the higher races. Sepúlveda was an advocate, therefore, of natural aristocracy; the government of the lower races by the higher, of the lower elements by the higher in each race. He even denied that a people might strictly be considered to have legitimate rulers—in modern terms, to be a state—unless it was governed according to the principles of *Jus gentium*; though he was quick to add that for purposes of maintaining the peace Natural Law enjoined obedience even to bad rulers, and rebellion could have no legal justification against a prince whose title was legitimate according to the particular laws and customs of his people.

Natural aristocracy implied natural servitude, since the more perfect should govern the less. The familiar Aristotelian dictum, as interpreted by Sepúlveda, was made to constitute a general mandate for civilised peoples to subdue by force of arms, if no other means were possible, those peoples 'who require, by their own nature and in their own interests, to be placed under the authority of civilised and virtuous princes and nations, so that they may learn from the might, wisdom and law of their conquerors to practise better morals, worthier customs and a more civilised way of life'. Sepúlveda was too restrained a polemist to level at the Indians such a battery of abuse as Oviedo had employed; but he did assert that the Indians lived in defiance of Natural Law, and pointed to their very inability to resist the Spanish invasion as further proof of their inferior state and their need of strong and wise government, for their own good. He might have drawn, from these premises, conclusions embodying a purely secular title for Spanish rule in the New World, but this he had no intention of doing. The spreading of the Faith appeared as a solemn duty to him as to all his contemporaries, and though his theological arguments were logically unnecessary in the general development of his thought, they presented no contradictions. *Compelle eos intrare* was his text. The forcible baptism of individuals, it is true, he considered unjust and useless; nor did paganism in itself provide ground for just war. The effective conversion of large bodies of pagans, however, could be achieved only after long contact with Christians. The Indians would not accept Christianity at once, on the mere word of strangers, nor change their way of life in a few days. In order that they might learn from missionaries and prepare themselves for entry into the Church, they must be brought, with or without their consent, under civilised government. Civilisation and Christianity went hand in hand. Conquest was a religious duty, an act of charity towards ignorant and unfortunate neighbours.

Unlike Vitoria, therefore, Sepúlveda had no squeamish misgivings about the justice of the war which his countrymen had waged against the American Indians. The principal rights entitling a nation to wage just war were four: the natural right of repelling force by force; the recovery of possessions unjustly taken; the necessity of punishing

criminals who had not been punished by their own rulers (since all
men were neighbours and mutually responsible one for another);
and the duty of subduing barbarous peoples by force if they refused
to submit voluntarily to government by a superior race. This last
right in its turn depended on four causes: the naturally servile nature of
barbarians and their consequent need of civilised masters; their habitual
crimes against Natural Law; the plight of the subjects of barbarian
rulers, who were the victims of oppression, unjust war, slavery and
human sacrifice; and the duty of making possible the peaceful preaching
of the Gospel. All Christian and civilised nations enjoyed these rights
and owed these duties. The special rights and duties of Spain in the New
World arose from three causes: the natural superiority of Spaniards
over other Christian nations; the right of the first discoverer to occupy
lands which had no legitimate ruler; and the decree of the Pope, at
once a spiritual commission to convert the heathen and a temporal
grant of legally unoccupied territory.

The just war of conquest had conferred upon the Indians not only
the blessings of civilisation and true religion but economic advantages
also. The Spaniards had introduced beasts of burden into the Indies,
had developed the mines and had taught the Indians profitable methods
of agriculture. Of course, they had profited themselves in the process;
though Sepúlveda had severe things to say about conquerors who were
inspired *auri inexplebili cupiditate*. He repeatedly and explicitly denied
the right of conquerors to seize the private property of the conquered.
Labour was another matter. In return for the services they performed,
the conquerors, in his opinion, naturally and rightly employed the
labour of Indians in performing those tasks necessary for civilised life,
exercising over them a 'mixed and tempered paternal authority'.

The force of Sepúlveda's arguments was undeniable. Their principal defect was that they tended to prove too much. His cold and harsh
reasoning roused few answering echoes (save among the more per-
cipient colonists, who rightly regarded him as the champion of their
interest; the town council of Mexico sent him a letter of congratulation
and thanks). Many of his contemporaries and most historians since his
time thought him an apologist for slavery. His theory of natural servitude was repugnant to most Spanish theologians and academic jurists.
The great Suárez disposed of it curtly: '*hactenus tamen, ut existimo, tam
barbarae gentes inventae non sunt*'. Certainly Sepúlveda wrote in ignorance of American conditions, and used theoretical arguments to sup-

port a system which lent itself in practice to appalling abuses. He certainly admitted the justice of enslaving prisoners taken in rebellion or in the act of unjust war—a right of the conqueror generally admitted at the time. He added to this admission, however, the warning that enslavement was no longer a reputable practice among Christian peoples, and that many Indians must have resisted in good faith, thinking that they themselves had just cause for war. The enslavement of these people would certainly be unjust. Sepúlveda protested bitterly in later works and in private letters against those who accused him of brutality in this matter. His proposal, he insisted, was not to enslave but 'to divide the Indians . . . among honourable, just and prudent Spaniards, especially among those who helped to bring them under Spanish rule, so that these may train their Indians in virtuous and humane customs, and teach them the Christian religion'. These exculpatory qualifications, however, did little to mollify those who differed from Sepúlveda and who vehemently rejected his central argument. The circulation of *Democrates Alter* in manuscript produced a storm of protest, especially from Dominicans. Las Casas and Melchor Cano both wrote violent refutations. Permission to publish the book was withheld, and discussion of the problems which it raised ran on until 1550, when they were submitted by order of the Emperor to formal debate, in which Sepúlveda and Las Casas argued face to face before a panel of eminent jurists convened at Valladolid. The proceedings were protracted and inconclusive. The judges never produced a final report; but Sepúlveda, by implication, lost the argument, since he never received permission to publish. *Democrates Alter* was not printed until nearly 200 years after its author's death.

Sepúlveda and Las Casas represented the two divergent yet complementary tendencies of the imperialist theory of their time. Both sought to modify royal policy and to limit the exercise of the royal will. The thought of both was rooted in the Middle Ages. Sepúlveda wished to interpose permanently between the Crown and the Indians a benevolent aristocracy, who might exercise at first hand a paternal authority which the Crown could not easily exert at a distance, and who would be entitled to use Indian labour in reward for their services. The feudal implications of this proposal in themselves made it unacceptable to a royal government always suspicious of aristocratic pretensions; but, further, to proclaim Indians slaves by nature was to disown much carefully drafted legislation, royal and papal, and to eat fifty years of royal professions. Las Casas wished to impose upon the Crown, in dealing with conquered Indians, the same limitations which, in his opinion, the law of God and the laws of the land placed upon it in governing Spain; and, further, to prohibit the use of armed force against Indian peoples in future. But a government which operated in the Indies in practice as an irresponsible, though conscientious, absolutism could hardly be expected to accept a theory which limited its sovereignty and might even cast doubt upon its right to rule. To insist with Las Casas that Indians should be won over by persuasion only was to abandon all future conquests and admit the injustice of past ones. The full implications of either theory were more than any self-respecting government of the time could stomach.

This is not to say that the debate at Valladolid was a mere academic exercise. No one knew how many Mexicos or Perus still awaited discovery. What of the Philippines? Of El Dorado? Of the seven cities of Cíbola? Charles V took the matter seriously, and even forbade further expeditions of conquest until the question of just war should be settled. It never was settled; but in the third quarter of the sixteenth century the interest of the Crown coincided with some, at least, of the views which Las Casas had put forward. The empire needed a period of consolidation and peace, in which the mineral wealth of the Indies could be exploited and their administration improved. In order to curb the restless mobility of the old conquerors and settlers, to prevent them keeping the frontiers in constant uproar, and in order to avoid further brutalities such as those of the early conquests which had received such unwelcome publicity, it was necessary to limit new *entradas* and to keep them under strict royal control. To this end, the *Ordenanzas sobre descubrimientos* of 1573 were promulgated. Juan de Ovando, the president of the Council of the Indies at the time—an outstandingly able and conscientious official—was an admirer of Las Casas (who had died, at a great age, in 1566). By Ovando's orders, Las Casas' manuscripts were brought from their monastic repository at Valladolid and utilised by the Council in the drafting of the new code. The *Ordenanzas* did not, it is true, entirely prohibit the use of force against the recalcitrant; nor did the suppression of the word 'conquest' and the substitution of the word 'pacification' necessarily ensure the use of peaceful methods. Nevertheless, the new rules emphasised, in words which Las Casas himself might have used, the royal preference for persuasion and agreement in extending the bounds of Spanish authority, and the importance of effective—because willing—conversion. They laid down stringent conditions for the grant of licences for new expeditions and sternly prohibited unauthorised *entradas*. To this extent, at least, the Spanish Crown disowned the ruthless methods by which the greater part of its possessions in the Indies had been acquired.

There remained the question of the treatment of conquered Indians; of the civil rights of those who lived peaceably under Spanish rule; of the spiritual standing of those who accepted Christianity. These were more intractable problems. Powerful vested interests were involved. Legislation about *encomiendas* could, and sometimes did, provoke dangerous outbreaks among the settlers. Legislation about forced labour affected an important source of royal revenue. In spiritual affairs many concientious churchmen found difficulty in accepting Las Casas' assertion that converted Indians were fully capable of understanding the Faith they had adopted and were entitled to all its sacraments. Yet the consciences of successive monarchs and the policies advocated by their advisers could not remain unaffected by the tenacious reasoning, the passionate propaganda and the fierce denunciation which had split the learned professions in Spain and spread unrest throughout the Indies. How effective were the theorists and propagandists in influencing public policy? To what extent were the activities and the organisation of Church and State in the Indies affected by considerations of responsibility towards the conquered?

CHAPTER 8

The spreading of the Faith

THE discoverers and conquerors of America were, for the most part, devout men whose devotion took forms at once orthodox and practical. Of the many possible forms of religious zeal, two in particular appealed to them and to the rulers and investors who sent them out. The first was the simple-minded desire, long familiar within Spain, to ensure by military and political means the safety and independence of their own religious community and, better still, its predominance over others; to defend the believer against interference and attack; to kill, humiliate or subdue the unbeliever. The second was the deeper desire to convert—to appeal to the minds and hearts of individual unbelievers by preaching, reasoning or force of example, by any means of persuasion short of force or threat, and so to bring unbelievers into the community of belief. These two possible lines of action might be confused or combined; it might appear politic, for example, to subdue unbelievers in order to convert them. In general, however, the two expressions of religious devotion in action were kept distinct in men's minds. The first, the politico-military expression, provided an excuse for conquest and plunder on a grand scale. The second called for intense effort, with little likelihood of immediate material gain. If in America conversion, no less than conquest—rather, perhaps, than conquest—was a Christian duty, upon whom lay the responsibility for carrying it out? It could be achieved only by a dedicated professional priesthood. Who could provide the organisation and direction needed for such a mission, and undertake the heavy expense which it inevitably required? Not, certainly, the *conquistadores*. Some of the more thoughtful among them, it is true, accepted both the desirability and the feasibility of an apostolic mission to the Indians, and some of the more pious were generous benefactors to churches and convents; but a makeshift government of military commanders and town-councils could not be expected to recruit, organise and support the large numbers of trained men needed for so immense a task.

The prime responsibility for encouraging and organising missions to the heathen lay with the Papacy, but the popes of the time had no adequate resources for the task in America, and no body of trained men effectively at their command to undertake it. Moreover, they lacked the necessary knowledge. Even for elementary geographical information, such as was needed for siting churches and delimiting the boundaries of dioceses, they were dependent upon the Spanish government. In America—as everywhere outside central Italy—the popes could make their will effective only by putting moral pressure upon temporal rulers. From the beginning they realised that an apostolic mission in America could be organised only by the Spanish Crown.

A commission to undertake the conversion of the natives of the newly discovered Indies was explicit in the bull *Inter caetera* of 1493. The sovereigns were to 'despatch. . . virtuous and God-fearing men endowed with training, experience and skill, to instruct the natives . . . and to imbue them with . . . Christian faith and sound morals'. Columbus accordingly took with him on his second voyage a small party of friars, about whom little is known except their names. What is known about Fray Bernardo Buil and his companions is that the sovereigns selected them, and that their instructions—to teach the natives Spanish, to preach to them and baptise them, to treat them kindly, and so forth—emanated from the royal chancery. The Crown defrayed the cost of the friars' journey to the Indies and paid their stipends while they were there. It was in recognition of this considerable and growing charge against the royal revenue that Alexander VI issued the last of his bulls relating to the Indies, *Eximiae devotionis* of 1501, which empowered the Spanish monarchs to receive all tithes levied from the inhabitants. Ovando, appointed in the same year as governor of Hispaniola on behalf of the Crown, was instructed to arrange the collection of tithes. Subsequent royal letters to Ovando contain detailed instructions for the ordering of ecclesiastical affairs—the payment of stipends, the delimitation of parishes, even the methods to be employed in evangelisation. In all this correspondence the Crown assumed without question its own entire control of the development of the Church within its newly settled dominions.

The constitutional position, nevertheless, was ambiguous. In one newly conquered kingdom—Granada—Ferdinand and Isabella held and exercised a degree of control over ecclesiastical affairs far greater than the Papacy was normally willing to concede; far greater than they possessed, for example, in Aragon or Castile. They held it, however, by virtue of a specific enactment: the famous bull of Granada, *Orthodoxe fidei propagationem* of 1486, which had granted to them the right of presentation to all episcopal sees, monasteries and other churches in the conquered Moorish kingdom. No such enactment existed for the Indies. The founding bull, *Inter caetera*, made no mention of presentation; but in their actions in the Indies the monarchs apparently assumed, as implicit in the general terms of that bull, a prerogative analogous to that which they undoubtedly possessed in Granada. Alexander VI made no difficulties. Throughout his pontificate he was extremely amenable to Spanish requests and suggestions, and in those early days the enterprise of the Indies was a very small affair. The Indies grew, however, and Alexander's successor, Julius II—whose character Pastor likened to that of Cortés—proved, despite his personal admiration of Isabella, initially somewhat less accommodating. In 1504, the Spanish sovereigns asked for papal legislation erecting, for the first time, episcopal sees in the New World. Julius responded with the bull *Illius fulciti presidio* of 1504, providing for three new bishoprics, but in terms which completely ignored the claims of royal patronage.

Illius fulciti presidio brought the whole question into the open, and convinced the sovereigns of the necessity of an explicit grant of patronage in the Indies. Action on the bull was delayed by Isabella's death shortly after its issue; by Ferdinand's difficulties with Philip of Burgundy, and with the Castilian nobility; and by his retirement to Naples. Throughout these difficult years, however, Ferdinand, through his ambassador in Rome, maintained diplomatic pressure upon the Pope, who, for his part, was encouraged to compliance by his need of Ferdinand's support against Louis XII. In 1508 Ferdinand, firmly in control of the regency in Castile and so of the affairs of the Indies, obtained all he had been seeking. The bull *Universalis ecclesiae regimini* of that year conceded to the rulers of Castile in perpetuity the privilege of founding and organising all churches, and presenting to all sees and livings, in all overseas territories which they possessed then or might acquire in future. This famous enactment was the legal foundation of the royal *Patronato* of the Indies. It was followed in 1510 and 1511 by bulls regulating the details of the tithes which the Crown was entitled to collect; exempting the production of precious metals from liability to tithe; recognising Seville as the metropolitan church of the Indies, and redrawing the boundaries of the original sees in accordance with the royal wishes, so as to include the new settlements in Puerto Rico and Cuba. Finally, in 1512, Ferdinand made his own royal gesture, the Concordat of Burgos, in which he declared the manner in which he proposed to exercise his new and wide prerogatives. In this detailed and highly significant agreement, almost every clause of which amounts to a *pragmática* on some aspect of ecclesiastical government, the most important single item was the re-donation of tithes. It had always been understood on both sides that the tithes which the Crown was empowered to collect would be spent in furthering the work of the Church. The Concordat made this understanding specific. The Crown delegated in perpetuity to the bishops in the Indies the collection and distribution of tithes on all products of the Indies save precious metals, which were exempt. The distribution was to be made according to the custom of the metropolitan province of Seville: so much to the bishops, so much to the cathedral churches, so much to the inferior clergy, and so forth, one-ninth being reserved to the Crown. By this far-reaching enactment the King provided the Church in the Indies with a permanent income; supported the collection of that income with the weight of royal authority; and ensured that the money would be spent by men whom he appointed, and according to rules which he approved.

The *Patronato*, thus amicably established, conferred upon the Spanish Crown an immense, a unique, authority. Except in the little kingdom of Granada, nothing like it existed in Europe; not until the eighteenth century did the Spanish kings secure a similar power in the rest of Spain. Neither Ferdinand nor Julius, of course, can have had any notion of the magnitude of the concession which the Pope had made. In 1508 'the Indies' still meant, effectively, the island of Hispaniola. As discovery, conquest and settlement advanced, however, the sweeping terms of the grant subordinated to the royal will the entire clergy of a great empire. The King was the patron; his administrative representatives, the viceroys and governors, acted also as vice-patrons, enforcing his will in ecclesiastical affairs. The central administration of the *Patronato* was entrusted to a committee, first of the Council of Castile, after 1524 of the Council of the Indies. Within the general structure of the Council the *Patronato* had its own departmental office, its own secretariat, its own archive; but the monarch often intervened personally in its affairs, exercising a quasi-pontifical authority even in matters of religion and of spiritual jurisdiction. Preachers might be admonished for 'pulpit excesses', bishops ordered to absolve officials whom they had excommunicated. In the way of privileged jurisdictions, the *Patronato* tended to become broadened and extended by usage and by construction. In the appointment of bishops, for example, the role of the Crown was limited to presentation, for no temporal ruler could confer spiritual authority; but in practice bishops were packed off to their dioceses in America unprovided and unconsecrated, and set to work immediately, confident in the assumption that the necessary documents would automatically follow from Rome in due course. The saintly first bishop of Mexico, Juan de Zumárraga—drawn unwillingly, without warning, from his obscure cloister, by Charles V's personal command resulting from a chance encounter—spent four difficult years as an unconsecrated bishop-elect, his provision and consecration being delayed first by the sack of Rome in 1527, and then by a fortuitious clerical mistake. During that time he felt obliged to take drastic and urgent measures for the protection of the natives, including the excommunication of Nuño de Guzmán and other high officers of the royal *audiencia*. His action was clearly non-sacramental; but it was supported by the Crown, and was effective. Zumárraga was a devoted priest, indifferent to the opinion of men and to threats of removal from office; but he was ready to obey the King's command as the command of God. Later, when he was involved in litigation with Vasco de Quiroga, the Bishop of Michoacán, about the boundaries of dioceses and other ecclesiastical matters, he had no hesitation in carrying his plea to Madrid rather than to Rome, and in regarding the Council of the Indies as a supreme ecclesiastical court. Even when appeal to Rome was desired—as it very rarely was—the *Patronato* made it extremely difficult. Further, the Crown controlled all movement to and from the Indies. No cleric could go there without the permission of the Council of the Indies; no direct contact was possible between Rome and the clergy in America; no document could be circulated in the Indies without royal approval. The *pase regio*, the royal permit for the presence of an ecclesiastical person or the circulation of an ecclesiastical document in the Indies, was a unilateral and drastic extension of the use of the *placet* and the *exequatur* by rulers in Europe; a use which had the sanction of diplomatic custom, but which itself was nowhere recognised by papal concession. The *pase regio* was never formally included in the grant of *Patronato*, nor did the Papacy ever accept the royal argument that it was implicit in the grant. Nevertheless, the promulgation of papal bulls and briefs in the Indies was frequently suspended, and sometimes stopped altogether, if the contents appeared likely to infringe the authority of the Crown. Among people devoted to the Church and proud of their orthodox piety, as Spaniards were, these were great powers; small wonder that the *Patronato* was among the most jealously guarded regalia of the Crown. Small wonder, also, that kings of Spain, supported by civilian lawyers, came by imperceptible degrees to forget that it originated in a papal grant, in theory revocable, and to regard it as a prerogative inherent in their sovereignty. Private infractions or criticisms of it were apt to be sharply punished. The only serious papal attempt to limit its operation—by Pius V in 1568—was tenaciously and successfully resisted.

The conflict of 1568 was exceptional. In general, the relation between the Papacy and the Spanish Crown concerning the religious affairs of the Indies was harmonious. The popes appreciated the sensitiveness of the Spanish kings in all matters touching their authority in the Indies, and their own powerlessness to act there. They usually accepted, at least tacitly, extensions of the *Patronato* beyond the already wide terms of the original grant. The kings, for their part, conscientiously and vigorously directed their extraordinary powers towards the attainment of general ends which the Papacy was bound to approve. The *Patronato* was not primarily a device for sanctifying, and so strengthening, the power of the Crown. Still less was it an excuse for plundering the endowments of religious foundations; in the early days of the Indies, indeed, there were no foundations worth plundering, and the Crown was put to expense in establishing them. The *Patronato* in those early days was what it purported to be: an arrangement to ensure efficiency and speed in establishing the Church in the Indies and in evangelising the Indians, without the certain delays and possible divided counsels which constant recourse to Rome would have entailed. The rulers of Spain throughout the sixteenth century, without exception, were firmly devoted to the ends for which the *Patronato* was established. They used their power to send into the mission field men of outstanding ability, experience and zeal; men who—considering the smallness of their numbers and the magnitude of their task—achieved an extraordinary degree of success.

The Church in Spain in the late fifteenth and early sixteenth centuries had experienced a wave of spiritual unrest, similar in many ways to the movement which was to shake the Church throughout northern Europe a generation later. The unrest was most pronounced among the friars of the Mendicant Orders, particularly among Observant Franciscans. The main characteristics of the Regular Observants for many years had been discontent with the relative ease of conventual life and determination to return to the strict rule of St Francis, with its renunciation of property. To this adherence to the original rule, the groups of Strict Observants, which emerged in Spain in the later fifteenth century, added the practice of austere spiritual retreat with extreme self-discipline, and, above all, a strong feeling of evangelical mission. The followers of the Blessed John of Puebla and of his disciple Juan de Guadalupe elected to preach their simple and austere Christianity among poor and neglected people, particularly the mountain peasants of western Andalusia and Extremadura, and among infidels. After the conquest of Granada the Strict Observants characteristically took as their mission the extremely difficult task of evangelising its Muslim population.

The movement for reform and the cult of austerity gained administrative form and added effectiveness from the direction and support of Cardinal Jiménez de Cisneros. Jiménez—confessor to Queen Isabella, Franciscan Provincial in Castile, Archbishop of Toledo, Primate of Spain, twice regent—sought throughout his public life to purify the Spanish clergy by strengthening the austerity and the preaching mission of the Mendicant Orders. Among his own Franciscans he naturally favoured the Observants against the Conventuals, so that in the year of his death no Conventual house remained in Spain. Corresponding reforms took place, with his approval, among the Dominicans and the Jeronymites. The numbers of the reformed Mendicant population increased enormously in his time, forming a trained and disciplined spiritual militia available for service anywhere in the world. To austerity and discipline, moreover, Jiménez—founder of the University of Alcalá, instigator of the Polyglot Bible, champion of the *Philosophia Christi* in pre-Reformation Europe—added another characteristic, humanist scholarship. His influence encouraged the emergence, among the reformed friars, of a spiritual and intellectual élite of evangelical tendency, which would sympathise with Erasmus and even, later in the century, come under suspicion of Lutheranism·

From among such men the leaders of the spiritual conquest of the Indies were largely drawn.

The Amerindian peoples encountered by Spaniards in Jiménez' day were weak and primitive, and in the islands their numbers declined, after the arrival of Europeans, with appalling speed. This pitiful attenuation provided little encouragement or opportunity for an evangelising mission. Nevertheless, even in these hopeless circumstances, the tradition of Mendicant reform made itself felt. The most vigorous, though not the earliest, missionary effort in the islands was that of the Dominicans. Among their most famous leaders, Domingo de Betanzos, later prominent in the mission field in New Spain, was known as a strict and austere reformer; he is said to have influenced Las Casas to take the Dominican habit, with momentous results. Another Dominican, Antonio de Montesinos, created an uproar by his sermons against the ill-treatment of Indians and by his efforts to stir the Crown to action on their behalf. Montesinos' journey to Spain led to well-meant legislation, but no effective action. Probably, in the circumstances, no action within the power of the Crown could have availed much. Nor did conditions in the isthmus, under the savage rule of Pedrarias Dávila, allow much scope for missionary endeavour. The first great opportunity and challenge to Mendicant zeal came with the invasion of New Spain, Guatemala and Yucatán. In dealing with the numerous settled peoples of these areas, missionary policy became an issue of burning importance. Their own religions included rites of horrifying savagery, but individually they appeared tractable and intelligent, and their agrarian collectivism seemed to provide a foundation upon which Christian communities could be built. Cortés himself wrote to the Emperor from Mexico asking for a Franciscan mission, and the decision to entrust the new field to the Mendicant Orders was taken immediately. For the Crown to prescribe the spiritual labours of the members of an Order chartered by the Papacy, and for the members of that Order to undertake the pastoral and sacramental duties normally entrusted to parish priests, special papal legislation was necessary. The required powers were readily granted, in the bull *Exponi nobis fecisti* of Adrian VI, commonly called the *Omnimoda*, in 1522. In 1523 the General of the Franciscan Order, Francisco de Quiñones—himself a Spaniard deeply interested throughout his career in the problems of the Indies—ordered Martín de Valencia, provincial of San Gabriel, to embark with his following on the Mexican mission. The province of

San Gabriel was one of the principal centres of the Strict Observance. It contained 175 friars, nearly all of whom had deliberately left the laxer life of conventual establishments for the rigours of the reform. Some, including Martín de Valencia himself, had been disciples of Juan de Guadalupe and had served in Granada. Fray Martín selected twelve of the ablest and most ardent—the number was, of course, deliberate —and in 1524 they crossed the Atlantic. They were received by Cortés in Mexico with impressive public humility, and embarked at once upon a methodically planned mission, establishing their houses in the principal centres of Indian population in the valleys of Mexico and Puebla. Other Mendicant groups soon followed. The first Dominicans arrived in 1526, also originally twelve in number, including Betanzos and four companions from Hispaniola; though their number was reduced by deaths on the way. They established themselves first in the densely populated Alta Mixteca, where they retained a virtual monopoly for many years. The Augustinians came in 1533. Less is known of their mission; but they were to build some of the most splendid churches in New Spain—Acolmán and Yuriria were among their foundations— and they included in their number eminent men of letters and learning. Among the best known of these scholar-missionaries was the theologian Alonso de la Vera Cruz, who had studied under Vitoria at Salamanca. Fray Alonso spent much of his long and productive career of preaching and scholarship in New Spain, and was the first Professor of Scripture in the University of Mexico, established by imperial decree in 1551. Bravely and publicly, before the whole university, he supported Luis de León when that ill-fated mystic—for belittling the text of the Vulgate and for translating the *Songs of Songs* in its literal meaning—was arrested by the Inquisition.

Most of the early bishops in New Spain were friars. The first, Julian Garcés, Bishop of Tlaxcala, was a Dominican, a staunch supporter of Las Casas, founder of a famous hospital for travellers at Perote on the road from Vera Cruz. The Franciscan Zumárraga, whom Charles V presented in 1527 to the see of Mexico, besides his personal sanctity, austerity and gift of command, brought to New Spain that other vital ingredient of the Mendicant reform, its humanism. He introduced, about 1534, the first printing press in the Indies, and later employed it to print doctrinal manuals: a *Doctrina breve*, intended for the instruction of priests in the diocese, and a *Doctrina christiana*, a simple catechism in Spanish and Nahuatl, for Indian use. The first consists chiefly of extracts from Erasmus's writings. Both insist on the primacy of faith over works and advocate the unlimited diffusion of the Scriptures. Zumárraga also read and admired the work of Thomas More—his annotated copy survives—and this admiration was shared by his friend the humanist lawyer Vasco de Quiroga, Bishop of Michoacán, who attempted, with influential success, to found self-supporting Indian communities based on the plan of the *Utopia* on the shores of Lake Pátzcuaro.

The list of names and of achievements is impressive. The men who led the spiritual conquest of the Indies were not simple friars; they were picked men, daring religious radicals representing both the austerity and the intellectual ferment of Church reform in Spain; many of them had training and experience highly relevant to the task which faced them. They were, moreover, a spiritual army whose commanders stood close to the throne; royal support gave them, in their extravagant humility, a masterful authority. Their mission was planned with the discipline and detailed attention of a military campaign. Like a campaign, it was, initially at least, destructive. A few dozen determined men among millions of Indians, the friars wished to begin their work with a clean sheet. They had no hope of making use of any elements which native religions might have in common with Christianity. Aztec notions of life after death, Aztec practices superficially resembling baptism and confession, seemed to them diabolical parodies. The more sophisticated interest of an ethnologist friar such as Sahagún belonged to the second generation of missionaries. In the early years everything which might perpetuate the 'idolatry' of the Indians was to be destroyed. To dismantle the major temples and expel the priests was simple prudence, for the great stone-faced pyramids were all potential fortresses; but to the friars it was even more important to destroy the shrines and the altars and figures which they contained. 'Idols', especially the little carved deities of village cults, could be concealed, and many were; but efforts were made to hunt them out, and the major effigies were systematically broken, either smashed with hammers or rolled down the pyramid faces. Zumárraga claimed, in a letter of 1531, that more that 500 temples and 20,000 idols had been destroyed in his diocese. To Zumárraga, also, as to other bishops, has been attributed the wholesale destruction of Indian manuscripts. The evidence for this is less clear. Manuscripts—many of which were tribute rolls of purely temporal interest—disappeared through many causes. Certainly very few survive.

After destruction, replacement. The friars quickly spread in twos and threes over vast territories, and wherever they went they founded churches, each church having associated with it a house or convent to accommodate the friars working in its area. The areas served by these houses were often very large, and the friars travelled constantly. The Franciscans alone established nine churches in New Spain in the first five years of their mission. By 1560 they had over eighty, with a total strength of about 380 friars. In all, about 270 churches were founded by friars in New Spain in the sixteenth century, mostly before 1576. Initially the churches were modest temporary structures; but having apparently unlimited labour at their disposal, including large numbers of men accustomed to building in stone, mortar and adobe, the founders from about 1540 onwards embarked on the construction of permanent churches, often of considerable size. Many of these churches occupied the sites of destroyed temples. An obvious reason for this lay in the symbolic significance of a Christian church surmounting an ancient pagan temple-mound, but there was also a more practical reason: the big temple-mounds were mostly in big centres of population. The teaching and baptism of many hundreds of thousands could be achieved, by the small numbers of friars available, only in urban communities close to the nucleus of church and convent from which the missionaries worked; naturally the friars settled in places where urban communities already existed. In many areas of New Spain, however, there were no such concentrations of population and the Indians lived in scattered villages among their cultivations. In these areas the missionaries devoted much energy to persuading or compelling the villagers to move into new towns built around church and convent and reserved for Indian habitation, often under systems of communal tillage and directed by themselves. By these means, they argued, new converts could have not only the moral advantages of urban life and missionary teaching, but also the economic and social advantage of segregation from lay Spaniards. A policy of racial segregation was advocated, not for the convenience of Europeans but in order to protect Indians from the exploitation and demoralisation which might follow from too close contact with Europeans, and to keep them under constant ecclesiastical supervision.

The mission churches were the bases for an extraordinary campaign of wholseale conversion. Martín de Valencia estimated the number baptised in New Spain by the Franciscans alone at more than a million by

1531. Motolinia put it at nearly 5,000,000 by 1536, and said that friars
had been known to baptise 1,500 in a single day. Indians presented
themselves for baptism every day and at all hours. The Franciscans,
more consistently than the Dominicans and Augustinians, made a rule
of never refusing them, and used a greatly abridged and simplified
ceremony for the purpose. They were even accused by members of
other Orders (though they denied the charge) of baptising by aspersion.
A high proportion of the neophytes were, of course, adults, and all
the Orders, in their different ways, struggled with the formidable task
of pre-baptismal instruction. A catechumenate in the modern sense
was out of the question. A general outline of the essentials of the Faith
was given to the candidates *en masse* before baptism. Some of the ad-
dresses used by the Twelve on these occasions were recorded by
Sahagún; they are masterpieces of simplification and compression.
Individual instruction by means of catechism and sermons was left until
afterwards, and great ingenuity and effort was expended in attempts
to make such instruction effective. All the early friars endeavoured to
master Indian languages, usually Nahuatl, though some acquired other
languages; the learned Andrés de Olmos, an early companion of
Zumárraga, was credited with ten. Music, painting, mime and morality
plays, all were freely employed. The friars even developed a specialised
architectural form to serve the needs of the great crowds demanding
attention: the *atrio*, an extensive walled courtyard, with open chapels
facing inward at intervals along the wall. The amount of instruction
needed before an Indian neophyte might be admitted to communion—
if he ever was—caused a great deal of controversy within the Orders,
and on this point the Augustinians early adopted the most liberal view:
that he might be admitted immediately after baptism if his confessor
was satisfied with his piety and his understanding of essentials. This was
the view which ultimately prevailed, in the bull *Altitudo divini consilii*
which officially settled the matter. All the Orders gave early attention
to the education of Indian children. Many missions included schools,
which not only gave religious instruction but taught Spanish and in
some cases offered training in European crafts. Most famous and most
controversial of all the missionary educational establishments was the
Franciscan college of Santiago Tlatelolco, opened in 1536 in the
presence of the viceroy; it included Latin in its curriculum, and was
deliberately designed to train a native priesthood.

The success of the friars in establishing their ascendancy over the

Indians was extraordinary. Making all due allowance for their ability
and devotion, for the prestige derived from their disinterested poverty,
this ascendancy can be explained only in terms of Indian psychology.
The Indians were accustomed to living in accordance with an intricate
and continuous ritual which governed all their communal activities,
including the all-important processes of agriculture. Ceremonial and
work were intertwined and inseparable. The Spanish conquest, with its
destruction of temples, its prohibitions of pagan dances, its forceful
proselytising, weakened and in some places destroyed the old ritual
organisation. Work—whether forced labour for an *encomendero*, or
wage labour, or even subsistence agriculture—ceased to be part of a
socio-religious ceremonial system and became a mere profane necessity.
A void was left in the spiritual and social life of the Indians, which
could be filled, though partially and often superficially, by the ritual
of the Church and the activities of church-building. The friars understood this necessity; and the numerous and sometimes very large
churches which were built all over New Spain, though they owed
their massive strength to considerations of defence, also owed their
magnificence to a desire to replace the lost splendour of the pagan
temples. Similarly, the splendour of ecclesiastical ritual—far more
elaborate than was usual in Europe—was an attempt to meet the
Indians' longing for the old ceremonial life which they had largely lost.

In New Spain, despite the friars' anxiety to exclude pagan elements,
those Indians who were in regular contact with missionaries—a
minority, of course—acquired a new theocracy, a new priesthood and
a hybrid religion. The cult of the Virgin was superimposed upon, and
confused with, the cults of earth-mother and corn-goddess. The war-
gods were forgotten, because they had proved so patently powerless
against Spanish steel. Pagan fertility rites were Christianised by the
inclusion of a preliminary Mass and a procession through the village
with the images of saints, or of local gods—for the distinction was often
little understood. Nevertheless, with all its inevitable mixtures and
dilutions, an extraordinary conquest had been achieved, no less remarkable than the success of Spanish arms. A new and living Church had
been created. Its outward signs can be seen to this day in sixteenth-
century churches, decorated by Indian craftsmen, where angels are
carved wearing feather bonnets and the Madonna is depicted with the
swarthy skin and lank black hair of an Indian.

Events in Peru pursued a different course. Peru was more distant, less accessible; its physical obstacles were more formidable, its native peoples more resistant. For reasons geographical, political and strategic, Spanish and Indian communities remained widely separate. More-over, the Peruvian enterprise began later. Whereas New Spain had been settled initially during a decade of humanist ascendancy in Spain, Peru was conquered in a decade of anti-humanist reaction. The Crown, in Cortés' time, was profoundly concerned over the spiritual welfare of new subjects. In Pizarro's day, while still concerned, it had many other preoccupations and, for a time at least, exercised less control over new settlements; nor, probably, could it have found enough men of the necessary quality to repeat the achievement of the spiritual con-quest of New Spain. By the time Peru was conquered, both Erasmian radicalism and apostolic fervour within the Spanish Church had lost much of their vigour; and the representatives of the Mexican missions were combing the Mendicant houses of Spain, and of other countries too, for suitable men. Peru, therefore, received no picked band of zealots comparable with the Twelve. The Quechua people were not effectively evangelised until the middle of the seventeenth century. Christianity, in so far as it was accepted at all, was accepted as a second and separate ritual, while the traditional worship was carried on as well, sometimes secretly and sometimes in the open. For 200 years after the conquest the ecclesiastical authorities found it necessary to send out periodical *visitadores de idolatría*, in a vain attempt to suppress pagan rites. Apart from these occasional persecutions, the Indians, so long as they paid their tributes and performed the labour required of them, were left to themselves. Peru became, and still remains, a country with a Spanish, devoutly Catholic, ruling class and an Indian, largely pagan, peasantry.

In New Spain the very success of the Mendicant missions brought its own problems. Their influence among the Indians, and the power which they derived from royal and papal support, gave them, for a time, virtually an independent authority, and made them the target of bitter local jealousy. Inevitably they became embroiled in a complex struggle for power, first with the leaders of colonial society, the *encomenderos*, then with the bishops and secular clergy. The differences with the *encomenderos* were obvious: the policy of the Orders necessarily interfered with the control of Indian labour upon which Spanish economic activity depended. It involved the preservation, indeed the extension, of Indian communal agriculture, for the support of the mission towns. The demands of the missions for Indian labour and their success in securing it, for the purpose of building churches, cloisters and new dwellings, competed directly with the demands of lay Spaniards. *Encomenderos* complained of the extravagance of the mission building programmes. They were particularly suspicious of the schools and of the proposal to train native priests. Gerónimo López, *procurador* of Mexico—an extreme example—thought it 'damnably dangerous' to teach Indians to read and write, and said so in a letter to the King. Worse still, they suspected that Mendicant influence lay behind instructions given to the second *Audiencia* in 1530 to reduce *encomienda* grants. Some friars certainly objected on principle to the *encomienda*, with its possibilities of local tyranny and ill-treatment, with its implication of a quasi-feudal lay control of Indian villages. The attitude of Las Casas— formed by his experience in the islands as a young man, and little changed thereafter—was an extreme example of this point of view. Influential though he was in Spain, however, Las Casas was not typical. Many friars, including his old mentor, the worthy but quarrelsome Betanzos, disagreed with him flatly. They recognised in the *encomienda* a uniquely effective instrument of Spanish settlement; they realised that without it there would be no settlement; they hoped that the great feudatories, so long as they received their tributes, would not interfere unduly with the internal life of the Indian villages. In the early 1540s, after more than a decade of mutual hostility, the two groups discovered a need for mutual help, and began to draw together. Mendicant churches began to receive financial help from *encomenderos*, some of whom took the initiative in asking for missions to be established. The more devout *encomenderos* admired the missionaries, as Cortés did. The more intelligent appreciated the stabilising effect of the missions, especially on the mining frontiers, and understood that prosperous Indian communities produced more tribute. They were, moreover, under an obligation to build churches and support parish clergy within the areas of their grants; if the friars would do this for them they would be saved responsibility and trouble. Most serious of all, their position and privileges were under increasing pressure from the Crown and its officials in the *audiencias*; they needed the influential and apparently disinterested support which the Orders could give. The Mendicants, for their part, seeking to allay civilian opposition to their work, saw the advantages of an alliance with leading colonists. In the crisis which arose over the promulgation of the New Laws in 1543 they sided with the *encomenderos*; in 1544 all three Orders in New Spain sent a delegation to the Crown protesting against the New Laws and urging the retention of the *encomienda* system.

An uneasy alliance with leading *encomenderos* was of little assistance to the friars in their trial of strength with the episcopacy and the secular clergy. Until the middle of the century the secular clergy played a minor part in the growth of the Church in New Spain. Reports of their ignorance, stupidity and general wickedness were written mostly by regulars and must be accepted with caution, but certainly they were few in number. After about 1555 their number increased; more livings were available for them; more Spaniards came over, and young Creoles came forward for ordination. They had the advantages of newly founded universities as centres of training in the Indies, and church councils in Mexico as local legislative bodies. The creation and administration of a parish system was the responsibility of the bishops, and as dioceses became more settled and organised the bishops sought to create new parishes in Christian areas and to place secular priests in charge of them. The friars, however, in addition to their work of evangelisation, also performed the duties of parish priests among Indians. As conditions became more settled and the number of Christians increased, the original pioneer missions became *doctrinas*—parishes in all but name; though many of them covered areas far too large for an effective parochial ministry. Fortified by papal privilege and royal favour, the friars could, if they chose, defy or largely ignore the jurisdiction of the bishops. They used their privileged position to resist by every possible means the creation of new parishes and the introduction of secular clergy, whom they considered unsuited both by character and by training to assume the spiritual direction of Indian converts.

The first specific point of difference arose over the payment of tithe. The friars had insisted from their first arrival that Indians should be exempt from tithe so that the Faith should appear to them a privilege and not a burden. The bishops pointed out that a diocesan and parochial system could not be supported without tithes. This was a matter for the *Patronato*, and decrees of 1533, 1534 and 1544 overruled the religious and ordered the Indians to pay. The friars resisted, and encouraged their Indians to resist, so that for years in many districts the tithes could not be collected. Their resistance, it was suspected, arose less from an objection to tithe in itself than from a desire to exclude the secular clergy.

Three factors in the situation for long inhibited the bishops from making a concerted move to bring the missions under their effective control: the marked favour shown to the Orders by the first two viceroys of New Spain; the fact that many of the bishops themselves were members of Mendicant Orders; and the shortage of secular clergy. Nevertheless, the Crown as patron could not tolerate indefinitely a state of acrimonious schism between the two branches of the clergy, especially in view of the decision of the Council of Trent that no cleric might have jurisdiction over laymen, with cure of souls, unless he was subject to episcopal authority. That decision was enforced without much difficulty in Peru. In New Spain it was resisted. Philip II was obliged to point out the impossibility of staffing more than a fraction of existing parishes with secular priests, and to seek from Pius V a new bull, *Exponi nobis fecisti*, which in 1567 confirmed the privileges granted by Adrian VI. Such privileges, however, could be nullified by the power of presentation under the *Patronato*. In 1574 the Crown finally came down on the side of the bishops. A *cédula* of that year gave to each bishop—subject to the approval of the viceroys as vice-patrons—complete control of the numbers of friars in his diocese, their movements and their presentation to livings. Already, three years earlier, the organisation of the Holy Office had been extended to the Indies. This formidable jurisdiction was primarily concerned with rooting out heresy and with the surveillance of the considerable numbers of Jews and *conversos* who had made their way to the Indies. It was also, however, a powerful instrument of discipline among the clergy; in particular, it greatly assisted the bishops by stiffening discipline and maintaining standards of conduct among the secular clergy. The claim of the regulars, that only they were capable of ministering to the Indians, became harder and harder to sustain. Eventually a decree of 1583 laid down that secular priests were to be presented to livings wherever possible, in preference to friars. There were then about 500 secular priests in the viceroyalty of New Spain.

The 1570s saw the end of the great age of missionary activity in New Spain. Their special privileges restricted, their sphere of action progressively confined, the friars faced a choice between retiring to their convents, settling down to routine parish duties under episcopal discipline until secular priests could be found to replace them, or going out to found new missions on the periphery of the colonial world. Their plight could not be attributed wholly to quarrels with the bishops and to royal legislation; these were the accompanying symptoms, not the underlying causes, of the decline in Mendicant activity. By 1570 the original zealots were all dead, and the excitement and fervour of the early days had largely disappeared. The letters of Mendieta, the author of the *Historia eclesiástica indiana*, and of other leading Franciscans are full of complaints, not only of persecution by the bishops, but of apathy and chaos within the provinces. Guardians were resigning and asking to return to Spain; few recruits were coming forward, and they were ill-trained and ignorant; of the friars who remained, few were willing to travel and none would take the trouble to learn native languages. Intelligent Franciscans even doubted the value of the work of the past: the writings of Sahagún are full of pessimism about the efficacy of the conversions which had been made. It was in the hope of increasing the effectiveness of proselytising, indeed, that he undertook the great study of Aztec culture, which brought upon him the displeasure of his more orthodox superiors. The marked falling-off in Mendicant building activity may also be evidence of decline; though this was affected much more by the disastrous epidemic of 1576, and by the fact that monastic building had reached the point of saturation in many parts of New Spain. The truth was that the Mendicant missions in the settled areas had outlived their primitive function. Just as the battle-scarred *conquistador* had been replaced by the official and the lawyer in the administration of the Indies, so the barefoot friar had to give way to the comfortable parish priest, once the spiritual conquest seemed secure.

In many respects the loss to New Spain was severe. The noble Franciscan plans for a native priesthood were abandoned. The college of Santiago Tlatelolco decayed for lack of support, and early in the seventeenth century its buildings fell into ruin. The idea of segregated Indian agricultural communities under religious direction lost favour, and with it was lost one more safeguard against the alienation of Indian land and the spread of Spanish-owned *latifundia*. In these and other ways the vision of the millennial Christian kingdom faded among the harsh realities of colonial life.

The decline of the Mendicants in settled New Spain was not, of course, the end of the missionary story in the Indies. The *Ordenanzas sobre descubrimientos* of 1573, which forbade armed *entradas*, placed the responsibility for the pacification of frontier areas chiefly upon the missionaries, and the missions of the regular clergy were the most characteristic institutions of the frontiers of the Indies down to relatively modern times. In the mining districts of New Galicia the development of Franciscan missions and convents—all on a relatively modest scale—went on to the end of the sixteenth century and beyond. In this great mountain area the general establishment of secular parishes was undertaken half a century later than in central New Spain. In the late seventeenth century the Franciscan missions pushed out still further, thinly strung out in a long chain from New Mexico to California. The country was wild and many of its inhabitants primitive and hostile, so that the friars themselves and the few hundreds of 'reduced' Indians living about each mission had to be protected by blockhouses and massive encircling walls. In the eighteenth century most of the frontier blockhouses were manned by small military garrisons or *presidios*.

Originally only three regular Orders had been allowed by the Crown to work in the Indies, but in the later sixteenth century, with Philip II's approval, other religious entered the mission field there. Of these the most active and successful were the Jesuits—an Order with strong Spanish connections, and a discipline, organisation and system of training more comprehensive than any of their predecessors had possessed. Of all the Orders the Jesuits were probably the most learned and intellectually the most active, and to them we owe nearly all the best accounts of the civil and natural history of the Indies in the seventeenth and eighteenth centuries. They were armed with papal privileges analogous to those conferred upon the Franciscans by the *Omnimoda*; but when they arrived in Peru in 1569, and were directed by the viceroy Toledo to take charge of *doctrinas* where no other priests were available, they demurred on the ground that their vocation was for work among the heathen. Philip II ordered them to comply, in a decree which marks an extreme extension of the prerogatives of a patron. Eventually they selected as their field the little-known forest region in the valleys of the upper Paraná and Uruguay rivers and in Guayrá, east of the Paraná. The Jesuit province of Paraguay was founded in 1607 and the first mission established among the Guaraní Indians in 1610. Forty-eight missions were started in the first forty years. Both the Guaranís and the Tapes of Guayrá took kindly to mission life, and the chief danger to the missions came not from Indian hostility but from armed parties of raiders from São Paulo seeking slaves for the Brazilian plantations. Of the first forty-eight missions, the Paulistas destroyed twenty-six, and the Jesuits had to seek the help of the govern-

ment of Peru to arm their Indians for defence. The missions displayed
great vigour and endurance. In the middle of the eighteenth century,
shortly before the expulsion of the Jesuits, there were thirty of them,
with a total Indian population of about 100,000. Their organisation
resembled that of the settlements established earlier by Vasco de
Quiroga in Michoacán. They were pastoral and agrarian communities
in which the principal assets—the cattle and the plantations—were
mission property, only houses and gardens being owned individually.
They were carefully segregated from the outside world, and the
Indians, ruled in every detail by the priests, were introduced only to such
elements of European culture as the priests thought compatible with
their primitive intelligence. Guaraní was the language both of worship
and of daily life. Just as the Franciscans, by their preaching, had helped
to spread Nahuatl as a *lingua franca* in New Spain, so the Jesuits helped
to spread Guaraní. Economically, the missions prospered. Exportable
surpluses of cotton, tobacco, hides and *yerba maté* were shipped downriver to Corrientes or Buenos Aires to be sold on account of the Order.
Socially, also, they seem to have been modestly contented, within the
narrow framework of priestly discipline. They had little power of
internal growth, however; the Indians in them were treated, kindly but
firmly, as perpetual minors; they were utterly dependent on the
leadership and initiative of the priests. When the Jesuits were expelled
from the dominions of the Spanish Crown the cloistered jungle Utopias
collapsed.

The frontier missions, from Texas to California, from Venezuela
to Chile, despite the quality of their achievements, were peripheral
phenomena. The people affected by their activities were relatively
primitive and relatively few in number. No other opportunities
occurred in the Indies comparable with those offered to the Mendicants
in New Spain and Peru; opportunities to evangelise populations of a
high level of cultural attainment, numbering many millions; opportunities seized eagerly in New Spain, tardily and half-heartedly in
Peru. The character of Christian society in these two central areas had
been decided, largely by the activities of the regular Orders, before
the end of the sixteenth century. In evangelising the Indians, the friars
had obeyed their own consciences and followed the vocation to which
their lives were dedicated; but they had acted also as the agents of the
Crown, armed with the prerogatives of the *Patronato*. Church and State
in the Indies grew up in a close and constant interrelation in which

each derived strength from the other. The friars, by the part which they played in shaping this complex system, enormously enhanced the power of the Crown and strengthened it, both spiritually and administratively, in its dealings with the restless feudatories who were its most troublesome subjects. They did more: they constantly reminded the rulers of Spain of their moral responsibility to strive for an order of society in the Indies which should be just and tolerable to conquerors and conquered alike.

CHAPTER 9

The ordering of society

THE Spanish community in the New World included no peasants and virtually no manual labourers. In all pre-industrial societies, communities established by fighting men tend to discount the social and ethical value of manual labour, and New World Spaniards displayed this prejudice in an extreme form. Their numbers included settlers— *encomenderos* and their followers, ranchers, mine-owners—a class of armed subjects of great privilege and in some instances, within a generation of settlement, of considerable wealth; a clergy numerous in relation to the total number of Spaniards, but mere drops in the ocean of the Indian population; a considerable and rapidly increasing body of officials, lawyers, notaries and miscellaneous quill-drivers; and the merchants, shopkeepers and craftsmen who provided European goods. The new Spanish economy in the Indies depended on the old Indian economy for much of its food—particularly grain, vegetables and poultry, all mainly produced by Indians—and for almost all its labour; for except in the islands and the major Spanish towns, the number of imported slaves was too small in the sixteenth century to be important. Without Indian labour the Spanish community could not exist. Most Indians, however, accustomed to a life of communal subsistence farming, would not willingly work for outside employers; and the Indians, by reason of their standing as Christian neophytes, by reason of their relatively defenceless condition, and in virtue of repeated royal declarations, had a special claim upon the Crown for protection. The agents of royal paternalism were expected to defend the personal liberty of the Indians, without denying the just claims of deserving conquerors and settlers; to ensure an adequate supply of labour for the Spanish settlements, while protecting the Indians in their possession of land, which relieved them of the necessity of working for wages; above all, to safeguard

and increase the revenue which the Crown derived from the Indies and
on which, throughout the sixteenth century, it came more and more
to depend. Clearly these objects of royal policy conflicted. The Crown
received annually hundreds of petitions from individuals or groups,
seeking favours which, in many instances, could only be granted at the
expense of someone else's interests. The answers to them could only
be yes or no; but in giving any answers the Crown, the fount of
justice, implied general guiding principles of social organisation. Dozens
of reports, complaints and recommendations, from clergy, officials
and municipal corporations, arrived with every fleet, suggesting from
every conceivable point of view what those principles ought to be. The
Crown endeavoured to select and decide, and to make its decisions
explicit, in a steady stream of legislation. Nothing in the story of the
Indies is more impressive than this immense body of Statute Law,
which in 1680 was collected, roughly collated and published as the
Recopilación de los leyes de las Indias. Many decrees concerned immediate
matters of detail, and consistency in them is hard to find. From time
to time, however, the Crown issued general legislative enactments
for the Indies as a whole. These general decrees or codes were serious
and conscientious attempts to reconcile conflicting interests. It is
possible to trace in them—though with many vacillations and incon-
sistencies—the development of conscious official policy in the ordering
of colonial society.

Almost every Spanish enactment concerning the treatment of the
Indians insisted that they were free men. There were slaves in the Indies,
of course, not only Africans imported as slaves but Indians who had
been captured in the act of rebellion and enslaved as a punishment;
but these latter were exceptions. The normal status of an Indian under
Spanish rule was held to be that of legal liberty, and it is essential to
an understanding of Spanish legislation to appreciate what 'liberty'
meant in this context. It meant freedom to move about, to change one's
place of residence at will; to own property (subject at times to certain
exceptions such as horses and fire-arms, for reasons both of security
and of social 'degree'); freedom to sue and be sued (subject to rules
defining the different value placed upon the testimony of different
classes of people) and unrestricted access to the appropriate courts;
freedom to choose an occupation, to change one's occupation and one's
employer. It certainly did not mean freedom to hold and practise false
religion, once the true religion had been revealed (though the bishops

treated Indians far more leniently in this respect than they did Spaniards, and the Holy Office in the sixteenth century had no jurisdiction over them). Nor—and this was the crucial point—did liberty mean freedom to be idle, to be left to one's own devices, to refrain from making any contribution to the well-being of society and the revenue of the Crown. The King protected his subjects, did justice among them, upheld their rights, according to their respective stations. In return, the feudatory, the *encomendero*, was expected to bear arms; the cleric to preach and pray; the peasant, the Indian villager, to work and to support the others by his work. In short, the liberty of the Indian, in the sense in which Spanish legislators used the word, meant, *mutatis mutandis*, the kind of liberty which a legally free peasant enjoyed in Spain; liberty within the context of the whole society to which he belonged, and subject to discharging the appropriate obligations towards that society, as laid down by custom.

Within a very few years of the first settlement in Hispaniola the Crown was made aware, by the settlers' complaints and petitions, of the difficulty of applying Spanish notions of social order to a people who habitually lived in 'idleness'; who lived, that is to say, by a primitive, hand-to-mouth subsistence agriculture supplemented by hunting and fishing. In these circumstances, compulsion, in order to make the natives do a reasonable amount of work in the public interest, was not thought incompatible with their free status. Compulsory labour of one kind or another was common in Europe, and those of whom it was required were not confused with slaves. The instructions given to Ovando as governor illustrate this point. On his appointment he was told to proclaim to the Indians that they were free men, and might move about the island as they wished. They were to pay tribute only as all the King's subjects did; they could be compelled to work only on royal service, either in the gold washing or on public works; no Spaniard was to rob or harm them. Within a few months of his arrival Ovando reported that the Indians, on being told they were free men, ran off into the bush and left the settlements without food or labour. His powers of compulsion, accordingly, were strengthened in a fresh series of instructions sent to him in 1503: the Indians were to be made to settle in organised villages; each village was to be placed under the protection of a Spanish patron, who was to provide a school and a priest; for convenience of employment, the villages were to be sited near the 'mines'—that is, near to gold-bearing streams; Indians could be ordered to work, when necessary, not only in 'mines' but in building and cultivation, and not only for the Crown but for private employers; periods of employment were to be moderate and wages reasonable; in addition to his employment, each Indian was to have a house and a plot of land, which he might not alienate; intermarriage between Spaniards and Indians was to be encouraged; and in all things Indians were to be treated 'as free men, for such they are'.

These instructions, needless to say, were completely at variance with Taino custom and quite beyond the power of a rudimentary colonial government to enforce. Ovando interpreted them as permission to extend the tentative *repartimiento* of Columbus's day: to divide up the entire male population of Hispaniola in lots of roughly 100 or multiples of 100, under the name and legal form (with which, as a *comendador* of Alcántara, he must have been familiar in Spain) of *encomienda*. Each group of Indians was assigned to a Spaniard who—subject to the obligations and limits set out in the instructions—might employ their services as he chose. To the *encomienda* in this crude and early form Ferdinand, as regent of Castile, gave legislative approval in a decree of 1509, which provided that on completion of any new conquest, the *adelantado* or governor might divide up the natives of the area among the conquerors.

The *encomienda* of Ovando's day infringed the legal liberty of the Indians, in that instead of laying on them a general compulsion to work (which was held to be compatible with liberty) it placed them in permanent *personal* servitude to individual Spaniards. It was open to grave objection, therefore, on grounds of principle. More obvious and immediate, however, was the human suffering which could be caused by such unlimited—because unsupervised—subjection. The Spanish settlers were themselves suffering severe hardships. Many died shortly after arrival. The energies of the survivors were concentrated primarily upon an eager search for gold; but they had also to keep alive, to find food, to build themselves habitable dwellings. Between their excited gold-fever and their fierce struggle to survive there was no room in their minds for sympathy or sense of responsibility. They could feel only a furious irritation towards impractical, unreliable savages, who had no notion of steady work, who were for ever running off into the woods, or else unpredictably dying. The Indians were indeed dying in great numbers; so their masters, to maintain the production of gold, drove and flogged the survivors in order to get the last ounce of work out of them before they died too.

These were the crimes which horrified the Dominican missionaries, fresh from Spain, who arrived in Hispaniola in 1510. Of the many causes of Indian depopulation, some—social disruption, infanticide, despair—were incomprehensible to Europeans; others—starvation and pestilence—were acts of God, the familiar, unavoidable lot of many, in Spain and everywhere. The missionaries had little to say about these. Their indignation was reserved for the horrors which they thought preventable: the flogging, the slave-driving and the institution of *encomienda* which permitted them.

The first open attack on the system by a Spaniard was made in 1511, in a series of indignant sermons preached at Santo Domingo by the Dominican Antonio de Montesinos, and followed by the refusal of communion to some *encomenderos*. The sermons created a great stir in Hispaniola, and, when reported, gave serious offence in official circles in Spain. The viceroy, Diego Colón, was told to put a stop to further public discussion of the subject by missionaries. Montesinos made a hurried journey to Spain in the hope of convincing the King's advisers of the seriousness of the situation. In this he apparently succeeded; as was customary in matters of public controversy of this sort, the Crown appointed a committee, whose members included both ecclesiastics and officials, to examine the allegations which had been made and to propose plans for reform. The result of their deliberations was the promulgation, late in 1512, of the Laws of Burgos, the first general code governing the status and treatment of the natives in the Spanish Indies. The *encomiendas* and the forced labour system in general were retained, except that the right to 'commend' Indians (which had been withheld from the viceroy in 1511) was now explicitly reserved to the Crown. Every male Indian was to be required to spend nine months of the year in Spanish employment, and one-third of the total labour force was to be employed in gold production. On the other hand, while legalising forced labour, the legislators endeavoured to limit its abuses. The code contained emphatic and detailed regulations prescribing the hours of work, the housing, clothing, feeding and instruction of Indian workers. Except in their codified detail, these two sections of the Laws contained little innovation; the first was a concession to colonial economic necessity and to the need for revenue, the second a concession to conscience and to humanitarian pressure. The principal innovation in the code concerned the concept of Indian liberty. The legislators accepted the liberty of the Indians in principle, but decided that most Indians were in practice incapable of making use of their liberty. A distinction was drawn between those who were *capaces* and those, the majority, who were not; the *capaces* being Indians who were able and willing to embrace Christianity and adopt a European manner of life, and who, within limits, could be trusted to govern themselves. These *Indios capaces* were to be 'set free'—free, presumably, from the *encomienda* system, since, being civilised, they would accept voluntarily the necessity of regular wage-earning employment. They were to be gathered in villages under their own headmen, subject to supervision by Spanish priests and officials. The *encomenderos* who lost their services were to be compensated from the tribute revenue. In order to increase the numbers of *Indios capaces*, intelligent Indians were to be selected for training as teachers, and the sons of chiefs were to be taught—among other things—Latin.

The Laws of Burgos, with their curious mixture of naïveté and cynicism, naturally proved a bitter disappointment to the Dominican pressure group, and attempts to enforce them—in so far as any attempts were made—were more disappointing still. In 1514 commissioners were sent out to revise the distribution of Indians on behalf of the Crown, but the only result of their activities was the suppression of some of the settlers' grants and the transfer of large numbers of Indians to absentee *encomenderos*, chiefly the royal secretary Conchillos and his Aragonese friends about the court, who employed colonial agents to keep their Indians at work washing for gold. The death of Ferdinand, however, the regency of Jiménez and the eclipse of Fonseca and Conchillos, brought a change of attitude at court. The mantle of Montesinos had fallen upon the formidable Las Casas, who in 1516 succeeded in enlisting the sympathy of the regent. Diego Colón was absent from his government and absorbed in litigation in Spain over his hereditary rights. Jiménez seized the opportunity to send out to Hispaniola a commission of three Jeronymite friars, to take over the government, to enforce the Laws of Burgos, in particular the clauses for the protection of Indians, and to report on the whole problem of native policy. The arrival of the triumvirate at the end of 1516 caused general alarm among the settlers, but little came of their mission. They cancelled the *encomiendas* which had been granted to absentees, but their conscientious efforts to gather 'capable' Indians in free villages were all failures; the Indians ran away as before. In their reports the Jeronymites confirmed that the colony could not survive without forced labour. Their principal positive recommendations concerned the emigration of Spanish farmers, to be encouraged by grants of seed and tools; and—with many misgivings—the import into the Indies of Negro slaves to relieve part of the burden of labour borne by the Indians. Spanish planters—many of them from the Canaries—and Negro slaves were in fact soon to form the chief elements in the Antillean population, as the Indians died out. In 1520 Diego Colón, having succeeded in some, but not all, of his claims, resumed his government. Las Casas, bitterly disappointed in Hispaniola, had gone back to Spain, and in 1521 embarked on a social experiment of his own: the settlement, upon the Venezuela coast, of a community of Spanish farmers and artisans living a common Christian life under priestly direction, supporting themselves by their own efforts without recourse to forced labour. The object of the enterprise was conversion by force of example. It failed as completely as the free villages of Hispaniola; the settlers were massacred by the local Indians. Even Las Casas' spirit was crushed, for a time, by this disaster. He took the Dominican habit and retired to a monastery in Santo Domingo, where he lived in seclusion for the next eight years.

Between the disillusion of Hispaniola and the catastrophe of Cumaná, however, Las Casas and other Dominicans about the court had achieved one important success. They had gained the ear of the young King Charles, and implanted in the King's mind a lasting disapproval of the *encomienda* system, with its feudal implications and its opportunities for abuse. This deep suspicion and dislike, shared by many of Charles's advisers, influenced official native policy throughout his reign. Among the many causes of Indian suffering, the *encomienda* was singled out— wrongly—as the principal, the most serious, grievance. The Council of the Indies were soon made aware of the unique efficacy of the *encomienda* as an instrument of settlement, but they thought of it as —at best—a temporary makeshift, to be abandoned and replaced by a purely official administration when the settlements were secure. Over and over again they made legislative or administrative attacks on the institution. The attacks were met by sulky non-compliance on the part of officials; by strident protests from *encomenderos*; by gloomy predictions of abandonment of settlements, of loss of revenue, of general chaos and disaster; sometimes by armed revolt. Alarmed by these demonstrations, the Council would retreat, restore some of the *encomenderos'* privileges, equivocate over others, sometimes even make further concessions. At the same time the royal conscience would be salved by more and more stringent rules against abuses. These repeated short-term vacillations of royal policy are confusing to the historian, and were extremely unsettling for the colonists; but the general tendency throughout the reign was consistent—to define the rights of *encomenderos* over their Indians in more and more restrictive terms. In the process the institution, though not formally abolished—government was never strong enough for that—became much modified, and lost much of its original importance. It was supplemented, however, and eventually largely replaced, by other systems of exploitation, economically more efficient but socially no less oppressive.

The *encomiendas* of New Spain, established as they were among numerous, vigorous and settled peoples, were far more remunerative and far less oppressive than those of the islands; but they were no less repugnant to Charles and his councillors. The suspicion with which Cortés was regarded at court throughout his active life arose in large measure from his action in granting *encomiendas* in New Spain without prior authority. In 1523 he was ordered to revoke his grants, and to make no more. He appealed against the order and postponed its enforcement, explaining—truthfully—that without *encomiendas* the conquest could not be held. His explanation was borne out by a series of indignant petitions from his followers. In a series of general ordinances issued from Granada in 1526, and elaborated in 1528 and 1529, the government reluctantly gave way: if it was thought necessary for their conversion, Indians might be distributed in *encomienda* 'as free persons'. They were not to be robbed, ill-treated or hired out to third parties; the tribute exacted from them must be reasonable, and their labour must be paid. Commended Indians might not be employed in mining, or made to carry burdens. Before the conquest almost all land transport had been on men's backs; but Spanish officials and clerics unaccustomed to this practice were shocked by the spectacle of trotting *tamemes*, balancing their immense shoulder-loads on tump-lines over their heads, much as modern Europeans are shocked to see coolies pulling rickshaws. They disliked the affront to human dignity; and they knew the solution. Just as rickshaws today can be towed by bicycles, so Indian porters could, in time, be replaced by mules. As for mining, it could be done by slaves, whether captured in rebellion, purchased from Indian chiefs or imported from abroad. Such arduous work was not for 'free persons'.

The exchanges of 1523–9 well illustrate the uncertainties of a colony which could not be sure, from one year to the next, of its labour supply. Wage-earning employment was, to the Indians, unfamiliar and initially unattractive. The *encomienda* was the only lawful device whereby individual settlers could exert pressure in order to secure the labour they needed for building a society of European type. The Crown might—at least in theory—abolish the whole system at any time by a stroke of the pen. Even while the *encomienda* was upheld in law, the control of labour which it conferred was too brief and impermanent to be satisfactory to the settlers. The duration of *encomienda* grants had never been clearly decided. Some of the island assignments had been for periods as brief as three years; and the determination of settlers to make the most of them while they lasted had been the cause of much heartless brutality. No time limit was set in the grants made by Cortés; they were generally assumed to be for life, and it would have been extremely difficult in practice to dispossess the recipients while they lived. *Encomenderos* repeatedly pressed for legislation making their grants hereditary and perpetual, like the *mayorazgos*, the entailed estates, which had been legalised in Spain by the Laws of Toro and which were rapidly gaining popularity among property owners there. Cortés, in his despatches, pleaded for perpetual *encomiendas*; so, curiously, did Zumárraga, who was officially protector of Indians for New Spain as well as Bishop of Mexico. Both argued plausibly that perpetuity would be a guarantee of social stability and economic development, and would encourage among *encomenderos* a sense of paternal responsibility for their Indians. These arguments were resisted, naturally, by Spanish settlers who had no *encomiendas* and hoped that their turn would come, and by the Crown, which wished to retain its control over the granting of *encomiendas* even if it could not, in practice, abolish them.

When the *audiencia* of New Spain was established in 1528 the instructions to its members included a census of Indians, to serve as the basis for a redistribution of *encomiendas*, which might then be made hereditary. The task was beyond the resources of the colonial administration; and Nuño de Guzmán and his colleagues were too busy feathering their own nests, creating *encomiendas* for themselves and prosecuting their vendetta against Cortés, even to attempt it. By the time of their dismissal and replacement by a new Bench in 1530, policy had changed again, largely as a result of Zumárraga's reports

of the brutalities which Nuño had permitted. Another royal committee, sitting at Barcelona, had reconsidered the whole question of
encomiendas and had pronounced against them. The second *audiencia*,
accordingly, was instructed in 1530—though the instruction was not
made public—to arrange for the resumption of *encomiendas* by the
Crown, beginning with new grants recently made by Nuño de
Guzmán, with a view to the gradual elimination of the institution. Crown
Indians, and ultimately all Indians, were to be placed in the administrative care of district officers, *corregidores*—the first mention, in legislation
on native affairs, of this important official. Slave-raiding in the frontier
districts, and the deliberate provocation of rebellion in order to justify
enslavement, were to be stopped.

The new *oidores* made tentative moves to carry out their instructions,
which naturally provoked opposition and protest; so, like most colonial
officials, they came eventually to the conclusion that the task was hopeless, and the project was again dropped. The instructions issued to
Antonio de Mendoza, who went out to New Spain in 1535 as the
first viceroy, marked a return of the *encomienda* to royal favour; and
general legislation of that year made a further important concession:
encomiendas might, on the death of their holders, be inherited for a
second life, provided that the heir discharged, or paid somebody else
to discharge, the obligations of military service. Mendoza himself was
expressly empowered to commend Indians. This change of policy
significantly coincided with the foundation of Lima and the opening of
another rich and populous continental area to Spanish exploitation.
The concessions, presumably, were made in order to attract more
settlers to the Indies. *Encomiendas* spread through the populous areas of
Peru as quickly as they had done in New Spain, and the institution
seemed to its beneficiaries to be accepted at last as a permanent feature
of their society.

That the Emperor would see matters in this light was in the highest
degree unlikely. Hapsburg persistence, Hapsburg tenacity of prerogative and principle, was certain in time to revert to standard traditional
policy. The events of the early 1540s showed how far creole society
had already diverged from the society of metropolitan Spain. The
leading colonists were as blind to the motive forces of Spanish politics,
as Spanish statesmen were to the realities of colonial life. The colonial
code of 1542, known as the New Laws of the Indies, with its drastic
curtailment of settlers' privileges, both appalled and astonished those

against whom it was directed, for there had been, in the Indies, no warning of a change of policy. In Spain, however, the indications of change had been accumulating for at least five years. Vitoria, lecturing at Salamanca, had been subjecting the Spanish title to the Indies to destructive analysis. The Pope, Paul III, was persuaded by Spanish Dominican missionaries in 1537 to issue a series of bulls concerning the Indies. Of these, *Veritas ipsa* was a severe condemnation of Indian slavery; *Sublimis Deus* condemned as heretical the opinion that the Indians were irrational and incapable of receiving the Faith. The Emperor, it is true, took exception on grounds of *Patronato* to the promulgation of these bulls in the Indies, but he did not disavow the principles which they proclaimed, and Las Casas and his friends distributed hundreds of copies before the royal prohibition could take effect. Las Casas himself—always at the centre of controversy, and with a reputation enormously enhanced by a successful mission in lowland Guatemala—returned to Spain in 1539, and was one of the expert witnesses regularly consulted during the next three years by the Council which sat at Valladolid to draft the new code. Finally, and perhaps most important, reports of the violence and anarchy which followed the conquest of Peru were received by the Emperor with profound disquiet, and convinced him of the need for comprehensive legislation and drastic action to enforce royal authority.

The New Laws formed a comprehensive code—the first complete and adequate code—for the governance of all the provinces of the Indies. They were not, in general, revolutionary; they represented the traditional policy of the Crown. Most of their provisions duly came into force and were eventually included in the *Recopilación de Leyes*. Of the fifty-four articles of the code, twenty-three concerned native policy, and of these only four were seriously contentious: the four which dealt with *encomiendas* and slavery. After many years of shifts and equivocations the battle between Crown and settlers on these crucial issues was now to be fought in earnest. Articles 31 and 35 in effect abolished the *encomienda*. Some grants were to be terminated immediately, in particular those held by officials, those held by corporate bodies, such as town councils or monasteries, and those of individuals who had taken part in the recent disturbances in Peru. This last clause, if strictly interpreted, would have deprived almost every *encomendero* in Peru. All other *encomiendas* were to run to the death of their holders, and then to escheat to the Crown. Similarly, Indian slavery was to disappear within a generation. Indian women and children held as slaves were to be liberated at once. Male slaves whose slave status arose from lawful cause (such as capture in rebellion) were to remain in slavery, but all others were to be released, and the burden of proof was to rest on the owner. No Indians were to be enslaved for any reason in future.

The time was singularly inopportune for the promulgation of such a code. In New Spain the *encomienda* system had recently been put to a severe test as an organisation for defence. The Mixton rebellion of 1540-1, which originated among the half-subdued tribes of New Galicia, had spread to New Spain and seriously threatened the Spanish government there. The *encomenderos* of both kingdoms had been called out with their men, under the personal command of the viceroy. The rebellion had been put down by difficult mountain campaigns, in which a number of Spaniards, including the famous Alvarado, had been killed. The *encomenderos* of New Spain were in no mood to be deprived of the rewards of courage and loyalty. In Peru the distribution of *encomiendas* among the conquerors was barely completed. The *encomenderos* had lately been more concerned with cutting one another's throats than in fighting the Indians, but Manco Inca was still at large. Fresh fighting, whether between Spanish factions or against Indian risings, might break out at any time. Men slept with their weapons within reach, and might use them against a government which sought to take away their livelihood.

The Council of the Indies knew from experience that colonial officials, when ordered to enforce unpopular enactments, tended to temporise, to find excuses for evasion. To ensure enforcement on this critical occasion, they sent out, in 1544, special commissioners to each of the major centres of colonial government, with full powers to remove recalcitrant or venal officials. In New Spain the *visitador*, Tello de Sandoval, had the good sense to consult Mendoza, and was quickly convinced of the dangers of the situation. He agreed to postpone enforcement pending investigation, and the answers to his inquiries, from all classes of Spaniards, including the missionary clergy, showed a remarkable unanimity. The submission of the Dominicans, in particular, gives a vivid impression of the fears of the Spanish community, numbering only a few thousand, hemmed in by Indians who had largely lost their fear of European weapons, who were crowding into the Spanish settlements, and who effectively controlled the greater part of the colony's food supply. All the petitioners agreed that without *encomiendas* the settlers would desert or starve. In Peru events pursued a very different course. No settled royal administration existed there. The first viceroy was appointed, and the *audiencia* of Lima created, at this time, with express orders to enforce the New Laws. Blasco Núñez' blind adherence to his instructions, as we have seen, provoked the armed insurrection of Gonzalo Pizarro, in which the viceroy himself was killed. This was the first major overt rebellion among New World Spaniards; it could be met in only one way: ruthless suppression, and the execution of the leaders. The skill of Pedro de la Gasca and the fears and factions of the rebels made this possible in 1548. Meanwhile, the existence of rebellion had stiffened the determination of the Crown to make its will effective. Instead of withdrawing its unpopular decrees in the face of resistance, as it had done on former occasions, the Council of the Indies looked for the minimum concessions which would make the New Laws enforceable without sacrificing any major principle. The results were embodied in a series of decrees between 1545 and 1549. The laws on Indian slavery were to stand, and were, within the next few years, substantially enforced, at least in New Spain and Guatemala. *Encomiendas*, on the other hand, were authorised once more, but with a vital difference: *encomenderos* were to be entitled only to the tributes of their Indians, tributes which at that time usually took the form of traditionally fixed amounts of maize, poultry, cotton cloth or *cacao*. They were forbidden to demand any form of labour or to claim any jurisdiction. In this way the central principles of the personal liberty of the Indians, and the direct control of the Crown over them, were preserved, while at the same time the 'old conquerors' and their descendants were assured of an income in consideration of their past exertions and their present liability to military service. This arrangement, with minor modifications, survived for many years. Perpetual inheritance, though often asked, was steadily refused. Only in rare and special instances were exceptions made. Two of Montezuma's daughters received Indian towns in perpetual *encomienda*; but the Cortés *marquesado* was the only perpetual hereditary *encomienda* ever granted to a Spaniard in the Indies.

Concessions were made: in New Spain a third 'life' was authorised in 1555, and a fourth in 1607. In Peru two lives remained the rule until 1629, when inheritance for a third was permitted in return for a money payment. *Encomiendas* were sometimes reassigned, especially in Peru, but more commonly they escheated, to be administered by *corregidores* on behalf of the Crown. In the 1550s and 1560s, the viceregal governments made determined efforts, through detailed *visitas* conducted by *audiencia* judges, to assess the tributes payable by all Indian towns, whether held by the Crown or by *encomenderos*. Miscellaneous and variable contributions in kind were commuted into fixed annual amounts of maize or money, known to the Indians. *Encomenderos* thus became a class of pensioners receiving, in theory, a fixed income. In fact, as a result of inflation and the decline of Indian numbers, their incomes steadily dwindled. From Philip IV's time, moreover, they became liable to a heavy, though intermittent, tax, the *media anata*. By the end of the sixteenth century the *encomienda* had ceased to be a major factor in the economy of the Indies. By the end of the seventeenth it had almost disappeared.

In its insistence on the personal liberty of the Indians the Crown had won a notable victory. As we have seen, however, liberty did not mean freedom to be idle. Colonies could not survive without labour, and the problem remained of inducing Indians to work for wages. During the dispute over the New Laws two events occurred which made this problem more acute than ever: the discovery of the silver veins of Potosí and Zacatecas greatly increased the demand for labour, and the disastrous epidemic of 1545 (in New Spain especially) greatly reduced the supply. One by one the Crown had prohibited the familiar methods of private compulsion in securing labour; it could not now avoid the use of public compulsion. A decree of 1549 required all unemployed Indians, whether tributary to the Crown or to *encomenderos*, to offer themselves for hire in the public places of their districts, 'without molestation or pressure except such as should be necessary to make them work'. They were to work for such employers as they chose, for a length of time agreed upon by free contract, and were to be paid wages according to a scale fixed by the viceroy or local governor. As might be expected, this naïve decree had little immediate effect, and certainly did not attract labour to the mines. A more specific form of compulsory recruitment was needed; and one was found in the system known in Peru (where it was inherited from the Incas) as *mita*, in New Spain as *repartimiento*. This was in essence a public *corvee*. It was not new; it had long been used in a casual and *ad hoc* fashion to recruit labour from the Crown *pueblos* for public works; but in the later sixteenth century it was made permanent, regular and general. Every settled Indian town or village, through its headmen, was required to send a fixed proportion of its male population out to work, for a fixed number of weeks, in rotation throughout the year. The labourers so recruited were allocated, by a local magistrate known as the *juez repartidor*, to works for which *repartimiento* labour had been authorised. Public works—roads, bridges, public buildings—together with churches, convents and hospitals, usually had first claim; but silver-mining counted as a public purpose for *repartimiento* labour, at the discretion of the colonial authorities, and *repartimientos* might also be authorised for large-scale manufactures, such as cloth and sugar, for estate labour and for porterage. Wages were payable, at rates fixed by the colonial authorities; as might be expected, the rates were low. Employers in favoured industries thus gained a cheap and regular but constantly changing labour force; Indians were compelled, for a part of every year, to do uncongenial work in strange surroundings, often far from home; and the villages lost a proportion of the men available for communal farming, so that those left at home had to work harder in order to live and to meet the continuing, inexorable demand for tribute.

The use of *repartimiento* labour was a privilege for which an express administrative order was in theory required in each instance. Such orders could be granted by viceroys, governing *audiencias*, or in New Spain by the *Juzgado general de Indios*, a special court of summary jurisdiction set up, after the second great epidemic of 1576, to deal with Indian affairs. The liability of villages to provide labour was assessed by the same authorities. The assessments, infrequently revised, tended to grow into bodies of local custom as complex as those which in former times had governed labour dues in the villages of Europe. In 1609, however, the Council of the Indies made a determined attempt to codify the rules, and the legislation of that year, with minor modifications, remained in force for some 200 years. The quota of men required from each village at any one time was limited to one-seventh of the male population; or for work in the mines, 4 per cent. Casual gang labour was unsuitable for the skilled and semi-skilled work of mining, and mine-owners were prepared to pay relatively high wages to skilled Indian employees. For pick-and-shovel work they preferred to employ Negro slaves, when they could get them. The Crown encouraged this, partly to lighten the burden of forced labour on the Indians, and partly to increase the revenue from the import duty on slaves. *Repartimiento* gangs were certainly used in mining—the Potosí mines had a particularly evil reputation as devourers of *mitayos*—but only for lack of slaves or free wage-earners. *Repartimiento* labour was prohibited, by the 1609 code, in certain arduous or unhealthy occupations: in sugar-mills, in textile workshops, in pearl-fishing and in the operation of hand pumps for draining mine shafts. These, presumably, were jobs for slaves or convicts; though in the seventeenth century the hand pump for draining mines was often replaced by the animal-powered whim or *malacate*. The employment of Indians as porters, save in certain special circumstances, was also forbidden. By this time, mules were plentiful enough to make such a rule reasonable, though not necessarily enforceable; in practice porters continued to carry burdens; in some places they still do. Spanish traders often complained that their Indian competitors, unfettered by sentimental prejudice, continued to employ porters and gained an unfair advantage by so doing, but official opinion remained adamant against using free men as beasts of burden. Agriculture and cattle-herding, on the other hand, were considered highly suitable occupations for Indians. Spanish-owned estates in the later sixteenth century relied heavily on *repartimiento* labour. Viceroys were given a wide discretion to vary the legal quotas, and naturally the heaviest demands came at the periods of the farming year when labour was most needed on the Indians' own land.

The obligation to provide labour rested not on the individual Indian but on the *pueblo*, the town or village to which he belonged. It must be remembered that forced labour was not only an economic convenience for the Spanish settlers; it was regarded also as part of a civilising, Hispanicising, process. For Spaniards, civilised life meant urban life; and so the inculcation of regular habits of work was associated in the official mind with the creation of a properly organised urban polity for the Indians. Many Indians, of course, already lived in concentrated settlements before the conquest. In these settlements the object of colonial policy was to make urban government conform as closely as possible to the pattern familiar in Spanish towns; to replace the traditional authority of headmen or *caciques*—who were often custodians of sacred ritual rather than political leaders—by town councils of Spanish type; to induce the councils to elect magistrates and constables, who should be responsible to the local Spanish governors for the collection of tribute, the organisation of labour and the maintenance of the peace. For those Indians—in some areas the great majority—who lived scattered among their fields, a more radical policy was devised for 'congregating' them in towns or villages planned on Spanish lines from the beginning. The Mendicant friars, as we have seen, early adopted this policy in order to facilitate their missionary work. In the second half of the sixteenth century, as Mendicant influence in the settled areas declined, the task of congregating the Indians was taken over by the civil authorities; though, of course, the building of a church and the provision of a priest were essential features of any new settlement. In Peru an extensive resettlement of scattered Indians was carried out by the viceroy Francisco de Toledo in the 1570s. The most ambitious 'congregation' was that undertaken in New Spain, after repeated prodding from Madrid, by Luis de Velasco II and the Conde de Monterey at the end of the sixteenth century and the beginning of the seventeenth. This operation covered the whole of settled New Spain and New Galicia. Apart from considerations of general policy, the depopulation of the viceroyalty by successive epidemics had made a concentration of the surviving population urgently necessary. Usually existing townships formed the nuclei of congregations, and received the people displaced from nearby hamlets; but some entirely new villages took root and are thriving communities today— evidence of the care with which their sites were selected. Some were deliberately planted—for obvious reasons—in the neighbourhood of mining settlements. The resettlement undoubtedly involved an immense upheaval in the life of the Indians concerned. The commissioners' instructions forbade them to use force in moving people into the new settlements; but most Indians, imbued with conservative traditions and an instinctive love of the soil, would not have moved willingly. The only contemporary general account of the proceedings is that contained in Torquemada's *Monarquía Indiana*. Torquemada was a friar, and a hostile witness. His evidence, like that of Las Casas in an earlier generation, must be treated with caution; but he was probably not far from the truth when he asserted that Indians were compelled to move to new homes chiefly by the deliberate destruction of their old ones.

The supervision of Indian communities, old and new, with the task of encouraging their members to adopt Spanish habits, techniques and forms of government, was entrusted to a staff of district officers known as *corregidores*. In the second half of the sixteenth century these officials took over the social responsibilities—not, of course, the military responsibilities—which in earlier years had been left to *encomenderos*.

Spanish legislators tended to assume, somewhat uncritically, that paid officials would always be more conscientious and more effective agents of the royal will than private feudatories. In the local government of the Indies this assumption was not always valid. There were two quite distinct kinds of *corregidor*. The *corregidor* of a Spanish town—in Spain or in the Indies—was the representative there of royal authority, a magistrate and a professional administrator of considerable dignity and power. Usually he was a trained lawyer. *Corregidores de Indios*, on the other hand, were amateurs selected usually from among settlers who had no *encomienda* or landed estates, and therefore no ready source of income. They had no particular training for their duties. They were appointed for short periods, usually two or three years, and were paid a small salary charged upon the local tributes. Inevitably they tended to regard their office as a personal perquisite, and to make the most of it while it lasted. The *corregimiento* was one of the least efficient and least reliable institutions of colonial government. Never adequately supervised, it could be made the excuse for a petty local tyranny more burdensome than the *encomienda* had ever been. As Torquemada sourly explained, the *corregidor* robbed in order to return rich to Spain; the *cacique* robbed to keep the *corregidor* quiet.

The whole system of native administration invited abuse. Our knowledge of its operation in New Spain comes mainly from the records of the *Juzgado general de Indios*, the vigorous summary court before which most of the disputes which arose were heard. The commonest complaints were of labour demands in excess of those permitted by law; of *corregidores* who extorted labour and tribute for their own private use; of headmen who used their powers of coercion to extort bribes or pay off grudges; of employers who withheld wages, seized the possessions of Indians to prevent them from running away, or kept them beyond the authorised time; of trespass by Spanish flocks and herds on Indian fields; of occasional physical ill-treatment. The *Juzgado* was remarkable, by seventeenth-century standards, for its accessibility to Indian petitioners and for the despatch with which it handled their complaints; but thousands of complaints never reached it. In Peru there was no *Juzgado*, and petitions had to go through the complicated and dilatory procedure of the *audiencias*. Throughout the Indies, legislation intended to soften the impact of forced labour and to protect recognised Indian interests lost effectiveness and force through lack of adequate local supervision.

The social abuses and the economic wastefulness of the forced labour system were well known to responsible officials and to the Council of the Indies. They were tolerated partly because there was no obvious alternative, partly because the *repartimiento* was regarded, as the old *encomienda* had been, as a temporary makeshift, until Indian society could be reshaped in a European mould. For the individual Indian the only way of escape from the alternating compulsions of *repartimiento* and village community was to accept the implications of a money economy, move to a Spanish settlement, put on European clothes and become a wage-earner, or, if his resources and skill allowed, a crafts-man or small capitalist. This, of course, was what Spanish legislators considered to be the ultimate and sensible outcome.

CHAPTER 10

The enforcement of law

THE Spanish Crown in the sixteenth and seventeenth centuries enacted a great body of statute law governing the relations between conquerors and conquered in the Indies, and asserting royal authority over both. Most of this legislation was carefully considered and benevolent in intention. Some enactments were models of enlightenment for their time. That they were imperfectly enforced is true, and not surprising. Most sixteenth- and seventeenth-century legislation was imperfectly enforced. It would be wrong, however, to dismiss the Laws of the Indies as mere exhortations. They were intended to be obeyed. An elaborate and very expensive governmental machine was built up to ensure that they were obeyed in fact. The effectiveness of this organisation has now to be considered.

One of the most striking characteristics of Spanish colonial government in this period was its heavy reliance upon judicial devices and procedures, and on legally trained officials. Spain itself set the example in this respect. The gradual development of a centralised legal system had been one of the most important factors in the unification of Spain. The law of medieval Spain had been derived partly from the ancient Gothic laws—the *Fuero Juzgo*—partly from the accretion of customary law, partly from many jealously guarded *fueros* ranging from the model *Fuero Real* of Alfonso the Wise down to the various local *fueros* granting special liberties to particular places and particular classes of people. From the thirteenth century, Civil Law, with its severe practice and authoritarian principles, and Canon Law, its ecclesiastical counterpart, were superimposed more and more upon the mass of native law. The famous code known as the *Siete Partidas* (1256–65) bore the strong stamp of the Civil Law, though it drew largely also upon the native *fueros*. The codes of the succeeding centuries showed the Civil Law

V *A sugar-mill in sixteenth-century Hispaniola*
 (*from an engraving by* T. de Bry *in* Peregrina in America)

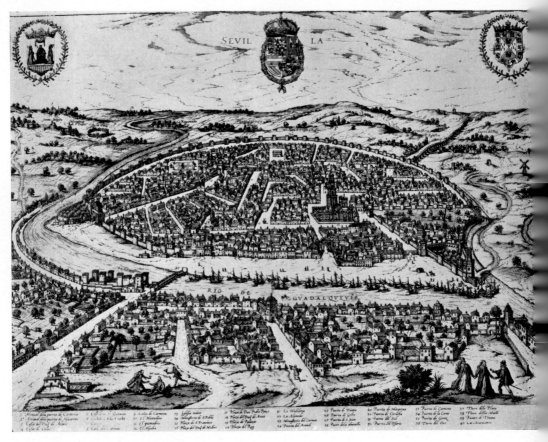

VI *A view of Seville in the sixteenth century*
(*from* G. *Braun,* Civitates orbis terrarum)

gaining ground steadily, though not unopposed. The Laws of Toro of 1505 are usually considered to mark the triumph of Civil Law in Spain. The permanence of its triumph, especially in matters of procedure and of legal theory, was assured by the great and growing influence of the law schools of the Spanish universities, which turned out year by year a class of professional lawyers thoroughly grounded in Roman jurisprudence. It was characteristic of Spanish legal development, however, that the earlier codes, particularly the *Siete Partidas*, remained in force, being amended but not superseded by the later compilations. Privileged classes and municipalities, moreover, clung tenaciously to their ancient *fueros* in the teeth of the growing autocracy of the sixteenth century. Similarly in the Indies: not only were special liberties granted to particular groups—the Columbus and Cortés families, municipalities, merchant gilds, the natives of Tlaxcala and so forth; Indian custom in general, where not clearly repugnant to Christianity or to Spanish legislation, was respected by Spanish courts.

The sixteenth century added to the existing tangle of law in Spain a long series of royal decrees (*cédulas*), the whole being collected and published in 1567 as the *Nueva Recopilación de Leyes de España*. This collection went through nine editions, down to 1774. A similar but separate process affected the Indies; though the corresponding collection of decrees relating to the Indies—the *Recopilación de Leyes de Indias* —was not published until 1681. The *recopilaciones* were designed as systematic summaries of statute law, but their contents were very miscellaneous, and the process of compilation did not always remove contradictions. They contained not only decrees of general application but also many rulings *ad hoc*, applying to particular places and circumstances, and dealing in some instances with quite trivial matters. They supplemented, but did not supersede, the mixture of *fueros*, Civil Law rules and local custom which the courts enforced. Throughout the sixteenth and seventeenth centuries, therefore, the empire was governed not by one but by several codes of law, all to some extent valid, and often conflicting one with another.

The interpretation of these various codes in Spain lay in the hands of a numerous and powerful judiciary, at whose head stood the King. Spain carried over from the age of feudalism into the age of sovereignty the notion of jurisdiction as the essential function of authority. Though he legislated continually, the King in the sixteenth century was still regarded primarily as a judge, the chief of judges. Even in the New

World, where everything was new and strange, this traditional attitude persisted. The principal task of government was considered to be that of adjudicating between competing interests, rather than that of deliberately planning and constructing a new society. 'The most serious obligation which Your Majesty owns in the government of the new lands of the Indies'—so runs a sentence often repeated in the *consultas* of the Council of the Indies—'is to provide an abundance of justice.' Administration, in the sense of the formulation of policy, was incidental to jurisdiction. The King's authority was most directly and characteristically represented by the high courts of justice and in the government of his dominions the school-trained lawyer was his most trusted servant.

The school-trained lawyer was an appropriate and willing agent of centralised authoritarian government. Though not always devoid of adventurous qualities, he had no excessive family pride, and as a rule no great ambition for military glory. His training gave him a deep respect for authority and for legal forms, and a habit of careful attention to detail, while it discouraged tendencies towards rash or un-authorised action. A judge, representing the jurisdiction of the monarch, could command the respect of swordsmen who would resent authority in the hands of one of their own class. The chancelleries of Valladolid, Ciudad-Real (later Granada) and Galicia, courts of appeal representing royal jurisdiction in their respective localities, had rendered important service in the unification of Spain under the Catholic monarchs. The conquest of the Indies represented to the legal mind an immense expansion of the area requiring unification, and offered, besides, special problems of its own. A connecting link was needed between a paternal royal authority and a subject people of alien culture, who were regarded as the direct subjects of the Crown and who were unprotected by capitulations such as those made with the Moors of Granada in 1492. The link must be sufficiently strong to resist the centrifugal tendencies of an avaricious and disorderly colonial society. The task of forging the link was naturally entrusted to benches of professional judges.

The Council of the Indies, which emerged between 1511 and 1519 as a standing committee of the Council of Castile, and which was constituted as a separate organ of government in 1524, was a predominantly legal body. The composition of the Council in its early days was variable, as was its place of residence—it followed the peregrinations of the Court; but the records of the first ten years show the payment of salaries to a president, four or five councillors, a secretary, a *fiscal*, a *relator* and a porter. In the first year for which a complete list is available the president was a prelate and four of the five councillors were professional lawyers. The number of councillors was increased to nine under Philip II, to twelve under his successor, and in the seventeenth century often included noblemen and royal favourites without legal qualifications; but lawyers always predominated. Many of them were drawn from among the judges of the chancelleries of Valladolid and Granada, from the *alcaldes de corte*, or from the *audiencias* of the Indies. Juan de Solórzano, the most distinguished of Spanish colonial jurists, the author of *Política Indiana*, had been an *oidor* at Lima before becoming a councillor of the Indies. The Council combined, in the manner characteristic of Spanish institutions, the functions of a supreme court of appeal in important cases with those of an advisory council and a directive bureau for the supervision of colonial affairs. As in law the Indies formed separate realms, linked with the kingdoms of Spain only through the person of the monarch of Castile, so the Council of the Indies was in most respects a separate organ of government. To this general rule there were only two important exceptions: the activities of the Inquisition in the Indies, after its introduction in 1570, were directed by the *Suprema*, the supreme council of the Inquisition, and the Council of the Indies had no control over them; and after the accession of Philip II, the administration of all royal revenue and expenditure, including the Indies revenue, was centralised in the Council of Finance. Before spending money in the Indies, therefore, the Council had to secure the agreement of the Council of Finance—a fruitful cause of dispute and delay, but obviously a useful arrangement for an autocratic and impecunious King. In every other respect, the Council was completely independent of the Council of Castile and the other royal councils and responsible only to the King.

The organisation and procedure of the Council in its early years were informal and flexible; the first formal ordinances for its guidance were issued in 1542, in the first nine chapters of the New Laws. In Philip II's reign, the growing importance of the Indies as a source of revenue brought the activities of the Council under closer royal scrutiny. A more comprehensive and detailed code of rules was promulgated in 1571, as a result of an inquiry conducted by Juan de Ovando of the Supreme Council of the Inquisition. Ovando

subsequently became president, and during his term of office brought
about a marked improvement in organisation and general efficiency,
especially in the administrative, as distinct from the judicial side of the
Council's work; for whereas the Council as a whole sat to hear appeals,
administrative problems—finance, native policy, naval defence and
so forth—were increasingly entrusted to smaller and more specialised
committees. The important responsibility of advising the King on
patronage and promotions in the Indies was confined, from 1571 until
Philip II's death, to the president alone, and was discharged by Ovando
and his immediate successors with conscientious care.

The Council of the Indies in Ovando's time was, by sixteenth-
century standards, a well-informed body. Ovando himself was
probably largely responsible for this. In his *visita* in 1569–70 he had
criticised the Council sharply for its ignorance of conditions in America,
and it was after his appointment as president that orders over the
King's signature began to go out to *audiencias* and officials demanding
detailed information on the history, geography, flora, fauna and population of all the settlements of the Indies. In 1571 the Council's permanent staff was increased by the appointment of a *cronista mayor*, whose
duty was to compile, from the answers to the King's questionnaires, a
General Description of the Indies. This great work was never completed; but the *relaciones* which came into the Council in the 1570s
and 1580s, many of them accompanied by maps and drawings, formed
—and for historians still form—a rich and comprehensive source of
information. They were turned to good account, not only by the
Council but also in the composition of specialised works such as the
Historia general of Antonio de Herrera, who was appointed *cronista* in
1596.

Ovando's reforms, together with the gradual establishment of
Madrid as a permanent administrative capital, enabled the Council of
the Indies, in common with the other royal councils, to develop an
adequate secretarial organisation and a comprehensive system of
record-keeping. Its archives survive today as impressive evidence of
its slow, thorough, bureaucratic efficiency. The Council collected
information voraciously, attended with judicial patience to all represen-
tations made to it, deliberated interminably, and advised the King with
conscientious care. Its *consultas* were, for the most part, the kind of
documents which a bench of experienced professional judges might
be expected to produce: lucid, balanced, closely reasoned judgements.

They were based on evidence and on precedent and were necessarily conservative. They rarely initiated action, or even proposed a positive and coherent policy. Ideas on constructive policy usually originated in the Indies. Viceroys and *audiencias* made proposals for action and sought, through the Council, royal authority for their proposals. The Council was not a ministry; it was a deliberating, not a deciding or commanding body. Its members were collectively responsible for giving advice to the King; usually they gave, according to their lights, sound advice; the King decided; and the Council transmitted his decision to the authorities in the Indies in the form of of *cédulas* or other formal orders. This, at least, was the theory; under a king such as Philip II, who had the industry to read all the papers, the intelligence to grasp the points at issue, and the will-power to make decisions, the system worked well. It applied, it is true, a restraining discipline rather than an inspiring leadership; a brake on rash violence, rather than a spur to creative action. In an empire full of violent conflicting interests restraint was sound policy; sixteenth-century Spaniards needed no spur. After Philip's death, however, restraint became frustration. His two successors had less intelligence and much less industry than he; in their reigns the conciliar system meant endless debate, procrastination, suspended judgement. Under the cretinous Charles II decision on any major matter became almost impossible. A well-organised bureaucratic machine will grind on for years, even under a weak and vacillating command; but, in time, lack of decision in policy becomes reflected in lack of efficiency in routine. The volume of papers passing through the Council increased year by year, and so did the staff which dealt with it. Under Philip II the King's own detailed and industrious supervision had imposed reasonable limits on this development, but under the flabby rule of his successors the growth of staff became much more rapid than the growth of business. The office of secretary was divided into two, one for each viceroyalty, in 1604. Ornamental offices made their appearance, such as that of grand chancellor, revived in 1624 as a hereditary honour for Olivares. Both the secretariat proper and the *contaduría*, the accounts section, became swollen by the addition of supernumerary officials. Between the death of Philip II and that of Philip IV the staff of the Council trebled in numbers. In the same period the length of time taken to answer a colonial governor's request for an instruction or a ruling approximately doubled.

'Inasmuch as the Kingdoms of Castile and of the Indies are under one Crown, the laws and the manner of government of the one should conform as nearly as possible to those of the other. Our royal Council, in establishing laws and institutions of government in the Indies, must ensure that those Kingdoms are administered according to the same form and order as Castile and León, in so far as the differences of the lands and peoples will allow.' This declaration, published in the *Recopilación de Leyes*, represented, at least from the accession of Philip II, the consistent policy of the Hapsburg monarchy in the New World. It is not surprising, therefore, to find many of the peculiarities of the Council of the Indies reproduced in those most characteristic colonial institutions, the *audiencias*. Ten *audiencias* were created in the sixteenth century, representing royal jurisdiction in the more important and populous provinces. They resembled the Council, and differed from the chancelleries of Valladolid and Granada, in that they were at once courts of appeal and cabinet councils, entrusted with many political and administrative powers. Each was a supreme appellate tribunal, under the Council, within its area; but in practice the degrees of independence enjoyed by the *audiencias*, and their combinations of judicial, administrative, military and financial power varied greatly. The two 'viceregal' *audiencias* of Mexico and Lima (after 1535 and 1543 respectively) in theory exercised only judicial authority, administrative and military power being in each kingdom in the hands of the viceroy, as governor and captain-general. The viceroy decided, in cases of dispute, whether a particular question was judicial or administrative. In making important political or administrative decisions, however, the viceroy was required to consult the *audiencia*; and during an interregnum, or prolonged absence of the viceroy, the *audiencia* temporarily exercised all his powers. At all times the *audiencia* might hear appeals against the viceroy's actions, and might draw up corporate complaints against his administration. The viceroy, on the other hand, might complain to the Crown against the conduct of any of the *audiencia* judges; an arrangement which fostered the mutual tale-bearing characteristic of the official correspondence of the Indies.

In New Spain and in Peru the area of the appellate jurisdiction of the *audiencia* coincided with the area directly administered by the viceroy. This arrangement was sometimes reproduced on a smaller scale elsewhere; in Guatemala, for instance, the appellate jurisdiction of the *audiencia* coincided with the administrative command of the captain-general. In other areas the division of duties was more complicated. The jurisdiction of an *audiencia* might cover a number of administrative provinces; in the central province the lawyer-president would also serve as governor, perhaps also as captain-general, while each of the outlying provinces had its own governor. This was the arrangement for many years in the *audiencias* of Santo Domingo and New Granada (Colombia). In Charcas (Bolivia) the president was governor throughout his jurisdiction, but the captaincy-general was in the hands of the viceroy of Peru. In New Galicia the arrangements, from 1574 onwards, were even more involved. The President was governor, but not captain-general, of New Galicia proper; the jurisdiction of the *audiencia* covered also New Biscay, New León and (later) New Mexico; but each of these provinces had a governor responsible —somewhat loosely—to the viceroy, who was captain-general of the whole area. The boundaries of jurisdictions, governments and commands were the subjects of constant disputes and petitions, and were frequently altered by royal decree.

Jurisdiction, even where not directly associated with administrative power, covered a very wide range of activity. All colonial *audiencias* exercised a general supervision over the conduct of inferior magistrates within their areas of jurisdiction. They were empowered to review the routine inquiries (*residencias*) into the records of retiring *corregidores* and other judges, which the law required. They might send out special commissioners (*jueces pesquisidores*) to make such additional investigations as they thought necessary. They possessed, in addition to their appellate powers, first-instance jurisdiction in cases concerning royal prerogative, patronage and revenue, and might take the initiative in investigating any usurpation of royal authority. They were responsible for enforcing the legal limits of other jurisdictions, in particular for the issue of writs of *recurso de fuerza* in restraint of illegal extensions of ecclesiastical jurisdiction. All legal fees, the fees charged by ecclesiastics for the administration of the various sacraments, the tributes paid by the Indians, were all supposed to be assessed by the *audiencias*, and the assessments published and enforced. Each *audiencia* was to sit regularly in committee (*acuerdo*) to discuss the administration of its area and to make recommendations; and in *acuerdo de hacienda*, jointly with the local treasury officials, to discuss financial questions. Finally, the supervision of Indian affairs—where not entrusted to special courts such as the *Juzgado general de Indios*—was laid under the especial care of the *audiencias*.

As might be expected, the organisation and conduct of the colonial high courts was the subject of constant legislation. Several attempts were made in the sixteenth century to codify the long series of decrees, the most important being the Ordinances of the *Audiencias* issued at Monzón in 1563. This comprehensive code was first drawn up for the guidance of the *audiencia* of Quito, founded in that year, but it was extended by degrees to all the *audiencias* except those of Mexico and Peru, in a resolute endeavour to preserve uniformity and check the growth of provincial peculiarities. Its provisions remained in force for many years, were frequently repeated and were eventually incorporated in the *Recopilación de Leyes*. Of the 311 clauses of the code, the great majority concern details of procedure; some, however, lay down rules of daily life for the *oidores*, the *audiencia* judges, and reveal these dignitaries as a highly specialised, highly respected professional group, upon which the Crown placed a particularly heavy reliance. Solórzano probably expressed both the official view and the general feeling when he declared, calling St Jerome to his support, that a viceroy who ill-treated a judge sinned most gravely: 'Why should I treat you with the respect due to a Prince, if you do not treat me with the respect due to a Senator?' The law prescribed a semi-monastic life for the *oidores* of each *audiencia*, in the interests of impartiality. With the *fiscal*—the public prosecutor—they lived together, usually in a house adjoining the court. They were forbidden not only to take gifts and fees, but also to hold land or Indians, to engage in trade, or to take part in enterprises of discovery or settlement; a provision recalling the early days, when ruffians such as Nuño de Guzmán or Pedro Morones had occasionally disgraced the Bench. The presence of *oidores* at bull-fights and similar public amusements, or even the exchange of visits with neighbours, might lead to the formation of friendships and the perversion of justice. Their very dress was prescribed. In strict law the only relaxation allowed them was attendance at religious festivals. Those not occupied with *visitas* or other special commissions were required to sit for three hours every morning and for two hours on Monday, Wednesday and Friday afternoons; and were to inspect the prisons—that of the *audiencia* and that of the local municipality—every Saturday afternoon. The other afternoons were reserved for *acuerdo* meetings. Each week one of the *oidores*, serving in turn, was expected to be constantly available for the issue of writs of course. For this somewhat dreary round, *oidores* received annual salaries much higher than those of any other colonial

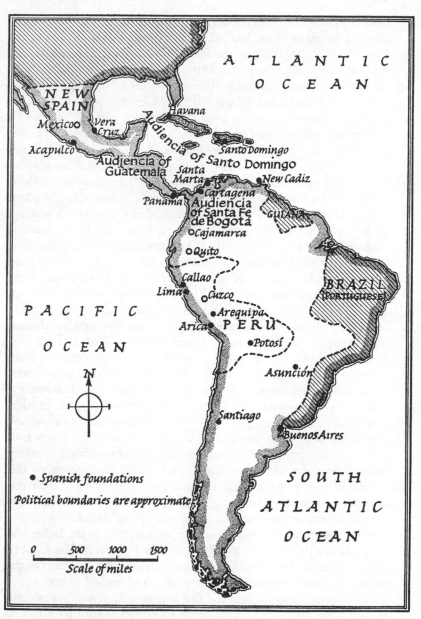

ATLANTIC
OCEAN

NEW
SPAIN
Mexico○ ○Vera
Cruz   ●Havana
Acapulco
Audiencia of Santo Domingo
Audiencia of   ●Santo Domingo
Guatemala   Santa
Marta   ●New Cadiz
Panama ●Cartagena
Audiencia
of Santa Fe
de Bogotá   GUIANA
○Cajamarca
○Quito
Callao●
Lima● ○Cuzco
Arica● ●Arequipa
PERU
●Potosí
Asunción●

PACIFIC

OCEAN

N

●Santiago

BRAZIL
(PORTUGUESE)

●Buenos Aires

● Spanish foundations
Political boundaries are approximate

0   500   1000   1500
Scale of miles

SOUTH

ATLANTIC

OCEAN

6. The Spanish empire in America in the late sixteenth century

officials except viceroys, considerably higher than those paid to corresponding judges in Spain, but still not over-generous in relation to the level of prices prevailing in the Indies. *Oidores* were not usually rich men, therefore. They were necessarily—in the absence of colonial law schools—peninsular Spaniards, differing widely in training, temperament and interests from the general run of settlers. Some of them, as might be expected, came to accept the interests and ways of life of colonial Europeans. Most career officials were thrown into daily contact with men who, by the exploitation of *encomiendas*, ranches and mines were becoming rich; inevitably they too acquired local points of view and were initiated into local rackets. An over-zealous official could have his life made unbearable, in a small community, by social ostracism; conversely, a more pliant official could make his fortune. There were always some *oidores*, however, who stood by the spirit of their training and the letter of their instructions, in the face of the most bitter local opposition and unpopularity. All in all, they formed the most consistently loyal and effective branch of the colonial bureaucracy.

Administration and jurisdiction were closely intertwined. It is not quite true to say that Spanish colonial government did not distinguish between them; the *Recopilación de Leyes* makes very intricate distinctions between *cosas de gobierno* and *cosas de justicia*. What is true is that from top to bottom of the colonial service the same people had a hand in both. All judges had some political responsibility; most senior administrative officials exercised some jurisdiction. Further down the scale, in many town councils the senior municipal magistrate, in addition to his judicial work, presided over the deliberations of the *cabildo*; and all the local *corregidores* and *alcaldes mayores* were both magistrates and administrative officers—as, indeed, are district officers in many colonial dependencies today. The only important exceptions to this general rule were the financial officers. The organisation of the royal *Hacienda* under the Hapsburgs was carefully separated from the general administrative and judicial system in the Indies.

In the sixteenth century the treasury organisation in the Indies was relatively simple. Each viceregal or provincial capital had its treasury office and its *caja real*. The office was staffed, and the several keys of the strong-box held, by treasury officers, usually described simply as the royal officials, *Oficiales Reales*. The senior officer was always the treasurer. He was assisted by a comptroller and usually by a factor. Sometimes there was a fourth officer with somewhat ill-defined duties known as the overseer (*veedor*), but this office disappeared from many provinces in the later sixteenth century The treasurer and comptroller usually had deputies stationed at the principal seaports and mining settlements, and some important harbours such as Vera Cruz came eventually to have separate offices and *cajas* of their own.

The heads of taxation were very numerous and very diverse. Some taxes were collected by the officials directly; in particular, they were required to weigh and stamp all silver ingots at the mines, and to take out the royal 'fifth'. Other taxes, such as the *alcabala* or sales tax, the *almojarifazgo* charged on imports, and the conceded religious tax traditionally known as the *cruzada*, were separately farmed. The sums paid over by the farmers—usually fixed rents—the proceeds of direct collections, the proceeds of the sale of offices, the moneys realised from the sale by the royal factors of Indian tributes in kind, were all paid into the *cajas*. The treasury officials were responsible for the whole to the accounts department, the *Contaduría*, of the Council of the Indies. They made such disbursements as the Crown authorised, in particular the payment of stipends to the salaried officers of their provinces; and they arranged for the shipment of the surplus by the regular fleets to the *Casa de la contratación* at Seville.

The organisation of the provincial treasuries was inadequate and the staff of royal officials too small for the handling of this great volume of work, even had the officials always been competent and honest. Being insufficiently supervised, they were often neither. The task of auditing their accounts and uncovering their mistakes or defalcations was a very considerable one. In the Indies it was entrusted in the sixteenth century to the *audiencias*. Until 1605 the Council of the Indies itself was the final court of audit. As might be expected, the work of auditing was always in arrear. Where as a result of urgent pressure from the Crown or its representatives, a thorough audit was held, huge sums were often found to be missing, and many thefts and frauds must have gone undetected. In 1605 the Crown tried to improve the accounting system by the establishment of *Tribunales de Cuentas* in the Indies, one at Lima, one at Mexico and one at Santa Fe de Bogotá. Each tribunal consited of three *contadores*. Their chief duty was to audit the accounts of all the Treasury officials in their districts, reporting annually to the Council of the Indies on the state of the provincial treasuries and the action taken to rectify mistakes or to punish frauds. They possessed, in conjunction with the *audiencias*, a wide jurisdiction in disputes over taxation and public finance. There was no appeal from their decisions.

The chief officers of the empire in America, in New Spain and Peru respectively, were the two viceroys. Peru, being the richer of the two commands, at least in terms of precious metal, was considered the senior, and viceroys of New Spain were often promoted to Peru, taking their crowds of clients and dependants with them; but each was responsible directly to the Crown. Viceroys might be lawyers, ecclesiastics or—more commonly—military aristocrats. The powers of a viceroy were great, and were reflected in the state which he kept. He presided over the viceregal *audiencia*, though without a vote in judicial matters, unless he were a qualified lawyer. He also presided— usually by deputy—in the *cabildo* of his capital city. He was at the centre of everything, and his stipend was generous enough to place him above petty venality. He was in no position, however, to make himself dangerously independent. The kings of Spain were determined to prevent repetitions of the financial importunity of a Columbus or the contumacy of a Gonzalo Pizarro. Since no payments might lawfully be made from the colonial treasury without the prior authorisation of the Crown, the viceroy could not spend public money on his own authority. Apart from insignificant jobs about his court, he had little patronage to dispense; civil offices were filled in accordance with a fixed routine over which, in law, he had no control. He was the King's vice-patron in ecclesiastical matters, but all appointments to sees and major benefices were made in Spain. He was the captain-general; but except for a small personal guard, he had no permanent force at his disposal. He could raise an army to repel invasion or put down insurrection by calling out the *encomenderos* and their men; but in order to raise paid troops he was required, at least in theory, to write to Spain for prior approval. Moreover, he was watched and to some extent checked by the *audiencia* judges, and like all other officials had to submit to a *residencia*, a judicial investigation of his tenure of office, at the end of his term. In practice the power of a viceroy depended largely upon his force of character and his administrative skill. Mendoza, Velasco, Toledo, Enríquez, exercised unquestioned authority throughout their viceroyalties and retained the confidence of the King; Falces and Villamanrique—to name only two examples—became involved in conflicts of jurisdiction with *audiencias* and suffered humiliating defeats. If a viceroy quarrelled openly with an *audiencia* he could not be sure that the Crown would support him. By this uncertainty, by setting everyone to watch everyone else, the Crown characteristically maintained its own control.

Not only did the Crown appoint the higher officials in courts and counting-houses; its surveillance extended more and more to the details of local government. In Indian districts the gradual resumption of *encomiendas* by the Crown, as we have seen, made way for the appointment of salaried *corregidores* to supervise the village headmen. In the Spanish communities, also, the Crown steadily broke down the power of the 'old conquerors' in their own strongholds, the corporate towns. The Hapsburgs had long memories. The revolt of the *comuneros* made Charles V and his successors intensely suspicious of the privileges and pretensions of municipal corporations, and of the local magnates who often controlled them. The towns of the Indies got titles and armorial bearings, but little else, by grant from the Crown. Their power of raising local taxes was severely limited, their *procuradores* were forbidden to meet together without express royal permission and any tendency towards concerted action was sharply discouraged. Nothing in the nature of a colonial assembly or *cortes* was allowed to develop. At an early date, also, the Crown secured control of the internal composition of the major town councils. Where at first the annual *regidores* had elected their successors year by year, subject to the governors' approval, the Crown increasingly appointed *regidores* for life. Many of the men who received these local offices from the Crown, it is true, were 'old conquerors' or settlers, but others came straight from Spain with letters of appointment in their baggage. Conscious of favours received, and hopeful of favours to come, they were unlikely to become champions of local independence.

Bureaucratic centralisation, in a vast and scattered empire with slow and hazardous communications, naturally created its own problems. In the Spanish Indies it was achieved at the expense of local initiative and speed of action. The Spanish monarchs—with some reason—never fully trusted their colonial officers. All important decisions, and many unimportant ones, were made in Spain. A request to Spain for instructions could not be answered in less than a year, at best. Two years was more usual; and the answer, when it came, might be merely a demand for more information. A system of checks and balances, of report, counter-report and comment, certainly ensured that all parties got a hearing and that government was fully informed; but equally certainly it impaired administrative efficiency, encouraged endless argument and led to indecision and delay. In the Indies there was no jurisdiction which could not be inhibited and no decision which could not be reversed. Appeals and counter-appeals might hold up essential action for years, until the occasion for it was forgotten. Even when the government had made up its mind and given a firm instruction the conventional formula 'obey but not enforce' might still excuse procrastination if the decision were unpopular.

The difficulties of the Spanish system of colonial government arose not only from its indecisiveness but from its size and complexity. The senior salaried officers—viceroys, *oidores*, governors, treasury officials—represented only a small fraction of the whole body of colonial officials. The empire was held together by chains of paper, chains which made up in number what they lacked in individual strength. A centralised bureaucracy required an immense body of secretarial officials—*escribanos*—to handle the paperwork. Every *audiencia* employed one or more *escribanos de cámara*—clerks of the court. Viceregal and provincial governments employed *escribanos de gobernación*—colonial secretaries. Every town council had its *escribano de cabildo*, its town clerk, who kept the minutes, drafted letters and deeds, witnessed the signatures of the *regidores* and often unobtrusively guided their deliberations. The provincial treasury offices, the mints, the gilds and chambers of commerce —every institution which conducted any considerable volume of formal or legal business—employed *escribanos*, often with large subordinate staffs. In a turbulent society, in which governors came and went, the *escribanos* represented permanence, order, routine. Their signatures on documents guaranteed to the Crown that prescribed procedure, administrative and legal, was being followed. Standing between their official superiors and the public, they often wielded great, though unobtrusive, power. They received no salaries. The King, it is true, could raise what taxes he pleased in America, and spend the money as he wished; but all the silver of the Indies would not have sufficed to pay salaries to all these officers out of royal revenue. As in Europe, they were remunerated by fees according to an official tariff. In the larger settlements these fees, together with incidental perquisites, assured a comfortable living. The more senior notarial offices in the Indies were valuable and coveted appointments. Conversely, it was always extremely difficult to fill notarial offices in small and backward settlements. The system of payment by fees, therefore, was an additional factor tending to concentrate European population and activity in the big towns.

The Crown of Castile possessed, in the Indies, an immense new range of patronage. In the distribution of this patronage, royal liberality and royal gratitude had to be reconciled with the aims of efficient administration and maximum revenue. Among the *conquistadores* and their descendants in the Indies, no less than in Spain itself, the Crown was confronted with a great number of eager claimants for office, most of whom based their claims upon services, military or otherwise, performed by themselves or their fathers. *Conquistadores* and their sons, however, rarely had legal or notarial training; they made indifferent quill-drivers. *Escribanos* in the early years had to be recruited in Spain. In Charles V's reign the appointment of fee-earning officials was largely handed over to private patronage in Spain. Colonial offices were given to claimants about the court as rewards for long service, for political good behaviour, or merely for persistent importunity. The members of the Council of the Indies in particular, and the King's secretaries, often secured grants of whole series of offices. The recipients of such grants also received the right to appoint deputies. In practice this meant that they sold leases of the offices in their gift, for life or for a term of years, to men who proposed to go to the Indies, do the work and collect the fees. In this indirect and haphazard way the secretarial staff of colonial governments, provincial treasuries and appeal courts was recruited. No attempt was made to establish a uniform system of appointment until Philip II's time. Philip, less imbued with the tradition of royal generosity, more interested in administrative routine, and more conscious of the revenue possibilities of America, kept colonial appointments firmly in his own hands. He endeavoured, with some success, to end the practice of titular officials serving by deputy. Where his father had given away fee-earning offices for lease or private sale, he usually had them sold directly to the men who were to perform the duties.

It is sometimes said that Philip II introduced the sale of offices into the Indies. It would be more accurate to say that he made the sale of some kinds of colonial office a Crown monopoly. In this sense his innovations may fairly be described not as an abuse, but as a reform. In the course of his reign most important fee-earning offices in the colonies—*escribanías*, police offices, offices in the colonial mints and a great range of municipal offices—were withdrawn from private or local patronage and made saleable on behalf of the Crown. They were to be offered publicly for sale in the provinces where vacancies occurred. Provisional titles were to be issued, usually to the highest bidder, except that the viceroy might in exceptional cases recommend a highly suitable applicant, though not the highest bidder. All titles required confirmation by the Crown; applicants were required to forward to Spain not only receipts for purchase prices, but also sworn testimony of their honesty, competence and purity of lineage, and in the case of *escribanos* their knowledge of the complexities of notarial procedure. From the Crown's point of view the system had important advantages. It helped to prevent provincial governors and viceroys from using public offices as rewards and pensions for their own private adherents, and it brought in revenue. Provided that judicial offices were excluded from the practice (as in law they always were) the idea of sale did not offend a public accustomed to regard fee-earning office as a form of property.

The administrative system created by Philip II survived in its essentials for a century and a half after his death. His seventeenth-century successors, however, both by legislative modifications and by laxity in enforcement, greatly weakened the Crown's control over the system as a whole. In 1606, in an attempt to make colonial offices more attractive, Philip III enacted that all saleable offices should be automatically renunciable also. This meant that the holder of an office might resign in favour of a successor of his own choice. The Crown, upon every renunciation, exacted a fee, usually one-third of the assessed value of the office, and always reserved the right to confirm, or to refuse to confirm, every transfer of office. This very important enactment had an immediate and profound effect upon the administrative service. Naturally it made offices more valuable and more expensive to buy; on the other hand, it made it easier to borrow money to buy offices. An aspirant to an official career could borrow the purchase price of an office, offering as security a mortgage upon the office itself, and engaging to renounce the office in favour of his creditor, should he default on the interest payments. This arrangement was perfectly legal. It called into being a whole class of speculators who might be described as office brokers, people who acted as middlemen for deals in public office and made loans to intending purchasers. Some offices were renounced from father to son and became hereditary. This was true especially of municipal dignities and other honorific posts; but in the administrative secretariat of the colonies such bequests were rare. In general, renunciation was a polite word for private sale. An aspirant to an administrative career in the Indies would buy a junior office with borrowed money. If he did well out of fees, in a few years he would sell his office, or turn it in in part payment for another more senior and more lucrative, and so on, until he was rich enough to invest in landed property, or lucky enough to secure a grant of *encomienda* or marry an heiress.

In the second half of the seventeenth century the system of sale and renunciation spread from fee-earning offices to the more senior salaried posts. For this there was no legislative sanction; it was an abuse by seventeenth-century standards and recognised as such. It was never very common. Records survive of the sale of seventeen provincial governorships and thirty-five reversions. Seats in the Council of the Indies were sold on two occasions, and once an *audiencia* judge was allowed to buy his appointment. These transactions were not only bad administration; they were bad finance, since they allowed officials to buy, for a very low cash price, fixed annuities charged against royal revenue. They nearly all took place in Charles II's reign, and are evidence of the financial desperation of the time, which the revenue of the Indies was quite inadequate to relieve.

The system of appointment by public sale and payment by perquisites outlasted the seventeenth century. It was modified, curtailed and reformed in the eighteenth, but it survived, at least in part, until 1812. It was generally accepted and little criticised. The great jurist Solórzano likened it to debasement of the coinage, legally permissible, politically deplorable, but unavoidable. It was an essential characteristic of the old colonial system, and to the historian of that system it suggests certain general reflections.

The Crown, having seized control of appointment to colonial offices in the sixteenth century, largely lost that control in the seventeenth. Most offices passed from hand to hand—from head to head, in the Spanish phrase—subject to a royal confirmation which became more and more perfunctory.

The great majority of colonial officials began their careers under heavy burdens of debt. They were not merely tempted, they were almost compelled to extort illegal fees, to take bribes, or to embezzle money from the royal chest, in order to make a living as well as keeping up their interest payments. The distinction between perquisites and bribes, to be sure, was difficult to draw exactly, but bribery in one form or another was almost universal in the seventeenth century. The unashamed openness of the sale of offices, the publicly accepted scale of charges, was matched by the openness of corruption and the cynically recognised scale of bribes; the two phenomena must have been connected.

Corruption would have existed whether offices were sold or not. A more direct consequence of the system of sale was the multiplication of offices. From Philip II's time onwards the Crown constantly created offices with no other purpose than that of selling them. This practice mattered little when the offices were mere honorific dignities. It became a serious nuisance when the Crown created new fee-earning offices and then, by legislation and by elaboration of procedure, compelled the public to employ the officers so appointed. It became financially self-defeating when the Crown, to raise ready money, offered for sale supernumerary salaried posts. The growing burden of bureaucracy was in part directly attributable to the growing practice of selling offices; and the actual income in ready money to the Crown from this source was in the long run hardly worth the trouble. It did not compare in importance with the main heads of taxation: silver tax, sales tax, native tributes, customs duties.

On the other hand, the system had its advantages. It discouraged nepotism among the high officials; this was one of Philip II's reasons for encouraging it. It offered the opportunity of an official career to men resident in the Indies; its restriction in the eighteenth century closed this avenue to many Creoles, and, as often happened in colonial circumstances, the reform was more unpopular than the abuse. It encouraged immigrants to settle down in the Indies and was an important source of capital for the economic development of the colonies. Many prosperous estates, especially in Mexico, originated in the profits of public office.

Despite all the abuses, the work of the administrative secretariat in the colonies throughout the seventeenth century showed a remarkable uniformity. The machine ground on, almost of its own momentum. These bureaucrats, passing their offices from one to another by private sale, were many of them the products of the universities and law schools of Spain or Spanish America. They might be rapacious and—within recognised limits—venal, but they had an *esprit de corps*, a training, a respect for precedent, a pride in their profession, which surmounted the shoddy, hand-to-mouth system which appointed them. The Spanish Empire in the seventeenth century suffered from a crippling lack of resources and faltering direction at the centre; its administrative procedure was pettifogging, complex and slow; but, subject to these defects, by the standards of the time the government was well served by its officials. It had detailed and accurate information, regularly supplied; on the few occasions when it succeeded in making up its mind to give a definite order it would usually in time get that order carried out, though only at the cost of immense persistence and effort. This degree of centralised control was dearly bought. Administrative costs absorbed an ever-greater proportion of the Indies revenue. For the private citizen the cost in time and money of even the simplest official business came near to prohibition. At the end of the century the whole life of the empire seemed in danger of strangulation, not only by external enemies preying upon its trade and cutting its communications but by the host of internal parasites preying upon the livelihood of its people.

CHAPTER 11

Demographic catastrophe

IN EVERY province of the Indies the European invasion was followed by a steep decline in the numbers of the native population. In the greater Antillean islands the decline began very shortly after the invasion and was clearly perceptible to Spanish observers within a decade or so of the first settlements. Missionary chroniclers attributed the high death-rate to ill-treatment and over-work. They hoped that legislation and stricter royal control would arrest the decline. Both missionaries and officials were struck by what they described as the physical weakness of the Tainos. They thought that a stronger race would be better able to bear the labour of cultivation and gold-washing, and for this reason advocated the import of African slaves to ease the burden upon the natives. Their hopes were disappointed. Within a century the Indian population of the greater islands was extinct.

On the mainland the *conquistadores* found, to all appearance, stronger peoples. Cortés and his companions were greatly struck by the warlike prowess of the Aztecs and their tributaries, and by the remarkable feats of Indian runners in carrying messages between the coast and the capital. In the area which became New Spain—roughly the area between the isthmus of Tehuántepec and the Chichimec frontier running in a sagging curve from Pánuco to Culiacán—the inhabitants at the time of the conquest formed sophisticated, settled, highly regimented societies, vastly different from the small and primitive groups in the islands. To the invaders the population appeared not only strong and well organised but also very numerous. All the early Spanish accounts stress the size of the towns and their proximity one to another, especially on the shores of the lake of Texcoco, the crowds thronging the markets, the streams of passers-by on the causeways, the great fleets of canoes on the lake. The lake-side towns, it is true, with their fertile *chinampas* and their abundant tribute income, were exceptional; but the countryside also was populous. Indian peasants lived on a simple and monotonous diet, consisting chiefly of maize; they had no domestic animals of consequence, and ate very little meat. Maize is a productive crop, and on such a diet two or three acres of reasonably good land sufficed to maintain an average family. Moreover, the methods of intensive hoe cultivation made it possible to till marginal land, which with more developed tools would have been unusable. Most cultivable land was in fact cultivated. Throughout most of the area, except in parts too high, rough and steep even for hoe cultivation, all the evidence indicates an extremely dense rural population; denser, indeed, in many places than it is today. Peasants were confined to a low level of subsistence, not only by pressure of population on land but also by the tribute exactions of their local nobilities and of the Aztec triple alliance, which took from them most of their surplus of food and almost all their production of valuable goods such as cotton cloth and cacao. In the last few decades before the conquest population probably was tending to increase, despite low living standards and despite the checks imposed by war and human sacrifice. These checks were powerful; wars were regularly undertaken not only to acquire land, slaves and tribute but also to procure captives for sacrifice. Major ceremonies often involved thousands of victims. Human life, then, was plentiful and cheap, and so was human labour. By means of closely organised communal and tributary labour, using hand methods, without the help of draught animals or mechanical appliances, Indian societies accomplished an astonishing amount of heavy construction, including irrigation systems, flood controls, aqueducts and causeways, and elaborate and massive public buildings.

Here was what the *conquistadores* had been looking for: not only land, food and gold but an apparently inexhaustible supply of docile labour. In the early years of settlement the Spaniards, having seized the main centres of government, took over the native system of tributes and services. They began almost at once to modify the system, partly because their *encomienda* grants did not always coincide with pre-conquest political or tribute groupings, partly because some forms of pre-conquest tribute—feather mantles, for example—were of no interest to them. In general, however, both from policy and through force of circumstances, they based their demands roughly upon the tributes and services formerly enjoyed by the Aztec triple alliance and by the Indian local nobility—still enjoyed, indeed, by many of the latter. Their declared policy was to demand somewhat less than precedent permitted, in order to reconcile the Indians to their rule; their practice, to drive the best bargain they could with the Indian headmen. Like their predecessors, they were great builders, and, like them also, they grew accustomed to an extremely lavish use of labour; but the reservoir of population from which the labour was drawn seemed boundless. Relieved of the drain of human sacrifice, indeed, and—once the conquest was accepted—of constant war, the Indian population, already vast, might have been expected to increase. Instead, just as it had done in the islands, it quickly began to decline.

Evidence that labour was becoming harder to get, that the tributary population in some areas was dwindling, began to be noticed in official reports and in the writings of missionaries such as Motolinía in the 1530s. Thereafter, complaints became progressively more frequent and more serious throughout the sixteenth century. Most modern historians, from Robertson and Raynal almost to the present day, belittled the complaints. To eighteenth- and nineteenth-century historians the estimates of numbers in early Spanish accounts were plainly incredible. *Conquistadores* and early missionaries, it was assumed, exaggerated the pre-conquest population either through naïveté or carelessness, or deliberately in order to magnify their own achievements in conquest or conversion; later missionaries exaggerated the decline, in order to secure legislation for the protection of their Indian charges; *encomenderos* and employers exaggerated their difficulties in obtaining labour, in order to secure wider concessions. In the last fifteen years, however, careful analysis of tribute assessments and parish counts has shown, beyond reasonable doubt, that the sixteenth-century reports were broadly correct. An astonishingly large population at the time of the conquest suffered a catastrophic decline in the course of the century. The Indian population in the early seventeenth century was probably less than one-tenth of what it had been 100 years before.

The pre-conquest population of New Spain has been roughly but credibly estimated at about 25,000,000. In 1532, when the second *audiencia* was trying to systematise the assessment of tribute and to restrict *encomiendas*, it had probably declined to some 17,000,000. So large a decline could not have been caused simply by ill-usage and over-work; though these were common enough, especially in the feverish rebuilding of the city of Mexico. The number of Spaniards was then small and their penetration of the country very uneven. Most of them were settled in highland areas, especially in the central valley, in or near Mexico City. In the coastal lowlands Spanish settlers were much fewer. Many areas, even fertile areas with large Indian populations, were hardly touched by Spanish settlement. The extent of the decline in the Indian population, as might be expected, varied greatly from one region to another. It was far more drastic in the coastal lowlands than on the plateau; on both the Gulf and Pacific coasts the available evidence suggests a decline of about one-half between 1519 and 1532. Even in areas where there was, as yet, no permanent Spanish settlement, and no forced labour exactions, populations declined. The decline bore no obvious and direct relation, therefore, to the amount of Spanish activity; it was caused chiefly by pestilence, by contagious diseases introduced by the invaders, against which the natives had no immunity. Smallpox entered Mexico with Cortés' army, and caused many deaths in the city in the early 1520s. The extraordinarily high mortality on the coast may have been caused by malaria or yellow fever, introduced from Europe but spread by indigenous insects. The precise nature of the lethal factors can only be guessed; what is certain is that they operated with increasing severity throughout most of the century.

The progressive decline of the Indian population caused marginal land to be abandoned and much even of the relatively fertile areas to be left untilled. The vacuum so caused was filled, for the most part, by grazing animals, horned cattle chiefly in the lowlands and valleys, sheep in the highlands, horses, mules and goats almost everywhere. These animals were all alien to the Americas and were introduced by Spaniards. Imports of livestock were particularly numerous in the 1530s; and, once introduced, the beasts multiplied prodigiously on land which had never before been grazed. They brought a new diversity into the economy of New Spain, and caused a major revolution in the use of land. Indians participated in this revolution to some extent. Apart from those who were employed as herdsmen or shepherds by Spanish masters, some rich individuals and a few communities, especially among the

privileged and enterprising people of Tlaxcala, ran flocks of sheep of
their own. Reference has already been made to Indian muleteers; and
probably, though not recorded, backyard goats were not uncommon
even in the 1530s. On the other hand, very few Indians went in for
cattle ranching. Possibly dislike and even fear of large, unfamiliar
animals deterred them. More probably, however, they were prevented
from running cattle by difficulty in securing title to areas of grazing
large enough to make ranching profitable.

Pastoral farming produced new commodities and new services which
became available, to a limited extent, to Indians. The use of pack
animals progressively replaced the wasteful demand for human carriers,
as depopulation reduced the supply of porters. For those who acquired
sheep and goats, mutton was a new source of protein in a hitherto
almost meatless diet. (In this connection it is curious that although the
pre-conquest Indians relied chiefly on fish for their supply of animal
protein, their range of devices for fishing—nets, traps, weirs, hooks,
spears and so forth—was very limited and lacking in ingenuity. The
Iberian peoples for many centuries have possessed a remarkable range
of these devices. Indian efficiency in fishing and in snaring *chichicuilotes*
—lake-side wading birds—improved greatly as a result of contact
with Europeans.) Beef, the mainstay of the Spanish community, was
little eaten by Indians except where they could afford to buy it or,
more commonly, contrive to steal it. Spanish ranchers on the northern
frontier sometimes complained of illicit slaughtering by 'wild' Indians.
Milk was unimportant. The Indians either did not like it or could not
get it; scrawny backyard goats and half-wild scrub cattle cannot have
yielded very much. More important than the change in diet was the
change in clothing. Many woollen mills were set up from the 1530s
onwards, a few owned by Indians, but most by Spaniards. In the highlands, woollen capes or blankets, forerunners of the modern *serape*,
soon began to displace the traditional *manta* woven from cotton or
other vegetable fibre. Cotton cloth had been a major item in many
tribute assessments at the time of the conquest. In the second half of
the century, as tributes were commuted to money payments, this
form of assessment tended to disappear. The area of land planted to
cotton in the warmer parts of the country grew progressively less
through the century.

In settled New Spain, in the 100 years between 1520 and 1620, the
viceregal government made formal grants totalling more than 17,000

square miles for cattle *estancias*, almost all to Spaniards, and more than 12,000 square miles for sheep farms, some to Indians, but the greater part to Spaniards. In addition, at least 2,000 square miles were granted to Spaniards for arable purposes; for the production, that is, either of crops such as wheat intended for Spanish consumption, or of fodder for animals. Well over 30,000 square miles, therefore, were officially converted to new uses. Most of this great area at the time of the conquest had been farmed by Indians and had subsequently either been taken from them or, more commonly, vacated by them because of the diminution in their numbers. In the course of the sixteenth century, then, a vast agrarian revolution took place; a wholesale substitution of an animal for a human population. The destructive effect of this revolution upon traditional Indian agriculture was in fact far greater than the figures suggest, for flocks and herds grazed over much bigger areas than the official grants. A cattle *estancia* was in theory a square tract, each side of which was one Castilian league, about 2·6 miles; its area was thus 6·76 square miles. On this, the grantee was entitled—indeed expected—to run 509 head of cattle, or seventy-four to the square mile. The corresponding figure for sheep was 666 to the square mile, which—even for scrub animals—meant heavy over-grazing. Each *estancia* was supposed to be one league distant from its nearest neighbour and one league from any Indian village. It was to be surrounded, therefore, by a belt of empty land. The large numbers of stock carried, and the rapid natural increase, made these territorial 'cushions' inadequate. The area actually grazed by Spanish stock was probably two or three times as great as that comprised in the official grants. The animals strayed freely through the peripheral belts and into Indian cultivations beyond. In Spanish practice this unrestricted grazing at certain times of year was customary and necessary. In Spain the law required most arable land to be opened to grazing after the harvest was gathered. In New Spain the same rule was enacted; but in practice vast, half-wild, untended flocks and herds, on unfenced range, might invade cultivated land at any time. Indians constantly complained to the courts about the resulting damage to their crops. Both the *Juzgado general* and the *audiencias* made many orders forbidding trespass and awarding damages, but often the means of enforcement were lacking. The cactus hedges now characteristic of the Mexican rural scene were a tardy and inadequate defence against this destructive invasion. Many Indian communities, seeing their crops repeatedly destroyed by great herds of grazing, trampling beasts, abandoned their cultivations in despair.

Against this background of destruction the depopulation of New Spain is easier to understand. To the steady attrition caused by debilitating disease and near starvation, moreover, were added the heavy and irrecoverable losses caused by major epidemics. One such epidemic ravaged the whole of New Spain in 1545-6, while the colony was still in a state of angry uncertainty about the future of the *encomienda* system. The precise nature of the disease cannot be certainly identified, nor can the mortality caused by it be accurately assessed, but reports reaching Spain so alarmed the government that Prince Philip, in the absence of the Emperor, ordered a detailed inspection of the entire colony, and reports on the tributary population and resources of every Indian community, with the express intention of reassessing tributes and services. A large number of *visitas* were actually made in or about the year 1548. The surviving summary of the reports, the *Suma de Visitas*, covers about half the area of New Spain. From the information contained in it and from other sources a careful estimate has recently been made of the total Indian population of New Spain in 1548. The figure is 6,300,000.

A declining Indian population was expected to support, by its tribute and its labour, both its own nobility and an increasing Spanish population. By the middle of the century decline had reached a point where the exaction of tribute and services was causing severe hardship to the surviving Indians. Spaniards were beginning to experience not, indeed, hardship, but some inconvenience, from shortage of labour. They were, moreover, seeking additional labour for the development of newly discovered silver-mines. The sweeping reforms of the tribute system carried out in the 1550s were designed primarily to relieve hardship, but also to increase revenue—or at least to prevent its reduction—by more rational and systematic assessment. The tribute exacted from each community, instead of being assessed as a total amount based either upon custom or upon a bargain with the *encomendero*, was now related directly to the actual number of heads of households, and was expressed in common terms, usually of maize or of money or a combination of the two: so many silver *reales*, so much maize, in respect of each tributary living in the town. As a result, the amount of tribute demanded would automatically be reduced where a decline in population could be proved to the satisfaction of an official *visitador*. On the other hand, large classes of people who had formerly been exempt were now included in the ranks of those liable to tribute, and privileged groups such as the Tlaxcalans lost their privileges. As for labour, *encomenderos* were forbidden to demand services by way of tribute; Indians were urged to undertake wage-earning labour; and, as we have seen, a beginning was made in the systematic organisation of *repartimiento* labour for public purposes. The import of Negro slaves was encouraged, and considerable numbers were in fact employed in Spanish households, in the mines and in the harbour at Vera Cruz. These measures may have had some effect in mitigating, or at least spreading, the burden upon the Indians, but they did not arrest the decline in numbers. A thirst for detailed information on the population and resources of the Indies was characteristic of Philip II's government. The assessments, reports and *relaciones* of the 1560s and 1570s which have survived are much fuller and more precise than any evidence for earlier years, and from them the movements of population can be traced in some detail. By 1568 the Indian population of New Spain was probably under 3,000,000. In 1576–9 another major epidemic, probably smallpox, swept through the colony. Contemporary accounts all agree that the rate of mortality in this visitation was heavier than in 1545–6. The Indian population in 1580 has been estimated at about 1,900,000. Further, the 1576–9 epidemic destroyed one optimistic illusion about labour in the Tropics: the mortality among Negroes was at least as severe as that among Indians.

In the last decades of the sixteenth century the Spanish population of New Spain began for the first time to experience serious hardship; hardship, at least, by contrast with the easy opulence of earlier years. The construction of churches and other major public buildings slowed down and in some places ceased. The recruitment of labour for mines and estates became increasingly difficult, and wages of free labour mounted steeply. The supply of food for provisioning the towns became increasingly precarious, and the prices of food also reached unheard-of heights. It is true that large arable areas were by now under Spanish control, and that the productivity of Indian holdings probably increased, since peasants, as their numbers declined, withdrew from marginal land and cultivated only the best. They also adopted some European technical devices for economising labour and increasing productivity; the *arado*, the simple wheel-less Andalusian plough, for example, was becoming fairly common. These improvements, however, were more than offset by the constant shrinking of the labouring population.

Supplies of maize, vegetables, fruit, fish, game, firewood, grass and hay were directly affected, since all these commodities were produced almost entirely by Indians, and brought to the cities by them either for sale or as tribute. At the same time, beef, mutton and wheat, the traditional foods of Spaniards in New Spain, chiefly produced by Spaniards, were also becoming scarcer. Over-grazing was probably the cause of the shortage of meat; the Spaniards were suffering from the prodigality of their grandfathers. Cattle and sheep, sheep especially, where grazing is uncontrolled, tend to multiply to the limit of sub-sistence, and then to destroy the means of their subsistence. In highland New Spain the more edible grasses and plants with edible seeds, such as mesquite, tended to disappear from the sheep ranges and to be replaced by intrusive palmetto and prickly pear. The annual burning of sheep pastures, and browsing by goats, destroyed forest and bush cover and prevented its replacement. Over-grazing and burning together, in a land of long dry seasons and torrential summer rains, led to erosion, to the silting of rivers and lakes, to the flooding of valleys, to the spread of semi-desert badlands. Naturally, the animal population near the cities began to decline as the grazing deteriorated. Viceregal legislation in the 1590s regulating grazing and prohibiting the slaughter of female animals came too late and was impossible to enforce. The big herds were moving north, to vast new ranges in the Chichimec country, where they were too far from the cities to be useful as a source of food, and where the chief profit came from the sale of hides and tallow.

Viceregal and municipal governments attempted to deal with food shortage and high prices by applying traditional sixteenth-century remedies—price fixing, the prohibition of engrossing, the restriction of all food sales to authorised market places, the establishment of state granaries which pre-empted large quantities of grain and sold it at fixed prices in times of acute shortage. These *alhóndigas* were first set up by Enríquez as an emergency measure in a year of pestilence, 1578; but they soon became permanent features of Mexico City and other large towns. In 1579 the system was supplemented by legislation requiring all *encomenderos* to sell one-third of their tribute maize to the *alhóndigas*, again at a fixed price. Efforts were made in the 1590s to compel Indian villages to pay a larger share of their tributes in kind and to produce more animal food, especially poultry; but little came of legislation to this effect, partly because of difficulty of administration, partly because of passive Indian resistance to new burdens.

The official remedy for the growing shortage of labour was, in effect, a system of labour rationing. So long as labour was plentiful, it could be levied from the Indian towns when and where it was needed. A populous town suffered no great hardship through being told to produce, even at short notice, a few hundred men for some particular task. After 1576, as we have seen, the *repartimiento* ceased to be a casual, *ad hoc* practice, whereby any Spaniard of standing could procure at least a temporary labour force through the authority of local officials, and became a rigid, highly organised system of periodical draft. A proportion of the adult male population was levied in rotation to work for Spanish employers. The proportion varied according to the type of work and according to the agricultural season, but subject to those variations was fixed by law. The actual number demanded each week from each town was computed on the basis of population counts made at frequent intervals for the purpose of assessing tribute. *Repartimiento* labourers could be used only by the employer to whom they were officially allotted, and only for specifically approved tasks. After 1580 *repartimiento* labour was rarely approved for churches or for private building. Partly for this reason, relatively few major building projects were undertaken, and those which were took many years to complete; a sharp contrast with the earlier period. The only major exception to this rule in seventeenth-century New Spain was the great undertaking of draining the lake of Texcoco, made urgently necessary by floods, which themselves were caused by silting consequent upon erosion. Early seventeenth-century legislation removed most manufactures, especially sugar and textiles, from the list of activities eligible for *repartimiento* labour. This left, in effect (apart from urgent public works), only food production and silver-mining—the two basic supports of the whole Spanish economy in the Indies, whose priority nobody could dispute.

As a device for making the most economical use of a dwindling labour supply the *repartimiento* was a failure. Apart from the opportunities which it offered for every kind of abuse, it was cumbersome and difficult to administer. When, as sometimes happened, Indian communities flatly refused to contribute their quota, the process of punishing and coercing them was troublesome and expensive. At best, the system produced unskilled, unwilling, constantly changing gangs. The brief working period and the rapid change-over entailed much waste of time in travelling. A week's work might involve two weeks' travelling or more, especially in the more remote mining towns—time lost to the Indians without being gained by the Spaniards. The ambitious 'Congregation' of the last years of the century was, among other things, an attempt—a quite inadequate attempt—to prevent this waste. The unrelieved pessimism of viceregal reports, the evidence of intense competition for labour among Spanish employers, the steady reduction in the size of labour drafts, based on frequent tribute counts, all point unmistakably to the fact that by the end of the sixteenth century the *repartimiento* was failing to draft enough labour from the steadily declining Indian population to meet even those demands which the Crown officially recognised as having a clear prior claim on whatever workmen were available.

At the beginning of the seventeenth century the settled Indian population of New Spain was little more than a million and a quarter. The white and near-white population was increasing steadily and may already have reached 100,000, most of whom contributed little directly to production and were, economically considered, so many mouths to be fed. Indian food production was quite inadequate for provisioning the Spanish towns; it became more and more necessary and more and more profitable to grow food crops on large multi-purpose estates, Spanish-owned and Spanish-managed. The proprietors of these *latifundia*, like the operators of manufacturing establishments, much more than the operators of mines, found themselves less and less able to rely on the official system of recruiting labour. More and more they were obliged to turn to free hired labour, to *peones, gañanes* or *laboríos*. In the acutely depressed conditions of Indian society in the early seventeenth century individual Indians were much more willing to take wage-earning employment than they had formerly been; and *haciendas* paid much higher wages than those fixed for *repartimiento* labour. Much of the labour required was casual, fluctuating with the seasons; but every *hacienda* needed also a permanent labour force, available at all times and preferably resident on the estate. *Hacienda* residence had its attractions for depressed Indians, hard though its conditions might be; at least they had a regular wage and, at need, a source of credit; and their employers, from self-interest, took steps to protect them from the demands of *repartimiento* and other community obligations. An *hacendado*, however, naturally wished to retain his labour force for his own exclusive use, and a *peón* who became resident on an *hacienda* often had difficulty in leaving it. Often, indeed, he had nowhere else to go. In the

more fertile areas, *haciendas* tended to enlarge their holdings by purchase or other means, until their boundaries were contiguous; or else
to press so closely upon the holdings of neighbouring Indian communities that no spare land was available for the extension of Indian cultivation. Apart from vagabondage and probable starvation, the *peón* had
to stay where he was, or seek employment on another *hacienda*. That,
too, could be prevented, by a range of devices borrowed from those
earlier employers of wage labour, the textile *obrajes*. *Hacendados* did not
lock up their labourers, as the proprietors of *obrajes* often did, but they
could hold them in debt-slavery. A *peón* whose employment, at least
in theory, originated in a free contract could be prevented from leaving
by reason of debts owed to his employer. Such debts could be incurred
in many ways. The employer might make loans or advances of wages
in money or kind, particularly clothing. A landless labourer would
be fed by his employer, but might have to buy food on credit, also
from the employer, for his family. Alternatively, the worker might
grow food for his family upon a plot of land allowed to him by the
employer; often an *hacendado* who acquired land by purchase or grant
in effect acquired also any Indians who might be living on it, since by
their inability to pay rent they became indebted to the owner. Throughout most of the seventeenth century, also, employers were often held
responsible for the payment to the Crown of their resident workers'
tribute; this arrangement meant an annually recurring debt to the
employer. These debts, however incurred, were payable in labour in
default of cash, and were inherited from father to son. No legislation
restricted the freedom of movement of *peones*, whatever their state of
indebtedness. The whole institution of peonage grew up outside formal
Spanish law. Nevertheless, by custom and in practice, debtors found it
extremely difficult to leave the service of the employer to whom they
were indebted, unless the employer sold the estate. When that happened
the purchaser was expected to take over the debts and reimburse the
vendor. The *peones*, in other words, were bound to the estate rather
than to its owner; in the seventeenth century, indeed, they were often
described as *adscripticios, adscripti ad glebam*.

In the course of the seventeenth century peonage replaced the *repartimiento* as the principal method of recruiting labour. In 1632 *repartimiento* liability was, indeed, formally abolished for all purposes save
public works and mining. From the employer's point of view peonage
had many advantages over the *repartimiento*. It was reliable and perma-

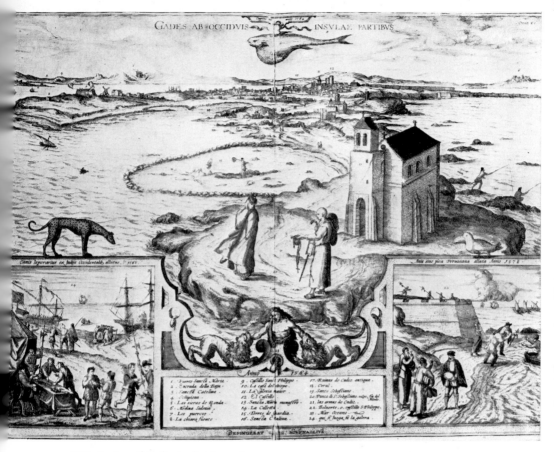

VII *A view of Cadiz in the sixteenth century*
(*from* G. *Braun,* Civitates orbis terrarum)

VIII–IX *The port of Cadiz in 1727*
(*from the MS collection of* Cartes Marines)

X *The spiritual conquest of Mexico*
    (drawings from the Codex Telleriano-Remensis)

nent, yet it avoided the heavy capital cost of importing slaves; towards the end of the century, indeed, the employment of Negro slaves was largely confined to domestic service, where their function was as much display of their masters' wealth as performance of work. Unlike the *repartimiento*, peonage could be used to bind workers in any employment—agriculture, stock-raising, mining, quarrying, sugar-making, weaving and so forth; it could, moreover, bind a wider range of people. *Mestizos*, for example, were exempt from *repartimiento*, but they could be held to debt-slavery, and many were; an important advantage at a time when they were increasing rapidly in numbers and swelling the ranks of the *léperos*, the vagabonds who thronged the streets of Mexico and other large towns. Even from the *peón's* point of view, peonage may often have been preferable to an alternation between life in a shrunken, indigent village and the recurrent harsh compulsion of the *repartimiento*; at least it represented security of a sort, and often some degree of personal obligation, even sympathy, between *peón* and *patrón*. The Crown never seriously discouraged peonage. It legislated against the more obvious abuses of the system, limited the extent of credit and forbade the use of coercion to get Indians to incur debts; but in general, on theoretical grounds, it wished to replace forced labour by free wage-earning labour, especially in the mines, and saw no compelling reason why debt should not be used to hold men to useful employment. Officials hunted down runaway debtors and returned them to their employers without criticism, overt or implied, from the viceregal governments or from the Council of the Indies. Peonage became an indispensable feature of the colonial economy, and a characteristic feature of the social life of New Spain. It removed many Indians from the continuing centres of Indian culture and settled them in centres of Spanish influence, where they tended to adopt Spanish as their language, intermarry with other tribes or with mixed bloods and to become absorbed in an emerging hybrid society. It continued in Mexico and Central America into the twentieth century and in many parts of Spanish-speaking America it persists to this day.

Through peonage the Spanish settlers of New Spain, and those of the Indian nobility who adopted their way of life, in large measure solved the critical labour problem posed for them by depopulation. The supply of food for the cities was maintained, though with recurrent periods of crisis and near famine; many contemporary accounts describe the squalor and disorder of the poorer parts of Mexico City. There were,

naturally, occasional years of abundant harvests; misery was not continuous, except for the Indians, who in the first half of the seventeenth
century seemed doomed to relentless extinction. The economy kept
working, but at a lower level and a more sluggish pace than formerly.
Compared with the exuberant vitality of the sixteenth century and
the wealth and brilliance which were to follow in the eighteenth, the
seventeenth ceutury was for New Spain a period of depression and
decline. Probably the lowest point was reached in the 1620s and 1630s,
when the enormous labour demands of the Huehuetoca drainage canal
near Mexico City coincided with a prolonged series of bad crop years.
Population was probably also at its lowest point about this time. The
decline had levelled out and eventually ceased. In the coastal lowlands
it probably ceased about the turn of the century, on the plateau twenty
or thirty years later. Shortly afterwards numbers began to recover,
but very slowly. Recovery was especially slow among Indians; the
moderate growth of the later seventeenth century and the much more
rapid growth of the eighteenth were chiefly among *mestizos*.

An indication of the movement of the colonial economy as a
whole—though still a scanty indication—is to be found in variations in
silver production. Mining was a favoured industry, enjoying an
unquestioned priority in the official allocation of labour; the more so,
since a large part of its product was sent, officially or unofficially, to
Spain. The records of official receipts in Spain suggest that production
expanded fairly continuously during the second half of the sixteenth
century and reached a peak between 1591 and 1600. From this high
level it declined slowly until 1630. From 1630 to 1660 the decline was
precipitous; in 1660 official receipts of silver in Spain were little more
than one-tenth of what they had been in 1595. This does not necessarily
mean, of course, that output declined in the same proportion. An
increasing share of the silver produced was doubtless retained in the
Indies, to defray the increasing cost of administration and defence;
and as the Spanish population there increased, more silver was needed
for ordinary business transactions. Some *reales*—Zacatecas notably—
seem to have maintained a fairly steady volume of production; but in
others, including Potosí, which was by far the most important,
output undoubtedly declined steeply. It is true that in the bad years of
the seventeenth century other factors besides labour shortage were
affecting output: the exhaustion of rich surface veins, the technical
difficulties of draining deep shafts, interruptions in the supply of

quicksilver for reduction. Depopulation, however—a desperate shortage of people—must have been a principal element in so drastic a decline. The depression of the whole economy of New Spain in the seventeenth century reflected a vast demographic catastrophe, one of the most severe, perhaps, in human history. The catastrophe, as far as the American natives were concerned, was permanent. A new hybrid society took their place and slowly grew in numbers; but only in the twentieth century did its numbers come to equal the great population which had inhabited Mexico when Cortés first landed.

The foregoing account of depopulation refers chiefly to New Spain, because the circumstances there are better known than elsewhere. A series of careful and extremely able studies have in recent years interpreted the mass of tribute assessments and population counts in New Spain in the sixteenth and seventeenth centuries. No comparable interpretations for other provinces have been attempted; nor have comparable data yet come to light. It is almost certain, however, that Guatemala, Quito, Upper and Lower Peru, New Granada and Tierra Firme suffered severe reduction in the numbers of their native inhabitants. Devastating epidemics were reported from all these areas. The extent of depopulation in the Andean provinces may have been less catastrophic than in New Spain. The country was more difficult and less accessible; the native population may have been less dense; the number of Spanish settlers was smaller; there was more vacant land, especially in the highlands, where domestic animals could graze without destroying cultivations; and racial mixture was less rapid and much less widespread. With all allowances made, however, the decrease in the labouring and tribute-paying classes in all these areas almost certainly entailed much the same consequences as in New Spain.

In the same period, from the late sixteenth century, Spain itself entered upon an economic and demographic decline which was not reversed until the beginning of the eighteenth century. Demographic data, curiously, are more scanty and more difficult of interpretation for Spain than for New Spain; but the evidence is clear for the decline in the population of most big towns and for a corresponding decline in economic activity, in sharp contrast with the steady growth of the early and middle years of the sixteenth century. As for the countryside, there is evidence that not only Spain but most countries bordering the western Mediterranean suffered severely from over-grazing, soil exhaustion, erosion and consequent depopulation in the seventeenth century. Pestilence also played its deadly part. Epidemics of unusual severity occurred in 1599–1600—accompanied by widespread crop failure—and in 1649–51. The second of these affected chiefly Andalusia, which for many months was commerciall; cut off from the rest of Spain. In Seville it caused 60,000 deaths, about half the total population of the city. Loss of economic strength in Spain caused additional difficulties in the colonies. The inability of Spain to absorb colonial exports of wool, hides, dyes and other products may well have contributed to a falling off in production of these commodities in New Spain and the Caribbean area. Similarly, the failure of Spanish industries to provide manufactured goods, in adequate quantity and reasonable prices, for the Spanish cities of America, aggravated the difficulties arising from deficits in colonial production. Contraction of economic opportunity and worsening of living conditions in Spain drove considerable numbers of Spaniards to America where, bad though economic conditions may have been, food was still more abundant than in Spain. It is noteworthy that the viceroy, Luis de Velasco, at the beginning of the seventeenth century, remarked in one of his most pessimistic despatches that he feared that food shortage in Mexico might soon become as acute as in Spain; but matters were never quite so bad, for Spaniards at least. Emigrants from Spain, as we have seen, made little immediate contribution to the labour force of the colonies, but they were lost to Spain. Finally, the desperate financial straits of the Crown in the late sixteenth century and throughout the seventeenth drove it to more and more determined attempts to extract money from the colonies. Additional taxes; gifts and loans demanded from individuals and corporations; the purchase prices of offices; payments for grants, pardons, dignities, favours of all descriptions; all placed further burdens on the Spanish cities in America at a time when they were becoming less and less able to bear them. Through their coincidence in time the economic and demographic crises of Spain and the Indies thus interacted to the disadvantage of both.

CHAPTER 12

Economic dependence

PHILIP II was the first sovereign to rule over the whole of the Iberian peninsula. In the latter part of his long reign Castile and León, Portugal, Navarre, Aragon, Catalonia and Valencia all did him homage. Outside the peninsula he was the effective master of Flanders, Artois and the Franche-Comté. Holland and Zeeland, it is true, were obstinate in revolt, but Philip never abandoned the hope of recovering them, and never foresaw the immense power which, through their shipping and their commerical skill, they were soon to acquire. England, too, once a satellite, was now an enemy with whom, so long as Elizabeth lived, no accommodation was possible; but though Englishmen could defend themselves against invasion, and could deal damaging blows against Spanish shipping when they took to the offensive, they were apparently in no position to do Spain lasting harm. In southern Europe Philip's power appeared impregnable. By his control of Milan he could maintain regular contact with his cousins in Austria and almost encircle France. His influence in central Italy was assured by *presidi* on the Tuscan coast; in the south he was King of Naples and Sicily and master of Sardinia. In North Africa he held Oran, Ceuta, Tangier and the Canaries. As King of Portugal, he ruled the other Atlantic archipelagos: the Azores, the Cape Verde Islands and Madeira. Great possessions naturally involved great responsibilities; and apart from incessant wars in Europe, particularly against France, Philip regarded himself, and his great empire in the western Mediterranean, as the chief bulwark of Christendom against that other, and infidel, empire, the Ottoman sultanate of the Levant. Against the Turk Philip's navies achieved at least one resounding success. In northern Europe his forces were less successful; but in his last endeavours to leave his son a legacy of peace he managed to extricate himself from his French adventure in the Treaty of Vervins, and negotiated in the Netherlands a settlement which gave the Flemings an appearance of sovereignty and saved face all round. Philip III succeeded to a kingdom which, though financially embarrassed, was the centre of a great empire, and was feared and respected throughout Europe. Spanish land forces, especially heavily armed infantry, enjoyed a reputation for invincibility, inherited from the time of the Great Captain, which had not yet been shaken. At sea Spain was more vulnerable; but the merchant fleet of Spain and Portugal combined was one of the largest, perhaps the largest, in Europe. It was not yet seriously outnumbered by the Dutch fleet; it was double the size of the German merchant marine, three times that of the English or the French; and the number of vessels armed for war was correspondingly large. Nor was Spanish ascendancy in Europe at the end of the sixteenth century merely one of military and naval strength. Spanish models of manners, deportment, above all of dress, were widely imitated throughout Europe. In the arts, especially in painting, in literature and in drama, the Spain of Philip II was entering upon a golden age: the age of Cervantes, of Lope de Vega, of Calderón; of Zurbarán, Velázquez and El Greco.

The history of Spain in the seventeenth century reveals a decline in wealth, influence and power, verging, in the later part of the century, upon collapse. The degree and speed of decline varied greatly, as might be expected, from one field of activity to another. In the arts and in the related fields of manners, dress and social behaviour Spanish influence and leadership survived well beyond the middle of the century. In literature and drama, in painting and allied arts, Spain continued to produce men of commanding and creative genius. Royal, noble and ecclesiastical support was maintained on a lavish scale, which increasingly exceeded what the country could afford. Neither artists nor their patrons seemed aware of the crumbling economic foundations upon which their greatness rested. In military power and diplomatic influence the process of decline was more rapid, though still not sudden or immediate. The first sign of faltering confidence came early. The Twelve-year Truce with the Dutch, negotiated in 1609 by Spínola, on Lerma's instructions, 'without seeming to desire it', left them in effective—though not yet recognised—independence. It left them, moreover, free to trade with Spain, and so indirectly to share in the profits of the Indies, to say nothing of the opportunities for direct illicit trade. Of more immediate importance, the truce left the Dutch in control of the mouth of the Scheldt, so exposing Antwerp (already twice devastated) and the whole of the 'obedient provinces' to a gradual impoverishment. Seventeenth-century Spain still commanded the services of admirals and generals of genius. Spínola's capture of Breda in 1625, commemorated in one of Velázquez' greatest paintings; Fadrique de Toledo's defeat of the Dutch fleet off Gibraltar in 1626; even later, in the Thirty Years War, the resounding success of the Cardinal Infante Ferdinand at Nördlingen in 1634—these were notable victories, won by Spanish forces against formidable adversaries. But though Spaniards in the seventeenth century won some victories, they lost every war. The shattering defeat of Rocroy in 1643 destroyed the reputation of the invincible *tercios*. Spanish tactics and organisation, which had dominated European military thinking for more than a century, had become static and out of date; they were quickly discarded after Rocroy, by most of the military states of Europe, in favour of the more flexible, more imaginative, methods of the French, who had learned their tactics from Gustavus Adolphus. After the Peace of Westphalia in 1648, which formally recognised the independence of the United Provinces, the confused disorders of the Fronde in France afforded some relief to Spanish arms; but the decisive Peace of the Pyrenees in 1659 finally revealed to all Spain's neighbours, allies and adversaries that they were dealing with a power of the second rank. The change in the temper of Spain itself was clearly shown by the peace-at-any-price rejoicing with which this humiliating treaty was received.

The sixteenth century had been for Spain a time of growing unification and discipline. Philip II in particular had achieved considerable progress in the assertion of royal authority thoughout the peninsula. It is true that he was punctilious in respect for the liberties and traditions of the coastal kingdoms,and treated their occasional disobedience with a politic clemency; but in general he was obeyed. The seventeenth century by contrast was a time of disintegration and revolt. The Basques of Vizcaya rose in the 1630s, and threatened to seek the help of the French. A far more serious revolt broke out in Catalonia in 1640—a civil war, in effect, which lasted twelve years and left the economic life of Catalonia in ruins. There were formidable risings also in Andalusia, Sicily and Naples; and in 1640 Portugal embarked on a successful war for independence of Spain. These movements, whether aristocratic, popular or national in character, all had some connection with the constant pressure of foreign war, with attempts to make the other kingdoms bear part of the brunt of the wars in which Castile engaged. One of the most serious complaints of the Catalans was against the billeting of Castilian troops on their way to or from France. The risings also reflected a deterioration in the personal quality of the rulers of the time. Throughout the sixteenth century Spain was governed by men of energy, capacity and stern devotion to duty. Charles V, at first an unpopular foreigner, came to be loved and admired. Philip II, though little loved outside his family circle, was justly feared and respected. Philip III, however, was incompetent and idle; Philip IV, despite good nature and considerable intelligence, was an unreliable dilettante in kingship. Both monarchs left their responsibility largely in the hands of ministers who were personal favourites, who, whatever their abilities, suffered inevitably from the jealousy of their fellow noblemen, and who in turn became unpopular scapegoats for the failures of government. These *validos*—Olivares in particular—with Castilian arrogance treated the coastal kingdoms as provinces, rather than as the separate realms which in law and tradition they claimed to be. It is true that the liberties of these kingdoms, especially those of Catalonia, if strictly interpreted reduced central government to impotence, and must have been a source of infuriated frustration to any vigorous administrator; but the attempts of ministers such as Olivares to override them naturally intensified resentment against Castile. Finally, Charles II was a pathetic idiot, incapable of governing, of selecting ministers, or of maintaining them in power. Strong kingdoms, however, have often survived the damage caused by weak rulers. The enfeeblement of Spanish government was due not only to the incompetence of the later Hapsburgs but to the circumstances in which they had to work: to the progressive impoverishment of the Crown and to the economic exhaustion of the country as a whole.

While the decline in Spanish political and military dominance revealed itself comparatively gradually, and was not obvious to the world until near the middle of the seventeenth century, the failure of Spanish wealth to keep pace with the immense demands made upon it became evident before the end of the sixteenth. The sixteenth century—certainly the first three-quarters of it—was on the whole a period of fairly rapid economic growth in Spain. Growth was especially evident in the population and industrial activity of many of the larger towns. Nevertheless Philip II—with mounting revenues in Castile and with a great and varied empire to draw on—several times resorted to bank-

ruptcy to escape from part of his enormous indebtedness to international bankers. His seventeenth-century successors were worse off
still, and were driven to more desperate financial shifts, including
repeated coinage debasement. Poverty of governments at that time did
not necessarily imply poverty of peoples. In nearly all European
countries methods of tax collection were wasteful and inefficient;
and in Spain, especially in the peripheral kingdoms, constitutional
tradition permitted considerable resistance to new demands. Throughout the seventeenth century in Spain, however, the evidence is overwhelming that not only the Crown but the country as a whole, and
most individuals within it, were becoming steadily poorer. The resources needed to support armies, navies, court and administration
were less and less available.

During the whole of this period of impoverishment the Spanish
Crown governed and taxed all the most densely populated regions of
the Americas. Its territorial losses there, though a cause of angry
humiliation, were trifling in themselves. From 1580 to 1640, in addition,
the Crown controlled, though indirectly, the Portuguese plantations
in Brazil and Portuguese forts, factories and slave barracoons in West
and East Africa, in India and in the Indonesian archipelago. Despite
territorial and maritime losses to the Dutch, the commercial poten-
tialities of these possessions were still great. To what extent did the
possession of the Indies contribute to the growing power and apparent
prosperity of Spain in the sixteenth century? To what extent did it
precipitate, or delay, or modify, the impoverishment, the military and
political decline of Spain in the seventeenth?

In any attempt to draw a balance it must be remembered that Spain
was not a populous country. Throughout the sixteenth century population increased in most parts of the peninsula, especially in the towns;
but at the end of the century the population of all the Spanish kingdoms
combined was still not more than half that of France, about three-
quarters of that of Italy. The total population of all Philip II's realms
in Europe and North Africa was approximately equal to the population
of France. The acquisition of Portugal added a million or so, but only
balanced the loss due to the revolt of the Netherlands. Contemporary
estimates of numbers—those, for example, contained in the reports of
successive Venetian ambassadors—are little better than guesses, and
material upon which modern research could base more accurate counts
is scanty. There is general agreement, however, that population declined

in the seventeenth century. The population of the Spanish kingdoms, exclusive of Portugal, in the last decade of Philip II's reign was probably about 8,000,000. Many estimates put it as low as 6,000,000 a hundred years later. As we have seen, Spain suffered from a series of very severe epidemics during this time. So did other European countries, but in Spain people appeared to lack the resilience which in other countries enabled populations to recover quickly from such disasters. The attrition due to constant war must have been among the causes of this debility. Armies, it is true, were small in relation to total populations, but losses were often relatively severe. The Spaniards lost at Rocroy 14,000 men of an army of 26,000. Such losses fell upon a vigorous and prolific section of the male population. Probably a more important cause of debility was chronic undernourishment, which affected almost all classes in some degree. Spain as a whole ceased to be self-sufficient in grain about the middle of the sixteenth century, and thereafter relied increasingly on imports; but Sicily and the other overworked wheat lands of the western Mediterranean had less and less to spare, and the abundant grain of northern Europe was controlled by Spain's enemies. In the seventeenth century the position grew worse. The picaresque literature of the time is full of references to hunger. The drawn, haggard faces familiar from paintings such as the *Enterramiento del Conde de Orgaz* do not reflect only the peculiarities of El Greco's style. Most Spaniards were hungry much of the time. They were undoubtedly worse fed, in general, than Frenchmen, Dutchmen or Englishmen. In bad years the country came near to famine. Hunger reduced resistance to disease. In the weary, despairing years which followed major epidemics, hunger prevented the rapid recovery which other parts of Europe managed to achieve.

In the general circumstances of hunger, war and pestilence, losses of population due to deliberate expulsion or emigration assumed added significance. The most important expulsion was that of the Moriscos in 1609–14, the most significant emigration that to the Indies. The deported Moriscos were mostly humble peasants, who had been the victims of social and economic discrimination for years. The number actually expelled was estimated by the commissioners in charge of the deportations as 101,694, exclusive of nursing infants. The commissioners' records probably were not complete; some economic historians have put the number as high as 400,000. The social and economic effects were felt most strongly in Valencia, especially in the production of sugar, rice, and wine; though the prices of these commodities in the country as a whole were surprisingly little affected. Land-owners in Morisco areas, however, lost rents and labour, and investors who had made loans or advances to cultivators lost their money. Opinions differ widely on the extent and significance of the expulsion. It was certainly a factor in the general decay of the Spanish economy. On the other hand, religious prejudice and social disunity were such that few people (except the land-owners directly affected, and presumably the Moriscos themselves) made any complaint. Most contemporary writers considered the expulsion to be both meritorious and socially beneficial.

The expulsion of the Moriscos was a single operation covering only five years. Emigration to the Indies, on the other hand, was continuous throughout the sixteenth and seventeenth centuries. Numbers, again, cannot be estimated with any precision. Of the steady increase in the white, or reputedly white, population of the Indies there is no doubt. In New Spain alone it rose from about 1,000 in 1520 to about 63,000 in 1570 (according to López de Velasco), to about 125,000 (according to Díez de la Calle) in the middle of the seventeenth century. How far this rate of increase was attributable to migration and how far to natural increase in the Indies is impossible to say. Emigrants leaving Spain were licensed and registered, but for many years in the sixteenth century the records are lost, and those which survive naturally do not include illicit emigrants, who may have been fairly numerous, deserting seamen from the *flotas*, and so forth. On the other hand, a considerable proportion of those registered as leaving Spain must have died at sea or shortly after arrival in America. At the roughest of rough guesses, perhaps 100,000 people—more rather than less—left Spain permanently for the Indies in the course of the sixteenth century. In the seventeenth century the rate of emigration may well have been higher. There are no adequate records on which even a guess could be based. Bad conditions and contracting economic opportunities in Spain encouraged emigration. On the other hand, shipping space was limited— increasingly so in the seventeenth century—the cost of passage was high, and there was no organised system of indenture comparable with that in the English or French colonies. The absolute numbers involved, then, were never very large; but they came from a population which was declining through other causes, and they must have included a high proportion of people of vigour and initiative. They came from all occupations and all classes of society save the higher nobility, who did not cross the Atlantic except very occasionally as viceroys. They came from all parts of Spain; Isabella's legislation confining emigration to subjects of Castile was never effectively enforced. The population of the Indies, in fact, was heterogeneous, including Portuguese and some accepted non-Iberian foreigners; but most emigrants, of course, were Spaniards. Castilians and Andalusians predominated, but there were also many Biscayans, Galicians and Canary islanders. Only Catalonia, Aragon and Valencia were relatively unaffected. Emigration must be reckoned among the factors contributing to the depopulation of Spain in the seventeenth century. Though the Spanish government on the whole encouraged emigration to the Indies, intelligent foreign observers considered it to be a serious loss. To quote only one example, John Evelyn, in a pamphlet in 1674 denouncing English emigration, referred to 'the ruinous numbers of our men daily flocking to the American plantations, whence so few return . . . which in time will drain us of people, as now Spain is, and will endanger our ruin, as the Indies do Spain'.

Spain was not only sparsely populated; in general it was poor in natural resources, and this too must be borne in mind in assessing the place of the Indies in the Spanish economic system. The cool moist valleys of Cantabria, it is true, supported prosperous, small-scale rainfall farming; Valencia and Murcia produced subtropical irrigated crops, only partly interrupted by the expulsion of the Moriscos; the rich plain of the Guadalquivir was full of vineyards, olive-groves and wheat-fields; but over the greater part of Spain food crops were poor and sparse at best. In the dry, rocky expanses of the central *meseta*, wealth was chiefly pastoral, horned cattle in the Andalusian uplands north of the Guadalquivir, sheep in Old and New Castile. Castile produced great quantities of high-quality wool, some of which was exported through Burgos and the Biscay ports, some made into cloth by the weavers of Soria and Segovia. Throughout the first three-quarters of the sixteenth century, sheep-grazing, wool-weaving and the wool trade expanded steadily. With the expansion, the numbers of sheep also increased. In an arid country, with sparse and short-lived herbage, much of the grazing was necessarily transhumant. The great flocks followed the young grass. The sheep-owners' gild, the Mesta, through its financial influence on the Crown, and through the pugnacity of its half-nomadic shepherds, secured many privileges for its members: the maintenance of open migration routes, hundreds of miles in length; rights of access to arable land after harvest; rights of wood-cutting in forests along the way. The privileges of the Mesta effectively impeded the development of arable farming and seriously aggravated the shortage of grain.

The sixteenth-century heyday of sheep and their owners was over by 1570. Towards the end of the century the system of markets and fairs, at which the wool was bought and sold, was dislocated by the long war in Flanders, and many dealers were ruined by royal bankruptcies. Both the trade and the industry entered upon a decline from which they never fully recovered. Meanwhile the sheep themselves, as they increased in numbers, had caused damage of a different kind. They destroyed herbage, damaged growing crops and encouraged soil erosion. By grazing down young seedlings they prevented the regeneration of forests. The late sixteenth century and the early seventeenth were a time of hard winters and long dry summers. In Old Spain, as in New, sheep in vast numbers destroyed the means of their own subsistence. The Mesta flocks declined rapidly in size, and the Mesta itself in importance, in the seventeenth century; but the damage had been done.

Against the background of the somewhat primitive rural economy of Castile, the remarkable growth of some of the industrial cities in the sixteenth century stands out in sharp relief. The doubling of the population of such centres as Burgos, Segovia and Toledo, the even more rapid growth of Seville, indicated an industrial and commercial expansion which, in part at least, must be attributed to the stimulating effect of the Indies trade. It is true that Spain remained, as always, primarily a producer of raw materials, exporting wine, olive oil and wool in return for foreign wares; and that oil and wine were among the commodities in chief demand in the Indies. At the same time, however, the silk, woollen cloth, glove, leather and cutlery industries not only supplied a large part of the domestic market but also furnished considerable exports to the Indies. Even Catalan cloth found its way in considerable quantities to the Indies, *via* Medina del Campo and Seville, in the middle decades of the sixteenth century. This striking industrial growth, however, proved to be a temporary phenomenon. Neither internal consumption nor the demands of the Indies trade sufficed to maintain its momentum. Since in the late sixteenth century the demand for manufactured goods in the Indies continued to increase, the failure of Spanish industry to profit correspondingly by the increase calls for comment.

The kingdoms of the Indies did not develop as a neat and effective economic complement of Spain or of Castile. The Seville monopoly has frequently been blamed for unreasonably constricting trans-Atlantic trade, and it is true that commercial monopolies as a rule prefer to deal in limited quantities of goods at high prices. The Seville *consulado* was no exception. Between 1529 and 1573, however, a number of other channels were legally open to export trade; but little use was made of them. Legal restrictions are only a partial explanation, therefore. It must be remembered that the native population of the Indies in the sixteenth century was declining catastrophically, and that most Indians had little purchasing power. The export trade to the Indies was almost entirely a trade in goods for sale to Spanish settlers. The early dependence of the island settlers on imported European foodstuffs, as we have seen, was a major factor in establishing Seville as the commercial capital of the Indies. The demand for grain fell away in time, partly because Spaniards began to grow wheat in favoured parts of the Indies, partly because some of them grew accustomed to eating maize. The sustained demand for wine and oil continued to bring profit to Seville and Cadiz shippers and to Andalusian land-owners. The profits in this trade, however, were relatively modest in relation to the volume of goods carried, and the trade was subject to serious uncertainties due to weather. Heavy casks and jars were difficult to transport overland to the ports of shipment or to river-side jetties; a wet winter could seriously delay, and in part prevent, the freighting of the Indies fleet. Manufactured goods were more profitable and easier to handle. Some of the manufactured articles in high demand in the Indies—pottery, saddlery, silk—were made in Seville and other Anda-lusian towns, and were exported from the Guadalquivir in consider-able quantities. Limits to the expansion of these exports were set less by legal restrictions and transport difficulties than by American com-petition. Ceramic industries of European type soon grew up in the Indies, and most of the American provinces produced great quantities of leather, some of which was used locally by emigrant saddlers. In the second half of the sixteenth century only the better qualities of European pottery and leather goods found a market; the ordinary workaday kinds were locally made. As for silk, rich men in the Indies used it freely for clothing; attempts to establish a silk industry in New Spain, after promising beginnings, eventually failed; but from the later sixteenth century the settlers of New Spain—and, for a time, those of

Peru—had access, through Manila, to supplies of Chinese silk, cheaper and of far better quality than that imported from Europe.

Of the other manufactured articles of European origin in high demand in the Indies—woollen and linen cloth and clothing, tools, weapons and general hardware, glass, paper and books—few were made in Andalusia. Woollens always sold well, especially the better qualities; the coarse woollen blankets used by Indians were mostly made, after the middle of the sixteenth century, in the Indies. The principal centres of good-quality wool-weaving were in Catalonia and Old Castile, far from the Guadalquivir, far from any harbour where goods could easily be shipped to America. The interior communications of Spain, even by the normal European standards of the time, were extremely difficult; and in the late sixteenth century the Castilian woollen industry was declining for other reasons. Internal customs duties, moreover, deterred the manufacturers of the rest of Spain from sending their goods to the colonies through the kingdom of Seville. The Seville merchants found it more economical to import cloth for shipment to the Indies by sea from the Low Countries or from France. In the iron and steel industries the story was similar. The products of Bilbao and Toledo were of excellent quality, but high costs and transport difficulties made them uncompetitive. Similar articles brought to Seville in Dutch ships from northern Europe steadily displaced them in the Indies trade. Already in the late sixteenth century, therefore, a considerable proportion of goods shipped from Seville to the Indies—with the continuing exceptions of wine and oil—was of foreign origin. In the seventeenth century the population and industrial activity of almost all Spanish towns, except Madrid, declined abruptly. The settlers in the Indies had then to get most of their manufactured imports from elsewhere. Dutch and English smugglers drove a thriving and increasing trade in the Caribbean ports. Foreign ships lying in Cadiz road transferred their cargoes illegally, often with the connivance of port officials, to the ships of the westbound *flotas*. Lawful exports of manufactured goods, which paid duty and were openly shipped from Seville, were commonly of French origin; in the later seventeenth century, indeed, the French controlled the greater part of the official trade; the merchant houses of the Seville *Consulado* lent their names, and acted for a commission as agents of French exporting firms.

Besides European food and manufactures, the settlers in the Indies

demanded African slaves. Spaniards had no lawful access to the Guinea
coast, the principal source of supply; Portuguese, who were the principal slave dealers in the sixteenth century, had no lawful access to the
Indies. Before 1580, apart from smuggling and apart from occasional
short-term individual licenses, slavers had to buy their slaves from Portuguese middlemen, and clear from Seville. The consequent charges,
inconveniences and delays added to the mortality of the slaves on passage
and to their price when they arrived. From this dilemma an escape
was suggested by the union of the two crowns in 1580. In 1595 the
Spanish government consented to the first of a long series of slave
Asientos. This was an agreement for farming out the slave-trade, or
the greater part of it, to a Portuguese contractor who was to organise
the whole business, maintaining his own stations in Spain, in Africa
and in the Indies. He and his sub-contractors might ship slaves directly
from Africa to America, making their own arrangements for convoy
and escort if necessary. The port of Buenos Aires, already the channel
of clandestine *peruleiro* trade between Brazil and Upper Peru, was
officially opened for the reception of slaves. In return for this concession the contractor undertook to ship certain numbers of slaves
to ports, designated by the Crown, where slaves were urgently needed.
In the early seventeenth century considerable numbers of slaves were
shipped to the Spanish Indies in Portuguese ships on these terms; but
Brazil competed strongly for the available supply, and there were
never enough. Participation in the Spanish slave-trade was the only
compensation the Portuguese received for the loss of national independence and for the disasters which befell their empire under Spanish
rule. The Spanish Crown, for its part, became dependent for the provision of essential labour to the mines and plantations of the Indies
upon a group of semi-foreigners who were temporarily and unwillingly
its subjects, and who were themselves soon to lose control of the
principal sources of supply.

The failure of the Spanish industrial and commercial communities
to provide the Indies market adequately with any of the commodities
most in demand there, was accompanied by a corresponding failure
to exploit the Indies as a source of tropical commodities for sale in
Europe. Seville never rivalled Lisbon, Antwerp or Amsterdam as a
centre for the import and redistribution of 'spices'. It had no pepper or
cloves to distribute. The 'spices' native to America were unfamiliar,
and demand for them grew very slowly. Cochineal was a valuable article

of trade, but it was a wild product collected by Indians, and the amount available was never large. Some native plants—sweet potatoes, for example, candied as a sweetmeat or tinctured with eryngium as an aphrodisiac—had a limited sale as curiosities. Cacao, later to become an enormously valuable commodity, though it caught the fancy of the conquerors of New Spain, was not imported into Spain until about 1580. It deteriorates rapidly when damp, moreover, and is therefore difficult to ship in good condition. Chocolate did not become a fashionable beverage until well into the seventeenth century. Tobacco, another native American plant, has made more fortunes than all the silver of the Indies, but not mainly for Spaniards. Some Spanish physicians credited it with medicinal properties, and small quantities were re-exported from Spain in the later sixteenth century; but tobacco-smoking did not become an established social habit in any part of Europe until the early seventeenth century. By that time other maritime peoples, commercially more enterprising than the Spaniards, were sailing to the Indies to buy tobacco from 'wild' Indians, or to grow it for themselves in areas unoccupied by Spain.

Most of the major native food plants of the Americas—maize, potatoes, cassava, *phaseolus* beans—were introduced to the Old World by Spaniards or Portuguese in the sixteenth and seventeenth centuries. Potatoes have become a major staple in northern Europe, cassava in West Africa. Maize is a fodder crop of the first importance, and is food for human beings also in parts of central and southern Europe, parts of Asia and much of Africa. The enormous contribution of these plants to the feeding of mankind in the Old World, however, was an indirect and incidental result of the Spanish conquest in the New. Spaniards in Spain, intensely conservative in their food habits, paid them little attention. It would have been impossible, in any event, to carry significant quantities of these bulky foodstuffs across the Atlantic in the available shipping. They were never regularly imported into Spain or sold abroad. Cassava almost certainly was introduced to Africa through its use in victualling slavers. The story which attributes the introduction of potatoes into Ireland, and thence throughout northern Europe, to Sir Walter Raleigh is at least plausible. Maize was first grown in Europe on a considerable scale in Lombardy in the late sixteenth century. The roundabout manner of its introduction there is suggested by its Italian name, *grano turco*.

Spaniards introduced an immense variety of Old World plants and animals to America. Some of the introduced products were commodities in demand in Europe, but their value in the official Indies trade was limited, because they competed with similar products in Spain. Sugar, for example, was grown in southern Spain and in the Canaries. Sugar from the Indies was imported into Seville from the 1520s, and some of it re-exported; but the quantity so handled was never very large. Sugar produced in New Spain was mostly consumed locally, though some was exported from the Cortés estates coastwise to Peru; the colonial sweet tooth was notorious. Much of the island production, from the later sixteenth century, was sold to foreign interlopers. It was the Portuguese in Brazil who, from the late sixteenth century, first produced American sugar on a large commercial scale for export to Europe. Among minor plant products exported from the Indies to Spain, dyestuffs were the most important; and though many of them were wild forest products, the most valuable, indigo, was an introduced cultivated crop. Its value in the Indies trade was limited by the languishing state of the Spanish textile industry in the late sixteenth century and throughout the seventeenth, but appreciable quantities were re-exported from Seville. Pastoral products, especially hides and tallow, were major objects of export from New Spain and the islands; but, again, they merely supplemented the similar products of Castile. The numerous cargoes of hides shipped in the *flotas* were relatively unprofitable, though certainly better than sending ships back in ballast. The demand for leather was far greater in northern Europe than in Spain; and from the later sixteenth century settlers in the smaller Caribbean colonies were able to sell hides as well as sugar to illicit English and Dutch traders, who found it more economical to run the risks of a direct voyage than to buy American produce in Seville.

Far more important than all these varied commodities—at least in the official trade—were the precious metals. The predominance of gold and silver—silver especially—among the products of the Indies is the most characteristic feature of the whole story of the Spanish Empire, and the feature which most caught the imagination of contemporaries. The literature of the time abounds in references to it; Cervantes' allusions in *Rinconete y Cortadillo* and *El celoso extremeño* are only the most famous of many. At no time in the later sixteenth and early seventeenth centuries did the proportion of gold and silver in the recorded eastbound cargoes amount to less than 80 per cent, computed by value. In 1594, the peak year of the sixteenth century, the proportions were: gold and silver 95·6 per cent, cochineal 2·8 per cent, hides 1·4 per cent, indigo ·29 per cent. All the complexities of the official Indies trade, indeed, can be reduced to three main groups: the supply to the Indies of certain foodstuffs and a limited quantity and range of manufactured goods produced in Spain; the import into the Guadalquivir ports, and re-export thence to the Indies, of a wider range and larger quantity of manufactured goods of foreign origin; and the import into the Guadalquivir from the Indies of vast quantities of bullion.

The proportions of gold and silver in the treasure shipments are difficult to estimate precisely from the available records; but from the middle decades of the sixteenth century silver greatly predominated, both in bulk and in total value. Between 70 and 75 per cent of the total shipments were the property of private firms and individuals. Crown treasure, the product of taxation in the Indies after the deduction of the costs of administration, accounted for the rest; though sometimes, in years of crisis, the Crown also sequestered, by way of forced loan or actual seizure, additional quantities of treasure belonging to private persons, a practice which added to the hazards of trans-Atlantic business and naturally encouraged fraud. The entire shipment in each east-bound fleet was under the care of a senior official, the silver master of the fleet, who was responsible for safe delivery in Seville, and who drew his remuneration from fees paid by the owners. The system leaked at every joint. Some silver masters were venal. Banditry, piracy and smuggling caused losses in the Indies and at sea. Silver passed secretly to foreigners in the Azores and in Cadiz, even in Lisbon, to pay for purchases of foreign goods and to avoid the dues levied in Seville. Some was smuggled into Seville in bags and casks containing other commodities. The officially registered shipments were landed at Seville, checked by officials of the *Casa*, and then, for the most part, sold to silver merchants. These middlemen were the financial princes of the Seville water-front. In the sixteenth century they were usually individual capitalists; but a decree of 1608 required them to be organised in firms of at least two partners—one of the first appearances in Spain of the limited partnership, the *société en commandite*. The principal function of the silver merchants was to arrange with the mint for the coinage of silver; the circulation of bar silver was prohibited. Once coined, the silver passed into general circulation.

The chief effect of this steady increase in the volume of silver coin upon the economies of Andalusia, of the whole of Spain, and by degrees of the rest Europe, is well known; a continuous, though fluctuating, rise in all commodity prices. The general level of prices in Spain rose by about 400 per cent in the course of the sixteenth century. The connection between American silver and rising prices was dimly perceived by some advanced theorists; Jean Bodin first drew attention to it in 1568, and his reasoning was followed by a few Spanish economists in the seventeenth century, of whom Moncada and Martínez de Mata were the most eminent. The Spanish government, however, remained unaffected by their arguments, and endeavoured by all possible means to increase the production and shipment of silver and to restrict its export from Spain. The restrictions were not, and could not be, generally effective; but they did to some extent impound silver in Spain, and so accentuated the difference between Spanish and general European prices. Wages naturally rose in response; but as always they lagged behind prices. This lag, together with technological advances, stimulated the industrial and commercial progress of Spain in the first three-quarters of the sixteenth century; but in Spain wages caught up with prices more rapidly than in the rest of Europe. In the first half of the seventeenth century, indeed, the index numbers of wages, calculated on a 1571–80 basis, were in some years above those of prices. In industries where this occurred business profits could be made only by means of continued technological progress to reduce costs; but the general illusion of prosperity, the feeling of easy money, the accompanying contempt for manual arts, discouraged technological advance precisely when it was most needed. By the early seventeenth century these processes, together with heavy taxation, had raised Spanish costs and prices so far above those of the rest of Europe that all industry was discouraged and export industry in particular was at a serious and growing disadvantage. Even the traditional export trade in raw materials suffered; in the course of the seventeenth century Irish wool and Swedish iron competed more and more successfully in northern Europe with the wool and iron exported from Bilbao. Among internal industries, one particularly affected was ship-building; Spain had always depended heavily upon imported sail-cloth and cordage; in the early seventeenth century rising costs, technical conservatism and the depletion of forests brought ship-building almost to a standstill.

Between a quarter and a third of the treasure shipped from the Indies to Spain was consigned on behalf of the Crown. From the crude

and incomplete accounts of the time, in the absence of anything resembling a modern budget, it is impossible to calculate precisely what
proportion of the royal income was derived from this source. The
proportion rose in the second half of the sixteenth century probably
from 10 or 12 per cent in the middle years of the century to as much
as 25 per cent in peak years in the 1590s. Apart from its absolute amount
the Indies revenue had a special value of its own. It was in the form of
bullion and immediately negotiable. It was—or appeared to be—
certain and predictable; the metal existed in the ground, and the power
of the viceregal governments to direct labour ensured that—whatever
hardships the Indies might suffer—it would be mined. The taxes on
it were collected by salaried officials, not by farmer-speculators. Fraud
and theft, banditry by land, piracy or enemy action by sea, naturally
took their toll, and a heavy one; but in the sixteenth century the
degree of success achieved in guarding against these losses was fairly
uniform. The Indies revenue was unconditional. The King, in order
to collect it, did not have to endure weeks of bargaining with *cortes* or
private corporations; or enter into undertakings to redress grievances;
or explain the purposes for which the money was needed. The treasure
was his, to use as he saw fit. The possession of a large unappropriated
revenue, however inimical to constitutional liberties, was an immense
administrative advantage, and was generally applauded by the King's
subjects. The amount of the Indies revenue, moreover, was greatly exaggerated by report, in Spain and elsewhere. Its possession encouraged
the Spanish Crown in an exaggerated estimate of its own international
responsibilities, influence and power; and, conversely, aroused in other
European countries an exaggerated fear and envy of Spain. It appeared,
even to professional financiers, a more valuable asset than it really was.
In borrowing the money and making the transfer arrangements necessary for the payment of garrisons in Italy and the Low Countries,
of armies campaigning in Germany and fleets in the Atlantic and the
Mediterranean, the Crown offered the Indies revenue as its principal
security. Large as it was, larger still as it was believed to be, the treasure
was never enough to secure these enormous borrowings adequately. It
was always pledged to international financiers long before it left the
Indies. Any interruption or delay in the silver shipments, accordingly,
damaged Spanish credit disastrously and caused repercussions in all the
financial centres of Europe. In 1592 Philip II—in a period when the
level of silver shipments was very high, and after twice repudiating

his debts and leaving a trail of financial ruin—was constrained to the public admission in the *Cortes* that he still owed more than 13,000,000 ducats.

Spain in the early seventeenth century, then, had slipped into a state of extremely dangerous economic dependence. The working of an inflated economy, the credit of the government, the maintenance of royal authority at home and influence abroad, had all come to depend on a steady influx of American bullion. This steady flow depended in its turn on the availability of shipping, much of it Portuguese or foreign-built; on a supply of slave labour, carried by the Portuguese; and on a supply of manufactured goods, mostly imported from France or the Low Countries and paid for in silver, both for the needs of Spain itself and for re-export to the Indies in order to earn more silver.

In the second and third decades of the seventeenth century the system began to break down. The terms of trade in Europe moved steadily against Spain. Incessant war with the United Netherlands and France, besides impoverishing Spain directly, made essential imports more and more difficult to obtain. The Portuguese under Spanish rule lost to Dutch and English aggression many ships and most of the factories and barracoons in West Africa upon which the supply of slaves to the Indies depended. In 1640 they revolted against Spain and asserted their national independence, so that their shipping was no longer readily available for Spanish purposes. Most catastrophic of all, the supply of American silver began to dry up at its source. To some extent this was due to depopulation and consequent shortage of labour in the mines, but even more to exhaustion of the easiest and most productive veins. As the rich surface deposits became worked out, the miners had either to work poorer ores near the surface or else sink deep shafts. The first alternative presented problems of reduction, the second problems of haulage, drainage and support, which seventeenth-century technology could not readily solve; both courses, moreover, added to the cost of production. Total recorded imports of precious metals into Spain reached their highest level in the decade 1591–1600. The annual average for those years has been estimated by E. J. Hamilton at just under 7,000,000 *pesos de minas*; the *peso de minas* being a bullion measure theoretically equal in value to the *castellano* or ducat. For the first six decades of the seventeenth century the corresponding estimates are: 1601–10, 5,580,853; 1611–20, 5,464,058; 1621–30, 5,196,520; 1631–40,

3,342,545; 1641–50, 2,553,435; 1651–60, 1,065,488; this last figure being almost equal to that for the decade 1541–50, in which the first big silver 'strikes' were made. The Crown share of these declining imports declined even more steeply, because of a steady increase in the number of officials and in the general cost of administration and defence in the Indies. The president of the Council of Finance reported in December 1616 that 'in the last two years hardly a million ducats have come each year', instead of the 2,000,000 ducats a year during the first years of the reign. By 1620 the Crown receipts had fallen to 800,000 ducats. As silver became scarcer, the Crown resorted first to debasement—a device which Philip II had always refused to contemplate—and eventually to the coinage of enormous quantities of *vellón*, coins either of pure copper or silver and copper alloy. The inflation caused by the influx of American silver was thus followed by a further inflation, caused by excessive issues of copper coins, but punctuated by sharp and disastrous deflations through arbitrary revaluations of coinage, mistakenly conceived as a remedy for high prices and general scarcity. While universally envied because of their monopoly of the American mines, Spaniards saw their precious metals driven out of circulation in the second quarter of the seventeenth century by a cumbersome and unstable medium of exchange. Even the supplies and munitions for the Indies fleets had to be purchased with *vellón*, and often the gold and silver which arrived in Seville never entered circulation in Spain. The private treasure was sequestered by the Crown for remittance abroad, along with the public treasure; and the owners were indemnified in *vellón*. Even copper was not always available for minting in sufficient quantity and at prices which the Crown could pay, especially in view of the enormous demand for copper for ships' fittings and for gun-founding, and of the difficulty experienced in importing European copper in time of war. In 1643, by a final irony, the *Armada*, the guardships of the Indies fleet, arrived at Seville with a cargo of American copper for the Spanish mints.

As the principal commodity in which it dealt became scarcer, the official Indies trade as a whole declined in volume. The turn of the tide, the moment when the tendency to expand became a tendency to contract, is difficult to fix precisely; the first two decades of the seventeenth century represent—albeit with many fluctuations—a statistical plateau, a period of hesitations and uncertainties. The average number of ships sailing annually to the Indies in the 1590s had been about 130, with a sharp drop in 1597–8. The drop was due to enemy action in the Caribbean and at Cadiz in 1595 and 1596, to a royal bankruptcy in 1597 and to the epidemic of 1596–7 which reduced the purchasing power of the Spanish community in New Spain. The trade recovered by the end of the decade and was well maintained in the early years of the seventeenth century. The year 1607, however, was a disastrous one with only thirty-seven ships west-bound; a crisis of confidence caused by reports of glutted markets in Peru (at the height of the Manila–Acapulco–Lima trade) and by another royal bankruptcy, which paralysed credit and delayed delivery, by the Fugger *concessionnaires* at Almadén, of essential supplies of mercury. By contrast—and due, no doubt, in part to delayed sailings left over from the previous year—1608 was the record year of the whole history of the *Carrera*, with over 200 west-bound sailings; and 1609 and 1610 also were years of big west-bound fleets. It might have been expected that the temporary cessation of war with the Dutch in 1609 would release the energies necessary for further expansion; but the will and the vigour to expand had been sapped by economic debility and by war. The truce, as it happened, coincided with a steep fall in prices in New Spain, to which the high level of Pacific trade at the time probably contributed. The effect of the resulting business losses was to reduce shipments in 1611. Many American markets, moreover, had been lost to competitors during the war, and because of high Spanish costs could not be recovered. Between 1610 and 1621—years of at least formal peace—the best the *Carrera* could achieve was a moderately prosperous stability: a moderate recession in 1611–12, a recovery about 1614, a further recession towards the end of the decade. In 1621 war was resumed with the Dutch, and the Crown embarked on its desperate experiments with copper coinage. Stability gave way to a violent seesaw of prices in Spain, and of annual volume and value of trade. The *Carrera* still had capital reserves and a considerable momentum to keep it going; but the confidence of exporters was shaken, and customers baulked at prices pushed up by soaring freight and insurance charges. Ominously, the demand for mercury in New Spain dropped alarmingly; a shrinking mining industry could not use the quantities which the government sent out. Although, therefore, the total number of sailings from Seville was surprisingly well maintained in the 1620s—taking the decade as a whole—an increasing proportion of the ships were costly and uneconomic men-of-war. The number of genuine merchant sailings progressively declined. Ironically, the *Consulado* members chose this time to elbow their competitors from the Canaries finally out of the trade by royal legislation; a Pyrrhic victory for the Seville monopolists, a loss of handy small merchant ships to the *Carrera*.

In the 1630s the decline in the total volume of the official trade be-became steep, continuous and unmistakable. The war with France which broke out in 1635 caused a serious loss of freight, since many of the goods normally carried were of French origin. The recruitment of trained seamen for the trans-Atlantic trade became more and more difficult. The most famous and comprehensive account of the *Carrera*—Veitia Linaje's *Norte de la Contratación*, published in 1672—sadly describes a trade which was a shadow of what it had been. In the 1650s official sailings to the Indies rarely exceeded forty in a year. In some years there were less than twenty, including warships. Admittedly the average size of ships had increased over the years, largely because warships formed an increasing proportion of the total number; but, even so, the average annual tonnage, again including warships, in the 1650s was less than a quarter of what it had been in the first decade of the century. The *armadas* in bad years actually outnumbered the merchantmen they escorted, and their cost rose year by year. The rates of duty levied to meet the cost rose correspondingly, and duties became more and more difficult to collect in the face of massive evasions. In 1660 the *Casa*, in despair, finally abandoned the whole system of *ad valorem* duties, and replaced it by the arbitrary lump-sum levy known as *indulto*.

Ships of any sort were hard to find in adequate numbers, even for the attenuated trade of the 1650s. Ship-building in Spain was a dying industry. The defection of Portugal in 1640 had deprived the *Carrera* of many valuable ships. It would have been difficult to maintain the trade at all, but for the increasing contribution of West Indian ship-yards, especially those of Havana. West Indian ships began to appear in the trade in significant numbers in the late 1620s. In 1650 less than a third of the ships in the *Carrera* were Spanish-built. About a third, mostly small merchantmen of Dutch origin, were foreign-built. A little more than a third, including many of the warships, were American-built; yet one more example of the dependence of Spain upon its Indies.

Economic and demographic considerations apart, to what extent did war, and the losses due to war, contribute to this catastrophic decline?

The myth of the inexhaustible wealth of the Indies died hard, and so did the envy and fear which Spanish power had provoked. As Spain became poorer and weaker, Spanish fleets and colonies became more vulnerable, and other seafarers, Dutch and English especially, became more eager and able to exploit or plunder them. The story of these depredations has now to be considered.

CHAPTER 13

Peril by sea

THE *Carrera de Indias* was always a hazardous trade. Those who invested in it, as we have seen, faced unusual business risks: wild fluctuations in prices, both in Spain and in the Indies, unpredictable gluts and scarcities, so that sometimes freights could not be had, while at other times goods had to be dumped, unsaleable, upon tropical beaches; back-door competition from unexpected—and not always illicit—sources; sudden changes in the financial and commercial policy of the Crown; occasionally, and worst, forced loans, tardily repaid, or sequestrations of bullion cargoes for a derisory compensation in debased copper. Even when all went well—when prices were stable and markets steady, when convoys sailed on time, when weather was kind and winds favourable—the owners and masters of Indies ships had to allow for the special conditions of the Tropics: the rank growth of weed on ships' bottoms, the secret tunnelling of the ship-worm, the general rot and decay of wooden ships in conditions of damp heat; worse still, the rot and decay of the men in the ships, from scurvy at sea, from yellow fever and malaria in tropical harbours. When winds were contrary and passages prolonged, hunger and thirst were added to the list of dangers. Weather itself could be dangerous. Much of the trade of the Indies, especially that to New Spain and the islands, passed through hurricane latitudes. Hurricanes could be avoided by carefully timed and punctual departures; but delays in fitting-out or freighting often made punctuality impossible, and even punctual sailings could not avoid the storms of the open Atlantic.

The *Casa de la Contratación* maintained a famous school of navigation in which navigating officers were trained, examined and licensed for the Indies trade; but there were never enough trained pilots, and the navigational practice of the sixteenth and seventeenth centuries in the ocean trades was rudimentary at best. It was based upon accumulated knowledge of wind systems, ocean currents and compass variations; a careful dead-reckoning checked by rough observations of latitude made with open-sight instruments; a good memory for coast-lines and a judicious use of the lead in approaching land. Charts were small in scale and based—in the sixteenth century at least—on magnetic compass bearings, a fruitful source of error; not until the very end of the century was a workable projection devised, whereby a chart could be based on a grid of parallels and meridians, and compass courses could be plotted accurately as straight lines. Even so, only the best seventeenth-century navigators understood the use of such a chart. Even the best officers were sketchily equipped for taking ships across great oceans and through waters studded with razor-sharp reefs. Harbours were more dangerous than the sea itself. To reach Seville, ships must pass a treacherous river bar; in the Indies they lay for weeks in unprotected roads.

In the face of these physical dangers the Indies fleets made their passages year after year. As might be expected, the toll of shipwreck was a heavy one. Among the most serious disasters were those of 1563—seven ships driven ashore at Nombre de Dios, fifteen wrecked in Cadiz harbour, five lost in the Gulf of Campeche; 1587—six ships grounded and broken up on the bar at San Lúcar; 1590—fifteen ships driven ashore by a 'norther' in Vera Cruz harbour; 1591—sixteen ships wrecked at Terceira; 1601—fourteen at Vera Cruz, again by a 'norther'; 1614—seven wrecked on Cape Catoche. In the seventeenth century the number of losses was smaller, but the number of sailings was smaller too; the rate of loss, despite accumulated experience, did not sensibly improve. Navigational errors caused many of the losses; but the frequency of groundings in familiar harbours provides a significant comment on the handling qualities of the ships. The employment of larger ships, beyond a point, gave no improvement in safety; on the contrary, thanks to the extreme technical conservatism of the Spanish ship-building industry in the late sixteenth and early seventeenth centuries, size outran design. The largest ships—unhandy, heavily armed, often overloaded—were far more dangerous than those of moderate size, especially in the crowded open anchorages which the Indies fleets had to use.

The Indies trade would have been hazardous for ships, seamen and investors even if seafarers of other nations had peacefully respected the

Seville monopoly. Inevitably, however, in the second half of the sixteenth century, it attracted foreign attention and suffered increasingly
from foreign interference. The main termini of the trade in New Spain
and Peru were inland and out of harm's way; but to approach them,
ships had to sail the thousand-mile length of the island-studded
Caribbean, an area where Spanish population and power were thinly
scattered. Many islands were unoccupied and many channels perforce
unwatched. Convoyed fleets were usually safe, but stragglers and
isolated shipping were constantly exposed to attack, by enemy warships in time of war, but also in peace-time by pirates, or by vessels
which were neither warships nor pirates but unauthorised, unavowed
privateers whom the Spaniards called *cosarios*. The bolder predators
attacked harbours as well as shipping. Sores' sack of Havana in 1556
and Drake's raid on Nombre de Dios in 1572 were classic examples of
this type of action—small in scale, limited in object, swift and successful. Not all *cosarios*, however, set out as raiders. Even Drake did not
initially. Many of them were commercial smugglers, trading in slaves,
hardware and textiles in exchange for sugar, hides and silver. They
usually went armed, and often traded at the pike's point, using threats
of force when necessary to secure the connivance of local officials.
Before 1580 many Portuguese slavers did business in this way, to avoid
the delays and costs of trading through Seville. This also was the
pattern of the slaving voyages which Sir John Hawkins made to the
Caribbean in the 1560s. Hawkins was no pirate but a business man who
delivered his goods and paid for his purchases.

The Spanish settlers in the West Indies, at least in the islands and
smaller mainland ports, on the whole welcomed such smugglers. They
wanted cheap goods and resented the high prices and infrequent
deliveries of the Seville shippers. On the other hand, they both resented
and feared the constant outbreaks of war in Europe, which loosed
fresh fleets of privateers upon the West Indies. They thought little of a
naval organisation which was largely ineffective against small raiders,
but which treated peaceful smugglers, when it caught them, as if
they were raiders, and so encouraged them to go armed and take to
raiding. They wanted local defence, for they never knew in those
small and ill-armed settlements, when a strange sail appeared, whether
it was to be welcomed officially as a Spaniard, received discreetly as a
foreign trader, or fired upon as a raider.

To the Spanish government these distinctions were unimportant.

Foreign ships, whether pirates, smugglers or men-of-war, were all enemies in the Indies, to be seized whenever possible. Above all—and this, since the navy could not be everywhere at once, was the overriding consideration—the routes and harbours of the silver fleets through the Caribbean and across the Atlantic must be kept clear. Any foreign presence along these routes was a potential threat. Hawkins discovered this: so long as he kept to the minor Caribbean ports he met with no obstacle save official disapproval, easily overcome by bribes or threats; but in 1568, under stress of weather, he called with five ships—one commanded by Drake—to trade and store at San Juan de Ulúa, the harbour of the New Spain *flotas*. There he encountered for the first time not venal local officials but senior officers whose careers were bound up with royal policy. He was trapped in the harbour by an incoming *flota* commanded by the viceroy Martín Enríquez in person. After a show of parley he was attacked and most of his fleet destroyed.

During the years when Hawkins was trading in the Caribbean, Menéndez de Avilés—captain-general, governor of Cuba and *adelantado* of Florida—was working out his reorganisation of the defence of the *Carrera*. His proposals included the provision of powerful escort for all trans-Atlantic fleets; a permanent naval patrol of the waters between the Azores and the Andalusian coast; the creation of *armadillas* —cruiser squadrons—permanently based in the West Indies to seek out and attack corsairs upon their arrival in the area, and to patrol the main trade routes all the year round; the fortification of all the principal harbours and the provision of regular garrisons. The most important harbours were Cartagena, guarding the eastern approach to the isthmus; Santo Domingo, the administrative capital of the islands and a considerable city; Santiago de Cuba; San Juan del Puerto Rico; and, strategically most important of all, Havana. Havana was to provide a safe place of assembly for homeward-bound convoys. To complete the defence and control of the Florida channel, another fortified base was to be constructed opposite Havana, on the coast of Florida. Menéndez made this suggestion in anticipation of French attempts to occupy that area; the actual settlement under Laudonnière naturally gave added force to his arguments. All these remedies, to be effective, had to be applied simultaneously, as parts of an overall plan. Such a project would necessarily be expensive, and attempts to pay for it by increased charges on lawfully carried goods would merely encourage smuggling.

Menéndez' proposals were accepted by Philip II and the Council of the Indies, and partially carried into effect. Havana became an almost impregnable fortress, safe against enemy attack for nearly 200 years, with a dockyard capable not only of repairing but of building fair-sized ships of local timber. Appropriately, the works were paid for by subsidies from the treasury of New Spain. Cartagena was fortified. The French settlement in Florida was destroyed and a Spanish fort built in its place. Santo Domingo and Santiago, on the other hand, though much more important as local centres of population, received relatively slight additions to their fortifications, sufficient to stand off casual raids, but not to face attack by organised fleets. Similarly, in operating against corsairs in the Caribbean, Menéndez and his successors were compelled by war and financial shortage to concentrate on the immediate problem of getting the *flotas* through, and to postpone the secondary task of protecting local shipping throughout the year. The sailing warships, which Menéndez initially proposed for his Caribbean patrols, could not pursue raiders of light draught in shoal water. In 1578 and again in 1582, galleys were sent from Spain to assist the patrols in performing this work; but galleys, whether based on Santo Domingo or, later, on Cartagena, proved only moderately effective. Oarsmen were hard to recruit and maintenance costs were high. The squadrons had only an intermittent existence. Despite Menéndez' vigour and ability, therefore, and despite his success in capturing some fifty corsair ships during his career, the minor harbours of the West Indies were never safe from raiding. Even the principal cities, though safe enough against mere pirates, were still vulnerable to attack by organised fleets in time of war. Their situation grew worse as relations with England worsened, as religious bitterness came to reinforce the rapacity of the corsairs, and as that other naval genius, Drake, was loosed upon the Indies in independent command of voyages of reprisal.

Drake's Indies voyage of 1585 was no mere raid but a full-scale naval operation carried out by a fleet of more than twenty sail. The plan included an attack on Santo Domingo and on the port towns of Tierra Firme, in particular Cartagena; then a land attack on Nombre de Dios and Panama in conjunction with local 'wild' Indians and a force of maroons—runaway Negro slaves—in order to control both ends of the land route across the isthmus; and finally the capture of Havana. Drake hoped to hold both Havana and Cartagena with permanent English garrisons. Success would break up the whole communication and supply system of the Spanish Indies. It would deny to Spain for years, perhaps permanently, the means of making war in Europe, and would throw the Indies open to English exploitation. In the event, Santo Domingo was taken and looted, its fortifications and principal buildings gutted, and a ransom exacted. Cartagena resisted stoutly before it, too, fell; but there the loot was disappointing, because most of the valuables in the city had been sent inland before the fighting began. Drake had not enough fit men left to hold Cartagena. He abandoned his attempt on the isthmus and made for the Cayman Islands, thence to Cape San Antonio where, with his ships refitted and his men refreshed, he hoped to intercept the *flota* from New Spain. The *flota*, however, slipped through in heavy weather, unmolested, to the safety of Havana. Judging Havana too strong to be attacked, Drake sailed for home in June 1586.

The Spanish authorities, despite the defeats and the heavy loss of ships which they suffered in their operations against England in 1587 and 1588, set to work to remedy the weaknesses which Drake's voyage had revealed. In the 1590s the defence forces of the Indies were greatly strengthened both by land and by sea. A beginning was made by Antoneli, the best military engineer of his day, on the immense fortifications of Puerto Rico, the windward bastion of Caribbean defence, not so much because of the direct importance of the place to Spaniards as because of the vital necessity of denying its use to Spain's enemies. At the same time communications between the Caribbean bases were greatly improved by the provision of fast despatch boats. When in 1595 another great fleet left England, under the joint command of Drake and Hawkins, on what was to be for both their last Indies voyage they found the Spaniards ready and able to resist. The English were defeated at San Juan del Puerto Rico. They abandoned their project for a second attack on Cartagena. On the isthmus they sacked Nombre de Dios so thoroughly that the Spaniards never reoccupied the place, but moved to the more defensible site of Puerto Belo. They failed to reach Panama, however; and after Drake's death off the coast of Veragua the fleet returned to England by way of the Florida channel, where it was engaged in a running fight by Spanish local naval forces. The operation achieved little directly, but its indirect consequences were serious for Spain. When the news of the English expedition reached Spain a formidable naval force had been hurriedly assembled and sent to the Indies in pursuit under Bernardino Delgadillo de Avellaneda. Avellaneda arrived too late to intercept the English—possibly the news

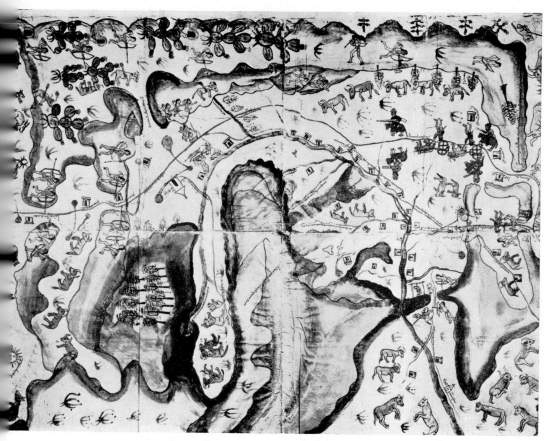

XI *Rural life in sixteenth-century New Spain: a plan of San Miguel in Michoacán and the surrounding country in 1580. Domestic animals include horses, bullocks, and dogs; wild animals, deer, puma and feral pig. A water-mill can be seen to the right of the plan*

XII *Title page of the Doctrina Breve of Fray Juan de Zumárraga, printed in Mexico in 1544: the first printed book in the New World*

of his presence hastened their departure from the Caribbean; but in order to provide him with ships a *flota* destined for New Spain had been denuded of its escort and many of its officers and men, and had been held back at Cadiz. This *flota* was still lying defenceless in Cadiz road when, in July 1596, a joint English and Dutch fleet attacked the port and destroyed the Indies ships at their moorings. As a result of this chain of misfortunes, communications between Spain and New Spain were cut for nearly two years; and in 1597 the Crown again declared its bankruptcy.

On the face of things, the attempts made by French, English and Dutch in the sixteenth century to break the Spanish monopoly of trade and territorial power in the West Indies were all failures; or at least their political and military successes were limited and temporary. The Spanish government refused to consider the open admission of foreigners to the Caribbean. In 1596, at the Treaty of The Hague, France, England and the Netherlands formed an alliance against Spain which seemed strong enough to dismember the Spanish Empire, but the French backed out and made their peace separately in the Treaty of Vervins in 1598. According to later accounts, Henry IV tried to secure a share of the American trade in this treaty. There is no contemporary evidence of these attempts; if made at all, they were unsuccessful, for the treaty is silent on the subject. The English and Dutch fought on; but in 1604, the pacific James I having succeeded Elizabeth, England also made a separate face-saving peace, the Treaty of London; and in 1609 Spain at last secured, in the Twelve Years Truce, at least a respite from wasting war in the Netherlands. The damage done to the Spanish Empire, however, the exhaustion caused by a military effort beyond the power of Spain to support, the depletion of resources in men, ships and money, the contraction of influence and commercial opportunity, were to have lasting and irreparable consequences.

In the *Carrera*, war obviously increased the rate of losses by enemy action at sea. It entailed also an increase in the number of warships escorting the convoys, and, consequently, a steep increase in costs. The best ships were requisitioned for fighting, and charges on the others raised to pay for it. The activities of enemy fleets delayed the sailing of convoys, sometimes—as in 1596—for many months. More serious still, by concentrating a large part of their marine resources upon the maintenance of the *Carrera*, the Spaniards to a large extent sacrificed their freedom to navigate in northern European waters. In order to obtain necessary supplies, including some of the goods which the *flotas* were to carry, they were forced to a humiliating dependence on Hanseatic shipping, and even, by a grudging toleration, upon Dutch ships which continued a risky trade with Spanish ports in spite of war and periodic sequestrations. The need for imports was so urgent that Dutch skippers could usually bribe themselves out of trouble. Most serious of all, perhaps, Spain was largely cut off from northern supplies of war material; of copper for founding bronze ordnance, of naval stores, timber, sail-cloth and cordage, all scarce in Spain, and throughout the Mediterranean. The fleets which crossed the Atlantic in the last decade of the sixteenth century and first decade of the seventeenth were composed increasingly of ageing, worn-out ships, and this naturally increased the rate of loss by wreck. Shortage of materials, together with the high and mounting cost of labour, was largely responsible for the decline of ship-building on the Biscay coast, where most of the ships in the *Carrera* were then built; a decline from which the industry never fully recovered.

Spain still disposed of an immense and formidable accumulated maritime strength. The conviction in official circles that the *Carrera* must at all costs be maintained gave its needs priority over almost all other demands and called forth tremendous and sustained efforts throughout the war. The efforts were remarkably successful. Large fleets crossed the Atlantic, in spite of all hazards, with reasonable regularity. The evidences of contraction and decline, as we have seen, did not become obvious to the world until after the resumption of war with the Dutch in the 1620s. There was still no question, in 1609, of Spain losing control of the main routes of the Indies trade. Spaniards were, however, already losing control of many of the marginal trades of the Caribbean. Heavy losses and high charges rendered the goods carried in the convoys more and more expensive, less and less competitive with goods brought to the smaller ports by smugglers. By the turn of the century the Dutch had supplanted the English as the chief contraband traders of the Caribbean. Deprived of much of their normal supply of Portuguese salt for their fishing industry, they discovered and exploited the vast salt deposits of the Araya lagoon on the coast of Venezuela. Araya became the centre of an illicit trade, enlivened by occasional raiding, more serious than anything the Spanish West Indies had yet known. Besides salt, the Dutch took back tobacco from Venezuela and Guiana, and sold European goods at small ports all along the Main. The pearl fishery of Cumaná was virtually closed by their interference; and the islands, outside the fortified bases, became heavily dependent on Dutch traders. In Hispaniola alone the Dutch hide trade employed twenty ships annually. The Spaniards could retaliate; the *armada* sent out under Luis Fajardo in 1605, with orders to surprise the Dutch at Araya, achieved a notable success, captured twelve ships and temporarily closed the trade. The governors of Venezuela, also, occasionally caught and hanged Dutch smugglers. In general, however, the measures taken by the Spanish authorities to curb smuggling were destructive, and damaged the interests of the colonists as much as those of the Dutch. Typical of such measures were the prohibition of tobacco-growing in Venezuela, to prevent sales to the Dutch; the proposal, made by Antoneli, to let in the sea and inundate the Araya lagoon; and the desperate decision taken in 1605 to depopulate the northern coast of Hispaniola. The settlers of Puerto Plata, Monte Cristi and Yaguana were ordered to leave their homes and move to the south coast, nearer to Santo Domingo and governmental control. Military force was needed to move them. Many fled to Cuba or turned pirate. Their cattle ran wild. The vacuum they left was filled by buccaneers, and later by the French.

The truce gave Spain a deceptive respite from overt hostilities, but not economic peace. The Dutch did not reduce the scale of their contraband trade in the West Indies; they increased it, and the Spaniards were no better able in peace than in war to dislodge them. At the same time they concentrated formidable naval strength against the Portuguese in the East. Portuguese merchants sought compensation in exploiting the trade of Brazil and in developing further contraband trade to Upper Peru, via Brazil and the Río de la Plata—the route of the *peruleiros*—all to the detriment of the official *Carrera*.

In itself, the truce was a bitter humiliation for the Spanish Crown. It was an agreement not with a victorious brother monarch but with heretic rebels; a major blow to Spanish prestige and self-confidence. Moreover, it stated a new and—to Spain—odious principle in international conduct. James I, when negotiating the Treaty of London in 1604, had announced that he would respect the Spanish monopoly of trade and settlement in all territories effectively occupied by Spain, but that he recognised no Spanish rights in unoccupied territory. This contravened a basic assumption of Spanish imperialism, and it was only after much haggling that the Spaniards agreed to a silence which their enemies could interpret as consent. The Dutch secured, in the 1609 Truce, a formal if ambiguous clause embodying the same principle. There had, of course, been attempts at settlement before these dates, but all had failed, either because the places were unsuitable; or because the settlers died or deserted or were driven away by Caribs; or because the Spaniards rooted them out. With suspended hostilities the pace quickened, and some settlements took permanent root, mostly, it is true, in remote places where they could be regarded, by a slight stretch, as compatible with peace with Spain. The French planted in Acadia, the English in Virginia, Bermuda and New England, and the Dutch beside the rivers of Guiana, the swampy 'wild coast' running between the Spanish possessions on the Orinoco and the Portuguese possessions on the Amazon. The promoters of these enterprises commended them not only as sources of 'spices' and naval stores, not only as 'vents' for the troublesome unemployed, but also frankly as possible bases for forays against the Spanish Indies.

Neither Spaniards nor Dutch expected peace to outlast the Twelve Years Truce. Shortly before its expiry, however, a political overturn in Holland displaced the republican oligarchy and the East India interest and brought the Orange party and the West India interest into power. When in 1621 the Dutch girded themselves for renewed war with Spain their West India Company received its formal charter. Here at last was an organisation capable of challenging Spain effectively in West Indian waters—no mere temporary association of partners in smuggling or raiding, but a great permanent joint-stock corporation with at least a nominal capital of over 7,000,000 guilders. It was to maintain its own fleet of warships, to be supplemented by the Estates General when formal war should be declared. It was to have the right to conquer, settle, build, administer and defend.

The directors of the company chose, as the primary object of their aggression, the Portuguese sugar-planting area on the north-east coast of Brazil. They proposed also to capture the Portuguese slaving stations of São Jorge da Mina and São Paulo de Luanda in West Africa, without which the Brazil plantations were unworkable. Secondarily, and simultaneously, a Dutch fleet attacked Spanish shipping and harbours on the eastern coast of Peru. To the Council of the Indies the Pacific threat naturally seemed the most serious, and they responded by desperate, though tardy, attempts to create a standing *Armada de la Mar del Sur*, a guardship squadron to escort silver shipments between

Callao and Panama. The Dutch did not long persist in the remote
Pacific. In Brazil, their first objective, the capital city of Bahía, proved
untenable. They captured the place in 1624 but lost it again in the following year. They did not renew the offensive in Brazil until 1630
and then against Recife, not Bahía. It was in the intervening five years
that the naval commanders sought to recoup their losses in Brazil by
raiding in the West Indies. In this they were overwhelmingly successful.
Successive Dutch fleets carried out sweeps in the Caribbean which
drove the local Spanish shipping from the sea. As for the official
convoys, freight and insurance charges reached almost prohibitive
levels; the Seville shippers became more and more unwilling to face
the risks of capture; more and more warships had to be found to escort
the fleets in order to get the silver home. In 1628, for the first time, they
failed to get the silver home. Piet Heyn, the ablest and most celebrated
of the company's admirals, surprised a homeward-bound *flota* off
Matanzas on the north coast of Cuba, and captured the whole sailing.
This triumph, achieved for the first time and not to be repeated for
thirty years, yielded booty worth 15,000,000 guilders, enough to pay
a dividend of 50 per cent to the company's shareholders and to finance
the new—and successful—offensive in Brazil. The psychological effect
of such a disaster, within a day's sailing of Havana, can be imagined.
The captain-general was tried and executed, an expiatory victim.
Financially, Matanzas ruined Spanish credit in Europe. In the West
Indies it paralysed for a time both communications and defence. It
was followed by several years of systematic pillaging by smaller fleets,
which drove local Spanish shipping from the sea. The armed convoys,
by a miracle of determination, continued their sailings; but an *armada*
of at least twenty warships was now considered necessary to escort a
merchant fleet of, at most, the same number. The war with France
which broke out in 1635 made matters worse, not only by interrupting,
at least temporarily, the supply of French goods for shipment to the
Indies, but also because of the need for warships to defend the harbours
of the Biscay coast. The *Casa de la Contratación* was forced in 1635 to
economise in warships by the inconvenient and uneconomic expedient
of sending out all ships destined for the Indies in one single convoy.

The depredations which followed Matanzas drove home an unwelcome strategic lesson. The *Armada de la Carrera* was needed constantly
for escort duties. However strongly reinforced, it could not be everywhere at once. For preventive patrol, the empire of the Indies needed

a navy of its own, and for a time it got one. In 1635–6 an exceptionally able and energetic councillor of the Indies, Juan de Palafox, persuaded Olivares to adopt the policy which naval commanders in the *Carrera* had been urging upon the Crown ever since the time of Menéndez de Avilés: the creation of a separate battle squadron permanently stationed in the West Indies. In the sixteen-forties the *Armada de las Islas de Barlovento y Seno Mexicano*, a small but formidable force of fast warships, at last took up the task of policing the sea lanes from the Windward Islands to Vera Cruz. The ships were built at Havana, based on Puerto Rico, victualled and stored from Vera Cruz and Santo Domingo. They were paid for by a specific tax; not the *avería* which financed the *Armada de la Carrera*, but a local sales tax, the *alcabala* of New Spain, the rate of which was doubled for the purpose. The plan was sound and well worked out; but it came too late. The situation in the Caribbean was already out of hand, and no Spanish fleet could do more than contain it. The *Armada de Barlovento*, in attempting this, laboured under special difficulties. It was, of course, an expensive weapon. The political difficulty, as well as the cost, of maintaining it permanently in the Caribbean was great. On the one hand, the Spaniards of New Spain resented paying a burdensome tax in order—as they saw it—to protect other peoples' property; on the other, the King needed every ship and every *peso* he could get, for the French war. Like the *Armada de la Carrera*, the *Armada de Barlovento* was the object of endless intrigue by home commanders, who coveted its ships for service in European waters. While it was on station the new fleet suffered in addition from appalling manning difficulties. Constantly depleted by tropical disease, it could not readily draw for replacement upon the motley seafaring population—Italian, Portuguese, even French, Dutch or English, as well as Spanish, whatever the law might say—which drifted in and out of the Atlantic ports of Spain and manned the ships of the *Carrera*. There was no adequate reserve of seamen in the Spanish Caribbean at that time; sometimes the *Armada de Barlovento* could not put to sea, for lack of men. Its periods of effective service, like those of its predecessors, the Cartagena and Santo Domingo galleys, were intermittent and short. It certainly achieved some local success; it probably helped to prevent a repetition of Matanzas; but it could not drive out the Dutch.

Dutch pressure on the defences of the Caribbean after Matanzas had another and more permanent consequence; it enabled other groups of foreigners to settle with impunity in unoccupied islands, and to pay their way by growing crops—first tobacco, later sugar—for sale to Dutch traders. Dutch naval and economic strength sheltered and encouraged the infant Antillean colonies of England and France—Barbados and St Kitts, Martinique and Guadeloupe. Nor was this all: success in settling unoccupied islands naturally encouraged the northerners to go further, and attempt the seizure of territory actually in Spanish possession. The great mainland viceroyalties were too remote and too strong to be attacked, and the Main harbours, though they could be raided, even taken, could not easily be held; some of the islands, however, increasingly neglected by Spain, were easier prey. In 1634 the Dutch seized Curaçao, valuable as a smuggling entrepôt, as well as for its salt-pans. An English company seized and settled Catalina Island—Old Providence—but this was over-bold, and in 1641 the Spaniards retook the island. It was left to Cromwell to plan the boldest of these island projects: an attempt in 1655 to capture Santo Domingo and the island of Hispaniola. The attempt failed. It was based on inaccurate and prejudiced intelligence (partly supplied by Thomas Gage, the renegade Dominican and author of *The English-American*); it was entrusted to an ill-armed, ill-led mob, largely recruited among indented servants in Barbados. The leaders, however, driven off from Santo Domingo, turned their attention to Jamaica in order to retrieve the expedition from total disgrace. Since 1536 the marquisate of Jamaica had been an appanage of the descendants of Columbus, as hereditary admirals of the Indies, but they had done nothing to develop the island. The Spanish inhabitants numbered about 1,500, living mostly by keeping or hunting cattle. They offered little resistance; nor could their neighbours in Cuba do much to help them. There was no hope of help from Spain; Blake's victory over the Spanish fleet at Santa Cruz in 1657 made the despatch of a relief expedition impossible. The beautiful and fertile island, 'lying in the very belly of all commerce', as a contemporary described it, became the chief centre of English wealth and power in the West Indies and a further potential threat to the Spanish colonial system. At about the same time, French freebooters operating from the pirate stronghold of Tortuga began to settle in the north-west of Hispaniola, an area which had been almost uninhabited, except for cattle-hunters, since the Spaniards evacuated it in 1605. The French settlers developed farms and ranches as a supplement to their primary occupations of hunting and piracy, and became so numerous that in 1665 the Compagnie des Indes appointed their first governor to take charge of what was already in effect (though naturally unrecognised by Spain) the French colony of St Domingue.

By the 1660s, then, instead of one territorial power in the Americas and one monopolistic trans-Atlantic trade, preyed upon but recognised, there were four or five territorial powers, four or five systems of trade. The mainland viceroyalties preserved their aloof integrity, and the convoys of the *Carrera*, reduced to a fraction of their former size, still plied between Seville and New Spain or the isthmus; but the Spaniards could no longer police the West Indies. Their *Armada de Barvolento*, for all the financial and naval effort which it cost, had been too weak and too short-lived for its enormous task. Their Caribbean settlements, except for the major bases, in practice were left largely to their own devices. As for the English, French and Dutch settlements, they were growing in population and (as soon as they took to producing slave-grown sugar) in wealth. Aggressive and greedy, they were suspicious and jealous of one another, still more suspicious and envious of Spain. Though subject, in theory, to strict mercantile regulation, they had little government, and usually no regular armed force at their disposal. They defended themselves by means of planter militias, and harried and plundered their neighbours, especially their Spanish neighbours, with the help of such mercenaries as they could hire. There ensued thirty years of extraordinary anarchy and violence, in which the leading figures were not so much the colonial governors as the buccaneer leaders with whom they allied themselves.

The word *boucan* means the process of curing strips of meat by smoking over a slow fire; and the *boucaniers* were originally men who lived by hunting and by selling hides and smoked meat to passing ships. All the islands of the Greater Antilles supported great herds of wild—or rather feral—pigs and horned cattle, the descendants of escapes from Spanish farms and ranches, which throve and multiplied upon the virgin savannahs. The pursuit of these ownerless beasts offered a rough but not unattractive living to masterless men—marooned or shipwrecked sailors, deserters, escaped felons, runaway indented servants and all such as disliked organised society; and many of them varied hunting with robbery by land or by sea. Spanish settlements and shipping, being nearest to hand, naturally suffered most. The Spanish governors did their best to round up these wild people living in the unsettled areas of the islands. In Hispaniola mobile lancer squadrons were employed against them from about 1640, and attempts were made to starve them into surrender by killing out or driving away the herds on which they depended. The only result was to drive the buccaneers to further piracy, and to turn their antipathy to government in general into a vindictive hatred of Spanish government. By the middle of the century they had come to form dangerous outlaw bands, accustomed to hardship, well armed and (for so long as they chose to obey) well led. Most of them were English or French; but they owned no political allegiance, except temporarily as bloodthirsty and unreliable mercenaries, paid by plunder. The presence of such bands in the heart of the Spanish Caribbean was a perpetual temptation to aggressive colonial governors, French or English. The buccaneers could provide the armed force which the governors lacked; the governors could provide harbour bases, letters of marque or reprisal, and organised markets for the sale of stolen goods.

The chief patrons of the buccaneers were the English governors of Jamaica and the French governors of St Domingue; their principal bases, Port Royal and Tortuga. Their activities were largely independent of formal states of peace or war in Europe. The Port Royal buccaneers under Morgan plundered Puerto Belo and massacred its garrison in 1668. In 1669 they sacked Maracaibo and captured three Spanish warships, carrying silver from Cartagena but diverted to intercept the marauders. In 1670 they burned Santa Marta and Río de la Hacha, paid Puerto Belo another devastating visit, marched across the isthmus and took Panama. Most of the inhabitants—those who failed to escape in the forest—were killed; many tortured to death. The city was destroyed by fire, and never rebuilt upon its old site. This was the climax of Morgan's bloodthirsty career; he retired from active buccaneering and eventually became lieutenant-governor of Jamaica. The Port Royal gang broke up and many of its members moved to Tortuga. The Tortuga buccaneers played a prominent part in the Caribbean fighting against the Dutch between 1672 and 1678, which in 1674 brought the West India Company to bankruptcy and ruin. After 1678 they again turned their attention to the Spanish possessions— though France and Spain were at peace—with savage success. Their most daring exploit was the capture and sack, in 1683, of San Juan de Ulúa, which until then had been immune from attack. The buccaneer fleet was surprised in harbour, as Hawkins had been more than a century earlier, by the arrival of a *flota* from Spain; but times had changed. The *flota* was now a small fleet, only fourteen sail, and the captain-general dared not engage, but stood off and on outside the harbour while the buccaneers loaded their ships with money, goods and slaves, and sailed away to a nearby cay to divide the spoil. There they fell to fighting over the division, and many died of their wounds; but enough survived to make another large-scale raid, against Yucatán in 1685, in which the city of Campeche was reduced to ashes. These exploits were only the most outstanding in a fearful tale of outrage. Hundreds of towns and villages were sacked, many of them repeatedly. Throughout the Spanish Caribbean the inhabitants of the coastal settlements grew so accustomed to raiding that a hasty retreat to the woods, followed by ransom negotiations, was the automatic reaction to the appearance of a strange sail. Rarely in western history can a few thousand desperadoes have created a reign of terror over so vast an area, or influenced so strongly the conduct of civilised states.

The depredations of the buccaneers, though chiefly aimed against Spanish settlements, spared no ship which looked a likely prize. They became so serious an international plague that eventually even their employers turned against them, and brought in naval forces to put down those who could not be persuaded or bribed, as Morgan was, into landed affluence or respectable employment. The sugar-based wealth of Barbados and Martinique showed what Jamaica and St Domingue might become; but the development of the Greater Antilles as productive settlements was impossible while the buccaneers continued to receive support. Their suppression, delayed by strategic and political needs, was economically essential to merchant and planter alike; and West Indian planters and merchants were beginning to exert an influence in economic affairs. The English government was the first to grasp these facts, and to discover that an enfeebled Spain would be willing, in return for an end of raiding, to recognise effective English possessions in the Americas, including even Jamaica. An agreement to this effect, the Treaty of Madrid, was concluded in 1670, the very year of Morgan's sack of Panama. Enforcement was another matter; it was easier to disown buccaneers than to control them; but in 1680 the Treaty of Windsor reaffirmed and strengthened the agreement, and in 1685, for the first time, an English naval squadron was sent to Jamaica to hunt buccaneers. The Dutch—their power in America now relatively much reduced by their wars with England and with France—made a similar agreement at the Treaty of the Hague in 1673. They and the English had no longer much to fear from Spaniards in the Caribbean; common fear of France, indeed, was drawing them together, and ranging them, at least temporarily, on the side of Spain. With new-found virtue they both protested vigorously against the crimes of the French buccaneers. Louis XIV still employed them, convinced that an enfeebled Spain could be bullied into ceding St Domingue and granting to France a share of the supposed riches of the Indies. At Nijmegen in 1678 the Spanish government rejected these demands with unexpected obstinacy. In 1683, however, at the Truce of Ratisbon, the two governments agreed that 'all hostilities shall cease on both sides, both by land and by sea and other waters . . . within Europe and without, both on this side of and beyond the Line'. The possibility was opening before Louis XIV of acquiring the whole of the Spanish Indies by inheritance from the sickly idiot King Charles II; or else of imposing a successor who would grant the French a privileged position in the American trade. This was a more attractive prospect than mere casual plunder or piecemeal conquest. Administrative and naval action against buccaneering followed the truce. The new policy was not at first consistent, but eventually it prevailed. The last employment of buccaneers by a European government was in the successful and immensely lucrative French capture of Cartagena in 1697. The force so employed was disbanded immediately afterwards. Some became planters and some pirates; but with naval squadrons constantly in the area they ceased to influence policy and were never again a serious menace. The Treaty of Ryswyck of 1697, by which Spain formally ceded St Domingue to France, also marked the end of buccaneering.

Not, of course, the end of Caribbean fighting; the age of the buccaneers was followed by the age of the admirals. From the beginning of the eighteenth century the West Indies were brought within the normal conventions of peace, war and diplomacy in Europe. Irregular continuous marauding had been shown to be self-defeating, but formal wars were frequent. The death of Charles II in 1700 and the accession, according to Charles's will, of the Bourbon Philip V ranged France firmly on the side of Spain in America and made the forcible dismemberment of the Spanish Empire impossible. The English, therefore, while maintaining powerful naval forces in the Caribbean and engaging in periodical wars with France over the possession—among other things —of valuable tropical islands, reverted in their American dealings with Spain to an earlier and more limited policy: to that of 'forcing a trade'.

Of all the possible trades with Spanish America at that time, the most promising and lucrative in the eyes of contemporaries was the trade in African slaves. Slaves were essential to a booming sugar industry, and the difficult, dangerous and speculative business of importing them across 4,000 miles of ocean became a trade second only in importance to that in sugar itself. The trade demanded vast capital investment in ships, forts and barracoons; an expense justified only by a very large volume of business, and possible only under the protection of monopoly. Inevitably, in a mercantilist world which regarded monopoly as an essential measure of defence, and commercial competition as a mild form of war, the slave-trade gave rise to incessant international dispute. The Spaniards, possessing by far the largest and most populous colonial empire, had no foothold on the slave coasts, and were dependent on foreigners for their supply of slaves. When the Portuguese *Asiento* ended with the revolt of 1640 the trade became almost wholly contraband, chiefly in Dutch hands; but in the last quarter of the century the English Royal Africa Company and the French Guinea Company between them ousted the Dutch from most of their stations in West Africa. The Spaniards greatly preferred an agreed monopoly to unorganised contraband, and were well aware that a revived *Asiento* would have to go to a foreign company. The English and the French were the obvious competitors. Their trade plans were similar: to retain the monopoly of the supply of slaves to their own colonies; to sell a surplus to foreign colonies wherever possible; and above all to secure a share—or, better still, a monopoly—in the supply of slaves to the Spanish colonies. In fact the Spaniards in the West Indies did not need, and could not afford to buy, very large numbers of slaves in the seventeenth century; the great days of Cuban sugar were still to come. The mining industries on the mainland, however, were beginning to show signs of revival; and an exaggerated notion of the importance of the Spanish Empire as a source of wealth and as a market for goods and slaves was prevalent throughout northern Europe. It persisted, indeed, until the nineteenth century. Trade was the mercantilised version of the legend of El Dorado—a coveted prize, equally elusive, and no less a cause of misunderstanding and war.

By the late seventeenth century the *Asiento* had come to be regarded as so valuable a concession that its grant acquired all the characteristics of an international treaty. Inevitably it was used as an instrument of

Spanish foreign policy. Charles II and William III of England both failed
to secure the *Asiento* for their subjects. Political circumstances—the
likelihood of a union of the two Crowns, or at least a Bourbon prince
on the Spanish throne—favoured the French. Eventually, in 1702,
an *Asiento* was concluded with the French Guinea Company. A
Compagnie de la Mer Pacifique was formed in France, largely to give
employment to Breton ships which until the Peace of Ryswyck had
operated as privateers and pirates in Spanish American waters. During
the years of war which followed, French skippers, clearing mostly
from St Malo, used the *Asiento* as a cover for smuggling at Buenos
Aires. From there they rounded Cape Horn and, with the encouragement of a series of francophil—or merely venal—viceroys, drove a
thriving trade in the Pacific ports of South America. At the same time,
the French advisers surrounding Philip V at Madrid gained more and
more control over the direct trade to Puerto Belo. The only official
convoy sent to the isthmus during the war sailed under French escort.
The Peruvian market became, for a time, the ground for competition
between the trickle of French goods crossing the isthmus lawfully
and the much larger supply of much cheaper smuggled French goods
brought round the Horn. Naturally this arrangement did not suit the
English or the Dutch; and while, no doubt, the principal concern of
the English in the war of the Spanish Succession was to keep Louis
XIV and his relatives off the thrones of Spain, the Netherlands and
the Indies, at least a subsidiary motive was to prevent the French Guinea
Company from keeping the slave *Asiento*.

The war was fought mainly in Europe. In the West Indies, it is true,
the Spaniards, with the help of their new French allies, were able for the
first time for many years to take the offensive against the English.
Benbow had difficulty in defending Jamaica, and English commerce
and settlements suffered severely at the hands of French and Spanish
privateers. The only serious attempt at retaliation was Wager's successful attack on the galleons off Cartagena in 1708; a catastrophe for the
Carrera, for which mutual suspicion between the Spaniards and the
French was at least partly responsible. It was successful fighting in
Europe which eventually enabled the English, at the Treaty of Utrecht
in 1713, to extract from France and Spain the objects for which they
had been fighting: a firm assurance that the Spanish Netherlands and
Spanish America should not fall under French domination; and the
transfer of the slave *Asiento*, together with certain other trading rights

in Spanish America, to an English concern, the South Sea Company, floated expressly for the purpose.

Only exhaustion and defeat could have induced the Spanish government to consent to these concessions. The Spanish Crown still claimed a general lordship over all the Americas, except in those few places where it had expressly acknowledged the rights of others. This claim, in many parts even of the Caribbean, was an empty pretence. On the mainland, in provinces unquestionably recognised as Spanish, great tracts of mountain and forest had never been occupied or even explored. Unsubdued and often hostile Indian tribes lived upon the isthmus of Panama itself, within striking distance of the main treasure route from Peru to Spain, and of Puerto Belo, where the greatest trade fair in the Americas was held. Small bands of English settlers lived in scattered camps at Belize in Honduras and at Black River. These Baymen, as they were called, made a hard living by cutting and selling logwood for the dyeing industry. They received intermittent support from the government of Jamaica, and although well within Spanish territory they could not be dislodged. Among the islands, Jamaica, Curaçao and St Domingue were irretrievably lost. Most of the Lesser Antilles, including some of the best sugar lands in the New World, never occupied by Spaniards, had been settled by English, French, Dutch or Danes, and were to be throughout the eighteenth century the scene of a new international rivalry in which the claims of Spain were hardly even considered. But Spanish claims were not thereby abated; for Spanish statesmen, what Spain had not expressly granted was still hers by right.

Similarly in commerce: if the Spanish government could not prevent foreign settlements in the islands, still less could it prevent the foreign settlers trading with its own colonial subjects. But Spain insisted, in the face of facts, upon an exclusive monopoly of trade, and in the attempts to enforce that monopoly found it necessary to claim in general the right of regulating seaborne traffic in the Caribbean, of defining the courses to be followed by *bona fide* traders between other European countries and their respective colonies, and of stopping and searching foreign ships which deviated from those courses.

Such being still the official policy of Spain in the Caribbean, Spanish statesmen were bound to grudge the concessions which they had been bullied into making at the Treaty of Utrecht. The French even more bitterly resented seeing a privileged postion, which they had secured by negotiation, taken from them as a result of war. The South Sea Company now had its foot in the door, as it were, while all other foreign traders had to smuggle their goods through the back windows. Sooner or later the privileges of the company were certain to be challenged, and the result would again be war between England and Spain. Spain could now usually count on the support of France; but the Spaniards were to discover that the support of powerful allies entailed its own perils.

CHAPTER 14

Decline and recovery

THE long attrition of the seventeenth century affected the great vice-royalties much less than the Caribbean coasts and islands; less, indeed, than Spain itself. Secure in their remoteness, they suffered little from the direct effects of unsuccessful war. The indirect effects—the interruptions of communication, the constriction of the normal channels of trade—though serious, were less disastrous for them than for Spain. Already they were less dependent upon Spain than Spain on them; and to a considerable extent they could compensate for the decline of Spanish trade by doing business elsewhere. The very serious social and economic crisis through which New Spain, in particular, passed in the early seventeenth century, because of decline in native numbers, was surmounted by a brutal social and technical reorganisation, by the creation of self-sufficient *latifundia* under Spanish management. Ploughs and draught animals on the one hand, debt-slavery on the other, made this reorganisation possible. Rural reorganisation was accompanied by a steady growth in urban concentrations, relative to a depopulated countryside. Craft gilds, in full decline in seventeenth-century Spain, remained vigorous in the cities of the Indies, and many of them freely admitted *mestizo* or Indian craftsmen. Urban growth had its unhealthy side. Social prejudice, lack of adequate financial machinery, limited scope for productive investment, together encouraged private display, lavish public provision of bread and bull-fights, expensive and ceremonious viceregal courts, and most serious of all, an increasing concentration of wealth in ecclesiastical hands for the maintenance of

religious establishments. These were all characteristics which the
Indies shared with Spain. Correspondingly, the bigger cities developed
populous and sinister underworlds of *léperos*—beggars and petty
thieves. Mexico was not only the largest city in the Spanish world; it
was one of the most disorderly, and even viceroys were sometimes put
in fear of their lives by hungry and mutinous mobs. In general, however, the impressions of outside observers, such as Thomas Gage of
The English–American, do not suggest that Spaniards in the Indies in the
mid-seventeenth century lived in misery. They had lost the easy
affluence of the post-conquest generations, but compared with
Spaniards in Spain they were prosperous.

Remote viceroyalties; a ravaged and perilous Caribbean; an impoverished and enfeebled metropolis desperately struggling to maintain
communication: these were the main components of an empire in
danger of dislocation, increasingly lacking a firm central authority.
When, in the later seventeenth century, population, especially population of mixed blood, began slowly to revive in many parts of the Indies;
when silver production, at its lowest level about 1660, and economic
activity generally, once more increased, the revival was an entirely
American phenomenon. Spain contributed little to it and for years
profited little from it. Nevertheless, the empire did not break up, and
the Spanish Crown, apart from minor losses, never entirely lost
control. Some of the factors holding the empire together were politico-
military and external: the tenacity and courage of Spain in defeat, and
its refusal to accept the implications of defeat; the mutual jealousies of
Spain's enemies; and finally the intervention of France, through the
Bourbon succession. Other factors, more difficult to assess, were
internal: colonial loyalty; and the conserving inertia of a cumbersome,
elaborate administrative machine.

Riots, armed revolts and conspiracies were not infrequent in the
Indies in the seventeenth century, but their causes were usually local,
often merely personal or factious. They never—or very rarely—implied
conscious rebellion against the Crown or against the tie with Spain.
There were no Massachusetts separatists, no premature mutterings of
colonial self-government, of independent kingdoms or common-
wealths. Religious dissidence was comparatively rare and politically
unimportant. Though Judaising New Christians, some of them Portuguese, found their way to the Indies in some numbers, they kept their
views to themselves and rarely engaged in subversive conspiracy.

An alliance with heretics, Dutch or English—which would have been an essential factor in any serious rebellion against Spain—would have been abhorrent to Spaniards; the whole idea of disloyalty to the Crown, indeed, was abhorrent. Spaniards, it is true, in Spain and in the Indies, tended to be undisciplined individualists, ready enough to cavil at the orders of the King's representatives; but the King himself—though sometimes misinformed or ill-advised—was sacred. Even the battle-cries of rioting mobs, in times of civil tumult, had an apologetic note: *Viva el rey y muera el mal gobierno*. In normal times deeply ingrained loyalty and reverence for monarchy protected also the persons and dignities—though not always the decisions—of the senior officials, viceroys, governors, appeal judges, who were the acknowledged leaders of social as well as public life and who were almost without exception peninsular Spaniards. A 'palace' society, revolving about the viceroys, was normal and accepted. Though to an increasing extent the Indies in the seventeenth century became economically independent of Spain, they were far from being socially or intellectually independent, and educated and intelligent Creoles displayed little desire to become so. Most of the books they read, the plays they attended, were written and published in Spain. In these respects seventeenth-century Spain had much to offer; and the Indies also—New Spain especially—made their contribution to the literature of the Golden Age. The nostalgic Royal Commentaries of the Inca Garcilaso de la Vega, written in Spain, enjoyed a considerable vogue on both sides of the Atlantic. Alarcón and Balbuena were Creole-born, and divided their time between Spain and New Spain. Mateo Alemán, Spanish-born, came to live in Mexico. There was, as yet, no Creole 'school'. Spanish literature was still one body.

On paper the administrative machinery of the Indies was equally Spanish, equally unified. The structure of colonial administration had been created, and the general principles of colonial law laid down, under Charles V and Philip II. The reigns of the later Hapsburgs produced few major innovations. The l gislative processes of the empire—the careful consideration of petitions, opinions and support-ing evidence, the leisurely deliberations of the Council of the Indies, culminating in the presentation of documents of reasoned advice, *consultas*—demanded on each major question a decision, a yes or no, from the King himself. All the later Hapsburgs lacked, in varying degrees, the capacity for decision. The personal favourites to whom they entrusted much of the conduct of affairs did little, as far as the Indies were concerned, to supply the deficiency. Even Olivares, the ablest of them, showed little consecutive interest in colonial affairs; indeed the civil war in Catalonia, which his arrogance helped to precipitate, was the occasion of a very dangerous reduction in the forces provided for the defence of the Indies fleets. In these circumstances any major reshaping of the government of the empire to deal with successive crises as they arose was out of the question.

The early seventeenth century, on the other hand, was a great age of theoretical jurisprudence in Spain, and eminent jurists were employed, under the Council of the Indies, in an immense labour of refinement, interpretation and codification. The most outstanding work of Spanish colonial jurisprudence, the *Política Indiana* of Juan de Solórzano—a magisterial and immensely erudite analysis—was published in 1647. In the same period a whole series of specialised codes were issued dealing with particular subjects—forced labour, the sale of offices, mining rights and so forth. No official who took the trouble to study these codes need be in any doubt of the principles of the law which he was to administer. The codes, however, with their air of leisurely theoretical deliberation and their meticulous attention to detail, were ill-suited to times of crisis and change. They smelled of the lamp. Even their consistency, moreover, was impaired by a steady stream of subsequent legislation, issued in answer to petitions from interested parties, dealing *ad hoc* with minor questions, and introducing in the process constant contradictions in matters of detail. In the monumental general code known as the *Recopilación de Leyes de Indias*, finally published in 1681, many of these contradictions were incorporated but not resolved. A conscientious senior official in the Indies, therefore—a viceroy, or the president of an *audiencia*—confronted with a situation requiring action, and guided by a series of *ad hoc* decrees conflicting both with a general code and with one another, had either to write to Spain for further instructions or to risk making a decision himself.

The Hapsburg system of government was, on paper, highly centralised, in the sense that no decisions of more than trivial importance might be made, and no money spent, without reference to the Council of the Indies. There was no overriding authority in the Indies; all the various ill-defined and overlapping branches of government there corresponded directly with the Council. To write to Madrid for a decision was the correct procedure. An answer, however, might not be received for several years. A study of the dating of the Council's correspondence throughout the seventeenth century shows a steady increase in the length of time taken to answer letters. The indecisiveness of governments, the frequent interruptions of seaborne communications, the inadequacy of the central offices to deal with the volume of paper they received, all contributed to increasing delay. When the decision arrived circumstances might have changed. Our official would then have to decide whether it was possible or expedient to enforce the decision. Administrative convention, as distinct from law, allowed colonial officials a very wide discretion in postponing the enforcement of orders, pending further consideration or appeal. The system, in fact, was far more flexible than it appeared on paper. In practice an official confronted—as officials often were—with a number of conflicting decrees could often choose for himself which order he would obey, which principle—if any—he would apply. Confronted with a definite order or decision which he considered unenforceable or inexpedient, he could invoke the conventional formula of 'obedience without compliance' and, again, write to Spain. Usually the worst risk he ran was that of receiving—again several years later—a written reprimand. Philip II had usually been able to secure reasonably prompt obedience in matters of importance. His successors were less successful. In the seventeenth century more and more far-reaching decisions were either shelved or else taken on the spot by viceroys or governors with the help of their judicial advisers. The centralised system of Hapsburg administration became more and more a sham.

In the absence of decisive leadership at the centre, the burden of holding the empire together and keeping the administration going rested more and more upon civil servants, many of whom were school-trained lawyers, accustomed to respect precedent and to proceed by consultation. Viceroys might make decisions without much effective interference from Spain, but not without consultation and discussion locally. In particular, the *oidores*, the judges of appeal—whose functions, as we have seen, included advisory and administrative duties as well as jurisdiction—were greatly respected figures, and they were supported by a numerous notarial hierarchy with a strong professional *esprit de corps*, constantly recruited from Spain. A soldier-viceroy whose tenure of office was short and who was expected at every turn to consult a conservative bench of judges was unlikely to do anything very decisive or heroic, but on the other hand would be restrained from doing anything very silly. The compelling force of routine, the ingrained habits of consultation and discussion, respect for precedent and the forms of law, combined to keep things going, but also inhibited conscious organised innovation. The courts sat, the taxes were collected, public works—though in a slovenly and dilatory fashion—were maintained, the royal silver—what there was of it—was shipped to Spain. On the other hand many difficult or embarrassing problems were either ignored or endlessly discussed without solution. Royal legislation whose enforcement might lead to trouble, even to revolt— the decrees on Indian forced labour of 1601 and 1609, for example— were quietly set aside. A similar passive resistance inhibited new developments in public works. Almost the only new and bold public project initiated in the course of the century was the vast undertaking of draining the Lake of Mexico, begun in the viceroyalty of the second Velasco, in the teeth of steady obstruction from the Spanish government and from local people. It proved far beyond the technical resources available, and was, in the main, a costly failure; its objects, indeed, were not fully achieved until the nineteenth century.

The stagnation of colonial government did not, of course, prevent change in colonial society. The growth of peonage—to mention only one example—was a social and economic development of great significance, about which the Crown occasionally showed signs of mild concern. Any attempt to restrict or control it, however, would have led to trouble; so the viceregal governments ignored it, allowed it to happen. Even if a conscientious viceroy, in response to proddings from Madrid, tried seriously to enforce legislation in a matter of this sort, affecting the livelihood of Spanish settlers, the means of enforcement at his disposal were inadequate. Just as the empire as a whole lacked effective articulation, so vital links were missing in the chain of command within the Indies. Responsible and highly paid functionaries in the capital cities—viceroys, governors, *oidores*, treasury officials—had little day-to-day control over the rural *corregidores*, the district officers. *Corregidores* were numerous and—except in a few Spanish towns— poorly paid. Most of them governed comparatively small areas and had no training in law or administration. Being inadequately supervised, many of them governed badly. Their untrustworthiness bore most hardly upon the Indians, who were moreover the people least able to avail themselves of the remedies offered by the appeal courts.

The *audiencias*, though specifically charged with the protection of Indian interests, were few in number and their procedure was complicated and expensive. The summary Indian court, the *Juzgado general de Indios*, provided only a partial remedy, and existed only in New Spain. The *encomienda* had lost its original character of a quasi-feudal bond, and gradually died out in the course of the seventeenth century. For most Indians the *corregidor* was the Law, the only Spaniard with whom they had regularly to deal. Many *corregidores* practised rapacious and ingenious local tyrannies with impunity. They supervised the collection of tribute by Indian officials, and delivered the proceeds to the Treasury. In their capacity as magistrates they levied fines and court fees. All these duties offered opportunities for peculation and extortion. Moreover, *corregidores* exercised—also, confusingly, under the name of *repartimiento*—a commercial monopoly of certain classes of manufactured goods. This *repartimiento* was intended originally as a means of making European tools and other useful articles more readily available to Indian cultivators. In the hands of an unscrupulous *corregidor* it became a means of forcing a variety of useless and highly priced articles upon the Indians to the private profit of the *corregidor*.

Cut off in large measure from adequate supervision, seventeenth-century colonial government displayed two familiar characteristics of bureaucratic deterioration: a steady increase in the number of officials; and a decline in the trouble taken over selecting them, hence—though this obviously cannot be firmly established—a decline in their personal quality. Both were connected with the growing practice of selling offices. Viceroys, it is true, did not purchase their places; *oidores* very rarely did—only one instance is mentioned in surviving records, late in the century. Seventeenth-century viceroys on the whole were reasonably respectable if not particularly distinguished officers. Among seventeenth-century *oidores* were some men of great distinction, learning and probity—Solórzano, who later became a councillor of the Indies, was an outstanding example; so was the historian Antonio de Morga. Some *oidores* were venal and negligent, however; and lower in the hierarchy were many idle and ingenious rogues who regarded their offices primarily as an investment. The law governing the auction of offices by the Crown's representatives was set out in compendious decrees of 1581 and 1591, which restricted the practice to posts remunerated by fees rather than by salary; chiefly notarial offices—some of which were important and highly lucrative—and municipal dignities. A further decree of 1606 made all such offices renunciable, which in practice meant that their possessors might sell or lease them by private arrangement on payment of a further fee to the Crown. It meant also that royal control over the selection of such officials, which Philip II had been at pains to establish, was now whittled down to a power of veto, very rarely invoked. Under Philip IV and Charles II, without any formal legislative sanction, many senior salaried offices also came to be sold. Treasury officials often bought their places and provincial governors not infrequently; and reversions were offered for sale. The dangers of this abusive extension were obvious; the Council of the Indies disliked it, both on administrative and financial grounds, and sometimes protested to the King, but without result. Under Charles II, indeed, seats in the Council itself were sometimes sold. At the same time, the detailed evidence of the suitability and competence of purchasers, which the law required, and on which Philip II had always insisted, became more and more perfunctory.

The sale of offices was not a simple transaction between the Crown and its servants; it was a highly organised business in itself. Offices could not only be bought; like other forms of property they could be bequeathed, mortgaged or seized for debt. Often they were bought as a speculation, with borrowed capital; sometimes they were given to court favourites, who leased them or sold them privately to the highest bidder. The money-lender and the dealer in offices played a considerable part in the business. Many of the Crown's servants in the Indies were perpetually in debt to such people and looked to fees, tips or less legal exactions to pay the interest. It is not surprising that the standard of honesty, initiative and diligence among seventeenth-century colonial officials declined, and that a creeping paralysis afflicted the whole administration.

For a wealthy settler aristocracy living under a metropolitan administration, lethargy and venality among junior officials are often conveniences rather than otherwise. Seventeenth-century Creoles accepted the situation as normal and paid bribes when necessary. Metropolitan Spaniards who knew the system were less complaisant. Many sensitive Spaniards in the later seventeenth century were oppressed by a sense of decline, born of poverty, defeat and discontent. The vogue long enjoyed by the brutal and pessimistic satire of Quevedo is evidence of this. The instinctive reaction to this sense of decline was a withdrawal into defiant isolation, a stubborn clinging to ancient ways and a refusal to accept or recognise foreign ideas. The main stream of European thought in the seventeenth century, with its great developments in philosophy, mathematics and natural science, passed Spain by. Both Spain and Spanish America were intellectually, economically and politically backward by the standards of the time. Thoughtful Spaniards felt this backwardness as a bitter humiliation, and writers such as Martínez de Mata accurately analysed its causes in treatises which an inert government persistently ignored.

The shock of the Succession War with its destructive fighting on Spanish soil, and the humiliating concessions, particularly in the colonial field, extracted from Spain at Utrecht, all deepened the sense of pessimism. The glaring contrast between the wealth and potential power of the Indies, and the feebleness of Spanish administration, was increasingly noted in the early eighteenth century, and was coupled by some writers with a sense of guilt concerning the manner in which the Indies had been acquired. Macanaz in his bitter *Testament of Spain* makes dying Spain bequeath to her successors '. . . some valuable possessions which a Genoese acquired for me, dethroning emperors and depriving of their liberty peoples over whom I had no better rights than they over me. . . . I now declare that I possess such vast domains by usurpation and fraud. . . .' And later: 'It is true that I really control but little [of the Indies] besides the bare minimum on the coasts; and a very small portion is owned by France and England; but the industry of those Powers has enabled them to develop the inner part of their colonies by their activity and my negligence.' Still more pointed, and more specific, were the words with which Jorge Juan and Antonio de Ulloa began the preface of their *Noticias secretas de América* of 1749: 'The countries of the Indies, fertile, rich and flourishing . . . distant from their Prince and from his principal ministers, governed by persons who often regard no interests but their own, are now reduced to such a condition . . . that justice has no authority, and reason no power, to make any stand against disorder and vice.' The report which follows is one of the frankest and most detailed exposures of petty tyranny and administrative corruption ever written; it was, moreover, a secret report, written for the Crown by two naval officers who had been sent to South America on a scientific mission and who had no motive for blackening the government.

It was the function of the Spanish Bourbons to bring Spain back for a time into the main stream of European development and to

reorganise the government of the empire on modern—which at that
time meant French—lines. Initially, however, the movement towards
administrative and economic reform affected the Indies very little.
The theorists who lectured the government on how to reanimate the
stagnant economy of Spain, and the ministers who struggled with the
problems of applying their theories, all certainly assumed that the
Indies had a part to play in the process. They believed, rightly, that the
economies of the Indies, despite the wretched conditions in which
many of the inhabitants lived, were more buoyant and lively than that
of Spain. They saw that exports of leather from northern New Spain
and the Río de la Plata, of cacao, cotton, indigo and sugar from the
Caribbean, were growing. Silver production, also, the most convenient
measure of economic activity, was increasing once more; in New Spain
annual production in the 1690s had regained the level of the 1580s,
and the increase accelerated in the new century. All too little of it
reached Spain; much was spent in the Indies, and much went in trade
with foreigners. The problem for Spain was how to regain, if not an
effective monopoly, at least a greater share in this relatively prosperous
commerce. Measures designed to make Spanish industry and shipping
efficient enough to compete openly with foreigners—many of which
were discussed—would be, at best, long-term remedies, as Spanish
economists, in their franker moments, fully recognised. On the other
hand, some leaks could be stopped almost immediately, some waste
and extravagance prevented, some illicit traffic barred, by improvements in the machinery for gathering the profits of the Indies into the
hands of the Spanish Crown, or of its subjects. The attention of government, therefore, was directed not so much to the stimulation of the
economy of the Indies or to the reform of the administrative arrangements within the viceroyalties, as to the reassertion, on Colbertian
mercantilist lines, of Spanish political, military and economic control.

Under the early Bourbons the success achieved in this direction was
relatively meagre. Spain at the beginning of the eighteenth century
was economically and politically bankrupt. To the combination of
chronic unemployment, large untilled estates, a chaotic currency and
lack of industry, war added a final burden. Despite the sound advice of
imported French economists and of Frenchified Spaniards such as
Ustáriz, Spanish conservatism imposed upon Philip V's government
a hand-to-mouth struggle with adversity, leaving little scope for long-
term planning for the Indies. A departmental ministry for the marine

and the Indies was created in 1714—an important step, at least on paper, towards administrative modernity; but the duties of the new minister were not defined and the old Council remained as a clog upon any reforming zeal which he might display. Nevertheless, even in these unpromising circumstances, a number of significant reforms and changes were initiated, all pointing the way towards more drastic action later.

One of the earliest symptoms of the growth of a new spirit in colonial government was a series of enactments aimed against the wealth of the Church. The large numbers of conventual clergy, the vast area of land held in mortmain, the heavy burden of tithe and other ecclesiastical taxes, were all familiar economic grievances in the Indies as well as in Spain. A decree of 1717 rehearsed these complaints and forbade the foundation of new conventual establishments. In 1734 the Orders were forbidden to admit any novices in the Indies for ten years; and in 1754 legislation was enacted—curious and significant necessity!—prohibiting regular clergy from taking any part in the drafting of wills. This last enactment was clearly unenforceable; nor is there any evidence of a significant reduction in the power and wealth of the conventual clergy in this period. In general—except for such obvious measures as the restriction of rights of asylum and a very necessary extension of the powers of civil courts to try criminous clerks—the anti-clerical legislation of the early Spanish Bourbons was half-hearted and only occasionally effective. Nevertheless, the influence of Gallicanism was already at work. The Bourbons, unlike their predecessors, always claimed the ecclesiastical *patronato* as a direct consequent of their own sovereignty and not by virtue of a papal concession. Throughout this whole period, royalist sentiment in the government of the Church steadily increased. Eighteenth-century monarchy grew impatient of states within the State, and the power of the Crown over the Church was to find expression in drastic measures against some of the Orders in the second half of the century.

Another highly characteristic Bourbon experiment, in a different field of Crown activity, was a radical reform of the colonial coinage carried out under ordinances issued by Philip V in 1728. The effect of these ordinances was to take the mints out of the hands of the contractors who had formerly operated them. The government was to purchase and coin the output of the mines on its own account, and coinage on the individual account of miners or bullion merchants was

no longer allowed. Elaborate regulations governed the design of the
new coins, to discourage clipping and counterfeiting. The gold *escudo*
was made of equal weight and fineness with the silver *real*; and when in
1750 a fixed gold-silver ratio of 16:1 was introduced, the *escudo* came
to be worth two 'pieces of eight'. The new rules were put into practice
almost immediately in New Spain (1732–3), but did not become effective in Peru until 1748. They did not entirely stop debasement and
bullion smuggling—complaints continued throughout the century—
but they effected a considerable improvement and saving of expense.
On the other hand, no solution was ever found for the chronic shortage of small change in the colonies. There was no copper currency
there, and Indians continued to use cacao beans for their petty
transactions throughout most of the century.

The process of recoinage coincided with a great increase in bullion
production, especially in Mexico, where the amount of silver coined
at the mint doubled between 1700 and 1770. Most of this bullion,
however, came from a few very rich mines. In a country where wealth
was usually invested in land, the supply of liquid capital was insufficient
to finance mining operations adequately, and to provide the necessary
machinery for the drainage and support of deep mines. *Aviadores*,
merchant money-lenders, often provided loans or equipment on credit
to refiners, but rarely to miners, unless the borrowers could offer other
property—an *hacienda*, for example—as security. There were three
bancos de plata, banks which specialised in loans to miners, operating in
Mexico in the middle of the eighteenth century, but their resources
were limited and their financial stability doubtful. Mining methods,
moreover, were backward and slovenly. In consequence, only those
mines where rich veins lay near the surface could be sure of success.
The industry as a whole was inefficient; the majority of mines were
small and highly speculative enterprises, and financial disaster constantly overtook them. The increase in silver production in the first
half of the eighteenth century was a consequence more of an easier
labour supply than of technical advance. It was not until Charles III's
time that government took steps to organise this vital industry, in order
to ensure a better supply of capital for the mines and to provide proper
technical training for those who operated them.

Although the early Bourbon governments did little directly to
foster the mining industry in the colonies, they showed a lively interest
in the channels through which the products of the mines reached

Spain. The regulation of trade between Spain and the Indies claimed, as it had always done, a large share of the attention which government devoted to economic affairs. Foreign economic theories were not yet influential enough to break the Andalusian monopoly of the main trade route to Vera Cruz and Puerto Belo; but an important step towards greater efficiency was taken in 1717, when the *Casa de la Contratación*, the *Consulado* and the whole administrative machinery of the *Carrera* was moved from Seville to Cadiz. The move was over-due; for many years the volume of shipping using Cadiz had consider-ably exceeded that proceeding upriver and in 1680 Cadiz had been recognised as the official port of the Indies. The quantities of native Andalusian products exported to the Indies had steadily dwindled; more and more the trade consisted of the re-export of manufactured goods brought in to Cadiz by sea; more and more it was confined to a small number of big ships. The vested interest of the Seville shippers, however, had served to keep the *Casa* and all the official business of the *Carrera* at Seville—an inconvenient survival which merely made smuggling at Cadiz easier; but finally the silting of the Guadalquivir had rendered access to Seville not only dangerous, but impossible to big ships, without constant expensive dredging. The two cities exchanged roles—Cadiz the bustling port, Seville the splendid but somnolent backwater. Apart from this obvious move, the main cares of govern-ment were to reduce smuggling and to revive the old system of convoyed fleets, which had languished under Charles II and ceased altogether during the early years of the wars between 1701 and 1706. The suppression of smuggling was now entrusted mainly to an irregular force of *guarda-costas*, fitted out privately and paid out of the proceeds of the prizes brought in. They were more effective than regular naval forces for this particular service, but difficult to control; their depre-dations caused constant trouble with other maritime powers. As for the fleets, between 1706 and 1713 four small convoys had got through to Vera Cruz and one to the isthmus, all escorted by French men-of-war, and occasional *azogues*—quicksilver ships—had also reached Vera Cruz. Otherwise, all the imports of the colonies had come in foreign ships. The established mercantile interests of Cadiz, bitterly resentful of French interference, demanded the resumption of the galleon sailings and the Puerto Belo fair. At the end of the war, however, there were very few merchant ships available for the *Carrera*. All the avail-able warships, also, were fully employed, first in Philip V's attempt

to reduce Barcelona—long loyal to the Austrian Hapsburgs—to
obedience; and subsequently in Alberoni's Mediterranean adventures. As
a stop-gap measure, the Crown made a series of short-term contracts
with private capitalists, each for the fitting-out of a single fleet. Every
one of these sailings was a financial failure. The southern viceroyalty
in particular had been so well supplied by French smugglers throughout
the war that there was little sale for goods brought officially to Puerto
Belo, and Spanish shippers had now to face the open competition of
the English South Sea Company. As for New Spain, the market there
was spoiled by the steady influx of oriental textiles from Manila.
Private fleets, moreover, could not be relied on either to supply quicksilver to the mines or to bring the royal silver home. In 1720 a new
series of regulations, the *Proyecto para galeones y flotas*, appeared,
ordering the resumption of regular sailings escorted by royal ships.
Little regularity was achieved. Small fleets sailed to Vera Cruz at
intervals of two or three years between 1715 and 1736. Sailings were
then suspended for twenty years because of war or threats of war.
During the same period only five fleets sailed to the isthmus. In 1740
these sailings also were suspended and were never resumed. From 1740
ships were allowed to sail round Cape Horn to Peru. Eighteenth-
century improvements in design and rig, particularly the introduction
of fore-and-aft headsails and spankers, made this passage relatively
safe; some foreign ships, Frenchmen especially, had been trading to
Peru by this route since the turn of the century. Spanish vessels headed
for the Horn were usually granted leave to store and water at Buenos
Aires, though that port was still officially closed to general traffic.
The Puerto Belo fair came to an end when the *galeones* ceased to
use the place, and with it ended the prosperity of the presidency of
Panama. The New Spain *flotas* were restored in 1754, for there was no
alternative route to Mexico, and sailed intermittently until 1789, when
the convoy system was finally abandoned. It had long outlived its
usefulness; in war it had become inadequate, in peace unnecessary.

The breakdown of the convoy system under the early Bourbons
meant an increased freedom of trade, in the sense that an increasing
share of the lawful trade was carried in 'register ships', which sailed
singly and achieved a more rapid and efficient turnover. These register
ships, however, might still legally be freighted only by members of the
Cadiz *Consulado*. The monopoly of the *Consulado* was curtailed in law
only by the creation of other monopolies. In the 1720s the Spanish

government, long after the rest of Europe, sought a remedy for the prostration of trade in the creation of joint-stock companies. Limited groups of private capitalists received commercial, and sometimes administrative privileges in particular regions of the Indies, in return for developing the resources of those regions and putting down smuggling. These privileges were granted in backward areas where goods from the fleets rarely penetrated and where smugglers had operated undisturbed. Thus in 1728 the Caracas Company was created, with a monopoly of trade on the Venezuelan coast. In 1734 the Galicia Company received the privilege of sending two ships a year to Campeche. The Havana Company was incorporated in 1740, and in 1755 the Barcelona Company for trade with Hispaniola and Puerto Rico. Most of these ventures were started by syndicates in the north of Spain, where hitherto there had been little direct contact with the Indies. They were bitterly opposed by the Andalusian monopolists; and though they all played a part in the slow revival of Spanish trade, all except one eventually proved, through bad management, ill-luck or government interference, to be financial failures. The exception was the Caracas Company, which lasted until 1785 and was eventually merged in the Philippine Company. The Caracas Company policed the Venezuelan coast and suppressed much of the foreign smuggling there. It doubled the shipments of cacao to Spain and reduced the price; it also developed a lucrative trade in tobacco, cotton, dye-woods and indigo. The company was hated by the colonists, as monopolies usually are; but the prosperity of Venezuela began with this monopoly.

The Creole merchants in the colonies gained nothing by these developments. The *Consulado* at Cadiz, despite the creation of the companies, or perhaps because of it, kept up strenuous efforts to monopolise the main routes of the American trade. In 1729 it secured a decree confining the shipment of goods in *galeones* and *flotas* to active voting members of its own body; significantly, its jealousy was now directed as much against American competitors as against other Spanish firms. In the same year it issued regulations prohibiting merchant houses in America from acting as agents of the exporting firms. In 1735 the inhabitants of the Indies were forbidden to remit bullion to Spain for investment in goods for export to the Indies. Creole merchants might do business at Cadiz only through *Consulado* members; and though this rule was formally revoked in 1749 it remained in practical effect for thirty years after that date.

In the realm of political administration the early Bourbon governments were equally conservative. They showed more care than their predecessors in the selection of high officials for the colonies, and this alone was enough to secure an improvement in the quality of administration. Otherwise they made few changes of importance in administrative methods. They did, however, carry through a drastic regrouping of some of the administrative units of the Indies. In North America the viceroyalty of New Spain and the captaincy-general of Guatemala remained intact. Plans prepared in 1751 for the creation of a separate viceroyalty in northern Mexico were never put into effect; the arid northern provinces could not, in any event, have supported the expense of such an establishment. In South America the viceroy of Peru had been responsible for the government of Spanish territory through-out the continent, even for the remote, though growing, community on the Río de la Plata. In the eighteenth century the single viceroyalty was split into two, eventually into three. The vast area of the northern Andes was detached from Lima, temporarily in 1717 and permanently in 1739, by the creation of a new viceroyalty governed from Santa Fe, modern Bogotá. The purpose was at least partly military, to provide better defence for the Tierra Firme coast and stronger support for the isolated fortress of Cartagena; but the new arrangements also reflected the rapid growth of Spanish population, as the fertile and temperate farmlands of Antioquia were opened up. Antioquia was settled largely by northern Spaniards and was one of the few genuine colonies of agrarian settlement in the Indies. The presidencies of Quito and Panama were at first left intact, though subject to the new viceroyalty; but Panama lasted as a separate jurisdiction only until 1751, when its judicial and administrative business was transferred to Santa Fe. With the galleons gone, Puerto Belo a ghost town and Panama a backwater, there was little for its *audiencia* to do. Venezuela, on the other hand, enjoying its new prosperity, was declared in 1742 to be a separate province under its own governor and independent of Santa Fe. Except for Bolívar's short-lived union, it has remained separate ever since.

The small, primitive, but lively settlements on the Río de la Plata grew steadily in importance throughout the eighteenth century, and the estuarine colony, once merely a clandestine back door to Upper Peru, gradually became a centre of some importance in its own right, attracting the trade of Asunción, of the mission plantations upriver, and of populous Tucumán with its settled Indians and its textile industry. There were no settled Indians (though many 'wild' ones) near Buenos Aires, so that in the seventeenth century very few Spaniards had settled there. Commerce and cattle were the bases of its eighteenth-century growth. The estuary was disputed territory, and the administration of the area was complicated by quarrels between Spain and Portugal over the possession of the east bank. The Portuguese had maintained a small fort opposite Buenos Aires intermittently since 1680. Montevideo, the first formal Spanish settlement on the Banda Oriental, was founded in 1729. After much bickering and some actual fighting a boundary treaty was agreed in 1751, based partly on actual possession, partly on geographical convenience, and giving Portuguese America approximately the boundaries which Brazil has today. The treaty was abrogated when Spain entered the Seven Year War in 1761, but its terms were repeated in subsequent agreements. The outcome was that the territory now known as Uruguay was colonised by Spaniards and not by Portuguese. The decision to create a separate viceroyalty of Buenos Aires was dictated largely by the need to resist any renewal of Portuguese claims.

The rearrangement of the old-established governments of the Indies was accompanied by renewed expansion on the frontiers of the settled provinces. Most of this expansion was the work of missionaries who pushed into desert and forest far ahead of other explorers at this time. The most famous and most successful missions were those established by Jesuits among the Guaranís and related tribes in the Paraná-Uruguay basin; but industrious and orderly communities were also formed in the early eighteenth century among the Mojos and Chiquitos to the east of the Andes and among the warlike and recently subdued Araucanians of southern Chile. These were all Jesuit fields of activity. The Capuchins founded a number of successful missions from 1724 onwards on the Lower Orinoco. At the northern extremity of Spanish territory, on the desert frontiers of northern New Spain, the Franciscans were similarly extending the area of their missions. During the seventeenth century the task of policing and defending these frontiers had become increasingly difficult, partly because of the abandonment of worked-out mines, partly because of the acquisition of horses and European weapons by the Chichimecas, the 'wild' Indians of the northern hills. Some territory, indeed, had actually been lost. After the turn of the century the process was reversed. New Mexico, which had been the scene of a destructive Indian rising at the end of the seventeenth century, was slowly resettled in the first half of the eighteenth by a series of missions strung along the Río Grande. Successful missionary work began in Texas in 1716 and in Nuevo Santander, between the Pánuco and San Antonio rivers, in 1746. Meanwhile Jesuit missionaries pushed up from Sonora to Lower California, and thence later in the century to Upper California. Unlike the Guaraní villages, where the Jesuits usually succeeded in excluding Spanish laymen from the mission areas, most of the northern missions were protected by *presidios*, frontier blockhouses manned by small parties of soldiers. Apart from this difference the missions throughout Spanish America were all organised on much the same lines. All practised communal agriculture and minor ancillary industries—weaving, tanning and the like—under the direction of the mission fathers. Many of the missionaries were enthusiastic innovators in agriculture; they introduced stock-rearing and fruit-growing in many districts where the people knew nothing of these arts, and in many ruined missions today the walls of derelict orchards can still be traced. Some missions—those in the Upper Río Grande *pueblos* for example—grew up among agriculturalists of long standing; but many depended for success on the ability of the friars to persuade semi-nomadic peoples to settle permanently in villages near church and mission-house, and to adopt settled agriculture. In a sense the mission of the eighteenth century was the successor of the *encomienda* of the sixteenth. Among primitive peoples and on remote frontiers it was a far more efficient instrument of settlement. After the expulsion of the Jesuits, and with the decline of interest in missionary work in the later eighteenth century, many of the missions sank into neglect and ruin; but the work of settlement in many areas was continued by the ranchers and prospectors who followed the missionaries and enjoyed the same military protection. The eighteenth century, therefore, was surpassed only by the sixteenth in the discovery of new mines and the founding of new towns. San Francisco, Albuquerque, San Antonio, Pensacola, Montevideo, Cúcuta, Copiapó, Rancagua, and many smaller places, all date from this period of active frontier expansion.

The gradual growth of the strength and prosperity of the Indies in the early eighteenth century, the fumbling and only partially effectual attempts of the Spanish Crown to reassert its control, were watched with greedy and sceptical eyes elsewhere in Europe. 'The weakness of the Spaniards is, properly speaking, the weakness of their government.

There wants not people, there wants not a capacity of defence, if the governors and other royal officers were not so wanting in their duty, and did not thereby set so ill an example as corrupts and effeminates all who are subject to them.' These sentences occur in *The Spanish Empire in America*, by 'an English merchant' (John Campbell) published in London in 1747. They are typical of many such pamphlets. The author gives a list of foreign attacks on Spanish colonial possessions, of which some succeeded, but more were beaten off by a spirited local defence, and he concludes: 'So it seems to be a thing out of dispute, that it is not so much the weakness of the Spaniards, as the weakness of their councils, which have occasioned their losses in these parts.' These are, admittedly, the opinions of a man interested in a war against Spain for the sake of trade; but, as we have seen, they were corroborated by intelligent Spaniards. The empire was vulnerable. Most Spanish statesmen in the eighteenth century were obsessed by the fear, not merely that their efforts to regain control of the Indies trade might be defeated by the economic or naval aggression of other maritime powers, but that the Indies themselves, or parts of them, might be detached from the Spanish Crown. This fear helps to explain the shrill emphasis with which Spanish governments reiterated the rights which prior discovery and papal grant had given them in America. It explains also the readiness of the ruling classes in Spain to accept a considerable degree of French tutelage, while deeply resenting both the tutelage itself, and the obvious intention of the French to manipulate the Indies administration for their own commercial advantage. Fear for the Indies, together with the hope of recovering Gibraltar and Minorca, led Philip V's ministers, Patiño especially, to give the rebuilding of the navy priority over most other charges on the royal revenue. From 1717 onwards an increasing number of new and up-to-date warships, designed on French lines, were laid down at Cadiz, Coruña and El Ferrol. A broken and half-forgotten naval tradition could not be rebuilt in a few years, and the ships, initially at least, were better designed than manned; but by 1740 much had been achieved. The fleets with which Spain was to confront England in the Caribbean in the 'war of Jenkins' ear' and the Seven Years War were far from negligible. A new navy, a French alliance and strong ties of loyalty in the Indies themselves were to keep the empire intact—contrary to many expectations—for another century.

CHAPTER 15

Caribbean conflicts

SPAIN in 1713 appeared to retain its American empire through the forbearance of the rest of Europe. Though many outside observers thought that the Indies, or parts of them, could easily be detached from Spain, the attempt was not made. Spain was supported politically—dominated, indeed, for a time—by France, and the enemies of Spain wanted an extension of their trade rather than an extension of their colonial possessions. Spanish America remained Spanish; Jamaica and St Domingue were still the only New World outposts of any importance permanently ceded to foreigners. A breach, however—the first open and admitted breach—had been made in the Spanish monopoly of the main routes of the Indies trade. The novel privileges conceded to the English South Sea Company were embodied in a major international treaty. To the Spanish government they represented not only dangerous commercial competition but a bitter humiliation, a departure under duress from established policy and traditional principle. To the English they were a disappointment, an inadequate prize for a long and successful war. Between Spanish resentment and frustrated English greed they were a fruitful source of future conflict.

In fact the English had made a bad bargain. The peace settlement had assigned the *Asiento* for the supply of slaves to the South Sea Company for thirty years, together with facilities at certain Spanish ports—Cartagena, Vera Cruz, Panama, Buenos Aires, Puerto Belo, Havana and Caracas—for the 'refreshment' and sale of slaves. In addition, the company secured the novel privilege of sending a shipload of general merchandise to Spanish America every year. These concessions—though impressive enough to send the price of shares soaring—were much less than the English at one stage had hoped for, and the opportunities of profit which they offered were limited. The size of the annual ship was restricted, and the King of Spain was to have a quarter share in the cargo and 5 per cent of the profit on the rest. The cargo was to be sold at the Puerto Belo fair at the same time as the goods from the galleons, or at Vera Cruz at the same time as goods from the *flota*. When—as often happened—there were no galleons or *flota*, presumably there was to be no annual ship. The company could not select the place and the time for selling at the best prices, as the smugglers could, so that its profits from general trade were—at least in theory—limited; it suffered, indeed, from some of the economic disadvantages which handicapped the merchants of the Cadiz *Consulado*. In 1716 the English secured by the supplementary agreement known as Bubb's treaty, interpretations in their own favour of a number of points left vague in the 1713 treaty; in particular, the Spanish government agreed that the annual ship might sail even in years when there were no *galeones* or *flota*. It was this concession which prompted the anxious but ineffectual Spanish attempts to achieve annual sailings of fleets from Cadiz, for fear of the official markets of the Indies being monopolised by the South Sea Company. Each annual ship, however, had still to be authorised by an express *cédula*, and the Spanish government always made difficulties over the issue of these permits. As for the *Asiento*, it obliged the company to supply only slaves of a certain quality; so long as this undertaking was observed, the company's cargoes could be undersold by smugglers who shipped inferior slaves of a quality which the Spanish colonists could afford not only to buy but to pay for.

In making its distasteful, even though limited, concession to the company, the Spanish government hoped for one compensating advantage: a reduction in the volume of English smuggling. In its treaty with England in 1670 the government had recognised English possession of those territories in America which England actually occupied. Further, it had recognised the right of English shipping to sail unmolested to those possessions, including, of course, Jamaica. To that limited extent, and only to that extent, Spain had accepted the presence of English shipping in the Caribbean as lawful. Nevertheless, an extensive illicit trade, mainly in slaves, had quickly grown up between Jamaica and the Spanish West Indian ports. The Spanish authorities at first had done little to stop this trade. Charles II had needed English support against France; in the later part of his reign, and during the early years of the Succession War, the Indies trade had been in such chaos that Jamaican smuggling was not much resented or much noticed in Spain. Philip V, however, was under no obligation to England. He no longer possessed Flanders. He was anxious, and increasingly able, to reassert control over the affairs of the Indies. His determination to stop smuggling was expressed, at least by implication, even in the 1713 concession to the South Sea Company. The company itself undertook, in return for its slaving monopoly, to refrain from illicit trade; and it might have been expected, in its own interests, to take steps to prevent other, unprivileged, English shipping from engaging in such trade. Because of its official concession, its large stocks and its expensive establishments in America, the company was vulnerable to Spanish resentment. Its directors knew that any irregularity committed by an English ship, or any reprisals taken by English interests against Spanish attacks on English shipping, might be punished by confiscation of the company's property. The company, however, had no effective force at its disposal for the protection of its monopoly, and it was so unpopular with its own countrymen in the West Indies that it could not easily secure local naval co-operation to this end. It certainly used its influence with the English government to discourage an aggressive naval policy, and sometimes it dissuaded naval commanders from taking perfectly proper action to protect legitimate English shipping. To this extent, the interests of unprivileged traders were sacrificed to those of the company. Many English smugglers, however, were willing to risk a brush with the *guarda-costas*. As an auxiliary *guarda-costa* the company was almost useless.

Nor did the company's own agents always honour its undertaking to refrain from smuggling. Spanish officials had reason to suspect that the *Asiento* and the annual ship, instead of being accepted as substitutes for illicit trade, were used as a cover. In the Río de la Plata area the slave-trade never amounted to much. The despatch of slave caravans to Upper Peru or over the Andes to Chile was not really an economic proposition, and there was little demand in the estuary. Nevertheless, the company maintained a considerable establishment at Buenos Aires. Its concession permitted it to acquire land. It had a *factoría* on the south side of the town, and in 1717 it bought outright the suburban estate of Retiro—formerly held on lease by the French under their 1702 *Asiento*—as a barracoon for the 'refreshment' of slaves. The relations of the company's agents with the local authorities were close and cordial. They speculated heavily in land and building development in the growing town, and made acceptable profits. The name of the

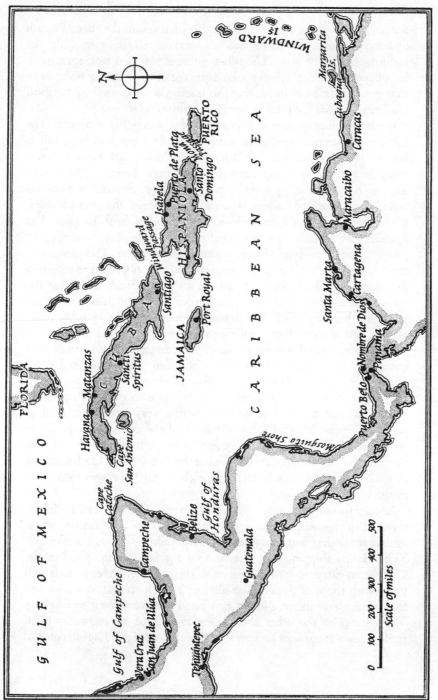

GULF OF MEXICO

FLORIDA

VeraCruz
San Juan de Ulúa
Tehuantepec
Campeche
Gulf of Campeche

Cape
Catoche
San Antonio
Cape
Havana
Matanzas

Belize
Gulf of Honduras
Guatemala

Mosquito Shore

Santi
Spiritus
B
A
C

JAMAICA
Port Royal

Santiago
Windward Passage
Isabela
Puerto de Plata
HISPANIOLA
Santo
Domingo

Nombre de Dios
Puerto Belo
Panama

Santa Marta
Cartagena
Maracaibo

PUERTO
RICO

CARIBBEAN SEA

Caracas
Cubagua
Margarita
Is.

WINDWARD
IS.

N

0   100   200   300   400   500
Scale of miles

7. The West Indies circa 1680

district still known as Retiro de los Ingleses dates from the 1720s. English influence in Buenos Aires was to survive all the vicissitudes of eighteenth-century wars. Though positive evidence is lacking, it may be supposed that the agents took advantage of their strong position to engage in contraband trade, that this trade was welcomed by the local residents and that the local authorities connived at it.

In the Caribbean area the position was somewhat different. The company genuinely traded in slaves and sold large numbers, but it bought many of them in the British West Indies and its slave-sloops from Jamaica notoriously carried other goods besides. The annual ships, also, sailed accompanied by provision ships which carried contraband. The Spaniards alleged—with reason—that the annual ships, while discharging off Puerto Belo, were reloaded from Jamaica. The Spanish government also suspected that the company concealed its profits in order to defraud the Crown of its dividend. The company's steady refusal to produce its accounts for inspection lent some colour to this suspicion. The smuggling and the suspected frauds intensified the government's dislike of a concession to which it had always, in principle, been opposed. The company for its part constantly complained that it made little profit by the annual ships and none by the *Asiento*. The complaints were somewhat insincere. The *Asiento* may have been financially risky and disappointing, but the annual ships, despite obstruction and levies of *alcabalas*, did well. One in particular, the *Royal Prince* of 1723–4, sold over 1,000 tons of merchandise in Vera Cruz and returned to England with a very large sum in silver *pesos*, to say nothing of other products of the country—a profit of several hundred per cent. On the other hand, the trade was interrupted, not only by difficulties over *cédulas* but by two outbreaks of war, one in 1718 and one in 1727. In fact only eight 'annual' voyages took place in the whole life of the concession.

Local Spanish governors were faced with a difficult and invidious task. Their home government pressed them to take firmer action against smugglers, but smugglers were increasingly difficult to identify. The colonial shipping of three or four foreign nations plied in the Caribbean, carrying lawful trade with their own colonies or unlawful trade with those of Spain. Law-abiding French traders, under orders from their government, usually gave bond not to engage in smuggling. The Dutch, on the other hand, went armed for an avowedly illicit trade; they were at least known for smugglers on sight. English colonial ships were far more numerous than either, but the English government would never accept the suggestion that their shipping should give bond as the French did. English shipping in the Caribbean included the South Sea Company's ships and slave-sloops carrying a lawful, or ostensibly lawful, trade with Spanish America; ships engaged in normal traffic between England or North America and the English islands; and smugglers to Latin-American ports. No treaty to which Spain was a party—certainly not the crucial treaty of 1670—condoned such smuggling; but nor did any treaty lay down the methods by which, or the areas in which, Spanish officials might proceed against suspected smugglers. Spain, however—while naturally keeping so immense a claim in the background of its diplomatic exchanges—still claimed a general overlordship in the Americas, on land and at sea, wherever it had not explicitly recognised exceptions. The government considered itself entitled—subject again to explicit exceptions—to stop and search foreign ships anywhere in the western hemisphere; and in order to distinguish between fair traders and smugglers it instructed its officers accordingly.

In the early eighteenth century regular Spanish warships were few, and rarely appeared in the Caribbean. The enforcement of trade regulations there was entrusted mainly to *guarda-costas* fitted out in colonial ports and carrying commissions from the local governors. These ships were manned by ruffians trained in the long war against the buccaneers. They were fitted out privately, and received their remuneration from the sale of the prizes they brought in. They cruised in the regular routes of colonial trade, stopping every English ship they met, and searching for 'contraband'. The *guarda-costas* and the colonial courts accepted the presence in a foreign ship of any Spanish colonial produce—indigo, cocoa, logwood or Spanish money—as evidence of unlawful trade. It was flimsy evidence, for Jamaica produced indigo and logwood in small quantities and had produced cocoa; and Spanish money was the commonest means of exchange almost everywhere in the Americas. Moreover, a foreign ship might be seized and condemned merely because its position at the time of encounter was—in the opinion of a Spanish court—off the direct course to a lawful destination. This, again, was flimsy evidence; ships approaching Jamaica necessarily passed close to Hispaniola, and ships leaving there had usually to sail round Cuba and beat out against the trade-wind through the Florida channel. Colonial governors received a share of prize-money; there was much collusion between the governors, the courts and the captains of the *guarda-costas*. Not only smugglers but many peaceful and lawful traders, mostly English, were seized, condemned and sold in prize.

The result of these arbitrary seizures was a long list of financial claims, and a mounting wave of national indignation, piled up in England against Spain. The English West India merchants clamoured for redress; the South Sea Company demanded compensation for property which had been seized in the brief wars of 1718 and 1727; and the English government supported its claim. The Spanish government retorted with complaints about continued smuggling and with demands for payment of the company's debts to the King of Spain— slave duties, share of trading profits (if any) and so forth. Since the company never allowed these to be ascertained, estimates of them varied widely. Besides these financial disagreements and the perennial dispute about free navigation, there was the problem of the logwood-cutters in the Bay of Honduras, and a boundary dispute between Florida and the newly settled English colony in Georgia. None of these disputes need have led to war, but war was forced by the truculence and clamour of the 'trading part of the nation' in England, and in particular by the intransigence of the South Sea Company. In 1738 the English House of Commons resolved that 'it was the undoubted right of British subjects to sail their ships in any part of the seas of America'. Letters of reprisal were distributed to English merchants—a slightly ridiculous revival of a maritime custom of 100 years earlier—and a British fleet cruised menacingly off the coast of Spain. In face of these provocations the Spanish government at first displayed considerable patience. A draft agreement, worked out with Walpole by the ambassador in London, was accepted in Madrid and actually ratified as the Convention of El Pardo. By its terms Spain was to pay £95,000 —the estimated excess of Spanish over English depredations; but the South Sea Company and its supporters opposed the agreement because it did not expressly recognise the company's right of navigation nor guarantee a renewal of the *Asiento*. The £95,000 was never paid, and in 1739 war was declared between England and Spain.

In the ensuing trial of maritime strength between Spain and England in the Pacific and the Caribbean the French government showed no haste to assist Spain, apart from an ineffectual show of naval force in the Caribbean in 1740. The Spanish Indies, however, again displayed a remarkable capacity for resistant endurance. The resistance was largely local. The government in Spain could not hope to send out naval forces capable of defeating the English fleets at sea. In the Pacific, Anson's squadron took a number of small harbours on the coast of the viceroyalty of Peru, and later off the Philippines captured the Pacific galleon carrying silver from Acapulco to Manila. Had Anson's ships been better found and better manned, and had he arrived earlier, his expedition might have had more lasting and damaging consequences; in conjunction with Vernon he might even have seized control of the route across the isthmus; or possibly established an English base in the South Pacific. In the event, he returned to England by way of the China coast and the Indian Ocean, having eluded a fleet sent round Cape Horn in pursuit, acquired a vast deal of plunder and set the whole Pacific coast in high alarm. In the Caribbean the defences of the major harbours stood up well enough, on the whole, to the test of war. Vernon's initial success in capturing Puerto Belo and destroying its fortifications was not repeated, despite the great force sent out to reinforce him in 1740. Havana was deemed too strong to be taken. Cartagena, where a few belated galleons lay, was chosen instead as the first object; but the combined military and naval attacks on Cartagena, and afterwards on Santiago de Cuba, were failures. The English, though they took many prizes, failed to stop three small fleets eastbound and one westbound between Havana and Spanish ports. There were no Isthmus fleets during the war, however, east or west. The Puerto Belo galleons were never restored, and the little remaining lawful trade to the isthmus was left to register ships. The smugglers throve by the war, and the English government instructed its naval commanders to do all they could to protect and escort English trade with the Spanish colonies.

Meanwhile the question of the Austrian succession had called most of Europe to arms, and soon drew English naval attention away from Spanish America, to Europe and to Canada. Formal war was declared between France and England in 1744. The sporadic fighting between them in the West Indies was governed not by desire to acquire new trades or territories but by bitter rivalry between two existing groups of sugar colonies. Any tenuous claim which Spain might profess to some of these islands was ignored. Neither side gained a clear and conclusive advantage, and the Treaty of Aix-la-Chapelle, which ended the war in 1748, was little more than a truce. The commercial treaty of 1750, which supplemented the general European settlement and wound up the maritime quarrel between England and Spain, was similarly inconclusive. It contained no reference to the freedom of navigation upon which England, in going to war, had so loudly insisted. The South Sea Company had almost ceased to present a problem. It no longer traded; its last 'annual ship' had sailed in 1733; its slave-trade ended with the outbreak of war in 1739. Under the treaty it received £100,000 for the surrender of all claims under the *Asiento*. Thus the English gave up the long attempt to force or persuade the Spaniards to allow direct trade to their colonies. The Spanish government, both during and after the war, maintained and expanded its policy of entrusting selected colonial trades to joint-stock companies. The trade of Cuba, for instance, was officially throughout the 1750s a monopoly in the hands of the Compañía de Comercio de la Habana, which undertook in exchange to build warships and suppress smuggling. Illicit trade went on between English islands and Spanish colonial ports, but it remained as illicit as ever, and could no longer be hidden by the *Asiento*. The Spanish government doggedly intensified its efforts to reorganise and protect its colonial trade system. What the English lost in the process the French gained. Though ousted from direct permitted trade in 1713, and subsequently outdone by the English in competitive smuggling, they were still active and successful in trade through the lawful and traditional channels of *flotas*, galleons and register ships. They continued to send goods to Spanish America through Spanish merchants at Cadiz, and the greater part of this business remained in their hands.

The disappearance of the South Sea Company made possible a period of civil relations with England which the Spanish government needed if it was to achieve much in the reform of colonial administration and trade. Such relations were further encouraged by the determination of energetic ministers such as Ensenada and Carvajal, and their Spanish-born master Ferdinand VI, to demonstrate that their foreign policy was not dictated from Versailles. The questions still at issue between Spain and England in the Caribbean, however, though individually petty, were highly irritating in sum. Colonial governors still commissioned *guarda-costas* of insufficient fortune and repute, and still got a share of forfeitures. The *guarda-costas* still arrested English ships upon flimsy legal pretexts, and sometimes plundered their prey without awaiting the formality of condemnation. English men-of-war, instead of putting down English smugglers, still sometimes gave them escort, and even—so Spanish officials alleged—smuggled on their own account. More serious, because it involved territorial sovereignty, was the question of the logwood camps. The Treaty of Aix-la-Chapelle had provided for mutual restoration of conquests; but the English government did not regard the camps as a conquest, and had taken no steps to evacuate them. The governors of Jamaica, indeed, had continued to support the cutters after the end of the war, and the Belize settlement now housed some 500 people, with a rudimentary local government. Further south, on the Mosquito shore of Nicaragua, English agents continued to intrigue with the Indians against Spanish government. Successive governors of Yucatán tried every method, from peaceful penetration by missionaries to armed expeditions, to win over the Indians and to evict the Baymen from their settlements. The Spanish government was prepared to offer supplies of logwood on reasonable terms in return for the evacuation of the camps, but this the English would not accept, being naturally unwilling to depend on a Spanish monopoly for a dye essential to their textile industries. In 1753 an armed attack, believed to have been ordered by Ensenada in Madrid, was launched against Belize, and the Baymen were driven away to Black River. They soon returned, and rebuilt their settlement with the help of soldiers from Jamaica; and English indignation over the attack helped to bring about Ensenada's fall from office. The dispute continued to disturb Anglo-Spanish relations, even after the appointment of the anglophile Wall as Foreign Minister.

After the outbreak of the Seven Years War, with France and England locked in bitter conflict in Europe and America, other disputes emerged. Even in peace the English had done little to restrain their smugglers. In war they showed the arrogant disregard of the rights of neutral shipping which belligerent naval powers commonly display. The Admiralty either could not or would not control the activities of privateers. Spanish merchant shipping was repeatedly molested, even in Spanish territorial waters. The situation grew worse when the English, after the initial disasters of the war, began to win victories at sea, and the hard-pressed French threw open the trade of their starving Caribbean colonies to neutrals; for the English, under their own 'rule of the war of 1756', considered that any Spanish ship suspected of having touched at a French colonial port was liable to seizure. Worse still, as the tide of war turned in favour of England and against France, it seemed clear that Pitt intended, if he could, to seize all the French possessions in North America and the Caribbean, including the neutral islands in the Windward group, to which Spain still made some shadowy claim. If England and France made peace upon such conditions Spain would be left to negotiate alone with an England all-powerful in North American and Caribbean waters, and the maintenance of communications and control in the Indies would depend on English goodwill. Choiseul, in order to let this lesson sink home, embarked in 1761 upon abortive and insincere haggling over peace, playing for time by demanding terms which England would not accept, in the expectation that Spain would be brought in on the French side. It was in these circumstances that the Spanish government agreed to the Family Compact of 1761, which bound Spain to declare war by May 1762 if peace had not been made between France and England. Peace was not made, and the English government anticipated events by declaring war on Spain in January.

The entry of Spain into the war brought no relief to France in the Caribbean. Rodney, fresh from England with a powerful fleet, took Martinique in the month that war was declared, and St Lucia, St Vincent and Grenada soon afterwards. Of all the French possessions in the West Indies only St Domingue remained. Meanwhile Spain, far from helping to save the French colonies, began to lose its own. The English government at once prepared an attack on Havana. This time the attack succeeded. The powerful French West Indies fleet under Blénac, short of victuals and with many men sick, remained at Cap Français and made no move to help. Havana had been thought by the Spaniards—reasonably, on past experience—to be impregnable. Its fall in 1762 made a great stir. The captors destroyed a considerable Spanish naval force and collected great sums in prize-money, and English politicians were encouraged to raise their peace terms higher. The other colonial disaster which befell Spain in 1762 was the loss of Manila, taken by a British fleet sailing from the East Indies. The captors of Manila received some assistance from the Chinese trading community there who, chiefly because of Spanish jealousy of their skill in getting Mexican silver into their hands, had been the victims of periodic persecution for many years. Manila did not enter into the negotiations for the Peace of Paris, because the news of its capture was not known in Europe at the time. The English held the place for two years, did much profitable business there, and some even, for a short time, entertained the possibility of keeping it permanently.

In Europe, Spanish arms were no more successful. The invasion of Portugal, planned as a diversion to assist France, proved an unexpected failure. In October 1762 Charles III capitulated. The French had been pressing him for some months to make peace. After the fall of Havana, Choiseul had to admit that France and Spain together were no match for England at sea. In the American field France secured moderate terms at the peace. The English politicians themselves were anxious for peace; many of them, in addition, felt nervous about the tremendous ascendency achieved in the colonial field, and hoped by concessions to reduce the danger of a future combination of all the other colonial powers against England. The English government agreed to restore Guadeloupe and Martinique, but insisted on keeping the Windward Islands and all French territory on the continent of North America east of the Mississippi. With the cession of territory was to be included the right of navigating the Mississippi itself. These proposals were, in the main, accepted by France, but they ignored the claim of Spain to be considered. Spain had been dragged into the war in the interests of France, had suffered serious losses and was now being urged to make a hasty peace, also in the interests of France. Charles III and his ministers faced the disquieting prospect of English ships plying regularly in the Gulf of Mexico, running their smuggling trade under cover of the Mississippi navigation, intercepting the Mexican *flotas*, in the event of future hostilities, with greater ease than before. Choiseul was obliged to recognise the force of the Spanish protests, and decided eventually to buy Spanish acquiescence by ceding Louisiana to Spain.

The old disputes between Spain and England were settled, for the time being, without much difficulty. The logwood settlements in Honduras received for the first time a precarious recognition. Spain agreed to tolerate the presence of the cutters and to respect their property; England agreed not to fortify the camps. Spanish sovereignty in the area was not put in question. Neither the boundaries of the settlements nor the rights of the cutters were defined, and the precise standing of the English in Honduras remained a matter of dispute. Finally, England restored Cuba to Spain and obtained Florida in exchange; and Spain renewed the treaties of commerce with England—none of them particularly favourable to England—which had been in force when the war began.

For Spain, Florida was a humiliating but not a crippling loss;

Louisiana was a large but not an immediately valuable gain. Spaniards did little to develop this acquisition, and their enemies commented that Spain had added another desert to her empire. Of more immediate importance was the recovery of Cuba, with interest; for many of the British and colonial forces who occupied the island acquired a taste for Cuban cigars, the best in the world, and for Cuban snuff; their return home was the beginning of the spread of that taste through northern Europe and North America. The occupation was important in another direction also: in fostering the development of a young but growing sugar industry. Tobacco, the principal Cuban export crop, was grown on small properties. The large slave-worked sugar plantation was comparatively rare; but during the British occupation optimistic traders, who thought that England might keep the island, had introduced some 10,000 slaves, all or almost all destined to work on sugar plantations. The influx of slaves continued after the peace, under an *Asiento* granted in 1763 to a Spanish company; and many were also introduced by smugglers, English and Spanish. In general the events of 1762 accelerated, if they did not originate, a striking development and a significant change of direction in the economic activity of Cuba. At the same time, however, a more ambitious and flexible strategy of defence, together with the virtual abandonment of the old convoy system, caused a decline in the purely military importance of Havana and a great increase in that of Puerto Rico, far out to windward. In the post-war years the immense forts of San Cristóbal and San Felipe del Morro were developed, on plans derived from Vauban, into the most powerful stronghold in all the Americas. Like the Morro at Havana, these works were paid for by *situados* from Mexico.

The territorial acquisitions of the English in the Caribbean were more extensive than immediately profitable; nor were their commercial gains particularly impressive, in view of the money and effort which had been put into the fighting in the area. In the trade of Spain itself France still held the advantages of the most-favoured nation. Choiseul had persuaded the Spanish government to reduce drastically the duties on the direct trade between Cadiz and the Spanish-American ports, a reduction which further favoured France indirectly, since most of the goods carried were French. The English were no nearer than they had ever been to an open and permitted trade to the Indies. Illicit trade between the British islands and Spanish America had flourished greatly during the war, but declined with the peace. A general tightening of

Spanish administration made smuggling more difficult. The rapacious and venal irregulars who manned the *guarda-costa* service were being replaced by paid men recruited in Spain, and regular warships were increasingly employed. In 1766 the English tried a new device: the opening of certain harbours in the British islands as free ports, to which Spanish traders could resort to buy slaves and British manufactures. In Jamaica a considerable amount of export business was done with Cuba under this arrangement, chiefly in slaves, who were sold to the Spanish *Asiento* Company, and with Puerto Rico; but the arrangement threw upon Spanish traders the risk of seizure by their own *guarda-costas*, and provoked the Spanish authorities to counter-measures, such as procuring copies of the Kingston customs-house register and prosecuting Spaniards recorded as trading. Naturally Spanish skippers were wary of such risks. The Free Ports Act revealed that Great Britain would no longer go to war to protect British subjects in illicit trade; it came too late to arrest the decline in trade with the Spanish colonies and its consequence, the acute shortage of silver currency throughout the British colonies. Once more, English mercantilists were being driven to the conclusion that the only way to force an open trade with Spanish America was by detaching parts of the Indies from Spain, but the likelihood of success in such an enterprise seemed much less in Charles III's time than it had been in Charles II's or Philip V's.

The House of Bourbon had not been crushed by the Seven Years War. Its members were firmly seated on the thrones of France and Spain, united by the Family Compact, guided for the most part by men whose ruling passions were dislike of Great Britain, desire for revenge and longing to regain what had been lost in the colonies and at sea. Choiseul at once set about rebuilding naval and military strength, a task in which he achieved notable success, and repeatedly urged his Spanish colleague Grimaldi to do the same. For the French, the resumption of war was certain. It awaited only financial recovery and a suitable opportunity. Such an opportunity was presented by the revolt of most of the British North American colonies in 1776. France declared war against England in 1778, Spain in 1779. The French fleet was at the peak of its fighting strength; the Spanish fleet, though less efficiently manned, included many new ships of excellent design, built under French influence. For the first time in 100 years the French and Spanish navies were able to establish, temporarily at least, a superiority of forces in the Caribbean; a Spanish force, operating from New

Orleans, took Pensacola in 1781, and reconquered Florida, which was formally restored to Spain in the treaty of 1783. For this success, however, the Spanish Crown unwittingly paid a heavy price in authority and prestige. The authoritarian monarch of a great and scattered colonial empire had set a dangerous example by helping the subjects of a neighbouring empire in rebellion against their king.

CHAPTER 16

Growth and reorganisation

THE fall of Havana and the bustling, riotous trade fair conducted there for the best part of a year by the merchants who followed the English fleet into the harbour, destroyed any remaining illusion of an Atlantic monopoly regulated from Spain. What occurred in Havana after its capture was merely a concentrated and openly acknowledged version of what was going on, to a greater or less extent, in most of the harbours of the Indies. The economies of Spanish America, largely isolated one from another, were all tied by many and diverse threads to the various economies of Western Europe. Whatever impediments Spanish regulation might interpose, the prosperity of the Indies depended increasingly on contact, direct or indirect, with the growing industrial and commerical wealth of Europe, particularly of England. The remarkable growth in the productivity of mining, cattle-raising and plantation agriculture in some parts of Spanish America in the later eighteenth century, the steady increase in the export trades of the Indies, reflected the growth in the industrial productivity of northern Europe, in the demand there for raw materials, tropical crops and pastoral products, and in the carrying capacity of European merchant fleets. Spaniards as individuals, and Spanish firms doing business in the Indies, naturally played a prominent part in these developments, but the economy of Spain itself profited only to the limited extent that Spain participated in the general quickening of European economic activity.

The most remarkable commercial development in the Indies in the later eighteenth century was that of the leather trade from the Río de la Plata. The incipient industrial revolution in Europe greatly increased the demand for leather, not only for boots, shoes and saddlery but for the moving parts of machinery, for forge bellows, for springs and coachwork and for many other purposes. Vast herds of feral cattle grazed across the *pampa* of what is now Argentina, even to the foothills of the Andes—an apparently inexhaustible supply. The permission granted in 1735 for Spanish 'register ships' to use the port of Buenos Aires—hitherto officially closed to most traffic—gave a useful facility to a trade which would probably in any event have developed illicitly without it. Buenos Aires became one of the major sources of leather in the world. Until about 1770 the exploitation of the herds was largely a matter of unregulated hunting of wild animals. About that time shortages occurred, due to the indiscriminate slaughter of cows; and the character of the business changed from free-for-all hunting to deliberate conservation, herding and raising on established *estancias*. A similar development took place in the older cattle areas of northern New Spain; though since those regions had no harbour comparable in convenience with Buenos Aires, their export trade was much smaller. The average annual export from Buenos Aires in the 1770s was about 150,000 hides. By 1790 it had risen to nearly a million and a half. At the same time, a solution was found for a problem which had plagued the cattle business in the Americas ever since the sixteenth century: the problem of what to do with the meat. In the early days, apart from tallow—always a valuable commodity—and apart from the relatively small quantity of beef which could be consumed immediately in nearby towns, carcasses had been left to rot. In the eighteenth century, however, the steady increase in the volume of shipping, and particularly the great growth of permanent navies, had created a heavy demand for salt beef. The first large-scale *saladeros*, salting beef for export, were established at Buenos Aires about 1776. They were run chiefly by immigrants from Spain, who supplied both the capital and the skill. Their operation was made easier by the discovery, near Buenos Aires, of extensive salt-mines, the *Salinas Grandes*—an essential source of supply, since the traditional method of making salt by evaporating sea water would have been impossible in the muddy estuary, and long-distance carriage by sea prohibitively expensive. The beef-salting business was officially encouraged, and the product exempted from export duty. Considerable quantities of dried salt beef were shipped to the Caribbean, especially to Cuba, for victualling the Havana garrison and for feeding slaves. The European demand was chiefly for beef pickled in brine and barrelled. Much of this went to Spain; but much also was sold to English and other foreign merchants, whose access to the many private jetties belonging to the proprietors of the *saladeros* was difficult to prevent; especially since the *saladeros* depended upon imported barrel staves, many of which came from North America.

The development of the South American fisheries in the later eighteenth century followed a somewhat similar pattern. The cold water off the Chilean coast produced a prodigious abundance of fish, and small-boat fishing for local needs had been carried on since the sixteenth century. In the 1770s enterprising Catalans established permanent bases in Chiloé, from which they operated considerable sea-going fleets. The catch—sea-bream and conger seem to have been the favoured species—was dried and salted and shipped up the coast for sale in the mining towns of Upper Peru. About the same time another Catalan concern, the Real Compañía Marítima de Pesca de Barcelona, was formed to organise the Patagonian whale fishery. The whales were towed into one or other of the bleak little ports—San José, Río Negro, Puerto Deseado—on the Patagonian coast; the blubber was rendered on the beaches and the oil shipped to Barcelona. Even more than other monopolies, however, a high-seas monopoly was difficult to defend. The coast of Patagonia has many inlets, and French and English poachers took their share of this valuable trade.

Like stock-raising, agriculture in most parts of the Indies was inefficient, slovenly and wasteful. In areas of concentrated Indian peasant settlement much land had gone out of cultivation in the fearful mortality of the late sixteenth and early seventeenth centuries; native agriculture had declined in quality as well as in extent, through lack of leadership, destruction by domestic animals, drafting of labour and many other causes. When, in the eighteenth century, population began to rise rapidly once more, many Indians still used their traditional methods of hoe culture, but less efficiently than their ancestors had done. The elaborate irrigation works, the careful organisation of communal labour, the delicate balance of traditional crops, had largely disappeared. The Indians had lost many of the skills of their ancestors; their acquisition of European tools and techniques, though it accelerated in the course of the eighteenth century, was still partial and slow. Peasant agriculture, in general, used inferior land, and in itself was unproductive and poor. Many Indians—in New Spain most—lived not as free peasants but as *peones* on big estates. Most of these *latifundia* were inefficient also, but for different reasons. The passive resistance of the Indian labour force to wage-earning discipline was one reason. Another was extravagance in the use of land. In a continent of vast spaces and poor communications, where over-grazing and erosion had already destroyed much good land, every estate sought to be as self-supporting as possible. This process, which had been going on in spite of legal obstacles since the sixteenth century, accelerated greatly in the eighteenth. Proprietors took in great tracts which they could not fully cultivate, partly in order to emphasise their own social prestige, partly to reserve their future supply of rough pasturage, water, firewood and game. Much land, in consequence, lay unused; what was used was carelessly cultivated by unwilling, inadequately supervised Indian labour. The *hacienda* system was not necessarily oppressive. Its easy-going inefficiency helped to make it tolerable, and in favourable circumstances a mutual liking and loyalty could develop between *hacendado* and *peones*, especially if the *hacendado* were a good horseman. *Hacendados* were not, as a rule, permanently resident, and their visits were usually the occasion of estate festivities.

These generalisations apply chiefly to the temperate highland areas of New Spain and the Andean provinces. In the hot lowlands, valleys and coastal plains the pattern was somewhat different. There, given active management, adequate labour and—where necessary—irrigation, large self-contained estates, though never very efficient in terms of crop per acre, could produce very large quantities in sum, and in the later eighteenth century some of them did. The insistent, mounting demand in Europe for tropical products; the growing interest in improved agricultural methods fostered by local Economic Societies; the increased facilities for the purchase of imported slaves; all these factors contributed to a remarkable growth in the production of cash crops for export. The successes of the Caracas Company, in developing an export trade in cacao from Venezuela, have already been mentioned. From about 1770 coffee, in Venezuela and also in Cuba, joined cacao as a valuable and expanding export crop, whose cultivation spread rapidly through the highland areas of the Spanish Caribbean. Tobacco was less successful; despite the high and deserved reputation of Cuban tobacco, its marketing was impeded from 1764 by a particularly close and burdensome government monopoly (which, incidentally, left a legacy in the form of one of the most notable eighteenth-century buildings in Seville). For foreign traders the effort to circumvent this monopoly was hardly worth while, since they had access to abundant supplies of much cheaper tobacco from the North American mainland. On the other hand, the production and export of sugar increased prodigiously. Sugar was grown in all the larger Antillean islands and at many places on the coast of the Gulf of Mexico; but in the later eighteenth century Cuba became by far the largest producer in the Spanish Indies. Between the outbreak of the Seven Years War and the end of the century, production there increased more than tenfold. Cuban sugar by the early 1790s was flooding the Mediterranean market and making great fortunes in Barcelona.

The tardy and uneven agricultural improvement of the later eighteenth century was not entirely confined to cash crops for export. Many of the common food crops, whether native, such as maize and cassava, or introduced, such as rice and bananas, extended their range as a result of increased communication between the provinces of the Indies. The potato, for example, a native Andean staple of great importance, made its appearance in Mexico at this time; while maize spread southward as far as the Río de la Plata. More significant still was the spread of wheat, the favoured cereal of the Creole. The preference for wheat over maize had nothing to do with nutritive values and not much to do with taste; it was a matter of social status. Wheat was grown chiefly by Creole farmers in areas of moderate-sized, often irrigated farms. The Puebla valley in New Spain was such an area; Antioquia was another; wheat-farming spread in both areas in the eighteenth century, and in Antioquia was the basis of a considerable movement of new settlement. Wheat also grew alongside maize in the Río de la Plata area, and from about 1780 began to be shipped upriver; though nobody visiting Buenos Aires at that time could have foreseen its later development as one of the major cereal exporters of the world. Few European countries imported wheat regularly in the eighteenth century. Only the thrifty North Americans—and they only towards the end of the century—thought of carrying so bulky a commodity across the Atlantic to sell in the Spanish Mediterranean ports.

What everyone wished to carry across the Atlantic, as always, was silver. The decline of silver production in the Indies in the middle decades of the seventeenth century had been a major factor in the disorganisation of the Spanish economy and had, indeed, slowed down the economic activity of all Europe. For more than half a century there was little change in this respect. Brazilian gold, rather than Mexican or Peruvian silver, was a principal stimulating factor in the growth of European economic activity in the late seventeenth century. By 1700, however, signs of a silver recovery were evident, and by about 1740

Spanish America was again becoming, as it had been in the sixteenth century, the source of a seemingly inexhaustible flow of silver. In this second and far more productive silver age New Spain was the principal producer. In the middle of the century rather more than half, at the end nearly two-thirds, of the total amount of silver produced in the Spanish Empire came from the northern viceroyalty. A number of factors contributed to this steady growth: increase in the population from which labour could be recruited; the discovery and exploitation of new veins, in turn made possible by the improvement of public order in the frontier areas; improved techniques; and more efficient organisation of the mining industry. Technical and administrative improvement, as well as improved public order, were in considerable measure the results of government initiative. José de Gálvez, reporting in 1771 on his visitation of New Spain, recommended the establishment of a mining gild. The *Real Cuerpo de Minería* was incorporated in 1777. Its activities included an appellate jurisdiction in mining disputes, and the operation of a miners' bank to finance exploration and development. The whole conduct of the industry was regulated by a celebrated and comprehensive code, the *Ordenanzas de Minería*, promulgated by Charles III in 1783, which served as the basis of the mining law of most Latin-American countries until the later nineteenth century. The Crown did its best to make up-to-date skill and knowledge available to the colonial miners. A number of German experts, and Spaniards trained in Germany, were sent to the Indies in Charles III's time. Fausto de Elhuyar, appointed Director-General in New Spain by Gálvez in 1786, and Thaddeus von Nordenflicht in Peru, each with a team of technicians, achieved considerable success in persuading mine-owners to modernise their operating methods. The School of Mines which Elhuyar founded in New Spain in 1792 was the pioneer centre of engineering education in the Americas. It was well staffed and equipped, and its courses combined theoretical instruction with practical experience and research.

The effectiveness of all these reforms was limited by general technical conservatism, by financial mismanagement and by the incorrigible royal habit of demanding forced loans at moments of financial crisis. Another serious obstacle to efficient organisation lay in the operation of the law governing inheritance of real property. In the absence of a *mayorazgo* or entail—a complicated and expensive device rarely applied to mines—an estate had to be divided among the heirs of its deceased

owner. Shares in silver-mines thus tended to be increasingly fragmented
and unified management increasingly difficult. Most of the major mines,
even in booming New Spain in the later eighteenth century, passed
through long periods of financial crisis and waterlogged neglect for
this reason. The principal exception was the famous Valenciana mine
in Guanajuato, sunk in 1769. The Valenciana was exceptionally productive, lucky in the continuity of its management and ruthless in its
exploitation of labour. It showed consistent profits, and for several
decades provided much of the loan capital needed for the running of
other mines in the Guanajuato *real*. Due chiefly to the production of a
few such exceptional mines, the inefficiency of much of the industry
passed almost unnoticed. The flow of silver steadily increased; it
irrigated the economic soil of Old and New Spain, and enriched Cadiz
and Barcelona. Together with the gold of Brazil, it helped to finance
the early industrial revolution of northern Europe; and since the highest
demand for silver was felt, and the highest prices paid, in the Far East,
it helped also to finance the commercial and military operations of the
East India Companies, and to quicken European maritime trade all
round the world.

With all these developments, the kingdoms of the Spanish Empire
remained, as they had always been, chiefly producers of primary goods,
whether agricultural, pastoral or mineral. There was no general
development of manufacturing industry. In Spain economic theorists
were well aware of the importance of industry as a factor in holding
empires together, and in the later eighteenth century government
was more willing than it had ever been before to pay attention to
economic theory. The example of the incipient industrial revolution
of northern Europe inspired many plans—often sponsored by government—to import foreign machinery and foreign technicians. The most
successful mechanised development was in the cotton industry of
Cataluña, which had grown up early in the eighteenth century, partly
as a result of Philip V's prohibition of the import of oriental silks.
As a substitute, a number of small firms in Cataluña began to make the
gay printed cottons known as *indianas*. The raw cotton was imported
from the Indies, as were many of the necessary dye-stuffs, and much
of the finished fabric was re-exported there. In 1771 the government
was persuaded to prohibit absolutely the import of cotton prints into
Spain, and to admit raw cotton free of duty. The industry throve under
protection, and in the 1780s both the spinning and weaving processes

were widely mechanised, using imported English machines. At the end of the eighteenth century there were more than 3,000 textile factories in Cataluña, employing about 100,000 people, mostly women. This industry, however, was exceptional. In most fields the import of foreign machines and the employment of foreign experts provoked jealous hostility among Spanish craftsmen; and neither the government nor private capitalists had the resources or the experience to exploit machinery adequately. The early industrial revolution in Spain was thus tentative and very limited in its effects.

In the Indies there was no industrial revolution at all. This is not to say, of course, that there was no industry. The eighteenth century was a time of great prosperity for skilled independent craftsmen in the Indies, especially for silversmiths and saddlers in Mexico, for the weavers of complex and beautiful cotton fabrics in Peru. Certain industries closely associated with agriculture also did well: sugar-making, distilling and—until the *estanco de tabacos* slowed it down—the manufacture of snuff and cigars. These agricultural industries produced on a fairly large scale and exported a large part of their product. Craft industry, on the other hand, was necessarily small in scale, and much of its product was for a limited market among the relatively rich. Humboldt, writing of the very end of the eighteenth century, estimated the annual value of agricultural produce in New Spain at 30,000,000 *pesos*, minerals at 25,000,000, manufactures at 7,000,000 to 8,000,000. Many factors combined to prevent the adoption of large-scale and mechanised methods of manufacture: mercantilist legislation intended to protect the interests of Spanish manufacturers, especially in the textile industries; the official emphasis on mining rather than manufacture; the restrictive influence of the craft gilds; poor transport facilities; above all, perhaps, lack of investment capital. There were plenty of rich men in the Indies; but Creole social convention not only called for lavish and ostentatious expenditure—it also placed narrow limits upon the range of investment. Land was the first choice, the safest, socially the most desirable; after land, trade. In such a society industry could not hope to attract any considerable amount of capital, even had the organisation, the equipment and the skill been available. As the Indies grew richer and more populous, new demands grew up; demands for manufactured goods in quantities and at prices which neither Spain nor the Indies themselves could provide.

Such was the economic background to the determined efforts of

Charles III's ministers to strengthen and rationalise the commercial, administrative and military structure of the empire. Economic imbalance was not the result of indifference, of lack of intelligent theoretical analysis, nor of lack of legislation. The Age of Reason had a strongly practical bent. The current vogue among the well-to-do for the study of natural philosophy and political economy was neither purely an academic exercise nor purely a dilettante amusement. It arose from a sincere—if optimistic—desire to improve the lot of man by organising society according to rational and orderly principles. This sincere faith in the effectiveness of informed rationality explains the enthusiasm which often pervaded discussion groups and societies for the study of natural science and for the application of scientific knowledge in useful inventions. A similar enthusiasm, a similar wish to apply knowledge usefully, animated the many *sociedades económicas de amigos del país* which sprang up all over the Spanish world in the second half of the eighteenth century. The activities of such groups did not end with discussion and with privately organised experiment and application—they could influence government. Eighteenth-century ministers, even monarchs, paid attention to economists, and some very gifted economists—Campillo, Campomanes, Jovellanos, for example— became ministers. The learned, voluminous and influential writings of Jovellanos, the briefer, more pointed and more practical tracts of Campomanes, all dealt almost entirely with Spain, with remedies for Spain's industrial lethargy, and neglected America. An earlier writer, José Campillo—economist, statesman, Minister of War and Finance in 1741—spread his interests wider. The celebrated *Nuevo sistema de gobierno económico para la América*, attributed to him and probably written in 1743, is devoted largely to urging upon government an active policy for the encouragement of productivity in industry and vigour in trade, in place of a passive policy of regulation. To be sure, Campillo wanted some colonial manufactures restricted in order to protect the market for Spanish manufactures; this was orthodox mercantilism. On the other hand, he advocated extensive training schemes for improving the skill of Indians and *mestizos* as cultivators and craftsmen. This was orthodoxy of a different sort; emphasis on education as a means of increasing production was characteristic of the Enlightenment. Campillo was aware also of the economic waste and social discontent caused by untilled *latifundia*, and the deadening effect of mortmain upon the sale and use of land. He suggested tax-free grants of land to Indians, conditional upon cultivation, and a system of agricultural credits. In the field of trade he saw that an expanding volume of business was more important to Spain than sterile attempts, by regulation, to monopolise a dwindling volume. He advocated the establishment of a regular royal mail service to the Indies; the termination of the Cadiz monopoly; the abolition of convoys and of the taxation which paid for them; even the reduction of duty on foreign imports destined for re-export to America.

The disasters of 1763 provided the shock necessary to start the government upon a career of drastic reorganisation. A royal commission appointed shortly after the end of the war recommended commercial legislation similar to that suggested by Campillo, and in the course of Charles III's reign most of its recommendations were put into effect. In 1764 regular monthly mail packets were inaugurated between Coruña and Havana; the trade of the Caribbean islands was opened to seven other Spanish ports besides Cadiz and Seville; a complex series of duties formerly levied on this trade was abolished and replaced by a simple 7 per cent *ad valorem*. This concession was originally intended as a special encouragement to a poor and backward area; but it came at a time when the production and export of sugar was beginning to expand, and was followed by an astonishing growth in the volume of the island trade. In 1760 half a dozen ships a year carried all the trade of Cuba; in 1778 over 200 were engaged in it, and liberal legislation was given the credit. The 1765 concessions, accordingly, were extended step by step to other provinces: in 1768 to Louisiana—which, with a French population accustomed to French goods, was always pampered by the Spaniards—in 1770 to Campeche and Yucatán, in 1776 to Santa Marta and Río de la Hacha, and in 1778 by a general *reglamento* to all the American provinces except Venezuela and New Spain. These were the most prosperous of all, too valuable to be lightly made the subject of radical experiment. For some years a share in the New Spain trade was allotted to Spanish ports outside Andalusia by a quota system. Meanwhile, by a series of decrees beginning in 1772, duties were further reduced and some products, both Spanish and American— notably wine west-bound, raw cotton east-bound—were placed upon a free list. Eventually, in 1789, the trade of New Spain and of Venezuela (the Caracas Company having meanwhile ceased to exist) was opened, like the rest of the Indies, to the shipping of all the major Spanish ports; and in the following year the *Casa de la Contratación*, for 287

years the principal agency for the regulation of the Indies trade, closed
its doors.

There was no question of free trade in the international sense; the
trade of the Indies was still confined to the Spanish flag. The exceptions
to this centuries-old rule were trifling, and all made for special reasons:
the permission granted, for example, to the French inhabitants of
Louisiana to import goods from France, and the facilities allowed to
Spanish Caribbean harbours to buy slaves from the French West
Indies. The Spanish government, like all colonial powers at that time,
was chronically suspicious of the commercial activities of its colonial
subjects. If they traded with one another they could not easily be
prevented from trading with foreigners. To the very end of its imperial
career the government forbade, though it could not effectively prevent,
all inter-colonial trade in certain classes of commodities—those exported in large quantities from Spain, or of particular value or interest
in Spain: wine, raisins, olives, almonds; or gold, silver, silk and china
goods. Restrictions on the interchange of ordinary American products,
on the other hand, were progressively reduced in Charles III's reign.
The reductions were of no great economic significance, since the products of the colonies were for the most part mutually competitive
rather than complementary; but at least the government demonstrated
its desire to remove unnecessary grounds of complaint. In 1768 legislation authorised trade between Peru and New Granada. Trade between
Peru and New Spain, prohibited since 1631, was legally reopened in
1774. In 1776 the Río de la Plata was opened for trade with the rest
of the Indies. The merchants of Lima lost their privileged position and
their protection against the competition of Buenos Aires in the markets
of Upper Peru; though this amounted to little more than recognition
of existing facts. The old traditional route of trade across the isthmus,
once dominated by the Lima merchant houses, had long lost its importance. European goods destined for Upper Peru now came mostly
overland from Buenos Aires; those for the coastal towns by sea round
Cape Horn.

Throughout the 1780s and 1790s trade between Spain and the Indies
steadily increased. Detailed statistics are lacking, but all contemporary
writers on the subject agreed upon the fact of increase, and even the
most conservative estimated a fourfold growth between 1778 and 1788.
The benefits of the trade, as might be expected, were unevenly spread
in Spain. Catalonia profited most, with its great port of Barcelona

virtually monopolising the import of sugar and the export of *indianas*; but Coruña, Vigo and other northern ports also traded widely, especially with Buenos Aires, and the northern ship-building industry received a powerful stimulus from the trade. Cadiz—despite wails of protest over the closing of the *Casa de la Contratación*—had no real ground for complaint. Its harbour remained busy and prosperous, at least until 1796. More surprising was the part played by Madrid capital in the Indies trade in Charles III's reign. The members of the Five Great Gilds of Madrid, enriched originally by retail trading among the swollen spendthrift population of the capital city, disposed of large sums of investment capital and from the middle of the century had formed the habit of combining in joint-stock enterprises of a general kind. In 1763 the gilds established their *Compañía general y de comercio* which under Charles III became for a time the largest and most powerful trading concern in Spain. It had branches at Cadiz and Barcelona and agencies at Mexico, Vera Cruz, Guatemala, Lima and Arequipa, as well as London, Paris and Hamburg. It invested largely in the manufacture of the goods it exported, and controlled factories making pottery at Talavera, silk at Talavera, Valencia and Murcia, cloth at Cuenca and Ezcaray, hats at San Fernando, printed cottons at Barcelona. It owned much of the share capital of the Manila Company, which at that time was doing very well, exporting Mexican silver to China, Chinese silk and muslin to Mexico. Unlike the Manila Company, the *Compañía general* held no monopoly of the trade of any particular region; it owed its success rather to the breadth and variety of its enterprise. Like other such concerns, however, it became involved in the risky business of lending to government, and bad debts, after the outbreak of the revolutionary wars, were its undoing. It came to an end in 1808, when the invading French seized its assets and burned its factories.

Madrid, Cadiz and Barcelona all benefited, in their Indies trade as in other respects, from the efforts of government under Charles III to improve internal communications. Notorious for many years as having the worst road communications in Western Europe, Spain shared in the general late eighteenth-century enthusiasm for road- and bridge-building. The *caminos reales* radiating from Madrid to the coasts, constructed by Floridablanca in the 1780s, were the first paved roads to be built in Spain since Roman times. In the Indies also, where the difficulties and distances were vastly greater, analagous improvements

were made. On the route of the *peruleiros*, the long and difficult road
from Buenos Aires, wheeled traffic could go as far as Tucumán. The
Andes defeated road-builders; from Tucumán to Potosí was possible
only for pack animals, usually mules; and on the mountain routes from
Potosí through Cuzco to Lima llamas were still in common use. North
of Lima, however, a cart road was kept open as far as Paita; from there
mules to Quito and on into New Granada. Similarly in New Spain
roads good enough for carts were built at this time from Mexico to
Jalapa in the east and to Guadalajara in the west; though pack mules
were still needed through the Sierra Madre to either coast. Rough and
precarious communications, indeed; but better than they had ever
been, at least under Spanish rule, and safer and surer in time of war
than coasting by sea, at the mercy of privateers. In the Indies, as in
Spain, the building of roads and the clearing of tracks supported the
royal policy of freeing and stimulating trade.

The enormous growth of trade between Spain and the Indies was
attributed by admiring economic theorists to the effect of liberal
legislation, in particular to the so-called Free Trade decree of 1778.
Certainly the lowering of duties and the removal of irksome restrictions
encouraged commercial enterprise. Spain, however, was merely
sharing, tardily and partially, in a growth of commercial and industrial
activity (and incidentally of inflation) common to most of Western
Europe. If Spain's trade and industry grew, England's grew faster; if
Spaniards did well in trade to the Indies, so, illegally but notoriously,
might foreigners. In time of war—between 1779 and 1783, for example
—England, despite defeats, interfered so seriously with Spanish shipping
that the old, familiar dearth of European goods reappeared in the
Indies, to the great profit of illicit traders. In peace-time, it is true, the
general lowering of duties served to reduce the difference in price
between lawful and smuggled shipments; but, on the other hand, the
easing of restrictions, the improvement of communications, the growth
of inter-colonial trade, in themselves made smuggling physically easier
and control, at least by traditional methods, physically more difficult.
This, of course, was no part of the royal intention. The purpose of
liberal commercial legislation was to improve the competitive position
of Spain in trading with the rest of the world, including its own
colonies; to get a bigger share of the Indies trade—if not, indeed, all
of it—back into Spanish hands; and to increase the royal revenue and
the national power by levying taxes, albeit at lowered rates, on a greatly

enlarged volume of business. To achieve these ends it was thought necessary, while lowering the barriers against trade within the empire, to raise and strengthen the fiscal and commercial fence which enclosed the empire as a whole. This in turn involved an attempt to tighten and rationalise the general administration of the empire, in particular to improve the machinery of tax-collection and accounting, and to strengthen the arms of imperial defence.

All this was normal eighteenth-century doctrine. Most rulers of the time pursued an ideal of government which should be rationally planned, consistent, tidy, authoritarian. The ideal was unattainable in any complete form in eighteenth-century conditions, especially in America; but Charles's ministers pursued it diligently and with some measure of success. At the centre, as we have seen, Philip V in 1714 had created four ministries, including one for Marine and the Indies. The ministry was to take over much of the work of the old Council of the Indies, though leaving intact the Council's jurisdiction as a supreme court of appeal. The functions of the ministries, and the relation between them and the Councils were not defined with any precision, however, until after 1763. Charles III, by consulting ministers separately as appropriate, gave a strong impulse towards departmental special-isation. At the same time, ministers themselves, at first meeting informally, endeavoured to co-ordinate the activities of their depart-ments by means of a committee or *junta*. Floridablanca, chief minister from 1777, encouraged his ministerial colleagues to meet more fre-quently and more regularly. He also impressed on the King the need to give the *junta* a formal and permanent existence, and to lay down rules governing its procedure. This was done in a comprehensive and carefully drafted decree of 1787. In place of a network of councils with ill-defined and overlapping jurisdictions, Spain had now a cabinet composed of departmental ministers collectively responsible to the King. The growth of the departmental effectiveness of the Ministry to the Indies, in particular, together with the emergence of the *junta*, robbed the Council of the Indies of more and more work, including even much judicial work. The Council lingered on into the nineteenth century, but after 1787 it was consulted only formally, perfunctorily and rarely. In place of a slow-moving deliberative bench, which had usually acted only on consultation or petition, the colonies had now to reckon with a powerful single minister, in close touch with the King, fully empowered to initiate policy and to direct its execution.

XIII *New World Baroque*
   a *The Church of Santa
      Prisca in Taxco*
   b *The Torre Tagle
      palace in Lima*

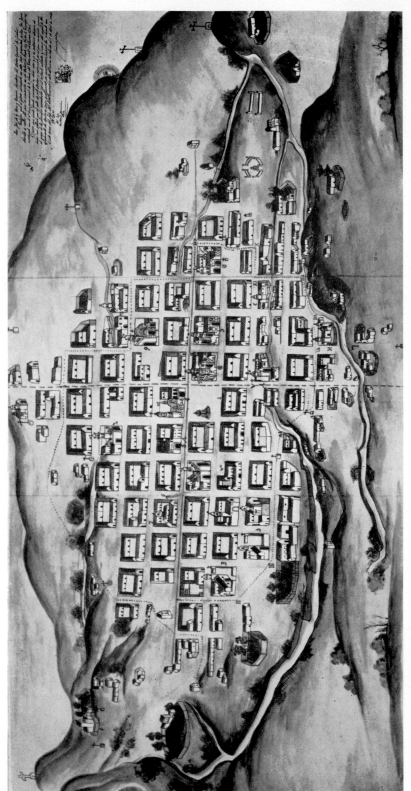

XIV Colonial town-planning: the city of La Plata

(drawn by Ildefonso Luján, oficial pintor, about 1778)

To make ministerial policy effective in the Indies it was first necessary to rearrange and subdivide, in the interest of administrative convenience and geographical fact, territorial units originally shaped by the hazards of discovery and conquest. The grotesque sprawling extent of the viceroyalty of Peru, intersected by great mountain ranges, had been curtailed in 1739 by the creation of New Granada. In 1776 yet another South American viceroyalty was detached from Lima, that of the Río de la Plata with its capital at Buenos Aires. In its origins the new viceroyalty was a temporary, *ad hoc* device, designed to meet military needs. The estuary was not only a convenient route for contraband; it was vulnerable to foreign aggression. In 1771 the British had stationed a garrison in the Falkland Islands, in defiance of vehement Spanish protest; from this remote base they could prey upon shipping bound for the Pacific, or equally well threaten Buenos Aires and the trade route to Upper Peru. More serious still, the Portuguese, pressing south from Brazil, could use their southernmost settlement of Sacramento as a base from which to intercept shipping going up the river, and were believed to be planning an assault on Montevideo. In 1776—the attention of Great Britain being engaged in North America—the Spanish government decided to mount a major naval and military expedition against the Portuguese forts in the area, in order to establish full control of both shores of the estuary. To provide a political and economic base for this expedition, its commander-in-chief was made temporary viceroy of the Río de la Plata provinces, which for this purpose were extended to include the district of the Audiencia of Charcas, Upper Peru. The expedition was a success, and so was the new viceroyalty. By 1777 the delighted merchants of Buenos Aires were petitioning the viceroy-commander-in-chief to extend the Indian frontier southwards, establish an *audiencia* and a university, and authorise the construction of docks. The viceroy, for his part, proved as able in economic conflict as in war. In the same year he placed an embargo—ostensibly to prevent fraud—on the carriage of bullion from Upper to Lower Peru. The centuries-old struggle between Buenos Aires and Lima was finally settled. Buenos Aires on its Silver River became the main outlet for the treasure of Potosí. The Río de la Plata provinces were far better administered from Buenos Aires than they had been from distant Lima. What had begun as a military improvisation became a permanent administrative unit and a standing bastion of defence.

Significantly the new viceroyalty, with its rapidly growing economy

and its disorderly cowboy population, was the area first selected for
the wide introduction of an important new administrative device, the
intendencia. Before Charles III's time the chief administrative defect
in each viceroyalty had been the gulf which separated the viceregal
court from the localities. The viceroy had governed with the advice
of the *audiencia* judges, for whom political and administrative work
was secondary to judicial duties; he had exercised a perfunctory supervision over the treasury officials, who constituted a separate branch;
he had had the services of a secretariat which in the course of the eighteenth century had become departmentalised and had increased greatly
in numbers; save for the occasional visits of *oidores* on circuit, however,
the viceregal centres had lacked direct contact with the district administrators, the *corregidores* and *alcaldes mayores*, who were mostly local men,
manning small districts on a small salary, relying for much of their
income on local perquisites or exactions, especially on the notorious
repartimiento of goods to Indians. The fault lay in the system, not in the
viceroys. Charles III throughout his reign appointed notably able and
conscientious men to these high offices; but no viceroy could govern
consistently and efficiently through an administrative system which
apart from the courts and the treasury consisted of a network of
petty local tyrannies, largely concerned with the forced sale to Indians
of European goods which they did not want and could not afford to
pay for. By the 1780s this haphazard system of district administration
was replaced throughout the Indies by *intendencias*. An intendant was
a provincial administrator with general supervisory powers over all
the main branches of government: public order, public works, finance,
economic regulation, defence. Such offices had been established in
Spain under Philip V in imitation of the system already in force in
France. José de Gálvez, among the findings of his general *visita* in New
Spain, recommended the appointment of intendants in the Indies, and
proposed the abolition of *corregimientos* and *alcaldías mayores*. In their
place the authority of each intendant was to be represented in each of
the Indian towns within his province by a *subdelegado* responsible for
the major *causas*—subjects of government: finance, defence, public
order and justice. In Spanish towns possessing formal municipal
corporations the *alcaldes ordinarios* were to be retained, and increased
powers were to be entrusted to the *cabildos*. They were to be supervised
by *subdelegados* with somewhat more limited powers. All *subdelegados*
were to be nominated by the intendants and formally appointed by

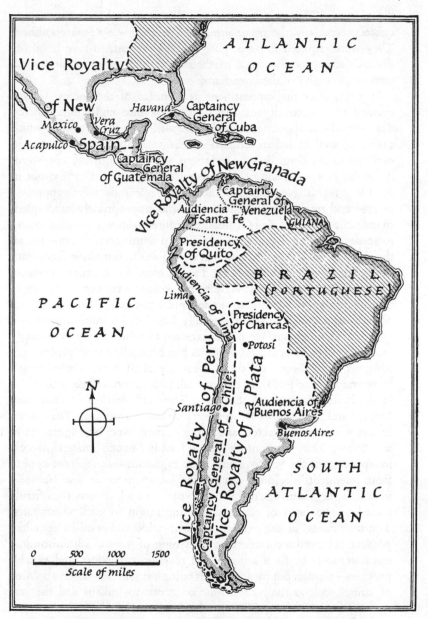

8. The Spanish empire in America in the late eighteenth century

the viceroys. They were to receive salaries; the old system of perquisites, especially the *repartimiento de comercio*, was to be abolished. They were required to be of pure Spanish descent, to give bond for the satisfactory performance of their duties and to work under the direct supervision of the intendants.

In 1782, after his appointment as Minister of the Indies, Gálvez divided the viceroyalty of Río de la Plata into eight intendancies. The intendants appointed *subdelegados* with full powers, in Spanish towns as well as Indian, and the *subdelegados* appointed deputies in outlying areas. Both these innovations were subsequently approved. A similar reorganisation of administrative districts was carried out in Peru in 1784. In New Spain some 200 *corregimientos* were suppressed in 1786 and replaced by twelve *intendencias*, appropriately subdivided. In the same year a detailed Ordinance for Intendants was issued, running to some 400 printed pages, comprising an administrative code for all the colonies which, with changes in detail, was to remain in force until the break-up of the empire. By 1790, except for frontier provinces administered by military governors, *intendencias* were general throughout the Indies. For the first time the empire possessed a rational system of territorial divisions and a centrally appointed administrative civil service. The intendants were not magnates like the viceroys, nor needy local place-seekers as most *corregidores* had been; they were professional administrators. Some of them were recruited from the viceregal secretariats, some from the treasury administration, either in Spain or in the Indies, many from the army. Their appointments issued from Madrid and nearly all of them were peninsular Spaniards. They were, on the whole, well selected, and many of them were intelligent, active and honest. They were, moreover, at least in financial matters, largely independent of the viceroys with their rapacious *entourage*; for appeals from intendants' decisions went to the *Junta superior de Real Hacienda*, in which the viceroy had only one vote, and which was thus firmly placed at the head of financial administration in each viceroyalty. The intendants, in the exercise of their wide and semi-independent powers, achieved a considerable tightening of general administration, improvements in fiscal control and revenue collection, and notable progress—though not by any means complete success—in the abolition of abuses such as the *repartimiento* of goods to Indians and the *mita* system of forced labour. They prodded the municipal *cabildos*, many of which had been in cataleptic trance for many years, into renewed activity in public works and local government generally. They were cordially detested throughout the Indies.

Both the economic and the administrative reforms introduced in the Indies under Charles III were designed to increase the royal revenue; one of the main purposes to which that revenue was to be devoted was imperial defence. It is curious that the Spanish Indies—reputedly so rich, so envied, so repeatedly attacked—possessed, until the Seven Years War, no standing army. Naval defence, it is true, the provision of convoy escort and cruiser squadrons, had always been given high place in the order of financial priority. The rebuilding of a 'line' navy—a major preoccupation of many of the ablest eighteenth-century ministers—was undertaken largely in order to defend the Indies without reliance on France. Land forces, on the other hand, were negligible. The old practice of calling out the *encomenderos* and their dependants did not long survive the sixteenth century and the decay of the *encomienda* system. In the seventeenth century key places such as Havana and Cartagena were garrisoned, and the viceroys had personal guards of halberdiers; but to meet emergencies—Indian risings or attacks by foreign corsairs— local forces had to be raised and paid for the occasion. In the eighteenth century a slow but steady process of militarisation began. A small frontier army was maintained in Chile, a few *presidios* in New Mexico; the viceregal halberdiers were replaced by companies of infantry— *compañías de palacio*; and in the major cities the merchant communities, or sometimes the *gremios*, the craft gilds, raised and maintained private local militias, usually, no doubt, ill-armed and ill-drilled. The entry of Spain into the Seven Years War and the consequent danger of English attack, emphasised by the fall of Havana, impressed upon government the need for a more permanent military force in the Indies. Such a force was organised hastily in 1762, and was kept in being after the end of the war. Originally it included both colonial levies and professional regiments sent from Spain, but in peace-time it was maintained chiefly by local impressment. In New Spain the normal establishment in Charles III's time was about 6,000 men: four line regiments, two regiments of dragoons, a brigade of artillery and a company of engineers. A whole regiment was now normally stationed at Havana. In addition to this professional army, a permanent militia was established, numbering in New Spain about 20,000 men, distributed by battalions throughout the provinces. The militia was recruited chiefly among Creoles and *mestizos*; Indians were, at least in theory, exempt from impressment. Most of the officers were leading Creoles, land-owners, mine-owners and the like, who bought their commissions. In South America the forces, both regular and territorial, were smaller, but all the viceroys had some military force at their disposal. The army affected not only colonial capacity for defence but also, through its Creole officers, the colonial social order; for professional and territorial officers alike claimed, and were accorded, a privileged position, legal, social and economic.

The army grew up beside the Church—indeed, to some extent replaced the Church—as a major prop and support of civil administration. In Hapsburg times obedience to law and to the royal will had been secured at least as much through the persuasion of the Church as through enforcement by secular sanctions. Royal administration, also, had relied heavily upon advisers and officials recruited from the clergy. The massive reorganisation of colonial life in the eighteenth century drastically altered this pattern of support. Royal administration relied less and less upon the Church, while controlling it ever more strictly through the *Patronato*. Sometimes the Crown came into serious public conflict with the Church, as, for example, in its quarrel with the Jesuits in 1767. One of the offences, or alleged offences, of the Company was its protest against the return of the Sacramento colony to Portugal in the peace treaty of 1763. The Jesuits were accused, absurdly, of seeking to establish an independent kingdom in the Paraguay missions; they were expelled, and great tracts of cultivated land went back to bush. Instead of relying on the Church, Bourbon government looked to the army; the bureaucracy was recruited increasingly from soldiers. The favoured standing and the political influence thus gained by military men was to be consolidated, a generation or so later, by civil war.

Administrative efficiency is rarely popular in colonial societies, especially when it is displayed by metropolitan officials. The colonial administration of the later Bourbons, admittedly, was not outstandingly efficient by European standards of the time. In many places, especially at the lower levels, it remained venal and slovenly, as it had always been. Nevertheless, it was more efficient, more tightly centralised, than any government which the Indies had known before; and the men who ran it and drew their livings from it were, as a matter of policy, nearly all peninsular Spaniards. The rift between Spaniards and Americans, which had long existed, but which Bourbon efficiency helped to widen, has now to be examined.

CHAPTER 17

Spaniards and Americans

THE Spanish Indies in the late eighteenth century—if so perceptive and so thorough an observer as Humboldt is to be believed—presented an impressive appearance of prosperity, stability and order. Colonial society—at least the European and Europeanised groups which formed the most influential and most articulate section of it—might be supposed to have strong reasons for loyalty and contentment. Population, productivity and trade were all increasing, and if a large part of the trade was directly or indirectly with foreign countries that did not worry the colonists; they had a reasonable supply of European goods and good markets for their own products. Administration was reasonably effective by the standards of the time, and not unduly oppressive; dilatory and pettifogging, no doubt—it had always been that—but probably not less effective nor more oppressive than in Spain; and taxation was lower. The military establishment seemed adequate but not excessive, and the provinces seemed reasonably secure against internal disaffection or external attack.

The wealth, the self-confidence and the pride of the Indies were reflected in the splendour of the principal cities. Spanish society, in America as in Spain, was urban by preference, and had been so since the first conquest. Prelates and senior officials toured their dioceses or provinces occasionally, as their duty required, but necessarily maintained their headquarters in the capital cities. The owners of mines, plantations and ranches similarly lived in the towns for most of the year, and visited their properties only for occasional rural diversion

or for necessary supervisory inspection. The preference for urban life
became accentuated in the eighteenth century and was clearly reflected
in the architecture of the time. Eighteenth-century *hacienda* houses
were large, and often stoutly built in order to resist, if necessary, local
riot or disturbance, but they tended to be sparsely furnished, comfort-
less, containing more storage space than living room. They had none
of the architectural elegance of the country houses of Virginia, Carolina
or the British West Indies. Rural church-building, similarly, in most
parts of the Indies at this time was on a very modest scale. The towns,
on the other hand, were magnificent. The culmination of late baroque
throughout Spanish America, and particularly in New Spain, between
1700 and 1780, produced a great number of buildings in which the
magnificence of the structure was matched by the luxury of the orna-
ment. These buildings influenced architectural forms in Spain, a reflux
particularly noticeable in Andalusia. It has been said that of the eight
masterpieces of baroque in the world four are in Mexico: the Sagrario
beside the metropolitan cathedral, the Jesuit seminary at Tepozotlán,
the convent of Santa Rosa at Querétaro, and the soaring church of
Santa Prisca in the silver city of Taxco. After about 1780 the baroque
style in the New World gave way to the more severe, more academic,
classicist. The best illustration of the change is in the work of the architect Francisco Tresguerras, who was born and worked throughout his
life in Mexico. Of Tresguerras's two most famous buildings one is
typically Mexican baroque: Santa Rosa at Querétaro. The other, the
Carmen at Celaya, is classicist, and splendid of its kind.

Ambitious scale and distinguished design were not confined to
churches. Many fine secular buildings date also from this time, especially
in Mexico City; the mint, the custom house, the tobacco factory, the
school of mines, the Academy of San Carlos, are all notable examples.
A great deal of public money was spent—chiefly as the result of viceregal initiative—upon improved town-planning in the late eighteenth
century. In Mexico City immense improvements were made in street-
paving and lighting, in policing and in water supply; the *quemadero* of
the Inquisition was removed, the Alameda enlarged, new streets laid
out and avenues of trees planted along the *paseos*. Humboldt is an
enthusiastic witness of these new civic elegances. As for Lima, the city
was almost totally destroyed in the catastrophic earthquake of 1746,
and was rebuilt in a similarly elegant, though in general less monumental, style. Among the most characteristic features of eighteenth-

century Lima were the great town houses—palaces, rather—built for private people. Some of them—the Torre Tagle palace and the house of the Perrichole, for example—still stand, with all their shuttered elegance and massive charm. The architectural splendours of the viceregal capitals were imitated, sometimes in only slightly lesser degree, in the chief provincial cities. Guadalajara, Puebla, Quito, Arequipa and many other towns are full of magnificent eighteenth-century buildings.

The spacious and lovely towns of America were inhabited by a rigidly stratified urban society. A few towns of comparatively recent growth, such as Buenos Aires, had populations which were racially homogeneous (except for slaves) and commercially oriented; here social intercourse could be, by Spanish standards, relatively free and easy. These towns were mostly small places, and were not typical. In the older viceroyalties most of the towns had large non-white populations, Indian, Negro or of mixed race; close-packed masses, inarticulate save in occasional outbreaks of rioting, elaborately classified according to race or racial mixture, each 'caste' identified by a precise, often contemptuous, collective name. The *gente distinguida*, the articulate, the well-to-do, the individually recognised, were relatively few in number and almost all white or near-white. A few ancient and distinguished *mestizo* families retained their wealth and social prominence in both New Spain and Peru; their menfolk wore knee-breeches and powdered wigs, and were accepted socially, as their ancestors had been; but in general the old easy racial intermixture of the immediate post-conquest era had long ceased to be acceptable to the ruling class. The *gente distinguida* included senior officials; ecclesiastics; a few professional men, lawyers and doctors; a few learned, especially in places where there were universities; major land-owners and mine-owners who ran town houses; merchants; in some places and for some purposes a few prosperous master craftsmen. In a place like Taxco, for instance, a successful silversmith could be a considerable local figure. There was, of course, a middle class of shopkeepers and artisans, mostly of mixed race, clearly distinct from their social superiors. There were also, inevitably in such a society, many 'poor whites', characteristically determined to insist upon their whiteness and their social standing and to avoid manual labour. This fierce insistence was made possible partly by the cheapness of Indian labour, partly by the availability, under a bureaucratic system of government, of a great number and variety of minor offices.

Empleomanía, the persistent and often pathetic scramble for office characteristic of Spanish colonial life, though certainly not confined to 'poor whites', was among them particularly bitter and intense; it reflected the predicament of men clinging to the fringe of an aristocratic society.

A self-conscious aristocracy, the white society of the Indies was intensely conservative, formal in its manners, on the whole parochial in its interests and outlook, and limited in its forms of social intercourse. The public centres of official life—the viceroy's or governor's palace, the *audiencia* for the legal fraternity, the municipal *cabildo*, the *consulado* (where there was one) for the commercial community, the cathedral or parish church for almost everyone—were naturally centres of social life as well. People met and gossiped in or about the church, and at the ceremonies, processions, bull-fights and the like which were organised in connection with ecclesiastical or secular festivals. There was much talk, and sometimes serious quarrelling, about precedence on such occasions; a preoccupation long characteristic of the Indies, and indeed of Spain. The other major focus of social life was the theatre. Mexico City and Lima each possessed two permanent theatres, the *Coliseo* at Lima having been nobly rebuilt after the earthquake. Universities and convents often staged theatrical performances; viceroys, even archbishops, allowed plays to be performed for select audiences in their *patios* or in the state rooms of their palaces. Apart from the theatre the arts in general did not provide many occasions for social gathering. Music was not greatly cherished, save as a ladylike accomplishment in convent schools, and there were no major colonial composers. As for painting, it exhibited, though with much less distinction, some of the characteristics of colonial architecture. It consisted chiefly of officially commissioned portraits, conspicuous for their grandeur and their size rather than for any subtlety in the delineation of character.

Between the superficial and formal intercourse of public gatherings and the guarded privacy of upper-class family life, there were few half-way houses, and consequently few opportunities for serious informal talk about matters of general concern. The genial society of club and coffee-house, which in Europe contributed greatly to the shaping of informed public opinion, hardly existed in the cities of the Indies. Learned academies and dilettante societies, of the kind which in Europe fostered upper-class interest in science, scholarship and the arts, in the Indies were few and short-lived. Official distrust of meetings behind closed doors may to some extent have discouraged them, but the main difficulty was the small number of their supporters. The Creole male tended to be more interested in horses than in ideas. For the most part, matters of general interest were discussed seriously only in gatherings for conversation in private houses; but it was difficult for anything in the nature of a *salon* society to develop when most upper-class women had little education and led comparatively secluded lives.

The universities, the official repositories of learning—some of them already ancient and famous—could not adequately fill the gap. The eighteenth century was not an age of conspicuous intellectual liveliness in universities anywhere in the European world. The universities of the Indies, moreover, had suffered a serious loss in the expulsion of the Jesuits. In the middle decades of the century the systems of Descartes, Newton and Leibnitz, in so far as they were known in the Indies at all, had been expounded by Jesuit lecturers at Lima and Quito. Enlightened viceroys, such as Amat in Peru between 1761 and 1776, had pressed the universities to include modern science and philosophy in their *curricula*; but competent lecturers were few. A formal scholasticism pervaded most of the *curricula*, at least until the 1780s; the intellectual leadership which the universities offered to colonial society was, at best, tentative and uninspired.

Despite all the obstacles, however, the society of the Indies in the eighteenth century was not without an intellectual life of its own, and in the last decades of the century this life was noticeably quickened and extended. Mention has been made of the *sociedades económicas de amigos del país*. The very existence of these formal and self-conscious associations of public-spirited citizens in the last two decades of the century is evidence that rational inquiry and experimental investigation, independent of theology, were becoming fairly widespread; that the attitude of mind of the encyclopaedists, both in Spain and in the Indies, was accepted, within limits, as respectable. The societies, it is true, usually had practical ends in mind, and concerned themselves chiefly with agriculture, with popular education and with economic and social problems. The interests of some of their founders and members, however, ranged more widely and embraced medicine, the physical and biological sciences, even philosophy and economic and political theory. Many of the leading members were physicians. A number of well-qualified physicians found their way to the Indies, partly because the government ever since the sixteenth century had interested itself in public health, partly because viceroys, appointed to reputedly un-healthy stations, took their medical advisers out with them. As a result, both medical practice and medical education in the major cities of the Indies in the late eighteenth century was surprisingly up-to-date. Vaccination against smallpox, for example, was widely applied in the Indies very soon after its introduction in Europe. Gifted physicians often turned their attention to natural science. Such a man was the famous José Celestino Mutis, who corresponded with Linnaeus and whose vast project of a complete botanical survey was subsidised by a viceroy of New Granada. Mutis, though he lived in South America for most of his adult life, was a peninsular Spaniard; but he had several distinguished Creole pupils, of whom the most eminent was Caldas, for a time director of the astronomical observatory and botanical garden at Bogotá. Mutis was also one of the founders of the *sociedad económica* of Bogotá. The *sociedades* had a good deal to do with the dissemination of scientific discoveries and ideas. Most of them main-tained, or were connected with, periodical publications, of which the *Aurora de la Habana*, the *Gaceta de Guatemala* and the *Mercurio peruano* were perhaps the liveliest and most varied; these journals often contained serious articles on scientific subjects. In spreading scientific knowledge and encouraging discussion the *sociedades* usually had the support of colonial governments. The Spanish Crown throughout the eighteenth century was an enlightened patron of scientific investiga-tion in the Americas; it financed expeditions on its own account, and welcomed and encouraged the travels of European *savants* such as Humboldt and Bonpland.

The scientific side of the Enlightenment, then, came to the Indies largely from, or through, Spain, and with official Spanish blessing. Political and social theory was another matter. The writings of Feijóo, with their strictures on superstition and their insistence on rational method, were much read in America, despite the misgivings of the orthodox and the conservative. The liberal Madrid periodical *Espíritu de los mejores diarios* circulated freely, and the ideas which it contained were spread by the *sociedades económicas* and by the American journals which, though they were officially forbidden to discuss politics, could and did criticise the socio-political structure indirectly in essays on education. All this, however, was mild stuff by European standards. The most exciting political ideas of the time emanated from France, or—worse—from England or North America. In those countries writers were openly attacking all despotism save that of the 'people'. Spanish intellectuals, in close contact with France, were inevitably affected. The somewhat enlightened despotism of Charles III, and the much less enlightened (and less efficient) despotism of his successor, could be severe in dealing with public criticism of their policy or of the principles on which their authority rested, especially in the Indies. Both monarchs were less tolerant in this respect than their great sixteenth-century namesake.

This is not to say that the viceregal governments in the Indies were encouraged to embark on an ideological 'witch hunt', or that they did so in fact. Their attitude was eminently practical. Down to the 1780s, at least, they rarely prosecuted people merely for possessing radical books or even for discreetly voicing radical ideas, unless those ideas were connected, or believed to be connected, with subversive intent. Foreign books containing potentially revolutionary ideas—many of them officially prohibited—were in fact readily available. They entered the Indies not only as contraband supplied by foreign traders; they came from Spain—where they were current and familiar—in the baggage of Spanish officials and merchants; they were brought back by rich young Creoles sent to Europe to complete their education; sometimes, daringly, they were printed in the Indies. There was, it is true, a censorship, operated by the Inquisition, which had long given up burning heretics but still sometimes burned books. The censorhip was dilatory, exasperating and at times puritanically eccentric; it regarded *Tom Jones*, for example, with the gravest suspicion. On the other hand, it was sluggish and inefficient and could easily be evaded. Not only Diderot and Franklin, but Rousseau and Raynal were well known, and much discussed, at least in the small circles of intellectuals who studied such matters. The ideas of Rousseau notoriously challenged the assumptions of eighteenth-century political life in many parts of the world. For the Indies, Raynal was even more disturbing, because more specific. 'If ever a happy revolution takes place in this world', he wrote, 'it will come from America.'

The availability of prohibited literature and the mild excitement of its clandestine circulation partly accounted for the limited influence of the *sociedades económicas*. The societies were officially sponsored. They confined themselves to non-controversial matters and to cautious proposals for piecemeal practical reform. Valuable as they were as fora for intellectual discussion, they had little appeal for real radicals or malcontents, who were more attracted by semi-secret organisations such as freemasonry. They made no impact at all on the unintellectual majority of Creole society, while to conservative officials and ecclesiastics their rationalism made them objects of suspicion. Their membership was largely confined to officials of liberal inclination and to a small number of respectable local citizens with intellectual pretensions. They were almost the only secular associations in the colonies which included both Creoles and peninsular Spaniards; but this very fact made it difficult for them to take any effective line of action. Few of them lasted very long. While they existed, they partially and temporarily concealed, but quite failed to repair, a fundamental cleavage in the society of the Indies; the growing mutual hostility between Spaniards born in the Indies and Spaniards born in Spain.

Such tensions exist in all colonial societies. The old hand despises the greenhorn fresh from 'home'; though he may at the same time long for the security and urbanity which 'home' represents. The settler, who has committed himself to a new land and risked his capital, perhaps his life, in it, may resent the salaried functionary who comes out for a term of years and risks nothing. The established resident, perhaps of several generations' standing, who knows the country and understands —or thinks he understands—the natives whose labour he employs, is irritated by the metropolitan official who has to enforce a policy based on general theories of how 'natives' should be treated. The colonial merchant, dealing in highly priced imported manufactured goods, resents the metropolitan supplier, whether manufacturer or shipper; especially when, as often happens, a monopoly is organised to keep up prices. All these resentments appeared early in the history of the Indies. Within a few years of the conquest of New Spain, 'old conquerors and settlers' were complaining of royal favours shown to strangers fresh from Spain. Imperial Potosí, source of so much wealth, was notorious for its murderous feuds between the European groups. All Spaniards living in the Indies were united in jealousy of the mercantile monopoly of Seville.

In the eighteenth century these tensions became steadily more acute. Many observers commented on this mounting resentment. Ulloa and Juan in the middle of the century, Humboldt at its close noticed that Spanish Americans preferred foreigners to peninsular Spaniards. Significant changes of group names occurred. In the sixteenth and seventeenth centuries American-born Spaniards had usually called themselves Spaniards, associating themselves with peninsular Spaniards in pride of race and culture and distinguishing themselves from Indians; *mestizos* of good family often did the same. In the second half of the eighteenth century the American Spaniards became more self-conscious as a class, distinguishing themselves both from *mestizos* and from peninsular Spaniards. From about the time of the Seven Years War— according to Humboldt—they began calling themselves *Americanos*. They reserved the name Spaniard for peninsular Spaniards, to whom they also applied offensive nicknames—*gachupín* in resentment or *chapetón* (greenhorn) in contempt. At about the same time peninsular Spaniards began generally to use the term *criollo*, Creole, to describe American Spaniards, whom they thus associated with Indians, *mestizos*, Negroes, mulattos and so forth in a complex hierarchy of 'castes'.

The split in white society in the Indies was more than a matter of mere prejudice or name-calling. It was widened by specific grievances, political, economic and social. At the root of these grievances lay resentment against discrimination of one kind or another; in the political field, for example, discrimination in appointments to office. This was a perennial grievance, especially since such discrimination was contrary to repeated early legislation favouring the sons of Spaniards born in the Indies. The appointments in dispute were not, as a rule, to the highest offices; Creole society expected, and accepted, that the viceroys, the King's personal representatives, would usually be peninsular noblemen; individual viceroys might be wildly unpopular, but on the whole patrician Creoles paid court at the viceregal palace as a matter of course, with all the snobbish emulation of 'government houses' anywhere in the world. To some extent the same was true of senior judges; though in fact a considerable number of Creoles became *oidores* or *fiscales*; one or two, indeed, became viceroys. The real trouble, the agonies of *empleomanía*, occurred lower down in the official hierarchy, in competition for offices which were still regarded among eighteenth-century Spaniards (and Frenchmen and Englishmen) as places of profit rather than as posts of trust. Under the Hapsburgs, it will be rememberd, the answer to Creole *empleomanía* had been simple and unheroic. Fee-earning offices, the innumerable clerkships for example, had usually been sold, either by the Crown or by private treaty, and Creoles had as good an opportunity of bidding for them as *Pensinsulares*—better, indeed. Even when lucrative offices were sold, or given as gratuities, to people in Spain, the recipients commonly leased them to Creole deputies. Provincial governors and treasury officials, who received salaries, also often—though illegally—bought their posts. Local magistracies—*alcaldías mayores* and *corregimientos*—and most municipal offices were usually given to local people; poor Creole gentlemen commonly recruited their fortunes through tenure of such posts, and there were always long waiting lists of hopeful applicants. In the eighteenth century this comfortable, slipshod system of outdoor relief came under attack. Successive Bourbon governments tried to limit the practice of sale, with some success. It is often difficult in practice to distinguish between the lawful payment to the Crown of a purchase price for an office and the clandestine payment of a *douceur* to an official for his help in securing an appointment. The latter type of transaction is by no means extinct today; but the records indicate that recognised and lawful sales of office by the Crown were restricted by Charles III's time to fee-earning places and honorific dignities—chiefly *escribanías* and seats in municipal councils. Sales of this type survived to the early nineteenth century. It was left to a 'liberal' government, in 1812, to make all sales of office illegal, and to incur the full blast of Creole resentment. A more serious barrier to *empleomanía* was raised by the establishment of intendancies and the abolition of *corregimientos* and *alcaldías mayores* under Charles III. Many holders of these old offices, it is true, became *subdelegados* under the new system; but *subdelegados*, for a time at least, were denied the most lucrative of the perquisites which their predecessors had enjoyed—the *repartimiento de comercio*—and they were answerable to unsympathetic peninsular superiors, the intendants. The imperial government naturally regarded Creole officials with suspicion. Living in close-knit isolated communities, they could not escape local pressures and obligations; they tended, once they attained responsible office, to favour and promote their relatives and friends; and their attitude towards the Indians was notoriously harsh by European standards. Equally naturally, they reacted to government suspicion with aggrieved resentment. What to rationalising Spanish ministers seemed overdue reform was vindictive denial of legitimate opportunity in the eyes of office-hungry Creoles.

Similar rivalries and resentments arose over ecclesiastical preferment. The eighteenth century was not a notably spiritual age anywhere in the European world, and the Church in the Indies, unlike the civil administration, was little disturbed by reforming zeal. The clergy in the Indies, however, had always been a quarrelsome body; in the eighteenth century most of their quarrels were about temporalities. The *Patronato* never openly descended to the sale of benefices; nor did it overtly discriminate against Creoles. It tended, usually, to present peninsular Spaniards to bishoprics. This tendency was not greatly resented, nor, indeed, was it exclusive; some Creoles became bishops; Creoles often became canons, inquisitors, rectors of universities; there were even one or two Creole archbishops. The bitterest quarrels arose not over these high preferments nor over ordinary parish incumbencies, which by that time were usually filled by Creoles, by *mestizos*, or even occasionally by Indians. They arose over the posts of Provincials or heads of districts in some of the religious Orders. 'The rent of these Provincialates'—so Juan and Ulloa—'is so substantial that they are far more desirable in those lands and more likely to lead to strife.' They were, moreover, elective, so that the friars in each province tended to form two parties, the European and the Creole; the Creole party was usually more numerous, but the Europeans usually had the support of their superiors in Spain. The common *modus vivendi* was an arrangement whereby a province would be ruled in alternate periods of three years by a Creole and by a European. This, led, in many places, to recurrent conflicts between the 'ins' and the 'outs' and to strenuous efforts on the part of the 'ins' to prevent the 'outs' from succeeding them, so that tension between Spaniard and Creole was perpetuated, communicating itself to the inferior clergy and to society in general.

Economic rivalry followed a somewhat different pattern. For 150 years, from the formal organisation of the *Carrera* in the middle of the sixteenth century to the outbreak of the Succession War, a small number of merchant houses with their head offices in Seville held jointly a legal, and for many years a fairly effective, monopoly of the main Indies trade. Entrenched and confident, they restricted their shipments to the quantities which they thought they could sell without difficulty, and charged high and uncompetitive prices. In the Indies there were two corresponding groups of wholesale merchant houses, one concentrated in Mexico City, the other in Lima, each organised, like the Seville merchants, in a *consulado*. Most of the goods landed at Vera Cruz were sold to Mexico City merchants; at Puerto Belo to those from Lima. Smaller merchants from provincial towns also made direct purchases at the ports; but the big firms in the capital cities always had the advantage because, with their greater resources, they could afford to take their time, to delay their buying until the fleets were due to return to Spain, in the hope of bringing the prices down. European goods were distributed throughout the viceroyalties from warehouses in the capital cities by *aviadores*, merchants who often traded also as money-lenders. They operated strings of mules, purchased goods from the wholesalers on credit and sold them, again on credit, to ranchers, to miners on the silver frontier and to shopkeepers in the provincial towns. The wholesalers had as firm a grip on the internal trade of the viceroyalties as the Seville *consulado* had upon the trans-Atlantic trade. Consumers' complaints of high prices and irregular deliveries were directed at least as much against the colonial wholesalers as against the Spanish shippers in distant Seville. The principal and most obvious rivalry was not simply between colony and metropolis; it was between powerful groups of middlemen, the Creole groups of Mexico and Lima, and the peninsular group at Seville. They skirmished continually, not only to get the better of one another in business dealings but to secure legislative favours from the Crown; the Spanish group seeking to strengthen the legal monopoly of Seville, the colonial groups endeavouring to weaken it while retaining their own local advantages.

The increasing pressure of foreign competition naturally favoured the colonial groups, and the Succession War ensured their victory. The galleons and the *flotas* for a time ceased to sail. Foreign interlopers, who up to then had operated mainly in the Río de la Plata and the smaller harbours of the Caribbean, now boldly entered Vera Cruz and El Callao. The colonial wholesalers had a wide choice of supplies, and part at least of the interloping trade was legalised at the peace, in the concessions granted to the South Sea Company. The Seville–Cadiz shippers had to try to re-establish themselves after the war in a new and competitive world. The small fleets which sailed from Cadiz at irregular and lengthening intervals were mostly expensive failures. Often the goods they carried were rejected by the Mexico and Lima importers, or sold at a ruinous loss. The *flotistas* and *galeonistas*—the Seville or Cadiz merchants who accompanied the fleets to sell the goods—instead of being the representatives of a secure and restrictive monopoly, found themselves at the mercy of their customers.

The peninsular answer, as we have seen, was the gradual, but eventually complete, abandonment of the fleet system; the establishment of joint-stock companies in appropriate sections of the trade; ultimately the opening of all the ports of the Indies to merchants from any part of Spain. These measures, coinciding as they did with a reanimation of ship-building and shipping generally and with a notable development of some of the relevant manufactures in Spain, achieved considerable success. They were not, however, universally welcome in the colonies. The joint-stock companies were generally hated in the areas they served and exploited. The opening of the Río de la Plata was a severe blow to the trade of Lima, much resented there. Worse, the sluggish, custom-bound operations of the Seville–Cadiz monopolists, which had been conveniently supplemented by contraband, gave way in the later eighteenth century to the more aggressive methods of merchants from other parts of Spain: of frugal, pushing Basques; of wily Catalans whose business practices had been sharpened by centuries of chaffering in the Levant. These people were not content, as the old monopolists had been, to dump their goods on the beach and await purchasers. They went into the interior; they bought mules and went into business as distri-buting merchants and *aviadores*; they set up as shopkeepers, even as wholesale dealers, in competition with local traders in the towns; they penetrated into the *consulados*, even into the municipal *cabildos*, where they created peninsular parties and pressure groups, often with the tacit support of the officials. Naturally they were disliked by the local mercantile community, and their invasion was yet another cause of Creole–Peninsular tension.

To these specific grievances social resentment added a nagging daily irritant. The leaders of Creole society—the people who set the example of social behaviour for all colonial whites—were patricians. They regarded themselves as the spiritual, if not the lineal, heirs of the *conquistadores*. Many of them were rich. On their wide estates, among a semi-servile peasantry, they exercised unquestioned paternal authority. In the towns they formed close-knit oligarchies whose members were all well known to one another and respected by lesser townsfolk. They controlled most of the activities of local government, either through personal participation or indirectly through lesser people who were their clients. They used their control to resist innovation, to let sleeping dogs lie. Towards their distant king they professed—and felt—traditional loyalty, a formal, patrician loyalty based on the assumption that the King would not, in practice, interfere effectively with their interests and their way of life. They treated the viceroys—who were the King's personal representatives, and usually patricians themselves—with ceremonious respect. As good conservatives, they

respected the Church and the judiciary. The minor officials of central
government, on the other hand, they regarded with contempt, as
persons to be bullied or bribed when necessary, otherwise ignored.

Creole patricians in the later eighteenth century saw, with acute
distaste, the invasion of *their* Indies by an increasing number of
peninsular Spaniards of low birth and little fortune—assiduous shopkeepers, sharp business men, busy officious quill-drivers in government
offices, officers in the regular army. These people often made money
and secured rapid promotion. They had their own form of social
conceit, merely because they were metropolitan Spaniards and
despised, or affected to despise, colonial society. Much as the leading
Creoles disliked such upstarts, they could not avoid social contact
with them. In some circumstances they might become uncomfortably
dependent upon them; mine-owners, for example—usually Creoles—
depended for working capital on merchant-*aviadores*, many of whom
were *Peninsulares*. *Haciendas* offered as security for this purpose often
fell into the hands of peninsular Spaniards by foreclosure, bringing
their new owners into the circle of local land-owning society. Self-
made *Peninsulares* even pretended to marriage—this was a common
cause of outraged complaint—with the daughters of prominent Creole
families. Friction was especially acute in the army. The stationing of
of regular units in the Indies after the Seven Years War led to mutual
jealousy between the professional army, mostly officered by peninsular
Spaniards, and the militia, mostly officered by Creoles. Those Creoles
who took commissions in the regular army found—or thought they
found—their promotion blocked and their standing in the mess
belittled by peninsular officers who were often—so they thought—
their social inferiors.

This explosive mixture of envy and contempt was intensified by
the growing practice among leading Creole families of sending their
sons travelling in Europe. Spain, to these young travellers, seemed
poverty-stricken and backward. Like all colonials accustomed to
reliance on semi-servile native labour, they were shocked to see white
men in Spain cheerfully performing menial tasks which in the Indies
were left to Indians. As urban aristocrats, they were unimpressed by
the older Spanish towns with their cramped medieval—or Moorish—
mazes of streets. Even comparatively modern Madrid was a bitter
disappointment, meaner and dirtier than Mexico or Lima, meaner by
far and intellectually less lively than Paris or Versailles. Moreover,

rich and handsome young Creoles often received in Paris and in London a social attention which, if not entirely disinterested, was highly flattering, and a contrast with the more familiar indifference of their reception in Spain.

From dislike of peninsular Spaniards to open repudiation of Spanish allegiance was a long step, which few Creoles seriously contemplated before the turn of the century. Reverence for the Crown was a deeply rooted feeling in all classes of society in the Indies, including the Indians —Juan and Ulloa emphatically noted this last point—and the royal patronage dispensed both by ministers and viceroys had still many rewards to offer to loyal Creoles. Moreover talk of rebellion could be highly dangerous, quite apart from the risk of official detection and punishment, in a society stratified largely on racial lines. In the late 1770s and early 1780s, at the very time that Spain was supporting rebellion in North America, a series of Indian risings occurred in the viceroyalty of Peru. One in particular, led by José Gabriel Condor-canqui, who took the Inca name of Túpac Amarú, lasted for two years and was suppressed only with great difficulty and bloodshed, by regular troops. Condorcanqui was in fact a *mestizo*, a man of property and a trusted local magistrate. In calling the Indians to arms against the burden of tribute and the abuses of the *mita* system, he proclaimed himself a loyal subject—indeed a viceroy—of the King, and the enemy only of '*corregidores, chapetones* and tax-gatherers'. He called upon the Creoles of Peru, his countrymen, to join him. Naturally they were as alarmed by the course of events as were the officials themselves. They played their part in the operations against Condorcanqui, and made no protest, when the rising was over, against the frightful manner of his execution.

The threads of attachment, however, were stretching and some were beginning to snap. Outside Peru the Condorcanqui rising made little impression upon Creole opinion. Most Creoles were completely confident of their capacity for controlling Indians. Events in other parts of the world demonstrated that revolutions need not necessarily be destructive of property and social order. The revolt of the North American colonies was led by patricians: land-owners, slave-owners, prosperous merchants. Once the power of the Crown and the royal governors had been removed, these respectable people took over the government. The French Revolution, a little later, was more complicated; it beheaded a king; it was accompanied by the burning of châteaux, and gave Paris over to brief periods of mob rule. Nevertheless, although the privileges of birth in France were reduced, the rights of property survived unimpaired, perhaps even enhanced. The resounding declarations which accompanied these two revolutions, and the social and political writing which preceded them—the writing of Rousseau in particular—supplied articulate Creoles with a theoretical framework, a means of rationalising their dislike and envy of peninsular officials and of European Spaniards generally. Later events in France provided even more exciting and suggestive models of behaviour: Napoleon, First Consul and then Emperor, surrounded by satellite marshals, toppling effete thrones, uniting the French people and leading them to unexampled military success. These glittering figures were the models which ambitious, frustrated Creoles were to seek to emulate.

The Spanish government, for its part, was well aware of the dangers of French example. The disturbances of the 1780s were not all Indian risings. The revolt of the *comuneros* of Socorro, in New Granada, in 1781 was a Creole and *mestizo* rising, in a province where few pure-blood Indians remained. It was basically a protest against local taxation imposed by the provincial intendant for defence purposes. The demands of the *comuneros*, however, included the abolition of the tobacco monopoly and the enforcement of old laws giving preference to natives of the Indies in appointments to all offices, including the highest. The rebels were protesting, in other words, against peninsular encroachment upon their ancient rights. The local authorities were obliged to parley and to accede to the *comuneros'* terms; but since no faith need be kept with rebels, the viceroy subsequently repudiated the agreement, and the leaders of the rebellion were executed. Episodes of this kind naturally made the viceregal authorities nervous, and led them to take seditious talk more seriously. The fashionable table-talk about the Rights of Man—harmless enough, to all appearance, in Spain—if it became widespread among illiterate and excitable people in the Indies could indeed be highly inflammatory. Prosecutions became more frequent. Among outstanding victims was Francisco de Santa Cruz y Espejo, scientist, literary critic, founder of the *Sociedad patriótica* in Quito, editor of the first periodical and director of the first public library to be established there. Espejo died in prison in 1795. He was of humble origin, a half-Indian *mestizo*, and social slights may have contributed to his dissatisfaction with colonial government. Other malcontents had no such obvious excuse. 'Inside nations'—according to de

Tocqueville—'revolution springs not from despair but from rising expectations.' Espejo's contemporary, Antonio de Nariño, was a prominent Creole who received marked viceregal favour and made a fortune from the perquisites of office. He dabbled in private printing, and published at Bogotá a translation of the French *Declaration of the Rights of Man*, for which he was prosecuted. He defended himself by citing instances of equally daring pamphlets published by respected citizens—even officials—who went unpunished. The defence, though able, was irrelevant; Nariño was imprisoned because he was suspected of subversive intentions. He was sent to Spain, escaped with the help of powerful friends—like many such, he was a freemason—and soon joined a coterie of plotters against Spain in exile. He returned eventually to America, to join the insurgents at Bogotá in 1812.

The career of Francisco de Miranda is an even more famous instance of the way in which government severity converted minor malcontents into permanent enemies. Miranda was a Creole, born in Venezuela, the son of a well-to-do commercial family. He became an officer in the regular army and secured rapid promotion; he was a brevet colonel at the age of twenty-four. He was sent to Jamaica at the end of the war of North American independence to negotiate an exchange of prisoners, became involved there in financial irregularities and made matters worse by supplying military information of a trivial kind to the Jamaican authorities. He was tried in absence and sentenced to eight years' confinement in Oran. It was a severe sentence, the more so since Miranda had been led into these offences by convivial but disreputable acquaintances in Kingston. Miranda fled to escape capture. He attributed his misfortunes not to his own folly but to Spanish prejudice against him as a Creole. After futile attempts to get himself reinstated he repudiated his allegiance and devoted himself to conspiracy.

In the 1790s many of these aggrieved and exiled Creoles gathered in Paris, in London and in Washington, where they conspired in groups and tried to establish contact with sympathetic politicians, to persuade them to back revolutionary landings in Spanish America. In time of peace these amateurish *émigré* cabals could do little to harm the Spanish government. They could, and did, present a serious threat once Spain became involved once more in a major maritime war. Foreign statesmen, covetous of the reputed wealth of the Indies, were not unwilling to listen to them; were willing, even, to act, should a favourable opportunity occur.

CHAPTER 18

The Creole revolt

THE ties which bind the provinces of a colonial empire to their metropolitan government are never easy to define. Dependence upon the armed force of the metropolitan country for protection against outside attack is one obvious and powerful bond. Another is dependence on the producers and shippers of the metropolitan country for goods which the colonial populations cannot produce for themselves, or easily procure elsewhere. If the colonies are in no danger of attack and have alternative souces of supply, however, they may still be held to imperial allegiance by traditional family affection, by a common language and culture, and by loyalty to a common crown. Even when loyalty is strained and soured, the metropolitan government may still be able to isolate and coerce particular disaffected groups and prevent general rebellion. Finally, sheer inertia, social habit, administrative routine, can hold together groups of people who have lost all sense of active affection or cohesion. An imperial government can become useless, ineffective and unpopular in the eyes of its colonial subjects, and still survive for years; but only if it can avoid revolutions at home and major wars abroad.

Two European powers, France and England, were each in a position to make damaging attacks upon the Indies. Each was stronger at sea than Spain in the eighteenth century. England was navally and commercially the more aggressive and the more dangerous; but England and France were nearly always at odds, so that Spain could usually count on French support, direct or indirect, in defending the Indies against English attack. The arrangement did not always succeed, and Spain sometimes suffered damaging defeats. Although at the outbreak of the French Revolution the empire was still substantially intact, it was obvious to intelligent Creoles that Spain was unable, by its own unaided efforts, to provide for their defence. Similarly in commerce; Spanish shippers had succeeded, between the Seven Years War and the French Revolution, in recovering a large share of the Indies trade, but English goods, when they could be had, were still cheaper than Spanish. The Indies were dependent on Spain for their supplies, only to the extent that the Spanish government, by regulation, could keep foreign traders out. It was in the Creole interest to let foreign traders in.

Loyalty is more difficult to assess. A fierce loyalty to the Crown and its wearer had been traditional among American Spaniards ever since the conquest; it was one of the characteristic attitudes of a gentleman. It did not, of course, imply unquestioning obedience. It was, moreover, a loyalty to the King as King in the Indies; it did not necessarily imply loyalty to Spain—which in theory and in sentiment was a separate kingdom or group of kingdoms—or deference to Spaniards from Spain. Many Creoles disliked and resented the peninsular Spaniards, whether officials or business men, with whom they came into contact. This did not mean that they liked foreigners any better, or—*pace* Juan and Ulloa —that they would have preferred foreign rule to Spanish; it meant that for them Spaniards *were* foreigners. Even loyalty to the Crown was not universal; a minority of intellectuals, as we have seen, influenced by English, North American and, above all, French, political theory, opposed imperial rule on theoretical grounds; others conspired against it because of the slights and injustices, real or fancied, which they had suffered. In general, however, Creoles felt a genuine loyalty to their distant king, treated his senior representatives with guarded respect, and accepted, as a matter of habit, the bureaucratic hierarchy with its *paperasserie*. What the Indians and the poorer *mestizos* felt is difficult to say. Probably they tended to think of the King, his viceroy and his judges as well-disposed but inaccessible (and therefore ineffectual) protectors against local oppression. However this may be, the feelings of Indians had little influence on the course of events.

In 1796 the Spanish government, pressed by France, outraged by English maritime arrogance in war and suspicious, as always, of English intentions in America, overcame its repugnance to revolution and regicide, and by the Treaty of San Ildefonso entered into alliance with republican France against England. In challenging the leading maritime power in the world it put a heavier strain on colonial loyalty than loyalty could well bear. No one could then foresee that the French wars would last, with brief intervals, for another nineteen years; but in the event, from 1796 to 1814 Spain was in large measure cut off from the Indies. The viceregal governments had to handle an increasingly explosive situation as best they could. The home government—when there was one—could neither supply, nor defend, nor effectively coerce.

In 1797 the English seized Trinidad, and instructed their governor there to investigate the possibilities of supporting risings in the mainland provinces. The urgings of Miranda, who rightly regarded British sea power as the strongest possible weapon against Spain in America, were beginning to command attention in London. At the same time English fleets, blockading the Atlantic coasts of Europe from the Channel to Gibraltar, kept Spanish shipping bottled up in the Mediterranean. In order to keep the colonies supplied, the Spanish government was obliged, by a decree of 1797, to open the ports of the Indies to neutral ships. The immediate beneficiaries of this decree were shipping firms in North America. Exports from the United States to Spanish America in 1796 were worth about 400,000 dollars. By 1802 the figure had grown to over 8,000,000. Access to the ports, once granted, could not in practice be confined to neutrals; any lull in the fighting brought English ships in even greater numbers. Spanish control of the Indies trade effectively ended in 1797, and was never recovered. The 1797 decree was the first clear step towards open independence. Despite its great economic importance, however, it had no immediate political or military sequel. The British government was too hard pressed to fulfil any half-promises its members may have made to the Creole *émigrés*. Nelson's victory at Trafalgar ended the last attempt of the Spaniards, in alliance with France, to reassert their sea power in the Atlantic, and so further weakened Spanish control in the Indies; but apart from the capture of Trinidad, no British operation against Spain in America was mounted until 1806.

Popham's invasion of Buenos Aires in that year was, in essence, a filibustering expedition of the traditional type, undertaken without specific authority by an energetic officer bored with inaction on the South Atlantic station. Popham had been assured by *émigré* acquaintances in London that his intervention would be welcomed by the inhabitants of Buenos Aires. The city was indeed deeply divided between Creoles and Spaniards, between those with English contacts and those with French, between those who profited by contraband and those who wished to suppress it. The viceroy, Sobremonte—an able and energetic officer who had formerly served with distinction as intendant of Córdoba—had no troops at his disposal and doubted the will of the citizens to resist. He set out in haste for Córdoba, fifteen days' march inland, to raise an army. His action, like Popham's, was traditional, old-fashioned. Both Popham and Sobremonte had miscalculated, however. The Buenos Aires Creoles, despite their long-standing English contacts, had no wish to exchange Spanish rule for foreign domination, and were deeply affronted by Popham's cheerful assumption. In these circumstances Creoles and unofficial *Peninsulares* in the city could act in concert. A *junta* of leading citizens—a *cabildo abierto*, a kind of informal extension of the town council—quickly assumed the government, organised a local force and drove Popham's people out of the city only three months after his arrival. The immediate results were an immense increase in local self-confidence—the Crown itself truckled to success and appointed the local military leader, Liniers, as viceroy—and the opening of the river to British trade. The people of Buenos Aires, though quick to resent foreign invasion, welcomed foreign trade. The port remained open to ships of all nations, with a few brief intervals, from that day to this.

Popham's landing, and the equally unsuccessful expedition sent to Montevideo to support him, were psychological and strategic blunders. They were also deviations from normal and obvious British policy, which was not to annex territory but to secure the right to trade. If this could be extracted from the Spanish government, well and good. If not, Great Britain would encourage American independence, again with a view to trade. This was the purpose of the next British design against the Indies, the assembly of an army in Ireland under Wellesley, intended for an invasion of New Spain. Trade with a liberated and grateful Mexico, it was hoped, would earn silver to finance the war against Napoleon. Miranda, back in London after an inept attempt in 1806 to invade Venezuela and to raise the standard of revolt there, hoped to persuade government to divert Wellesley's army to Venezuela. Both possibilities were hastily abandoned in 1808, however, because of the unforeseen turn of events in Spain. Napoleon, suspecting the intentions of Charles IV's flamboyant favourite Godoy, invaded Spain; induced Charles to abdicate and Ferdinand, the heir apparent, to renounce his claim; and set his own brother Joseph upon the vacant throne. The higher aristocracy and senior officials for the most part accepted the *coup d'état*; in the presence of French armies they had little choice. The French quickly occupied Madrid and the big towns in the east and north of Spain. Reaction soon set in, however. Affronted national pride caused violent and spontaneous risings all over Spain. As always among Spaniards in times of crisis, *juntas*, miscellaneous, local and temporary collections of leading people, sprang into life. A Council of Regency was formed, to govern on behalf of the exiled Ferdinand. A central, or national *junta*, first at Aranjuez, then at Seville, established—with some difficulty—its leadership over the local and municipal *juntas* in other parts of Spain. This central *junta* for a time retained control, more or less, of part of the south-west of Spain, and fixed its headquarters at Cadiz. Most of the rest of the country was occupied, though never fully controlled, by the French armies. Spain thus entered upon a long period of savage guerrilla war. The British government, anxious to tie down Napoleon's armies in Spain and to exploit its own command of the sea, offered alliance and help to the central *junta*. The price which it demanded was, predictably, permission to trade with the Indies; a privilege obscurely granted, subsequently denied, but vigorously exercised then and later. Military designs against the Indies were abandoned. Wellesley's army went to Spain to fight the French and Miranda was left to invade Venezuela by himself.

These events in Spain presented difficult problems of loyalty in the Indies, not only to loyal Creoles but also to Spanish officials. The business of colonial officials was, as always, to enforce public order and maintain the routine of government. Joseph Bonaparte was *de facto* ruler of Spain; he might even be considered ruler *de jure*, since Charles IV, in abdicating, had made over his rights to Joseph and had instructed his subjects to obey. Orders emanating from Madrid now came in Joseph's name. The instinct of most officials was to obey orders, keep the machinery of administration running and hope for better times. In this they collided with Hispanic resentment, in the Indies as in Spain, against French arrogance, and with the cult—for it was no less—among unofficial Spaniards and Creoles of Ferdinand 'the well-beloved'. That unamiable royal lout, so pitilessly portrayed by Goya, then appeared as a romantic and pathetic figure, a prince forsaken by a senile father and exiled by a foreign usurper. In most parts of the Indies even those whose real object was complete independence joined, for politic reasons, in the chorus of generous and sympathetic loyalty; one could be loyal to an exiled and powerless prince without any serious sacrifice of liberty. But if Ferdinand were proclaimed King in the Indies who was to adminster the empire on his behalf? Who, effectively, was to give the orders? The central *junta* commanded little respect in the Indies. It was an itinerant hole-and-corner affair. In 1810 it was almost extinguished by French military operations. Its subsequent gradual acquisition of local territorial control appeared largely due to the support of Wellington's army. Its somewhat academic liberalism did little to enhance its prestige. It introduced representative government; it abolished the Inquisition and the censorship; it prohibited the *mita*, Indian tributes, the sale of offices and other ancient abuses; it embodied all these reforms in a formal document, the famous Constitution of 1812. On the other hand, in its attitude to the kingdoms of the Indies it was as centralist, as authoritarian, as any Bourbon, without the traditional right to be so. It showed less grasp of American realities than many of the Bourbons' ministers, less than Aranda, less even than Godoy, both of whom had toyed with the idea of devolution. Its attempts to attract Creole support by means of representation in the *Cortes* were inadequate and perhaps insincere. The interests of responsible Creoles were more practical, more local, more immediate. Most of them were conservative by temperament and force of circumstance. They wanted a government in Spain which would preserve the monarchy and the Catholic Church against the intrusion of Jacobins and military careerists from France; but also one which would leave them, under the general authority of Church and monarchy, to manage their own local affairs. They were not much more disposed to obey the orders of the central *junta* than they were to accept the rule of the Bonaparte. If the empire was to be run by *juntas*, they argued, American gentlemen could perfectly well form their own; and that is what they proceeded to do.

The confusion which followed is comprehensible only if the dispersed, the invertebrate, character of the imperial administration is borne in mind. Each viceroyalty was a separate kingdom, each captaincy-general dealt directly with the Crown. Provincial governments had little contact one with another; often, indeed, they were bitterly jealous one of another. The reforms of Charles III, by rationalising provincial boundaries and making them conform more closely with natural frontiers, had accelerated the process by which provinces grew steadily more separate and more distinct. In the absence of any coordinating authority in the Indies, when the central royal government collapsed each provincial government was left to solve its own local problems without effective consultation or guidance, and naturally the solutions varied. Moreover, within each province there was a multitude of unco-ordinated interests. The administrative hierarchy, staffed chiefly by *Peninsulares*, had drawn further and further apart from the Creole society which it governed; and Creole society also lacked any co-ordinating principle. It was a society dominated by territorial magnates, animated by local personal loyalties. This was especially true in the predominantly pastoral areas. It is not without significance that these areas—northern Mexico, Venezuela, Río de la Plata— where a formidable irregular cavalry could easily be recruited among *vaqueros, llaneros, gauchos,* where any local great man could maintain a private army of loyal followers, were the areas in which ideas of total independence first became widespread. Regions where a numerous and docile Indian peasantry existed were also, of course, dominated by big land-owners, but their influence was more conservative and more respectful of established order. In the pastoral areas the dangers and fatigues of herding, hunting and killing cattle inured the country- men to a life of perpetual campaigning. Men brought up to such a life made perfect material for revolution or war. For the same reasons, the pastoral areas were the scenes not only of the fiercest demands for in- dependence but also of the bitterest internecine fighting. If one local magnate or *caudillo* opted for independence his neighbour and rival would be likely to declare for the Crown. In these areas liberty was its own executioner.

Between 1808 and 1812 almost every province in the Indies was shaken by revolutionary movements of one kind or another. There was more enthusiasm for outright independence in the newer vice- royalties than in the older, but also more tendency for the revolution- aries to quarrel among themselves. In each province the course of events was influenced by local peculiarities and personalities. No two were quite alike. In Buenos Aires, Liniers, the expatriate Frenchman who had led the local resistance against the English, and who had been recog- nised as viceroy by Charles IV's government, was driven out in 1809 by the resident *Peninsulares* and their sympathisers, and replaced by another viceroy sent out from Spain by the central *junta*; but in May 1810, when news of Napoleon's successes against the Regency govern- ment reached Buenos Aires, this viceroy was in turn ejected, by a Creole *coup*, and deported along with the *audiencia* judges. A precarious agreement among the local notables—a *cabildo abierto*—produced a local government, the provisional *junta* of the provinces of the Río de la Plata; and though this *junta* did not immediately and formally renounce allegiance to the Spanish Crown, Spanish authority was never re-established in that area.

Though effectively independent of Spain, the provisional *junta* was quite unable to enforce its own authority outside the neighbourhood of Buenos Aires. Montevideo, the growing rival harbour across the estuary, almost automatically took a contrary line and declared for the Regency. Four years of intermittent war ensued between the two ports. The upriver provinces, while less loyal to Spain, were little more friendly to Buenos Aires. The huge, unwieldy viceroyalty broke into quarrelling fragments. The economic interests of the port and its immediate hinterland conflicted—as the subsequent history of Argentina was to show—with those of the inland provinces. In the shabby little upriver port of Asunción a *junta* declared Paraguay to be independent of Spain (in 1811) and of Buenos Aires (in 1813). In the equally remote but economically far more important area of Upper Peru the president and judges of the *audiencia* of Charcas were imprisoned and ejected in 1809. The provincial intendant followed them in 1810, after a rising in La Paz, and a 'protective *junta*' took over the government, protesting loyalty to Ferdinand but virtually independent. Its independence was short-lived, however. Officials and traders in Peru proper had never forgiven the detachment of Upper Peru from the older viceroyalty, and Charcas province was brought to obedience shortly afterwards by viceregal troops sent from Lima. A series of expeditions from Buenos Aires achieved nothing permanent; but counter-attacks from Upper Peru against Buenos Aires were equally unsuccessful, and a stalemate ensued. Peru itself remained relatively quiet. The viceroy, with the support of the more conservative elements among the local people, and with regular forces at his disposal, was able to maintain his administration in spite of a series of minor risings and conspiracies. The viceroy of Peru was also able, though with more difficulty, to suppress the much more determined risings in Chile. There events followed the familiar course—local assemblies of notables; *juntas* claiming local independence while protesting their loyalty to Ferdinand; the arrest in 1810 of the captain-general. Quarrels among the leaders paralysed the provisional government, however. Colonial rule was re-established in 1814. The insurgent leaders either were executed or fled over the Andes to Argentina.

The viceroyalty of New Granada, like that of Río de la Plata, was a comparatively recent creation, vast, diverse, without traditional cohesion. Not only did each province in the northern Andes act separately; each town became a law unto itself. The municipal *cabildos*, indeed, were the only established authorities left, in provinces where the intendants and the judges had been imprisoned or expelled. Their whole tradition was one of local separation, and they usually took the lead. Neighbouring towns and neighbouring chieftains took opposite sides and fell to fighting. In staid Quito a group of local magnates formed a *junta* in 1809, imprisoned the members of the *audiencia* and proclaimed themselves joint governors in Ferdinand's name; they were quickly overthrown by a force despatched from Bogotá by the viceroy, and most of them were executed. Quito thereafter remained quiet until 1821. In 1810, however, a rising occurred in Bogotá itself, and the viceroy was expelled by a *junta* which recognised Ferdinand but not the Regency. Tucumán went the same way, but Pasto supported the Regency. Santa Marta, on the coast, declared for the Regency; but Cartagena, with its fortress and garrison, expelled its governor and proclaimed itself, in 1811, a sovereign and independent city state, at war with Santa Marta. In Venezuela the garrulous, middle-aged Miranda and the young and tireless Bolívar arrived in 1810 to raise the standard of outright revolt. Caracas proclaimed itself independent in 1811; but the coastal towns of Coro and Maracaibo and the cowboy town of Angostura in the *llanos* declared for Spain and the Regency. A fierce civil war between rival chieftains ensued, in which Caracas—already devastated by an earthquake which many regarded as divine judgement on rebellion—was taken and sacked by an irregular band of self-styled royalists. The most memorable feature of this confused fighting was the astonishing forced march of a small army under Bolívar, who, setting out from Cartagena, temporarily recaptured Caracas in 1813. The end of this phase of the fighting came in 1814 with the arrival of General Morillo from Spain with a professional army. Bolívar fled to Jamaica in 1815; Miranda had already died in prison three years earlier. By 1816 the whole of northern South America was again reduced to Spanish obedience; many insurgent leaders were shot, and a Spanish viceroy was again installed at Bogotá.

In prosperous New Spain events followed a different course. The abdication of Ferdinand presented government there with the familiar dilemma. The *audiencia* proposed to accept the new government of Spain; the *cabildo* of Mexico to form a local government to act in

XV a *The great plaza of Mexico City in about 1800*

 b *A cable bridge of the Inca type, in use about 1800*

(from *A. von Humboldt,* Voyage aux régions equinoxiales du nouveau continent)

XVI *Early nineteenth-century Mexican types*

   a *Muleteers*   b *Indian charcoal burners*

(*from C. Nebel*, Voyage pittoresque et archéologique dans la partie la plus intéressante du Mexique)

Ferdinand's name. The viceroy, with somewhat premature foresight, supported the *cabildo* and summoned a general congress; but before this body could meet he was himself arrested by the order of the *audiencia*, supported by the European faction in the city. The central *junta* in Spain sent out a successor, who might well have had to deal with a Creole revolt. The movement for Creole independence, however, was in that year, 1810, interrupted and postponed by a rising among the peasants and mine-workers in the intendancy of Guanajuato, led by the idealistic and probably somewhat unbalanced priest, Hidalgo. Hidalgo's rebellion was one of the very few genuine popular outbreaks of the period. It was inspired more by land hunger and resentment against poverty and peonage than by desire for political independence. The depredations of the excited Indian mobs which followed Hidalgo threatened both property and public order, and the Creole upper class either stood aside, or rallied to the viceregal government, just as the Creoles of Peru had done against Túpac Amarú thirty years before. Hidalgo was executed in 1811. His successor in the rebel command, Morelos, maintained a *guerrilla* from a base at Acapulco until 1815, when he too was captured and shot.

The fragmentary and local character of the rebel governments, their mutual jealousies, their lack of solid general support, made the return of Spanish government comparatively easy, once Ferdinand VII, in 1814, had been brought back to his throne by Wellington's army. The restoration robbed all save confessed separatists of their theoretical ground for rebellion. It also released considerable numbers of experienced troops for service in the Indies. By 1816 the colonial administration, much as it had existed before 1808, was re-established everywhere except in the Río de la Plata basin. It might have been restored there, too, if the Spanish government had succeeded in getting the military help which it requested from other European monarchies. Great Britain, however, secure in control of the Atlantic crossing, refused either to intervene or to allow any other intervention. The resources of Spain alone were not enough to attempt the reduction of Buenos Aires, especially since loyal Montevideo had fallen to the *porteños* in 1814. Elsewhere in the Indies, Spanish governors governed again. *Guerrillero* bands, not always easily distinguished from bandits, maintained themselves here and there—in Mexico, more significantly in Venezuela; but everywhere these disorganised groups were contained, for the time at least, by the viceregal armies. It is interesting to speculate on what might then have been achieved by timely concession. Disintegration was in fact far advanced, despite the superficial restoration of imperial unity, and probably could not be halted for long; but armed rebellion and civil war might have been postponed, perhaps avoided. Great Britain, adamant against armed intervention by any European power, was willing to support European mediation, especially since the Duke of Wellington seemed to be the most generally acceptable mediator. A formula for compromise in the government of the Indies might conceivably have been found. Spaniards were not necessarily intransigent; Apodaca, the last effective viceroy of New Spain, showed himself both realistic and magnanimous. Nor were Creoles necessarily irreconcilable; most were conservative, many still sentimentally loyal. Godoy, before the Bonaparte invasion, had suggested the creation of independent kingdoms in the Indies under princes of the royal house. Many revolutionary leaders desired nothing better. As late as 1821 Iturbide in Mexico was suggesting something of the sort. San Martín believed in the value of monarchical institutions. Even the champions of independence in Buenos Aires—Belgrano, Moreno—were eager for reconciliation with Spain, provided their effective independence was recognised. Ferdinand, however, would have none of it. His restoraton was a return of the old régime, absolutism, Inquisition and all. Nor did the liberal revolutionaries, who in 1820 bullied him into a temporary and insincere acceptance of constitutional rule, show much more sympathy for Creole aspirations than Ferdinand had done. Their attitude towards the Americans was not so much repressive as indifferent. Between 1820 and 1823 colonial affairs were rarely debated, or even discussed in the Press. Viceroys and military commanders in the Indies got no reinforcements, supplies or even clear instructions. Liberal ministers, however, had no hesitation in rejecting Iturbide's Treaty of Córdoba. Their radicalism and anti-clericalism, moreover, profoundly shocked Creole conservatism and turned the Church in the Indies against the government of Spain. When in 1823 Ferdinand regained his absolute power in Spain, and embarked on a series of brutal reprisals, he did so with the help of the hated French. Neither monarchy, ministry nor Church in Spain could then either negotiate with Creole malcontents or provide a rallying point for Creole loyalty. Spain must either reconquer its colonies or reconcile itself to their permanent loss.

The wars of independence fall, then, into two distinct phases, from

1808 to 1814, and from 1816 to 1825. Each phase was accompanied by major upheavals in Spain itself, with consequent disorganisation and loss of morale in army, Church and civil service overseas. From 1808 to 1814 the story of the empire had been one of disintegration. Between 1814 and 1816 discipline and central government were in great measure restored by force, and in 1816 the viceregal governments were again formidable and well armed. The final chapter, from 1816 to 1825, was necessarily a story of organised conquest and civil war. Bolívar and San Martín were the chief *conquistadores*, their mounted followers the *llaneros* of Venezuela, the *gauchos* of Río de la Plata. Bolívar, the intellectual Creole patrician, had been convinced from an early age, even from before the abdication of Charles IV, that the aspirations of liberty-seeking Americans were incompatible with the imperial temper and tradition of Spain. It mattered nothing to him what kind of government ruled Spain; the imperial tradition, the ignorance of America, the lack of sympathy, seemed permanent. The events of 1814–16 confirmed for him the belief he had always held, that the face-saving formula of loyalty to Ferdinand was a cowardly pretence. Bolívar gave the revolution an intellectual core, a doctrine, which it had not before possessed. His passion for independence grew not from personal vanity or resentment against personal slights but from study of the French prophets of liberty and reason and from a romantic admiration of the supposed virtues of patrician republican Rome. He was a doctrinaire republican as well as a local Venezuelan patriot and an American revolutionary. He brought to the project of revolution a powerful personal magnetism; a gift of oratory and self-dramatisation; and an untutored military genius.

Bolívar returned to Venezuela from his West Indian exile late in 1816. He had collected an armed following and a large supply of arms and ammunition, with the help of Pétion, the dictator of Haiti; and Dutch merchants in Curaçao, scenting a change of wind, provided transport. His first important success was the capture of the river port of Angostura on the Lower Orinoco, formerly a royalist stronghold. Based there, he drew the various *guerrillero* bands of eastern Venezuela together into a small but formidable irregular army capable of challenging Morillo's professional forces. The army was stiffened and to some extent trained by a considerable number of English and Irish soldiers, unemployed since the European peace, some seeking loot or adventure, some animated by libertarian fervour or personal admiration for Bolívar.

This was the army, less than 3,000 strong, which in 1819 outflanked Morillo, crossed the eastern Andes by a high and appallingly difficult route and won the victory of Boyacá. The viceroy retired to Cartagena and Bolívar entered Bogotá as the 'Liberator of New Granada'.

Before leaving Angostura, Bolívar had issued, in his address to the Congress of the new and struggling republic of Venezuela, the most eloquent of all the manifestos of aristocratic republicanism in America. He had written confidently to Buenos Aires of 'an American pact, uniting all our republics in one political body, in a single society with the watchword of unity in South America'. The Spanish government, as we have seen, while endeavouring to rule them all from Madrid, had kept the kingdoms of the Indies carefully separate one from another. The new ideal of revolutionary unity, short-lived though it was to prove, was a powerful stimulus to effort. Events were moving also in the south. San Martín, the professional soldier, trained in the Spanish army in the peninsula, who now commanded the army of the Río de la Plata, saw that the new republics would never be safe until the power of the viceroy of Peru had been destroyed. He saw, too, that the direct route of attack through Upper Peru was too long and difficult, but that the deadlock of the 'northern war' might be broken by an assault by sea. San Martín's attention to logistics and cautious mastery of detail stood in sharp contrast to Bolívar's intuitive dash and magnetic leadership, but both men successfully led expeditions which recalled the exploits of the *conquistadores*. In 1817 San Martín led his army over the Andes into Chile, to defeat the Spanish forces at Maipú, and to create yet another republic. In Chile, San Martín sought means to create a fleet which could transport his army up the coast to Peru, and found an organiser and naval commander of genius in Cochrane. Of all the British mercenaries who offered their swords to Spanish-American chieftains, Cochrane is perhaps the most interesting. A radical patrician, a naval officer baulked of promotion, a Scot unfairly treated—so he thought—by English admirals, his feelings and attitudes closely resembled those of many leading Creoles. He should have felt at home in South America. He was in fact too restless a spirit to feel at home anywhere for long; he found it little easier to work with San Martín than with Lord Gambier; but he served San Martin's turn in the assault on Peru.

While Cochrane and San Martín were assembling their makeshift navy in Chile, and Bolívar—still harassed by Morillo's army—was trying to build the Republic of Gran Colombia from the fragments of the viceroyalty of New Granada, the power of Spain to intervene was once more paralysed in 1820 by revolution. A powerful army, assembled at Cadiz and intended for the Indies, promptly mutinied. Without hope of reinforcement, without confidence in their home government, the royalists were doomed. Morillo left for Spain, and his successor was no match for Bolívar. In 1820 San Martín left Chile by sea for the richer prize of Peru. The ancient viceroyalty was now caught in a vast pincer movement, between San Martín off the coast and Bolívar advancing through Colombia and Quito. The viceroy, Pezuela, seeking more defensible ground, withdrew to the hills. Pezuela had done his best to put his viceroyalty in a state of defence. He had about 23,000 men, many of them raw recruits. He had been in Peru for many years and was well aware of the rancour of the local people against Spaniards. In the manner of proconsuls in dying empires he had gone to much trouble to persuade his Spanish staff, the military staff especially, to be more polite to their colonial colleagues; an effort which only made his staff officers suspect him of weakness in dealing with insurrection. Insurrection, meanwhile, was gaining ground. Most of northern Peru, led by the Marquis of Torre Tagle, intendant of Trujillo, a trusted Creole official, defected to San Martín soon after his arrival. One whole battalion of troops, supposedly loyal, also defected. Lima contained many loyal people, or at least people who had no wish for upheaval; but it was difficult to defend. The viceroy therefore withdrew his forces to the *Sierra*, after an abortive attempt to negotiate with San Martín. His Spanish military staff then forced his resignation from office and his replacement by one of their own number, a professional soldier in whom they felt more confidence. The Crown had no alternative but to confirm this military *coup*. The new viceroy, La Serna, was to be the last viceroy of Peru. He was a capable and experienced commander, but the manner of his appointment was an ominous precedent both for Spain and for America. Meanwhile, San Martín was left to occupy the city, to proclaim a republic with himself as 'Protector' and to be received with sullen suspicion by an urban population who had no particular wish to be liberated; not, at any rate, by an Argentinian.

When the two chieftains met face to face, and played out—figuratively speaking—their lonely mysterious game of poker at Guayaquil, it was San Martín who was out-bluffed and out-talked, who retired to exile in France: it was Bolívar and his lieutenants who undertook to 'protect' Peru and to fight the viceregal armies there and in Bolivia. Three years of fierce resistance and hard fighting followed before Sucre's victory at Ayacucho and the viceroy's surrender; but the issue, though protracted, was not really in doubt. Only powerful reinforcements could have saved viceregal Peru. The French, who had restored Ferdinand to absolute authority in 1823, might have supplied such reinforcements, at a price; but Great Britain—supreme at sea, jealous of possible commercial rivals, expecting great things from trade with South America—would still tolerate no intervention there but that of Spain; and Spain, disorganised, had now no means to intervene effectively.

Mexico reached the same end as Peru, characteristically by a different route. After the execution of Morelos in 1815 the insurgents he had led split into a number of bands which maintained themselves by combining revolutionary fervour with brigandage and which were enough of a local nuisance to require regular forces to contain them. The principal leader among them was Guerrero, later to become President of Mexico. The officer commanding the operations against Guerrero was a prominent Creole named Iturbide, one of the class and type who became alienated from Spain by the extremism of the radical government of 1820. There is evidence that Iturbide had been planning a political *coup* for some time; however that may be, he defected with his troops in 1821 and reached an accommodation with Guerrero on the basis of the celebrated Plan of Iguala. This ingenious document proposed an independent constitutional monarchy under a Bourbon prince; the maintenance of the Catholic religion; and the legal equality of all citizens of whatever race. The new viceroy, appointed by the radical government in Spain to replace Apodaca, was induced to accept the plan; but the Spanish government repudiated the agreement, and Iturbide then proclaimed himself Emperor of Mexico. He did not last long; he was deposed in 1823 and shot in 1824; but the independence which he declared was never effectively challenged.

The wars of independence were the first major land campaigns which had been fought in the Indies since the middle of the sixteenth century. They were civil wars, with all the complexity and all the ferocity of civil wars; they bore a close similarity to those savage wars which followed the conquest of Peru. The armies were small—tiny, indeed, in relation to the vast, daunting terrain in which they operated. There were some disciplined regular troops on both sides, and some convinced volunteers. Almost all the combatants were Americans. Morillo originally brought regular troops with him from Spain, but as his men were killed off, or died, or deserted, they were replaced by local recruits. Only a few hundred peninsular Spaniards fought at Ayacucho. For the most part the rank and file on both sides were poor whites, Indians, *mestizos*, attached to their leaders by a semi-feudal obedience, some pressed, others moved by sectional jealousies or by hope of loot. Their allegiance was unreliable—not unnaturally, considering the infrequency with which they were paid—and mutinies and desertions were frequent. The royal armies, as might be expected, suffered more in this way than the insurgents, especially as the Americans disliked the formal discipline demanded by Spanish officers. San Martín's easy occupation of Lima was greatly helped by the defection of a regular battalion which Morillo—who could ill spare it—had sent there to reinforce the viceregal army; but not long afterwards the republican garrison at El Callao, composed of Argentinian troops, mutinied in its turn. Troops were particularly prone to mutiny or desertion when called to serve far from home. The ideal, the fighting slogan with which their leaders presented them, was commonly *la patria*; but theirs was a local patriotism, loyalty to *la patria chica*. They could fight like tigers when well led; and the conflict produced some remarkable leaders. Among these, especially on the royal side, some were professional soldiers who fought because they were paid to fight, because fighting was their duty; many more on both sides, but especially among the insurgents, were local chieftains. Some, like Bolívar, fought with their own intellectual style and emotional force, brandishing, so to speak, the sabre in one hand and the *Social Contract* in the other; but many more fought, just as their predecessors had done, first in the *conquista*, then in the wars of Chupas and Las Salinas, to carve out kingdoms for themselves. The *conquistadores*, often enough, had disregarded the wishes of a king whom they revered but would not obey; the king, in turn, had taken what steps he could to humble his over-mighty subjects. In the middle-sixteenth century the king, through his officials, had, on the whole, won the day. Viceroys and *oidores* had taken over from the *conquistadores* the government of the kingdoms they had conquered. In the early nineteenth century the successors of the *conquistadores* took their belated revenge and turned the officials out. The result, predictably, was chaos. The *conquistadores* had fought one another as fiercely as they fought Atahualpa or Manco

Inca. The liberators and their successors similarly shot or expelled one another as readily as they had fought the viceroys. Bolívar, like San Martín, escaped assassination; but both died in exile. Almost every country in Spanish America in the 1820s was torn by civil war between rival *caudillos*. In some the only possible outcome was partition; in others dictatorship. Spanish America was free indeed.

CONCLUSION

The aftermath of empire

IMPERIAL SPAIN had been dangerously dependent upon the Indies. Its economy, its social life, its political behaviour, had been profoundly affected and modified by this dependence, and by the consequent urgent need to maintain and strengthen administrative control. The separation of most of the provinces of the Indies from the Spanish Crown would in any circumstances have entailed a severe shock to Spain. The actual manner of the separation made it a disaster. Every stage in the process was accompanied by bitter and destructive war. As a result of maritime war with England, effective commercial control of the Indies was lost in 1797. As a result of French invasion of Spain itself, administrative control of the Indies was lost in 1808. There followed six years of savage fighting within the peninsula; six years of occupation by foreign armies, which lived at Spanish expense. Spain emerged from the war with its countryside devastated, its trade and industry at a standstill. Suffering was particularly severe in the west and south-west. Andalusia, the old cradle of the Indies, had lost its easy leadership in American trade in the eighteenth century. In the nine-teenth, with its vast, neglected estates and its landless, unemployed *braceros*, it became the problem area of Spain, backward and depressed. In mountain areas misery found expression in violence. The *guerrilleros* of one generation became the bandits of the next.

The profits of the Indies trade, the stimulus of American silver, were needed more urgently than ever for the rebuilding of a shattered economy. Neither the prestige of the Crown nor force of arms could recover them. The market of the Río de la Plata had been lost irretriev-ably in 1810. In 1818–20, as a result of Bolívar's campaigns, the valu-able cocoa and coffee business of Venezuela and Colombia was similarly taken out of Spanish hands. In 1825 the mines of Peru were finally lost;

those of Mexico had gone two years before. The losses included not only political control, the proceeds of taxation and much Spanish property, public and private—trade and goodwill were lost as well. The stubborn tenacity of the Spanish Crown in defending its position in the Indies, and the long delay in recognising the new independent states, all helped to intensify and prolong mutual enmity. There was no commercial *rapprochement* between Spain and the Indies comparable with that between England and North America in the late eighteenth century. Impoverished Spain had little to offer, in goods or markets, to its former colonies; and the Creoles were in no mood to offer reconciliation, help or sympathy. Spain in the 1820s and 1830s was divided, humiliated and hungry. Its plight—even the futile misery of the Carlist Wars—may be attributed, at least in part, to the twin catastrophes of French invasion and colonial rebellion.

Not all the Indies were lost, it is true. There remained the Antilles, with their trade in tobacco, sugar and slaves; there remained Manila, a busy tradesmen's entrance to the Far East. These were more than mere fragments. Moreau de Jonnès could still, in 1825, seriously compare the Spanish Empire with the colonial possessions of England and France, while pointing out, however, that both Manila and Cuba did considerably more business with Great Britain and the United States than with Spain. None of these remaining colonial possessions, in the years immediately after 1825, made any significant contribution to the relief of Spain's distress. The trade of Puerto Rico was very small; the island had always been valued more for its strategic than for its commercial importance. Cuba, also, though relatively prosperous, required initiative and capital for the development of its potential wealth, and some years were to elapse before Spain could provide either. The difficulties were psychological as well as economic. Bitterness in some circles over the loss of the major part of the Indies was quickly succeeded by disillusion with empire in general, and by a tendency to belittle the value of what remained. An expedition to Tampico in 1829, despatched with a view to the reconquest of Mexico, attracted neither support nor interest in Spain. Disillusion was reinforced by the current fashion o liberal economic theory. Canga Argüelles, the most distinguished Spanish economist of his day—who, significantly, had been a minister during the abortive constitutional interlude of 1820 to 1823—argued that Spaniards for more than 300 years had poured men, goods, ideas and experience into America, to the great advantage of the kingdoms of the Indies and to the impoverishment of Spain. Many Spaniards in the past, as we have seen, had suffered qualms of conscience over the conduct of empire. In every century some had asserted roundly that the Indies were unjustly acquired or tyrannously governed. To suggest, however, that the Indies had been unprofitable, that the cost of empire had been excessive, was something new. According to this reasoning, measures for the development of Cuba and Puerto Rico would benefit those islands more than Spain itself. Colonial investment would be throwing good money after bad. The Indies were well lost. Spain, released from its long thraldom to the responsibilities of empire, should concentrate on working out its own destinies and developing its own resources.

The problem confronting Spain was one of adjustment to reduced circumstances in a changing world. Even more complex problems faced the former kingdoms of the Indies; problems both of reconstruction and of improvisation. Their reaction to these problems, after the first excitement of constitution-making, was remarkably conservative. The wars of independence had been primarily a political revolution; not the overthrow of a social order but the replacement of one set of rulers by another within the same social order. In the colonial empire there had been two main sources of influence and authority, one local, the other general. Local power was the preserve of a Creole aristocracy. The successors or descendants of the earlier conquerors and settlers had exercised their authority through their ownership of land, flocks and herds, and mines; through their social and economic influence upon the people living on their estates; through their control, direct or indirect, of municipal government, and through the acquisition, by purchase, inheritance or viceregal favour, of local administrative offices. General power was the preserve of the Crown, the focus of loyalty and the guardian of order, operating through its permanent officials, lay and ecclesiastical, and legislating for the empire as a whole. Viceregal and provincial governments had depended upon the Crown; they did not derive from or represent the local structure of towns and *haciendas*. The two authorities had existed side by side, and in Hapsburg times had, on the whole, respected one another's prerogatives and spheres of influence. In the later eighteenth century the Crown, employing a professional standing army and a reorganised civil service, had tightened its centralised control and increased its power at the expense of the local magnates. The old society of conquest, in the wars of independence, had reacted violently against this tightened control, had defeated the Crown, expelled the royal officials, and established new, independent authorities under its own leaders. In this aspect the wars of independence can be interpreted as the revolt of a reactionary territorial aristocracy against an innovating, rationalising central government.

This, of course, was not the whole story. Independence also had its innovating aspects. Although much of the fighting had been done by local warrior leaders, each with his personal armed following, the general conduct of the war had been organised, and the final victories achieved, with the help of a small but influential urban intelligentsia who had supplied the political theories, the slogans, the necessary diplomatic and commercial contacts and much of the money. After the war, with the focus of loyalty lost, with the civil service disbanded and administration reduced to chaos, with localities ruled by local leaders—whether landed magnates, cowboy *caudillos* or mere bandits— these urban politicians directed their influence to the creation of national states of modern type, embracing whole viceroyalties, provinces or groups of provinces. Some of them—Rivadavia, for example, in Argentina, Portales in Chile and, of course, Bolívar himself—were men of great ability and imagination. They endeavoured to establish centralised governments based on the major capital cities. They drafted constitutions, importing into Spanish America all the modern para- phernalia of representative assemblies. They enacted declarations defin- ing the rights of citizens. They promulgated new codes of law which clearly derived from the principles of the French revolution rather than from the old royal codes. They sought—and in this they had more in common with the former Bourbon ministers than with their own *caudillo* associates—to work out the ideas of the 'Enlightenment' in administration and in social and religious life, and to apply rational ideas to such matters as economic and social improvement. Naturally they were resisted; the history of much of Spanish America in the first half of the nineteenth century is concerned with the constant, age-old struggle between innovating, rationalising (and tax-collecting) central governments on the one hand, and conservative, often primitive, local particularism on the other. Sarmiento's *Facundo* is the classical expression of this widespread conflict.

Centrifugal tensions and the personal rivalries of ambitious leaders were strong enough to break up some of the larger territorial units,

notably Bolívar's Gran Colombia. Some very large units, however—
the Río de la Plata provinces, for example, and New Spain which
became Mexico—held together; and within most of the national units
the centralising tendency eventually proved the stronger. In most
modern Spanish-American states the form of government is highly
centralised. Whatever the legal fiction of local autonomy, the cities
batten upon the country, provincial capitals capture power and revenue
from local units, national governments strip states and provinces of
independence and political vigour. National presidents, wielding an
authority not very dissimilar from that of their royal or viceregal
predecessors, exercise a wide power of personal dispensation in individual cases. This does not mean that central governments can always
count upon being obeyed. It does mean that no official decision can
be made locally, no discretion lawfully exercised, without reference
to the centre. In this respect Spanish America has largely returned to
the pattern of development laid down for it by Charles III's ministers.

Between the imperial centralisation of the late eighteenth century
and the national centralisation of the late nineteenth, however, a long
gap intervened. The achievement of unitary government within the
new states was a slow and often sanguinary process. Bolívar, the seer
of independence, did not foresee it. Indeed, in his disillusioned farewell
on renouncing the presidency of Gran Colombia, he predicted a future
in which petty tyrants 'of all races and of all colours' would divide
the continent between them. The chaos of the first three or four decades
of independence arose not only from personal rivalries, not only from
local resistance to central authority, but also from uncertainties about
the territorial extent of the new states. In northern South America
local feeling crystallised round the personalities of Bolívar's lieutenants,
who divided his Gran Colombia between them. The United Provinces
of Central America, formed in 1823 under the leadership of Guatemala,
broke up in 1838. In the Río de la Plata basin disputes over national
boundaries gave rise to years of war between the successor governments. Not until the 1830s did most states accept, in sheer weariness,
a return, in general, to the old colonial boundaries; the rough principle,
unknown to international law, of *uti possidetis*. The territories which
became national states, and which endeavoured to apply this principle
in settling disputes among themselves, were in many instances so
large that their national feelings were very slow to develop. The old
imperial provinces, of course, had been keenly conscious of their separate

existence; but a feeling of being different from, perhaps hostile to, the people of a neighbouring province is not necessarily the same as a feeling of unity and loyalty within one's own. Some of the successor states, moreover, incorporated each a number of different provinces whose association in colonial times had been purely arbitrary. Their nationhood was not inevitable; it had to be learned. National sentiment, indeed, in many countries was the consequence and not the cause of the achievement of effective unitary government, and did not reach its full stridency until late in the nineteenth century. It was then that history books began to be written in order to glorify the national past, that a cult of national heroes was promoted and that statues of liberators were erected up and down the continent on the sites formerly occupied by *rollo* and *quemadero*.

One of the most difficult problems confronting the political leaders of the 1820s, in their endeavours to create national unity and order out of provincial chaos, was the constitutional position of the Church. The difficulty arose from the close inter-penetration between Church and State in the Indies, under the common authority of the Crown, throughout the three centuries of imperial rule. Under the Hapsburgs the clergy had been indispensable agents of royal government, not only indirectly through their spiritual authority but directly through their employment in colonial administration. Prelates had served as *oidores*, as governors, as councillors of the Indies, even as viceroys. The Bourbon kings had gradually abandoned the practice of employing clerics as civil servants and in a variety of ways had endeavoured to limit the political and economic power of the clergy. At times they treated some sections of the Church, particularly the regular Orders, with notable harshness, extending in the case of the Jesuits to persecution and expulsion. On the other hand, they fully appreciated the crucial importance of the Church both as the spiritual support of their authority in the Indies and as a vital instrument of social order. The clergy played their part accordingly. The late eighteenth-century Church in the Indies, with few exceptions, was docile and dutiful, free from ultramontane fervour, noted more for its cultivated and prosperous decorum than for the vigour and intensity of its spiritual life.

At the time of the first outbreaks of revolt most of the higher clergy in the Indies were peninsular Spaniards and almost all were men on whose loyalty the Crown could rely. Several sees fell vacant during the first phase of revolutionary disturbance, but except in the Río de la

Plata provinces they were filled again between 1814 and 1816 by royal presentation; and in 1816 a papal encyclical, issued at Ferdinand VII's request, reminded the clergy of the Americas that part of their duty was to discourage rebellion. The bishops were bound publicly to denounce the new campaigns which, after 1816, were frankly directed against the Crown of Spain. As rebellion gained ground and insurrectionary governments were set up, many bishops left their sees, or were expelled, and returned to Spain. There were a few exceptions. Two of the bishops in Colombia allowed themselves to be persuaded by Bolívar to remain at their posts, though without compromising their views on the royal authority. The situation was confused, however, by the Spanish revolution of 1820 and the anti-clerical policy adopted by the *Cortes* and the new ministers. Spain and the Papacy were temporarily estranged and many of the clergy in America, hitherto loyal, became alienated from the Spanish Crown. When in 1823 Ferdinand recovered his absolute authority, with all the might of the Holy Alliance supporting him, most of the Indies were already as good as lost. The King, nevertheless, still thought that the position might be retrieved with the help of the Church. In 1824 he secured another encyclical supporting his cause, which had no effect other than provoking a storm of protest in America. By this time many sees were vacant. The procedure for filling them had become a matter of vital international concern.

The revolutionary leaders were keenly aware of the dangerous discontents which could arise among Catholic populations cut off from Catholic authority and leadership. They desperately needed bishops; but to receive bishops nominated by Ferdinand, in accordance with the ancient rights to which he still obstinately clung, would be to swallow an affront to independence and possibly to endanger the very existence of the new states. They argued that their republican governments succeeded to all former royal rights in their territories, including ecclesiastical patronage. In practice many of them were willing to accept almost any formula, save that of royal presentation, which would allow bishops to be consecrated. The papal authorities for their part were anxious to provide bishops, lest the Indies should become a prey to Protestants and worse; but they argued that the *Patronato*, if withdrawn from the King of Spain, would revert to the Pope. Moreover, in the political circumstances of the 1820s, to consecrate bishops who had not been presented by Ferdinand would be to provoke the fiercest resentment both of Spain and of Spain's powerful allies. This was made clear in 1827 when Leo XII preconised six candidates for sees in Colombia. Bolívar regarded the papal action as a triumph for his own government; Ferdinand protested angrily; and the Papacy was obliged to confirm its recognition of the royal right of presentation by a public notice to the effect that in the nomination of bishops it 'did not act on the proposal of any rebel chief'. Leo's successor, Pius VIII, consecrated no proprietary bishops in the Indies, giving as his reason for refusal the general disorder and the imminent break-up of several of the new states. It was not until 1831 that a new Pope, Gregory XVI, risked Spanish displeasure by announcing in the bull *Sollicitudo Ecclesiarum* his intention of entering into normal ecclesiastical relations with *de facto* governments which showed evidence of stability. Between 1831 and 1840 all the vacant sees in America were filled. The names of many of the new prelates were suggested informally by the republican governments, but in no case did the Pope formally recognise a right of presentation.

During the years of war and subsequent uncertainty the lower clergy had been left very much to their own devices. Without adequate leadership or administration, the Church in many places had become disorganised, its authority weakened, its prestige diminished. It was socially and economically open to attack because of its great and evident wealth. It was politically suspect because of its former association with the Crown. Nevertheless, there was no Voltairean attack on the Church, no official anti-clericalism comparable with that of the Spanish government in the early 1820s. The attitude of the political leaders of the new states, in this as in much else, was conservative. Only one of the republican constitutions—that of the Río de la Plata—included freedom of worship among the rights of citizens. San Martín lived and died a devout Catholic. Even free-thinking leaders, including Bolívar himself, formally attended Mass. Some of the cowboy *caudillos* were noisily pious; Facundo Quiroga, apparently without conscious irony, at one time displayed a black banner proclaiming 'religion or death'. Rosas was a great upholder of the privileges of the clergy, so long as they obeyed him; so were Iturbide and Santa Anna. An innovating liberal such as Gómez Farías, with his premature plans for secularising education and Church property in Mexico, was a rare exception among political leaders before the middle of the century; and even he was personally devout. In general the new rulers wished to respect and protect the Church, while at the same time restricting its independent political activities, controlling appointments to its higher offices, employing it as an administrative instrument and as a guardian of stability and social order. Some of the more earnest among them, it is true, wished to reform it by legislation; but even this was not particularly new. The views of a statesman such as—say—Rivadavia on the proper relations between Church and State—once the substitution of a republican government for the Spanish Crown was accepted—did not differ greatly from those of Charles III's ministers.

It was a matter of urgency for the Church in each of the new states to reach an understanding with these relatively sympathetic chieftains, for fear of worse, but for political reasons understanding proved extremely difficult. The former royalism of the higher clergy had given place, in many instances, not to republican loyalty but to ultramontane attachment; and the Papacy was not unwilling to recover some of the authority in America which it had conceded centuries before. The clergy in America tended, understandably, to be suspicious of the new governments. Republicanism was associated in their minds with free-thinking, with secularisation, with anti-religious and anti-clerical legislation. During the wars, moreover, military leaders had from time to time seized Church property and taxed Church revenues in order to pay their troops. These desperate measures might, in peacetime, become a habit. Governments, for their part, could never ignore the political influence of the clergy. Most of them were unstable and commanded little confidence. Party differences tended to crystallise round points of religious policy. Any declaration on a religious—or supposedly religious—matter might give a handle to political opponents and set off a popular demonstration. The attitude of the clergy themselves, backed by great endowments and expressed in hundreds of pulpits, might make or break a government. Politicians discovered that in order to secure the passage even of quite minor and perfectly reasonable measures they had either to placate the clergy or intimidate them; the clergy found that collaboration with today's government might entail the dangerous displeasure of tomorrow's. When in later years Spanish-American governments, in common with most Western states, began to assume many social functions—education, certification of births, marriages and deaths, care of the sick and the destitute—formerly discharged by the Church—when they endeavoured to reduce the pressure of religious compulsion upon their citizens, to abolish universal ecclesiastical taxes such as tithe, or to limit the amount of property in mortmain, they encountered almost everywhere strenuous and powerful resistance within a frame of relations still fluid and undefined. The policies of the Spanish-American republics in this matter, and their legislation defining the relations between Church and State, developed in the course of the nineteenth and twentieth centuries a marked and increasing divergence. In some countries—Argentina, Colombia, Peru—a relation similar to that of colonial times, but with certain modifications, was successfully re-established. In others, such as Chile and Uruguay, the connection between Church and State was legally dissolved. In yet others, of which Mexico is the outstanding example, the Church was not only disestablished but brought under close surveillance, amounting at times to persecution. No nineteenth-century government was strong enough to ignore the problem, to leave it to individual choice or conscience. In every country the clergy felt—and in many places still feel—a duty to guide their parishioners in making political decisions. In every country politicians thought—and in many countries still think—some degree of control over ecclesiastical affairs to be necessary in order to maintain the authority of government. Religious and political authority had been too closely interwoven, through three centuries of imperial rule, to be quickly or easily separated.

In the field of civil administration, similarly, the national governments of Spanish America displayed—and many of them still display—characteristics inherited from the colonial past, but strengthened and accentuated by the struggle to establish effective unitary government. The most striking was the militarisation of government. The colonial beginnings of this phenomenon are relatively modern; they date only from the middle of the eighteenth century. Charles III and his successors created both a standing army and a militia in the Indies, employed military officers widely in colonial administration and increased and extended the privileges of the *fuero militar*. Professional loyalty, royal power and the predominance of peninsular officers in the professional forces combined, however, to prevent the army in the Indies becoming anything which remotely resembled a praetorian guard until the very last years of imperial government. Iturbide, a professional officer, provided an early example of a military careerist defecting with his army, and employing that army to get himself into power. More respectable, but no less ominous for the future, was the example of military king-making set by the officers who installed La Serna as viceroy of Peru. This precedent was very soon followed by the opposing side; the first two presidents of the infant republic of Peru were both pushed out by their general staff. Once formed, the habit quickly grew. In the wars of independence many—perhaps most —Creole officers had taken the insurgent side, many Creole politicians had perforce taken up arms. The newly independent governments were run by men who, if not professional soldiers, had considerable military experience; the general disorder required armies to be kept in being; politicians who were also generals had a better chance of survival than civilians, provided that the army was well paid and content. Serving soldiers, however, taken into political partnership, quickly developed their own political ideas and their own characteristic impatience with political fumbling. The duty of obedience to a personal monarch had disappeared; the idea of loyalty to an impersonal, abstract republic, and obedience to those who, for the time being, formed its government, was slow to take root. The army itself thus became, in many Spanish-American states, the core of effective authority. It came to be regarded—or to regard itself—as the guardian of national integrity and of national interests in internal government as well as in defence. The tradition, with its associated privileges, has survived to this day. In some states, it is true—in Mexico, for example, in Chile, in Uruguay— civilian government has in recent times successfully asserted its control over the armed forces. In many others military men still commonly hold high civil and administrative offices; the armed services interfere constantly in political life, whether as organised pressure groups behind the scenes or as overt participants in a series of *coups d'état*; and no civilian politician can afford to act in open defiance of the wishes of the general command.

Military interference in political life usually takes the form of direct pressure upon the central government, and affects the life of provincial and local centres only indirectly. The extent to which the will of central government can be made effective in the provinces and localities depends upon the operation of another institution—if so formal a word can be used of so informal a phenomenon—highly characteristic of Spanish America, and deeply rooted in colonial precedent. This is *caudillismo* or *caciquismo*: the organisation of political life by local 'bosses' whose power and influence derive from personal ascendency, family or regional association. In most countries the concentration of formal authority at the centre, the weakness of lawfully constituted provincial and local authority, leave a wide scope for the activities of such people. The real effectiveness of central government may depend upon the nature of the bargain which it can strike with those who wield local influence and power; while the prestige of the *cacique* may be enhanced by the 'pull' which he can exert in the capital. This tacit bargaining between official authority and effective local power goes back to the very beginning of Spanish rule in the Americas. In the decades immediately after the conquest, as we have seen, colonial society was dominated by self-appointed captains, each with his band of armed followers looking to him for leadership and livelihood. The Crown had tried to prevent these captains from establishing themselves as permanent or proprietary governors, and on the whole it had succeeded. Conversely, although the colonial governors and viceroys whom the Crown itself appointed had often turned out to be rapacious and violent, they could not easily become *caudillos* because their terms of office were short and because the Crown could, to a considerable extent, hold them to account. The administrative reforms of the late eighteenth century further strengthened the hold of the central government upon its high officials, and further limited the power of private magnates in political, though admittedly not in economic or social matters. The wars of independence, however, and the proliferation of privately recruited bands which they encouraged, gave *caudillismo* a new lease of life, and created a state of affairs strongly reminiscent of the post-conquest era. New governments had to come to terms with locally powerful leaders, many of whom commanded armed followers. A Facundo Quiroga in Argentina, a Vidaurri in northern Mexico, were too strong to be ignored. The *caudillos* were so strong, indeed, that they were able to demand official recognition, as governors of states and provinces, to an extent which the Spanish Crown would never have tolerated. *Caudillismo* became embedded in the structure of government itself. In more modern times stronger governments have insisted that provincial governors and other powerful officials should be elected or formally appointed, and have endeavoured, as the Spanish Crown had done, to separate administrative office from personal power; yet the *cacique* remains an indispensable agent of government. He may be no more than a skilful party organiser with good local contacts; he may be a big land-owner controlling a semi-servile peasantry; he may be a money-lender or—in extreme cases—a director of local brigandage or terrorism. Everywhere in Spanish America he is a man to be reckoned with.

Another characteristic of Spanish-American government, with roots reaching far back into colonial times, is the phenomenon which may perhaps best be described as 'passive administration'. The citizen who wishes to transact any kind of public or legal business is expected to comply with exacting regulations concerning the issue of licences and permits and to supply detailed information on official forms. The numerous petty officials dealing with such matters are not expected to be actively helpful to the public; they are there to insist that the forms are observed. The idea is virtually unknown of a systematic procedure whereby the government itself sees that, once an application is filed, all steps follow automatically as a co-ordinated responsibility of its officials. The client himself supplies the initiative at every stage. He himself is responsible for carrying his papers from desk to desk and from office to office; for collecting from unconcerned officials all the stamps and signatures required for the completion of his business. Here the colonial precedent is clear. The Spanish Crown, deeply suspicious of its distant subjects, demanded detailed information of all their public activities. It created an elaborate bureaucracy to deal with the paper-work, and allowed most of the minor offices, and some of the major ones, within the bureaucracy to be purchased. Such offices were regarded less as posts of public responsibility than as property, as invest-ments from which an income was to be drawn in fees. The system of sale, though much restricted under the later Bourbons, lasted almost to the end of the colonial era, and the attitude towards minor office which it encouraged survived independence virtually unchanged. Its significance in everyday life has tended to increase because of the in-creasing number of points of contact between government and the individual citizen. Modern Spanish-American governments do not, indeed, offer minor offices for sale; but most of them pay their minor officials very poorly, if at all. They do not, and cannot, demand a high standard of public service. Hence the importance of the inter-mediary: of the notary, as witness of integrity and credibility; of the attorney, with his knowledge of forms and procedures; of the 'fixer'. Hence also the system of miscellaneous payments picturesquely known as *mordida*. The standard fee for a document entitles the applicant to nothing but the document in the official's good time. For extra help and advice, for more expeditious service, he must expect to pay extra.

Mordida may include anything from a gratuity for unusual helpfulness on the part of an official to an outright bribe for conniving at illegalities.

As in their political and administrative practices, so in their economic habits and attitudes the independent states and peoples of Spanish America tended, after the disturbances of the wars of independence, to revert to colonial precedent in many ways; sometimes to pre-eighteenth-century precedent. The last few decades of effective imperial rule had been a period of considerable prosperity and of relatively rapid economic growth in most parts of the Indies, especially in New Spain. The wars of independence inevitably caused losses, especially in plantation areas, by destruction or neglect. Independence brought fresh economic difficulties, especially for incipient industry. The new rulers hastened to adopt the latest fashion of economic liberalism. The result was the impoverishment, in many places the disappearance, of a well-developed artisan class, and the sharp decline of local industry, especially in ship-building, textiles and metal goods. In the eighteenth century artisan manufacturers in the Indies had been to a considerable extent protected by the Spanish commercial monopoly, incomplete though this was. In the first decades of the nineteenth century international war in itself afforded them a measure of protection. After independence they had no protection. Among them, moreover, were many peninsular Spaniards who, after independence, left or were expelled. Those who remained could not compete with a flood of cheap British imports. The only class in Creole society which might have developed habits of saving and provided a steady source of investment capital was thus largely eliminated. At the same time, the supply of labour in some areas, especially the Caribbean coasts, dwindled because of the abolition of the British slave-trade and the diplomatic and naval measures taken by Great Britain to hinder slaving under other flags. Apart from shortages of capital and labour, the prevailing uncertainty following the wars of independence in itself discouraged investment in industrial enterprise, or even in the more highly capitalised forms of plantation agriculture. The familiar economic characteristics of Creole society—its concern with static investment in land and cattle, its taste for conspicuous expenditure, its interest in fees, rents and salaries rather than in commercial or industrial profits—were emphasised and perpetuated. The avid continued demand for manufactured goods could be met only by continued concentration of the production and export of a few primary commodities, so that the 'colonial' character of the Spanish-American economy was also per-petuated, and in many countries survives to this day. As a consequence, the land-owning rich tended to become richer and the landless poor poorer.

A relatively rigid system of social classes had been characteristic of Spanish America ever since the conquest; was, indeed, an inevitable consequence of conquest. Whenever a technologically superior or more warlike group conquers a less powerful group, and sets itself up as ruler, caste differences tend to result. These differences were emphasised in the Indies by the close-knit, introverted character of the Indian communities, and by the assumption, in the late medieval Catholicism which the *conquistadores* took with them, of a society in which each group had a specific social and economic function. Royal government and royal courts attempted to restrict overt oppression of one group by another, but did not appreciably modify the class structure, which survived with comparatively little change through the centuries of imperial rule. After independence the action of republican legislatures in abolishing titles of nobility indicated hostility to the Crown rather than any egalitarian feeling. Apart from this superficial change, the process of independence did little to change the class structure, but rather reinforced it by removing the external authority of the royal courts and by retarding the development of an industrial and commer-cial middle class. Only in recent times has the structure begun to be seriously strained by the impersonality of growing industrial economies.

The rigidity of the class structure in most parts of the Indies helped to preserve a remarkable appearance of cultural homogeneity throughout the area. Spanish immigrants through three centuries had settled in the Indies with common assumptions of racial and social superiority. They had come from all parts of Spain; but in the process of migration and settlement they tended to forget the diversities of their provincial origins. Their common culture was a generalised and simplified *Hispanidad*, their common language the speech of Castile, with Andalusian modifications; to this day, spoken Spanish varies comparatively little, at least among educated people, and written Spanish hardly at all, from one part of the area to another. Their religion was the orthodox Catholicism of Spain, but, again, in a generalised and sim-plified form. They preserved the essentials of Christian doctrine; the cult of the Virgin Mary as a common core of loyalty; the principal festivals of the Church and the observances associated with them (which, naturally, were a means of teaching doctrine to the Indians). They built magnificent churches and maintained the full splendour of the major rites. On the other hand, they left behind the very numerous local cults and festivals, some of them, doubtless, of pre-Christian origin, which existed and still exist in Spain. In their social life they brought with them a predilection for urban dwelling; but in organising town governments they adopted, throughout the Indies, relatively simple formulae, and abandoned the complexity of the municipal *fueros* of Spain. Even the physical design of colonial towns, as we have seen, tended to a common pattern, which may have reflected current Spanish theory on town-planning and did, under Philip II, reflect Spanish legislation; but which certainly did not reflect the idiosyncratic diversity of actual Spanish towns. A similar process of selection and simplification affected the transmission of tools and techniques. To cite a simple example: Spain possessed, and possesses, many types of plough, but only one, the Andalusian *arado dental*, reached America and became diffused throughout the Indies as the general type. The story is the same in respect of carts and waggons, saddlery and harness, hunting and fishing methods, agricultural and pastoral practices, and the traditions and superstitions associated with them.

By the time of the wars of independence all of Spanish America from northern Mexico to southern Argentina and Chile was strongly marked by a common cultural stamp. A common heritage was recognised across all the divisions caused by local loyalty, personal jealousy and provincial hostility. Although, following separation from Spain, a series of independent nations emerged, each with peculiar geographical, economic and social characteristics and with local traditions and histories, the supra-national resemblances were so pronounced that in anthropological concept all countries together constituted, and in large measure still constitute, a single culture area. The cultural differences between modern Spanish-American nations—at least among the European and Europeanised sections of society—arise more from the nineteenth-century immigration of non-Spaniards into some countries than from the attainment of political independence.

Cultural homogeneity, however, was characteristic only of the European and Europeanised elements. It was in this sense that the rigidity of the class structure helped to preserve it. Among the indigenous or mainly indigenous sections of society—generally speaking, the poorest, least influential, least mobile sections—diversity, as might be expected, was far more pronounced. Conquest, alien rule and de-population destroyed much of the rich diversity of the indigenous cultures, but not all; and although Iberian culture was offered as a substitute in a common, simplified form, the manner and degree of its acceptance was far from uniform. Just as Spanish immigrants, con-sciously or not, selected from the wide diversity of Iberian habits and techniques a limited range suitable for transmission to the Indies, so the conquered Indians made their own selection of transmitted characteristics for acceptance and imitation. Selection in this context does not, of course, necessarily imply free choice. The Spaniards imposed, often with great brutality, the local administrative arrange-ments which they found most convenient in order to exploit the work-ing and tribute-paying capacity of the Indians. They urged Christian religious observances upon the Indians by all the means at their com-mand. The missionary activity of the sixteenth and seventeenth centuries, moreover, was succeeded in the later eighteenth century by vigorous and determined economic and technical proselytising. There remained, nevertheless, a considerable range of European cultural characteristics, particularly in fields where the interests of the Spanish settlers were not directly affected, available to the Indians for imitation, in so far as their means allowed, or for rejection.

Some Spanish habits and techniques were willingly adopted because they were congenial or convenient. In religious life the cults of the Virgin and of the saints made a strong appeal to many Indians, possibly because they could be roughly equated with the cults of local deities. Many shrines associated with miraculous appearances in colonial times are deeply venerated today. In economic life, farm tools and agricultural techniques, in many predominantly Indian communities, today reflect, and have long reflected, more of Spain than of native America. Old World oxen draw the Mediterranean scratch plough, even, in many places, to prepare the ground for maize. In house construction, similarly, though the adobe wall is Indian as well as Spanish, the ubiquitous red-tiled roof came from the Spaniards, who had it from the Moors. Fishing is an age-old Indian occupation; but the ocean or lake-shore fisherman, whether Indian or *mestizo*, draws in his catch in a net of Iberian type, and the hook-and-line fisherman uses the familiar peninsular trot lines.

Some Spanish devices were accepted slowly and reluctantly, under strong compulsion exerted by the conquerors, but took root in many

Indian communities, and survive today. An example is the *cabildo*, the Spanish type of municipal government, with its *alcaldes* and *regidores* elected for short terms and responsible to an appointed *gobernador*. Indian *regimientos*, unlike Spanish ones, never became proprietary. The *cabildo* organisation conflicted with Indian notions of life tenure and the rights of ruling lineages, but in many places it prevailed. A more trivial and homely example may be found, perhaps, in the substitution of trousers for the traditional breech-clout, insistently pressed upon Indian men by Spanish clergy in the supposed interests of decency.

Many Spanish customs were regarded by Indians as unattainable or rejected as undesirable. Many Indian customs were abandoned; others were suppressed, more or less effectively, by Spanish authority. Special interest attaches to a few Indian customs which actually became more widespread as a result of conquest. The most significant of these was the use of intoxicants and narcotics. Chicha-drinking and coca-chewing in the Andes, pulque-drinking in Mexico, had all been known before the conquest, but had been limited and to some extent ritualised by social control. Under colonial government the traditional controls were weakened, and intoxication became, for many Indian peasants, the easiest way of temporary escape from the hardships of their daily life. In Mexico many Spanish *haciendas* exploited the demand for pulque, since the maguey cactus from which it was made provided a profitable crop on land too poor or too exhausted for cereals. The attempts of Government and Church to prevent drunkenness and to control the retail sale of intoxicants were largely ineffectual. Drunkenness remains a major social problem in many places to this day.

The pattern of cultural acceptance, rejection or modification in Indian communities displayed great diversity. Some Indian groups were too remote to be much affected by Spanish influence, too primitive to adapt, or too insignificant to be worth coercing. Some, such as the Araucanians in southern Chile, met all Spanish influence with hostile and stubborn rejection. Some—the Tarascans of Michoacán, for example—though extremely tenacious of many of their own customs, made their selection of Spanish innovations with discrimination and intelligence. Even in the areas of dense population, where Spanish pressure was strongest, the pattern of selection varied considerably. Since in those areas the conquest destroyed the wide-ranging 'imperial' structures, and left only the local town and village communities more or less intact, the pattern varied not merely from province to province but almost from village to village. The extent of the acceptance and use of the Spanish language, in particular, varied from place to place. Throughout the colonial period, declared government policy required that Indians should be taught Spanish. In some localities, such as parts of central Mexico where contact with Spaniards was relatively close, a considerable number of Indians—chiefly, it may be presumed, the *principales*, the leading men of the Indian towns, together with those who sought employment on *haciendas* or in Spanish towns—did learn Spanish; but very few gave up their native speech. In Peru, Spanish was spoken much less widely. Even in central Mexico, throughout the period, Indian legal documents continued to be drawn in Nahuatl by professional native scribes. Spanish courts, and all colonial authorities in contact with native society, always needed the services of interpreters. Only occasionally in late colonial times did Indian witnesses depose wholly in Spanish. In many places there was stubborn passive opposition to its use. Witnesses who were known to understand Spanish would deny knowledge and insist on testifying through interpreters. The endurance of Indian languages naturally assisted the preservation of Indian custom and Indian diversity. Customs of which Spaniards actively disapproved were merely driven underground, and reappeared when official pressure relaxed. Many survive to this day.

The social, economic and political diversity of the nations of modern Spanish America, then, arises not only from differences in terrain and resources, and not only from the variety of immigrants, Spanish and non-Spanish, who came to them from Europe. It reflects also the diversity of indigenous peoples, and the differences in the past, from country to country, in the interaction between Indian and Spanish cultures. In most places the pattern of interaction was decided in the early days of settlement, and changed relatively little in essentials throughout the colonial period. Some features of it, of course, were common to all provinces. The social standing of the Indian peasant in relation to Creole society was almost everywhere subordinate. Political independence, in itself, affected this standing very little. It is true that in the early nineteenth century the incarceration of work-people in textile and other factories to prevent their running away—an ancient practice repeatedly and ineffectually forbidden—was at last abandoned. The Council of Regency in 1810 formally prohibited what remained of *mita* labour and abolished the tribute, that discriminatory tax which had been paid by Indians, and only by Indians, since the first conquests, and before. These were, in principle, major changes. In practice they were relatively unimportant, because poverty, peonage and informal bullying were more efficient means of keeping Indians in subjection. These were general. The significant diversities were in the character and the populousness of Indian communities and in the closeness of their contact with the rest of society.

Argentina is an example of a country where Indian influence is minimal. In so far as it exists, it is confined to the upriver provinces. The pampa was settled late. Primitive and intractable Indian groups survived there, almost untouched by Spanish influence, well into the nineteenth century. Then they were hunted down, like the Plains Indians of North America, and few survive. Bolivia and Paraguay are predominantly Indian areas. Apart from a small, mainly urban, professional or property-owning class, Hispanic influence is only skin deep. In lesser degree the same is true of Guatemala. In prosperous Peru two societies exist side by side. A society of long-established Hispanic culture possesses political power, social leadership and economic wealth. A decayed but numerous Indian society, only superficially Hispanicised, and to a considerable extent geographically remote, exists on the fringe of national life. In Mexico interaction, from the first days of the conquest, has been closer. The Spaniards dominated, proselytised, exploited; the Indians endured. Little though they understood one another, however, the two societies were always in contact. Mexico is the only major Spanish-American country where Indian or part-Indian leaders played any significant role in the wars of independence. Modern Mexico is a composite society in which people of mixed descent predominate numerically. Of all Spanish-American countries it is the one where the Indian element is most explicitly recognised and respected as a vital ingredient in a composite national character. The wars of independence, in Mexico as elsewhere, left political as well as social and economic power in the hands of the successors of the *conquistadores*, but in subsequent upheavals restitution has at least been claimed for the successors of the conquered. In the ordering of modern Mexican society a serious attempt has been made to revive social and cultural patterns which existed, or are supposed to have existed, before the *conquistadores* arrived.

The present diversity of nations naturally finds expression in a diversity of attitudes towards the past, and an indication of a nation's feelings about its own past can usually be found in its commemorative statuary. In Buenos Aires, as in many Argentinian towns, a dramatic San Martín commands the wide plaza which bears his name. In Lima the statue of Pizarro stands fiercely on guard in the Plaza de Armas. In Mexico—a much be-statued city—the pattern is more complex. A huge idealised Cuauhtémoc dominates a major central site. A fine eighteenth-century equestrian statue of Charles IV is still displayed, but explicitly as a work of art, and no longer in the Zócalo. Bartolomé de las Casas has a more modest but still a respected place. The bones of Cortés, after many vicissitudes, lie in the church of Jesús Nazareno, which his descendants endowed, beneath a simple stone slab bearing his name. Other than that he has no memorial.

Bibliographical notes

GENERAL

No attempt has been made in this book to cite authority for particular statements; thorough documentation, in a brief account of so vast a subject, would require a volume of footnotes out of all proportion to the length of the text. What follows here is a modest list of the published works which have been found most useful. Many of these works contain more detailed bibliographies, to which the reader is referred. B. Sánchez Alonso, *Fuentes de la historia Española e Hispanoamericana*, 3rd edn, Madrid 1952, is a most useful and comprehensive list. R. A. Humphreys, *Latin America, a selective guide to publications in English*, Oxford 1958, lists about 900 books with helpful comment. There are a number of periodical reviews devoted to Latin-American history, of which the most important for the colonial period are *Revista de Indias*, Madrid 1940—, *Revista de Historia de América*, Mexico 1938—, and the *Hispanic American Historical Review*, Baltimore 1918–22 and Durham, North Carolina 1926—. *The Handbook of Latin American Studies*, published annually since 1926, at present by the University of Florida Press, is an indispensable critical guide to current writings in almost every branch of Latin American studies. The best guide to the bibliographies themselves is C. K. Jones, *A bibliography of Latin American bibliographies*, 2nd edn, Washington 1942. Francisco Esteve Barba, *Historiografía Indiana*, Madrid 1964, is not a bibliography, but a comprehensive critical account of the historiography of the Indies.

An immense wealth of documentary material, still very imperfectly explored, is preserved in the Archive of the Indies in Seville and in the archives of the various countries of Spanish America. R. R. Hill, *The national archives of Latin America*, Cambridge, Mass. 1945, gives a brief but valuable survey of history, organisation, contents and publications. There is no adequate calendar or catalogue of the Seville archive. During the past 150 years a considerable number of published collections of documents have appeared, mostly drawn from the Archive of the Indies; together they amount to a large volume of material, but still only a very small fraction of the contents of the archive. A convenient list of the most important is in the bibliography of Harings' *Spanish Empire*.

Of general histories of the Spanish Empire in America, William Robertson's *History of America*, 2 vols, London 1777, may still be read with profit, certainly with pleasure. A standard modern work is R. B. Merriman, *The rise of the Spanish Empire in the Old World and the New*, 4 vols, New York 1918–34, but it takes the story only to the death of Philip II. C. H. Haring, *The Spanish Empire in America*, New York 1947, is a comprehensive study of the institutions of the empire. J. M. Ots Capdequí, *Instituciones sociales de la América española en el período colonial*, La Plata 1934, contains much valuable information. B. Moses, *The Spanish dependencies in South America*, New York 1914, consists of studies of various aspects of colonial life, and is still useful and suggestive. H. H. Bancroft, *History of Mexico*, 6 vols, San Francisco 1883–8, and *History of Central America*, San Francisco 1882–7, are full and accurate narratives. B. W. Diffie, *Latin American civilisation; colonial period*, Harrisburg, Pa 1945, is a useful and readable guide. Charles Gibson, *Spain in America*, New York 1966, is an admirable and illuminating brief general study.

Special mention should be made of the encyclopaedic series directed by Sr Antonio Ballesteros y Beretta, in course of publication at Barcelona under the general title *Historia de América y de los pueblos americanos*. The first volume was published in 1936 and volumes III, IV, V, VI, VII, VIII, XI, XIV, XXII and XXVII have since appeared. Those relevant to this work are mentioned separately.

Prologue: The tradition of conquest

R. Menéndez Pidal, ed., *Historia de España*, Madrid 1935—.

This great co-operative work on medieval Spain has an introduction by its editor, which has been published separately in English translation, and with an introductory essay by W. Starkie, under the title *The Spaniards in their history*, London 1950.

A. Ballesteros y Beretta, *Sevilla en el siglo XIII*, Madrid 1913.

R. Menéndez Pidal, *Castilla; la tradición; el idioma*, Buenos Aires 1945.

La idea imperial de Carlos V, Buenos Aires 1943.

A. Castro, *España en su historia, Cristianos, Moros y Judíos*, Buenos Aires 1948.

M. Ballesteros Gaibrois, *La obra de Isabela la Católica*, Segovia 1953.

J. H. Elliott, *Imperial Spain 1469–1716*, London 1963.

Chapter 1   Islands and mainland in the Ocean Sea

S. E. Morison, *Admiral of the Ocean Sea*, 2 vols, Boston 1942.

A. P. Newton, *The European nations in the West Indies 1493–1688*, London 1933.

384 Bibliographical notes

A. Melón y R. de Gordejuela, *Los primeros tiempos de la colonización. Cuba y le Antillas. Magallanes y la primera vuelta al mundo (Historia d América y de la pueblos americanos* vol VI), Barcelona 1952.

I. A. Wright, *The early history of Cuba 1492–1586,* New York 1916.

Fray Alonso de Espinosa, C. R. Markham, ed., *The Guanches of Tenerife* (1594), London, Hakluyt Society, 1907.

The Journal of Christopher Columbus, trans. C. Jane, rev. L. A. Vigneras, London, Hakluyt Sodiety, 1960.

C. O. Sauer, *The Early Spanish Main,* Berkeley 1966.

R. Pike, *The Genoese in Seville and the Opening of the New World,* Ithaca 1966.

F. G. Davenport, ed., *European Treaties bearing upon the history of the United States,* 4 vols, Washington 1917–37; vol I, for the texts of the bulls of demarcation and the treaty of Tordesillas.

Peter Martyr Anghieri, F. A. McNutt, ed. and trans., *De Orbe Novo,* New York 1912.

G. Fernández de Oviedo y Valdés, J. A. de los Ríos, ed., *Historia general y natural de las Indias,* 4 vols, Madrid 1851–5.

C. L. F. Anderson, *Life and letters of Vasco Nuñez de Balboa,* New York 1941.

Chapter 2   Seville and the Caribbean

J. Pérez de Tudela Bueso, *Las armadas de Indias y los orígenes de la politica de colonización 1492–1505,* Madrid (Instituto Gonzalo Fernández de Ovida) 1956.

Ursula Lamb, *Frey Nicolás de Ovando, gobernador de las Indias, 1501–1509,* Madrid 1956.

Ruth Pike, *Enterprise and adventure; the Genoese in Seville and the opening of the New World,* Ithaca 1966.

C. O. Sauer, *The early Spanish Main,* Berkeley 1965.

H. and P. Chaunu, *Séville et l'Atlantique,* 8 vols, Paris 1955–6.

This immense work is now the standard authority on the *Carrera de Indias,* and likely to remain so. It lists all sailings to and from the Indies of which record remains, and draws detailed conlcusions on the fluctuations of the trade, down to 1650. For readers with less stamina, however, earlier and shorter books are still of value.

R. Pike, *Aristocrats & traders; Sevillan society in the sixteenth century.* Ithaca 1972.

C. H. Haring, *Trade and navigation between Spain and the Indies in the times of the Hapsburgs,* Cambridge, Mass. 1918.

G. de Artiñano y Galdácano, *Historia del comercio con las Indias durante el domino de los Austrias,* Barcelona 1917.

J. Pulido Rubio, *El polito mayor de la Casa de la Contratación de Sevilla; pilotos mayores, catedráticos de cosmografía y cosmógrafos*, Sevilla, Escuela de Estudios Hispano-Americanos, Ser. 2 no. 19, 1950.

E. Schäfer, *El consejo real y supremo de las Indias*, 2 vols, Seville 1935–47.

Chapter 3   The kingdoms of the sun

L. Pericot y García, *América indígena (Historia de América y de los pueblos americanos* vol I), Barcelona 1936.

G. C. Vaillant, *Aztecs of Mexico*, New York 1941.

J. Soustelle, *La vie quotidienne des Aztèques à la veille de la conquête espagnole*, Paris 1959.

S. G. Morley, *The ancient Maya*, Stanford 1946.

J. Alden Mason, *Ancient civilisations of Peru*, London (Penguin Books) 1957.

P. A. Means, *Ancient civilisations of the Andes*, New York 1931.

L. E. Valcárcel, *Etnohistoria del Perú antiguo*, Lima 1959.

J. H. Steward, ed., *Handbook of South American Indians*, 5 vols, Washington, Smithsonian Institution, 1946–50; vol 2, 'The Andean civilisations'.

A corresponding series, a *Handbook of Middle American Indians*, is in preparation.

Garcilaso Inca de la Vega, H. V. Livermore, ed., *The royal commentaries of the Incas*, 2 vols, Austin 1966.

Fernando de Alva Ixtlilxóchitl, A. Chavero, ed., *Obras históricas*, 2 vols, Mexico 1912–13.

B. de Sahagún, M. A. Saignes, ed., *Historia general de las cosas de Nueva España*, 3 vols, Mexico 1946.

Chapter 4   The conquerors

W. H. Prescott, *History of the conquest of Mexico*, 3 vols, New York 1843.
History of the conquest of Peru, 2 vols, New York 1847.
These two famous books have gone through many editions and are in many respects out of date, but they will always be well worth reading.

Jacques Lafaye, *Les Conquistadores*, Paris 1964.

F. A. Kirkpatrick, *The Spanish conquistadores*, London 1934.
An able and very readable summary.

A. M. Salas, *Las Armas de la Conquista*, Buenos Aires 1950.

R. Konetzke, *Entdecker und Eroberer Amerikas, von Kristoph Kolumbus bis Hernán Cortés*, Frankfurt 1963.

This recent work is particularly valuable for its perceptive analysis of the. personalities of Columbus and Cortés.

M. Góngora, *Los grupos de conquistadores en Tierra Firme.* Santiago 1962.

A. de Altolaguirre y Duvale, *Descubrimiento y conquista de México (Historia de América y de los pueblos americanos* vol VII), Barcelona 1954.

J. E. Kelly, *Pedro de Alvarado, conquistador*, Princeton 1932.

R. S. Chamberlain, *The conquest and colonisation of Yucatán*, Washington 1948.

P. A. Means, *The fall of the Inca empire and the Spanish rule in Peru 1530–1780*, New York 1932.

J. M. Rubio y Estéban, *Exploración y conquista del Río de la Plata (Historia de América y de los pueblos americanos* vol VIII), Barcelona 1942.

I. W. Vernon, *Pedro de Valdivia, conquistador of Chile*, Austin 1946.

F. Esteve Barba, *Descubrimiento y conquista de Chile (Historia de América y de los pueblos americanos* vol XI). Barcelona 1946.

A. R. Pagden, ed., Hernán Cortés, *Letters from Mexico*, New York 1961.

F. López de Gómara, J. Ramírez Cabañas, ed., *Historia de la conquista de México*, Mexico 1943.

There is a recent and excellent translation of this book by L. B. Simpson: *Cortés, the life of the conqueror by his secretary*, Berkeley 1963.

Bernal Díaz del Castillo, J. Ramírez Cabañas, ed., *Historia verdadera de la conquista de la Nueva España*, 2 vols, Mexico 1960.

Of the several English translations of Bernal Díaz, none is entirely satisfactory. The best is still that by A. P. Maudslay, 5 vols, London, Hakluyt Society, 1908–16.

None of the contemporary accounts of the conquest in South America approach, in merit or interest, the three books last cited. For Peru, the sources are comprehensively described in R. Porras Barrenechea, *Los cronistas del Perú* Lima 1962. English versions of the most important are

C. R. Markham, ed., *Reports on the discovery of Peru*, London 1872.

Pedro Pizarro, P. A. Means, ed., *Relation of the discovery and conquest of the kingdoms of Peru*, New York 1921.

Pedro de Cieza de León, C. R. Markham, ed., *Travels . . . contained in the first part of his Chronicle of Peru*, London, Hakluyt Society, 1864.

Second part of the Chronicle of Peru, London, Hakluyt Society, 1863.

The war of Las Salinas, London, Hakluyt Society, 1923.

The war of Chupas, London, Hakluyt Society, 1908.

The war of Quito, London, Hakluyt Society, 1913.

L. L. Domínguez, ed., *The conquest of the River Plate, including the accounts of Ulrich Schmidt and Alvar Nuñez Cabeza de Vaca*, London, Hakluyt Society, 1891.

Alberto Mario Salas, *Las armas de la conquista*, Buenos Aires 1950.

Chapter 5   *The society of conquest*

M. Góngora, *Studies in the Colonial History of Spanish America*, trans. R. Southern, Cambridge 1975.

J. Lockhart and E. Otte, *Letters and People of the Spanish Indies*, Cambridge 1976.

P. Boyd-Bowman, *Indice geobiográfico de cuarenta mil pobladores españoles de América en el siglo XVI*, Bogota 1964.

L. B. Simpson, *The encomienda in New Spain; the beginning of Spanish Mexico*, Berkeley 1950.

M. Belaunde Guinassi, *La encomienda en el Peru*, Lima 1945.

C. Bayle, *Los cabildos seculares en la América española*, Madrid 1952.
Much work remains to be done on the Spanish *cabildos*. The main source is their own minute books, many of which have been published; the most complete series is the *Actas de cabildo de la ciudad de México*, 54 vols, Mexico 1889–1916.

L. B. Simpson, *Exploitation of land in central Mexico in the sixteenth century*, Ibero-Americana 36, Berkeley 1952.

F. Chevalier, *La formation des grands domaines au Mexique*, Paris 1952.

R. G. Keith, *Conquest and Agrarian Change*, Cambridge, Mass. 1976.

W. Barrett, *The Sugar Hacienda of the Marqueses del Valle*, Minneapolis 1970.

P. Boyd-Bowman, *Indice geobiográfico de cuarenta mil pobladores españoles de América en el siglo XVI*. Vol. I (Bogotá 1964) covers the years 1493–1519. Other vols. to follow.

R. Konetzke, 'La formación de la nobleza en Indias', *Estudios Americanos*, III (1951), 329–357.

José Durand, *La transformacion social del conquistador*, 2 vols, Mexico 1964.

G. Kubler, *Mexican architecture of the sixteenth century*, 2 vols, New Haven 1948.
This important (and very handsome) book deals not only with the design of buildings but with the lay-out of towns, building methods and the recruitment of labour for building, secular and ecclesiastical.
The accounts of New Spain by English captives are in

R. Hakluyt, *Principal Navigations*, 12 vols, Glasgow 1903–5, IX.

R. L. Lee, 'Cochineal production and trade in New Spain to 1600', *The Americas* IV, 1947–8, 205–24.

H. R. Wagner, 'Early silver mining in New Spain', *Revista de Historia de América* no. 14, 49–71.

Alvaro Jara, *Tres ensayos sobre economía minera hispanoamericana*, Santiago 1966.

P. W. Powell, *Soldiers, Indians and Silver, the Northward advance of New Spain 1550–1600*, Berkeley 1952.

W. H. Dusenberry, 'Woollen manufacture in sixteenth-century New Spain', *The Americas* IV, 1947–8, 223–34.

The Mexican Mesta, Urbana 1963

A. Lipschutz, *El problema racial en la conquista de América y el mestizaje*, Santiago
    1963.
C. E. Marshall, 'The birth of the *mestizo* in New Spain', *Hispanic American
    Historical Review* XIX, 161–84.
J. Miranda, *España y Nueva España a la época de Felipe II*, Mexico 1962.
J. Lockhart, *Spainsh Peru 1532–1560*, Madison 1968.
J. de Acosta, *Historia natural y moral de las Indias*, Seville 1590.

Chapter 6   The maritime life-line

Chaunu, op. cit.
Artiñano, op. cit.
Haring, op. cit.
    'Trade and navigation between Spain and the Indies: a Re=View—1918–1958'.
    Hispanic American Historical Review, XL (1960) 53–62.
J. Pulido Rubio, *El Piloto Mayor de la Casa de Contratación de Sevilla*, Seville 1950.
A. P. Canabrava, *O comercio portugues no Rio da Prata 1580–1640*, Faculdade de
    filosofia, ciencias e letras, boletim XXXV, Sao Paulo 1944.
W. W. Borah, *Early colonial trade and navigation between Mexico and Peru*.
    Ibero-Americna 38, Berkeley 1944.
W. L. Schurz, *The Manila galleon*, New York 1939.
C. Céspedes del Castillo, *La avería en el comercio de Indias*, Seville 1945.
    The book trade, which from an early date formed an important and interest-
    ing element in the export trade to the Indies, has been studied in a series of
    illuminating books and articles by I. A. Leonard, of which the most relevant
    to this chapter is
I. A. Leonard, *Books of the brave*, Cambridge, Mass. 1949.
The ordinances drawn up in 1564, on Menéndez' advice, for the regulation
of the *Carrera de Indias*, were published in Diego Encinas, *Cedulario Indiano*,
Madrid 1596 (republished in *fascimile*, A. García Gallo, ed., 4 vols, Madrid
1945), vol IV. A revised code of ordinances was promulgated in 1597 under the
title *Instrucción de Generales y Almirantes de las flotas de la Carrera de Indias*. Many
of the provisions of this code remained in force throughout the seventeenth
century and were incorporated in the *Recopilación de Leyes de Indias* of 1681;
but the code as a whole has not, as yet, appeared in a modern printing.

Chapter 7   Rights and duties

J. H. Parry, *The Spanish theory of empire*, Cambridge 1940.

"A secular sense of responsibility." in F. Chiapelli, ed., *First Images of America*, Berkeley 1976.

S. Zavala, *Las instituciones jurídicas en la conquista de América*, Madrid 1935.

New viewpoints on the Spanish colonisation of America, Philadelphia 1943.

Venancio D. Carro, *La teología y los teólogos-juristas ante la conquista de América*, 2 vols., Madrid 1944.

Luis Weckmann, *Las bulas alejandrinas de 1493 y la teoría política del Papado medieval; estudio de la supremacía papal sobre islas, 1091–1493*, Mexico 1949.

L. Hanke, *The Spanish struggle for justice in the conquest of America*, Philadelphia 1949.

M. Giménez Fernández, *Bartolomé de las Casas*, 2 vols., Seville 1953.

A. F. G. Bell, *Juan Ginés de Sepúlveda*, Oxford 1925.

T. D. Marcos, *Los Imperialismos de Juan Ginés de Sepúlveda en su Democrates Alter*, Madrid 1947.

J. B. Scott, *The Spanish origin of International Law*, Oxford 1924.

On Juan de Ovando and the influence of Las Casas, see

J. Manzano y Manzano, *La incorporación de las Indias a la Corona de Castilla*, Madrid 1948.

The text of Vitoria's *Relectiones de Indis* are printed in English translation in Scott, op. cit. A facsimile of the 1696 (Frankfurt) Latin edition of the *Relectiones de Indis* and *de juro bello*, with a Spanish translation, edited by J. Malagón Barceló, has recently appeared (Washington 1963).

The Spanish polemical treatises of Las Casas are printed in facsimile in *Biblioteca argentina de libros raros americanos* vol III, *Colección de tratados de Bartolomé de las Casas 1552–3*, Buenos Aires 1924. The most famous of these treatises, the *Brevísima relación de la destrucción de las Indias*, has had a long bibliographical history in all the major European languages. The celebrated Latin edition, containing seventeen plates of atrocities, drawn by Jodocus a Winghe and engraved by De Bry, was printed at Frankfurt in 1598 under the title *Narratio regionum Indicarum per Hispanos quosdam devastatorum verissima*.

Other works of Las Casas relevant to this chapter are

Erudita et elegans explicatio questionis utrum reges vel principes jure aliquo vel titulo, et salva conscientia, cives ac subditos a regia corona alienare et alterius domini particularis ditioni subjicere possint, Frankfurt 1571.

Obras escogidas, 5 vols, Madrid 1957–8   vol I *Historia de las Indias*   vol III *Apologética Historica de las Indias*.

A. Millares Carlo and L. Hanke, eds., *Historia de las Indias*, 3 vols, Mexico 1951.

The best edition and translation of Sepúlveda's treatise is by Angel Losada, *Democrates segundo o de las justas causas de la guerra contra los Indios*, Madrid 1951.

Chapter 8　　*The spreading of the Faith*

W. E. Shiels, s.j., *King and Church, the rise and fall of the Patronato Real*, Chicago 1961.

A. de Engaña, *La teoría del regio vicariato español en Indias*, Rome 1958.

Pedro de Leturia, S. J., *Relaciones entre la Santa Sede e Hispanoamérica 1493–1835*, 3 vols, Caracas 1960.

M. Bataillon, *Erasme et l'Espagne; recherches sur l'histoire spirituelle du XVIᵉ siècle*, Paris 1937.

R. Ricard, *La conquête spirituelle du Mexique*, Paris 1933.

J. L. Phelan, *The millennial kingdom of the Franciscans in the New World*, Berkeley 1956.

J. García Icazbalceta, *Don fray Juan de Zumárraga, primer obispo y arzobispo de México*, Mexico 1881.

M. Cuevas, *Historia de la Iglesia en México*, 4 vols, Mexico 1921–6.

A. Tibesar, *Franciscan beginnings in colonial Peru*, Washington 1953.

F. de Armas Medina, *Cristizaniación de la iglesia y órdenes religiosos en el virreinato del Perú el siglo XVI, documentos del Archivo de Indias*, 2 vols, Madrid 1919.

J. B. Iguíniz, *La imprenta en la Nueva España*, Mexico 1938.

On the Jesuit missions the best works are

P. Hernández, *Misiones del Paraguay, organización soical de las doctrinas guaraníes de la Compañía de Jesús*, 2 vols, Barcelona 1913.

M. Mörner, *The political and economic activities of the Jesuits in the La Plata region*, Stockholm 1953.

The organisation and activities of the Inquisition in the Indies are described in detail, country by country, in a series of histories by J. Toribio Medina, published in Santiago between 1890 and 1914. A shorter English account is in H. C. Lea, *The inquisition in the Spanish dependencies*, New York 1908.

The neglected but not negligible story of the secular clergy is told in C. Bayle, *El clero secular y la evangelización de América*, Madrid 1950.

Gerónimo de Mendieta, J. García Icazbalceta, ed., *Historia eclesiástica indiana*, Mexico 1870.

Juan de Torquemada, *Monarquía indiana*, 3 vols, Madrid 1723.

B. de Sahagún, M. A. Saignes, ed., *Historia general de las cosas de Nueva España*, 3 vols, Mexico 1946.

F. J. Hernáez, ed., *Colección de bulas, breves, y otros documentos relativos a la iglesia de América y Filipinas*, 2 vols, Brussels 1879.

Chapter 9   *The ordering of society*

S. Zavala, 'Los trabajadores antillanos en el siglo XVI', *Revista de Historia de
América*, no. 2, 31–68; no. 3, 60–88; no. 4, 211–16.

L. Hanke, *The first social experiments in America*, Cambridge, Mass. 1935.
'Pope Paul III and the American Indians', *Harvard Theological Review*
XXX, 65–102.

L. B. Simpson, *The encomienda in New Spain*, Berkeley 1950.
Studies in the administration of the Indians in New Spain: I *The Laws of Burgos
of 1512;* II *The civil congregation*, Berkeley 1934; III *The repartimiento
system of native labour in New Spain and Guatemala*, Berkeley 1938; IV
*The emancipation of the Indian slaves and the resettlement of the freedmen
1548–1553*, Berekeley 1940.

S. Zavala, *La encomienda indiana*, Madrid 1935.
De encomiendas y propiedad territorial en algunas regiones de la América española,
Mexico 1940.

M. Belaunde Guinassi, *La encomienda en el Perú*, Lima 1945.

J. Basadre, 'El régimen de las mitas', *Letras*, Lima 1937, 325–64.

J. Miranda, *El tributo indígena en la Nueva España durante el siglo XVI*, Mexico
1952.
For accounts of *visitas* conducted by *audiencia* judges for the adjustment of
tributes in New Spain and New Galicia, see

W. V. Scholes, *The Diego Ramírez visita*, Columbia, Mo. 1946, and

C. Gibson, *The Aztecs under Spanish rule*, Stanford, Calif. 1964.
This recent and very important work deals in great detail with Spanish
pressures upon the Indian population of the Valley of Mexico, and Indian
responses to those pressures, from 1519 to 1810.

A. S. Aiton, *Antonio de Mendoza, first viceroy of New Spain*, Durham, North
Carolina 1927.

R. Levillier, *Don Francisco de Toledo, supremo organizador del Perú*, 3 vols,
Madrid 1935–42.

M. Góngora, *El estado en el derecho indiano, época de fundación, 1492–1570*,
Santiago 1951.

Torquemada, op. cit.
Sahagún, op. cit.

L. B. Simpson, ed., *The Laws of Burgos of 1512–13*, San Francisco 1960.

H. Stevens, ed., *The new laws of the Indies for the good treatment and preservation
of the Indians . . . 1542–3*; a facsimile reprint of the original Spanish edition,
with English translation, London 1893.
Instrucciones que los virreyes de Nueva España dejaron a sus sucesores, 2 vols,
Mexico 1867–73.

R. Beltrán y Rózpide, ed., *Colección de las memorias o relaciones que escribieron los virreyes del Peru*, 2 vols, Madrid 1921–30.

J. Castillo de Bovadilla, *Política para corregidores y señores de vasallos en tiempo de paz y de guerra*, 2 vols, Barcelona 1616.

Chapter 10   The enforcement of law

C. H. Haring, *The Spanish Empire in America*, New York 1947.

J. M. Ots Capdequí, *El estado español en las Indias*, Mexico 1942.

E. Schäfer, *El consejo real y supremo de las Indias*, 2 vols, Seville 1935–47.

E. Ruiz Guiñazú, *La magistratura indiana*, Buenos Aires 1916.

J. I. Rubio Mañé, *Introducción al estudio de los virreyes de Nueva España, 1535–1746*, 3 vols, Mexico 1959–61.

J. H. Parry, *The audiencia of New Galicia in the sixteenth century*, Cambridge 1948.

The sale of public office in the Spanish Indies under the Hapsburgs, Ibero-Americana 37, Berkeley 1953.

Recopilación de leyes de los reinos de las Indias, 4 vols, Madrid 1681.

J. de Solórzano Pereira, *Política indiana*, Madrid 1647.

A. de León-Pinelo, *Tratado de confirmaciones reales de encomiendas, oficios y casos, en que se requieren para las Indias occidentales*, Madrid 1630.

A. de Herrera y Tordesillas, *Historia general de los hechos de los Castellanos en las islas y tierra firme del mar océano*, 4 vols, Madrid 1601–15.

M. Jiménez de la Espada, ed., *Relaciones geográficas de Indias*, 4 vols, Madrid 1881–97.

J. López de Velasco, *Geografía y descripción universal de las Indias, recopilada desde el año 1571 al de 1574*, Madrid 1894.

A. Vázquez de Espinosa, C. U. Clark, ed., *Compendium and description of the West Indies*, Washington 1942.

Chapter 11   Demographic catastrophe

W. W. Borah and S. F. Cook, *The aboriginal population of central Mexico on the eve of Spanish conquest, Ibero-Americana* 45, Berkeley 1963.

The population of central Mexico in 1548, Ibero-Americana 43, Berekley 1960.

The population of central Mexico 1531–1610, Ibero-Americana 44, Berkeley 1960.

L. B. Simpson, *Exploitation of land in central Mexico in the sixteenth century, Ibero-Americana* 36, Berkeley 1952.

R. L. Lee, 'Grain legislation in colonial Mexico, 1575–85', *Hispanic American Historical Review* XXVII, 1947, 647–60.

M. Carrera Stampa, 'El obraje novohispano', *Memorias de la Academía mexicana de la Historia* XX, 1961, 148–71.

F. Chevalier, *La formation des grands domaines au Mexique*, Paris 1952.

W. W. Borah, *New Spain's century of depression*, *Ibero-Americana* 35, Berkeley 1951.

J. Miranda, 'La población indígena de México en el siglo XVII', *Historia Mexicana*, XII (1962–63), 182–189.

H. F. Dobyns, 'An outline of Andean epidemic history to 1720', *Bulletin of the History of Medicine*, XXXVII (1963), 493–515.

G. Kubler, 'The Quechua in the colonial world', *Handbook of South American Indians*, vol. II, 331–410.

A. Rosenblat, *La población indígena y el mestizaje en América*, 2 vols., Buenos Aires 1954.

N. Sánchez-Albornoz, *The Population of Latin America*, Berkeley 1974.

E. J. Hamilton, 'Imports of American gold and silver into Spain, 1503–1660', *Quarterly Journal of Economics* XLIII, 436–72.

P. J. Bakewell, *Silver Mining and Society in Colonial Mexico: Zacatecas*, Cambridge 1970.

R. Mellafe, *La esclavitud en Hispanoamérica*, Buenos Aires 1964.

J. Vicens Vives, ed., *Historia social y económica de España y América*, 5 vols, Barcelona 1957–59, vol III.

Chapter *12* *Economic dependence*

J. Lynch, *Spain under the Hapsburgs*, 2 vols, Oxford 1964.
This recent careful study of Spanish history pays particular attention to the consequences, for Spain, of the possession of the Indies.

A. Domínquez Ortiz, *Política y hacienda de Felipe IV*, Madrid 1960.
La sociedad española en el siglo XVII, Madrid 1963.

E. J. Hamilton, *American treasure and the price revolution in Spain 1501–1650*, Cambridge, Mass. 1934.
La Monnaie en Castille, 1501–1650, Paris 1932.
War and prices in Spain, 1651–1800, Cambridge, Mass. 1947.

J. Klein, *The Mesta, a study in Spanish economic history, 1273–1836*, Cambridge, Mass. 1920.

J. H. Elliott, *The revolt of the Catalans*, Cambridge 1963.

C. Bermúdez Plata, *Catálogo de pasageros a Indias*, 3 vols, 1940–6.

L. Rubio y Moreno, ed., *Pasajeros a Indias*, 2 vols, Madrid 1930.

A. Girard, *Le commerce français à Séville et Cadix aux temps des Hapsbourgs*, Paris 1932.

G. Scelle, *La traite négrière aux Indes de Castille*, 2 vols, Paris 1906.

I. Wolff, 'Negersklaverei und Negerhandel in Hoch-Peru 1545–1640', *Jahrbuch fur Geschichte Lateinamerikas*, I (1964), 157.

L. Hanke, *The imperial city of Potosí*, The Hague 1956.

H. Lohmann Villena, *Las minas de Huancavélica en los siglos XVI and XVII*, Seville 1952.

Emilio Romero, *Historia económica del Perú*, Buenos Aires 1949.

J. Díez de la Calle, *Memorial y noticias sacras y reales del imperio de las Indias occidentales*, Madrid 1646.

J. de Veitia Linaje, *Norte de la contratación de las Indias*, Seville 1672.

S. de Moncada, *Restauración política de España* (1619), Madrid 1746.

F. Martínez de Mata, *Epítome de los discursos . . . en que prueba: como la causa de la pobreza y despoblación de España*, printed in P. Rodríguez, conde de Campomanes, *Apéndice a la educación popular*, 4 vols, Madrid 1775–7.

Chapter 13   Peril by sea

Chaunu, op. cit.

P. A. Means, *The Spanish Main, focus of envy, 1492–1700*, New York 1935.

J. H. Parry and P. M. Sherlock, *A Short History of the West Indies*, London 1963.

K. R. Andrews, *Elizabethan Privateering*, Cambridge 1964.

    Drake's Voyages, New York 1967.

E. Sluiter, 'Dutch-Spanish rivalry in the Caribbean area, 1594–1609', *Hispanic American Historical Review* XXVIII, 1948, 179.

Scelle, op. cit.

   The standard works on the technical aspects of Spanish maritime history are those of C. Fernández Duro:

Armada española desde la unión de las coronas de Castilla y León, 9 vols, Madrid 1895–1903.

Disquisiciones náuticas, 6 vols, Madrid 1876–81.

J. Esquemeling, *Bucaniers of America . . . by . . . one of the bucaniers who was present at those tragedies*, London 1684.

There are several more modern editions of this celebrated book.

Chapter 14   Decline and recovery

A. Cánovas del Castillo, *Historia de la decadencia de España desde el advenimiento de Felipe III al trono hasta el muerte de Carlos II*, 2nd edn, Madrid 1910.

W. W. Borah, *New Spain's century of depression, Ibero-Americana* 35, Berkeley 1951.

M. Carrera Stampa, *Los gremios mexicanos*, . . . *1521–1861*, Mexico 1954.

C. Gibson, *The Aztecs under Spanish rule*, S-anford 1964.

A. de Engaña, *La teoría del regio vicariato español en Indias*, Rome 1958.

A. Girard, *La rivalité commerciale et maritime entre Séville et Cadix jusqu'à la fin du XVIIIᵉ siècle*, Paris 1932.

R. D. Hussey, *The Caracas Company 1728–1784*, Cambridge, Mass. 1934.

E. W. Dahlgren, *Les relations commerciales et maritimes entre la France et les côtes de l'Océan Pacifique, commencement du XVIIIᵉ siècle*, Paris 1909.

G. Kratz, *El tratado hispano-portugués de límites de 1750 y sus consecuencias*, Rome 1954.

M. Mörner, *The political and economic activities of the Jesuits in the La Plata region*, Stockholm 1953.

A. Métraux, 'The contribution of the Jesuits to the exploration and anthropology of South America', *Mid-America* XXVI, 183–91.

H. E. Bolton, *The Spanish borderlands: a chronicle of Old Florida and the Southwest*, New Haven 1921.

T. Gage, J. E. S. Thompson, ed., *Travels in the New World* (first published in 1648 under the title *The English-American. A new survey of the West Indies*), London 1958.

J. de Solórzano Pereira, *Política indiana*. Madrid 1647.
Recopilación de leyes de Indias, 4 vols, Madrid 1681.

F. Martínez de Mata, op. cit.

M. de Macanaz, *Testamento de España*, Mexico 1821.

J. Juan and A. de Ulloa, *Noticias secretas de América* (1749), London 1826.

G. de Uztáriz, *Teoría y prática del comercio y de la marina*, Madrid 1724.

J. Campbell ('an English merchant'), *The Spanish Empire in America*, London 1747.

C. W. Hackett, ed., *Historical documents relating to New Mexico, Nueva Vizcaya and approaches thereto, to 1773*, 3 vols, Washington 1923–37.

Chapter 15   Caribbean conflicts

G. Scelle, *La traite négière aux Indes de Castille*, 2 vols, Paris 1906.
J. O. McLachlan, *Trade and peace with Old Spain, 1667–1750*, Cambridge 1940.
E. F. S. de Studer, *La trata de negros en el Río de la Plata durante el siglo XVIII*, Buenos Aires 1958.
G. H. Nelson, 'Contraband trade under the Asiento, 1730–1739', *American Historical Review* LI, 55–67.
R. Pares, *War and trade in the West Indies, 1739–1763*, Oxford 1936.
A. Christelow, 'Contraband trade between Jamaica and the Spanish Main and the Free Ports Act of 1766', *Hispanic American Historical Review* XXII, 309–43.
R. A. Humphreys, *The diplomatic history of British Honduras 1638–1901*, Oxford 1961.

Chapter 16   Growth and reorganisation

Jean Sarrailh, *L'Espagne éclairée de la seconde moitié du XVIIIᵉ siecle*, Paris 1954.
Richard Herr, *The eighteenth-century revolution in Spain*, Princeton 1958.
Sergio Bagú, *Estructura social de la colonia*, Buenos Aires 1952.
J. M. Ots Capdequí, *Nuevos aspectos del siglo XVIII español en América*, Bogotá 1946.
J. Vicens Vives, ed. *Historia social y económica de España y América* (5 vols, Barcelona 1957–59) vol IV.
D. A. Brading, *Miners and Merchants in Bourbon Mexico 1763–1810*, Cambridge 1971.
H. I. Priestley, *José de Gálvez, visitador general of New Spain, 1765–1771*, Berkeley 1934.
C. Gibson, *The Aztecs under Spanish rule*, Stanford 1964.
G. Céspedes del Castillo, *Lima y Buenos Aires, repercusiones económicas y políticas de la creación del virreinato del Plata*, Seville 1947.
M. Kossok, *El Virreinato del Río de la Plata, Su estructura económico-social*, Buenos Aires 1959.
Germán O. E. Tjarks, *El consulado de Buenos Aires, y sus proyecciones en la historia del Río de la Plata*, 2 vols., Buenos Aires 1962.
J. Lynch, *Spanish colonial administration, 1782–1810; the intendant system in the Rio de la Plata*, London 1958.
M. Bargalló, *La minería y metalurgía en la América española durante la época colonial*, Mexico 1955.

A. P. Whitaker, 'The Elhuyar mining missions and the Enlightenment', *Hispanic American Historical Review XXXI*, 557–85.

W. Howe, *The mining guild of New Spain and its Tribunal General, 1770–1821*, Cambridge, Mass. 1949.

R. C. West, *The mining community in northern New Spain; the Parral mining district, Ibero-Americana* 30, Berkeley 1949.

M. del C. Velázquez, *El estado de guerra en Nueva España, 1760–1808*, Mexico 1950.

L. N. McAlister, *The 'Fuero Militar' in New Spain*, Gainsville 1957.

F. de Fonseca and Carlos de Urrutia, eds., *Historia general de real hacienda escrita . . . por orden del virrey conde de Revillagigedo*, 6 vols, Madrid 1845–53.

J. Campillo y Cosío, *Nueva sistema de gobierno económico para la América*, Madrid 1789.

R. Antúñez y Acevedo, *Memoria histórica sobre la legislación y gobierno del comercio de los españoles con sus colonias en las Indias occidentales*, Madrid 1797.

Reales ordenanzas para la dirección, régimen y gobierno del importante cuerpo de minería de Nueva España, Madrid 1783.

Real ordenanza para el establecimiento y instrución de intendentes de ejécito y provincia en el reino de Nueva España, Madrid 1786.

Chapter 17 Spaniards and Americans

Diego Angulo Iñiguez, *Historia del arte hispanoamericano*, Barcelona 1945—(a multivolume history, still in process of publication).

Documentos de arte colonial. Publicaciones de la Academiá nacional de Bellas Artes de la República Argentina, Buenos Aires 1943. (Ten volumes so far published.)

P. Kelemen, *Baroque and Rococo in Latin America*, New York 1951.

M. Toussaint, *Arte colonial en México*, Mexico 1948.

G. Kubler and M. Soria, *Art and architecture in Spain and Portugal and their American dominons 1500–1800*, London 1959.

A. P. Whitaker, ed., *Latin America and the Enlightenment*, New York 1942.

J. T. Lanning, *Academic culture in the Spanish colonies*, New York 1940.
The eighteenth-century enlightenment in the University of San Carlos de Gautemala, Ithaca 1956.

J. Torre Revello, *El libro, la imprenta y el periodismo en América durante la dominación española*, Buenos Aires 1940.

R. J. Shafer, *The economic societies in the Spanish world, 1763–1821*, Syracuse New York 1958.

B. R. Hamnett, *Politics and Trade in Southern Mexico 1750–1821*, Cambridge 1971.

N. M. Farriss, *Crown and Clergy in Colonial Mexico, 1759–1821*, London 1968.

G. Desdevizes du Dézert, 'L'Eglise espagnole des Indes à la fin du XVIIIe siècle', *Revue hispanique* XXXIX, 112–293.

'L'Inquisition aux Indes espagnoles à la fin du XVIIIe siècle', *Revue hispanique* XXX, 1–118.

Lyle N. McAlister, 'Social structure and social change in New Spain', *Hispanic American Historical Review*, XLIII (1963), 349–70.

R. Konetzke, 'Sobre el problema racial en la América española', *Revista de Estudios Políticos*, Nos. 113–114 (1960), 179–215.

Robert S. Smith, 'The institution of the Consulado in New Spain', *Hispanic American Historical Review*, XXIV (1944), 61–83.

C. D. Valcárcel Esparza, *La rebelión de Túpac Amarú*, Mexico 1947.

B. Moses, *Spain's declining power in South America 1730–1800*, Chicago 1919.

W. S. Robertson, *The life of Miranda*, 2 vols, Chapel Hill 1939.

G-T. Raynal, *Histoire philosophique et politique des établissements et du commerce des Européens dans les deux indes*, Geneva 1780.

A. von Humboldt, J. Black, trans., *Political essay on the kingdom of New Spain*, 4 vols, London 1811.

A. von Humboldt, H. M. Williams, trans., *Personal narrative of travels to the equinoctial regions of the new continent during the years 1799–1804*, 7 vols, London 1814–29.

Chapter 18   The Creole revolt

J. Rydjord, *Foreign interest in the independence of New Spain*, Durham, N. Carolina 1935.

H. Bernstein, *Origins of inter-American interest*, Philadelphia 1945.

C. K. Webster, *Britain and the independence of Latin America*, Introduction, Oxford 1944.

W. S. Robertson, *Rise of the Spanish American republics as told in the lives of their liberators*, New York 1918.

Lucas Alamán, *Historia de México desde los primeros movimientos que prepararon su independencia en al año de 1808 hasta la época presente*, 5 vols, Mexico 1849–52.

Bartolomé Mitre, *Historia de Belgrano y de la independencia argentina*, 4 vols, Buenos Aires 1927–8.

Historia de San Martín y de la emancipación sud-americana, 4 vols, Buenos Aires 1890.

G. Masur, *Simón Bolívar*, Albuquerque 1948.

W. Pilling, *The emancipation of South America*, London 1893. (An abridged translation of Mitre's *Historia de San Martín*.)

A. Hasbrouck, *Foreign legionaries in the liberation of Spanish South America*, New York 1928.

R. Vargas Ugarte, *Historia del Perú* vol 5, 'Emancipación', Buenos Aires 1958.

B. Moses, *The intellectual background of the revolution in South America*, New York 1926.

V. A. Belaunde, *Bolívar and the political thought of the Spanish American revolution*, Baltimore 1938.

C. K. Webster, ed., *Britain and the independence of Latin America 1812–1830, select documents from the Foreign Office archives*, 2 vols, Oxford 1938.

R. A. Humphreys, ed., *British consular reports on the trade and politics of Latin America 1824–1826*, London, Royal Historical Society, 1940.

W. R. Manning, ed., *Diplomatic correspondence of the United States concerning the independence of the Latin American nations*, 3 vols, New York 1925.

Conclusion: The aftermath of empire

J. Canga Argüelles, *Diccionario de hacienda con aplicación a España*, 2 vols, Madrid 1833–4.

J. Arias y Miranda, *Examen crítico-histórico del influjo que tuvo en el comercio, industria y población de España su dominación en América*, Madrid 1854.

A. Moreau de Jonnès, *Le commerce au dix-neuvième siècle*, 2 vols, Paris 1825. *Statistique de l'Espagne*, Paris 1834.

J. L. Mecham, *Church and State in Latin America*, Chapel Hill 1934.

F. J. Legón, *Doctrina y ejercicio del Patronato nacional*, Buenos Aires 1920.

L. Ayarragaray, *La Iglesia en América y la dominació española*, Buenos Aires 1920.

Pedro de Leturia, S. J., *Relaciones entre la Santa Sede e Hispanoamérica 1493–1835*, 3 vols, Caracas 1960.

D. F. Sarmiento, *Facundo* (first published as *Civilización y barbarie*, Santiago 1845), Buenos Aires 1962.

J. Bryce, *South America, observations and impressions*, New York, 1912.

G. M. Foster, *Culture and conquest, America's Spanish heritage*, Chicago 1960.

S. J. Stein, *The Colonial Heritage of Latin America: essays on economic dependence in perspective*, Oxford 1970.

Index

A

Acadia, 260
Acapulco, 129, 132, 133, 299, 353
Acolmán, 160
acuerdo, 199
acuerdo de hacienda, 199
Adrian, Cardinal, 63
Adrian VI, Pope, 168
Africa, North, connections with Spain, 28 ff., 37
Africa, West, exploration of coast of, 40–5
  barracoons in, 233
agriculture, eighteenth-century plantation, 307, 309–11
  Moorish, in Andalusia, 29
  post-conquest, 103 ff., 218 ff.
  pre-conquest, 65 ff.
  Spanish influence on Indian, 376–7
Aix-la-Chapelle, Treaty of, 299, 301
Alarcón: Juan Ruiz de Alarcón y Mendoza, 275
alarife[s], 110
Alberoni, Giulio, Cardinal, 286
Albuquerque, 290
alcabala, 203, 262, 296
Alcaçovas, Treaty of, 42, 45
alcaldes mayores, 202, 322
alcaldes ordinarios, 102, 322, 378
Alcántara, Order of, 49
Alemán, Mateo, 275
Alexander VI, Pope, 46, 153–4
alféreces, 109
alguaciles mayores, 61, 109
alhóndigas, 221
alpacas, 80
Almadén, 248
Almagro, Diego de, 89 ff.
almojarifazgo, 203
Alvarado, Pedro de, 86–8, 91, 184
Amat y Yunient, Manuel, Viceroy of Peru, 331
Amazon, 93, 260
Amerindian cultures, 65 ff., 94, 97, 213–14
  Spanish influence on, 49, 112 ff., 161 ff.,

175 ff., 188 ff., 213 ff., 289 ff., 377 ff.
Amsterdam, 240
Anáhuac, 72–3
Andalusia, as base for exploration, 39 ff.
  as base for Indies trade, 53–5, 62, 115–16, 124–5, 238–9
  Castilian conquest of, 32–4
  economic decline of, in nineteenth century, 361
  epidemics in, 228
  Moorish, 29–30
  productivity of, 236
  risings in, 231
Andes, 66, 74, 76
  conquest campaigns in, 90 ff.
  independence campaigns in, 351 ff.
  native cultures of, 74 ff.
  transport difficulties in, 96, 319
Angostura, 352, 355
annual ship, 293, 294, 296, 300
Anson, George, Commodore (Admiral Lord Anson), 299
Antilla, 42–4, 47
Antilles, 45, 50
  Greater, 50, 134, 213, 264, 266
  Lesser, 47, 97, 270
Antioquia, 104, 288, 311
Antoneli, Juan Bautista, 256, 259
Antwerp, 231, 240
Apodaca: Juan Ruiz de Apodaca, Viceroy of New Spain, 354–5
Appalachians, 97
Aragon, 33, 37, 44, 154, 236
Aranda, Pedro Pablo Abarca de Bolea, Conde de, 349
Araucanians, 75, 97, 289, 378
Araya, 258, 259
Arequipa, 108, 113, 130
Argentina, 308, 351, 364, 370, 380
Armada de Barlovento, 262–4
Armada de la Carrera, 261 ff.
Armada de la Mar del Sur, 260
armadillas, 254
army, standing, 325 ff., 340, 363, 370
arrieros, 113